Reapproaching Borders

Reapproaching Borders

New Perspectives on the Study of Israel-Palestine

Edited by
Sandy Sufian and
Mark LeVine

ROWMAN & LITTLEFIELD PUBLISHERS, INC.
Lanham • Boulder • New York • Toronto • Plymouth, UK

"Seizing Locality in Jerusalem," by Alona Nitzan-Shiftan, was originally published in *The End of Tradition?* ed. Nezar Al Sayyad, copyright 2004, Routledge. Reproduced by permission of Taylor & Francis Books UK.

"Contested Bodies: Medicine, Public Health, and Mass Immigration to Israel," by Nadav Davidovitch, Rhona Seidelman, and Shifra Shvarts, forthcoming in *Hagar: Studies in Culture, Polity and Identities*, ed. Rebecca Kook, is reprinted by permission of Ben-Gurion University of the Negev.

ROWMAN & LITTLEFIELD PUBLISHERS, INC.

Published in the United States of America
by Rowman & Littlefield Publishers, Inc.
A wholly owned subsidary of The Rowman & Littlefield Publishing Group, Inc.
4501 Forbes Boulevard, Suite 200, Lanham, Maryland 20706
www.rowmanlittlefield.com

Estover Road
Plymouth PL6 7PY
United Kingdom

British Library Cataloguing in Publication Information Available

Library of Congress Cataloging-in-Publication Data:
Reapproaching borders : new perspectives on the study of Israel-Palestine / edited by Sandy Sufian and Mark LeVine.
    p. cm.
  Includes index.
  ISBN-13: 978-0-7425-4638-7 (cloth : alk. paper)
  ISBN-10: 0-7425-4638-1 (cloth : alk. paper)
  ISBN-13: 978-0-7425-4639-4 (pbk. : alk. paper)
  ISBN-10: 0-7425-4639-X (pbk. : alk. paper)
  1. Arab-Israeli conflict. 2. Palestinian Arabs—Social conditions. 3. Palestinian Arabs—Ethnic identity. 4. Jews—Israel—Identity. 5. Boundaries—Psychological aspects. 6. Israel—Ethnic relations. I. Sufian, Sandra M. (Sandra Marlene) II. LeVine, Mark, 1966–
  DS119.7.R364 2007
  956.9405—dc22   2007012483

Printed in the United States of America

♾™ The paper used in this publication meets the minimum requirements of American National Standard for Information Sciences—Permanence of Paper for Printed Library Materials, ANSI/NISO Z39.48-1992.

In memory of Dr. Aftim Acra, born in Jerusalem in 1922, a Palestinian/Lebanese pharmacist, environmental health scientist, and expert on Lebanese amber who built political and intellectual bridges and constantly searched to understand complex questions.

Contents

Acknowledgments

The idea for this volume came about many years ago when we were graduate students together at New York University. Sitting at a café on Bleeker Street, we asked ourselves: What new avenues are other young scholars taking with regard to the history of Israel- Palestine? What themes and methods are being used? How does this work differ from earlier scholarship? How does it point to future directions in the field of Israel-Palestine studies?

Since then, we continued to think through the project, identified the new issues being pursued, and worked slowly—given other professional commitments—to find fitting contributors (Israeli, Palestinian, and American) and a publisher excited about the book. Luckily, Brian Romer of Rowman & Littlefield quickly took this project and saw its innovative potential. We thank Brian for his support for this volume and for understanding its value as a text that deliberately crosses both Jewish studies and Middle Eastern studies.

Sarah Stanton and Karen Ackermann of Rowman & Littlefield have similarly been instrumental in helping us follow through on the project and bringing it to production. Sara Vogt at the University of Illinois at Chicago spent many painstaking days on the manuscript since its beginning. We express deep gratitude for her efforts. We also would like to acknowledge our respective university departments for their encouragement and assistance in completing this project.

The staffs of the Israel State and Central Zionist Archives, the Institute for Jerusalem Studies, Salim Tamari, Zachary Lockman, and Ilan Pappé proved invaluable for their early support for the project. The latter three scholars have influenced our own work and much of the contributors' work on Israel-Palestine. Without their cutting-edge perspective on the history of Israel-Palestine, the next steps that the chapters herein explore would not have been possible.

Finally, special thanks goes to our contributors whose creative, inquisitive minds have inspired new approaches to studying the complexities of life and politics in a land that has been embroiled in long-standing conflict and which will hopefully, one day, see the fruits of peace.

Introduction

Investigating Borders in the Case of Israel-Palestine

As its title suggests, this volume is dedicated to an interrogation of the notion of "borders." We use the case of Israel-Palestine to explore the concept of borders, particularly how this term is imagined and actualized in this specific contested land. Territorial borders, borders of identity, and other kinds of social and cultural borders are constantly questioned and contested in the case of Israel-Palestine, both in present-day sociopolitical life and throughout the historical landscape of the land and its peoples. Indeed, part of the contestation over Israel-Palestine is about cognitive and physical borders and the movement between and within those boundaries. Who gets included and excluded when those borders are defined and as they are resisted not only complicates questions about the ownership of or right to the land, but also raises questions about visions for its future.

Some borders, like those of identity or of jurisprudence, are hard to pin down; they are often vague, invisible, ethereal, or constantly shifting in nature. Others are made tangible by visible markers—border crossings or passport control. Like borders of identity, these visible, territorial borders are not natural or static; they too are subject to change according to state interests, demographic balance, and political negotiations. They may bear different significances at various historical moments and may be invoked or underplayed by political and social actors.

The contributors to this volume examine the notion of borders by asking a series of questions: How are borders of all types defined? How have they been defined historically? Who defines these borders and what are the ramifications of those definitions in the specific space of Israel-Palestine? Why are certain borders defined in specific ways, as opposed to other ways? How are borders upheld, negotiated, or resisted? Can they be crossed and if so,

1

how? Do or can such borders merge or are they always mutually exclusive? How have they been contested throughout the particular modern history of Israel-Palestine?

During a period in the Palestinian-Israeli conflict when literal walls are being built; employment, academic, and business exchanges are increasingly restricted and shifting; immigration and emigration have continued to occur; and political alignments are quickly changing; such questions have compelled us to organize the collection of essays contained in this volume.

Perhaps the one type of border given the most political and media attention in the Palestinian-Israeli conflict is the territorial border. Indeed, the ongoing conflicts in the Middle East revolve around definitions of territorial borders, as well as rights to land and sovereignty. These boundaries are themselves dependent upon such borders being drawn, recognized, and effectively policed. We feel that the centrality of territorial borders in the history of Israel-Palestine and in the region at large demands a stronger focus on the epistemological foundations of territorial borders and problems with their conception and deployment. Scholars need to revisit the issue of territorial borders to reassess and complexify previous analyses. Underlying assumptions about the variety of territorial permutations in the history of Israel-Palestine need to be uncovered, the social and economic ramifications of these borders (i.e. the interaction of these territorial dimensions with other areas of daily living) need to be evaluated in more depth, and ideas for creatively thinking about the future of borders need to be submitted and evaluated. Many of our authors touch upon these themes throughout different periods in the history of Israel-Palestine in their contributions, although their work is just one step toward a more wide-ranging new historiography.

There are many other types of boundaries that underlie the myriad conflicts going on within and between Palestinian and Israeli societies. These also demand more intensive examination. Many of our authors move beyond the dominant concern of territorial borders found in much of the scholarship on Israel-Palestine to an approach that looks at the interaction of several social, cultural, and communal borders within and between Palestinian and Israeli societies throughout their history together. These divisions, in and of themselves, can offer us a more multilayered understanding of the sociopolitical trajectories of these societies. They can also aid us in further appreciating how such factors intersect with, exacerbate, or alleviate territorial conflicts. Our inquiry therefore explores both the theoretical and practical manifestations of upholding or dismantling several of the foundational boundaries that have traditionally defined the Palestinian-Israeli conflict.

The volume not only looks at strict divisions but also at the crossing of boundaries and even a merging thereof. Our particular emphasis on the changing nature of Jewish-Arab relations has its basis in earlier scholarship that chipped away at the previous understandings of the Jewish and Palestinian Arab societies as essentially separate and autonomously developing entities. We reapproach the history of Israel-Palestine by exploring what Israeli geographer Juval Portugali has evocatively described as the "implicate relations" that have joined Palestinian Arabs and Jews throughout the century and a half of conflicted but mutually informative interaction that began during the late Ottoman period and continues to the present day. By focusing on implicate relations between Palestinian Arabs and Jews—and the shifting character of those relations—the contributions in this volume provide new insights into the origins and contemporary dynamics of the conflicts between them.[1]

Our discussion of implicate relations between Palestinian Arabs and Jews emphasizes the history of the nonelite members of both communities whose lives, views, and actions defined the history that emerged far more profoundly than has previously been understood.[2] Our contributors see the relations between Jews and Palestinian Arabs in the space of historic Israel-Palestine as embedded and reflected in areas of daily living, such as the spheres of architecture, commerce and commodities, health affairs and sexuality, the role of the court system in the past and present, and daily narratives. These areas of daily living have also gone relatively unnoticed by previous scholars.

Not only the word "border" in the book's title, but also the word "reapproaching," is key to our project. The title denotes the new ways in which these scholars approach the methodologies (and combinations thereof) of writing about Israel-Palestine. We reevaluate the disciplinary borders that have inherently driven the writing of certain types of scholarship on Israel-Palestine while leaving out other types of questions, themes, and interactions. As such, our discussion on the notion of borders spans the territorial, relational, and methodological aspects of the concept. All of these areas require a combination of historical, sociological, and anthropological methodologies in order to capture the richness of their contributions fully. The volume therefore crosses disciplinary boundaries by presenting together a collection of methodologies used in the humanities and social sciences; it embarks on a new type of scholarship that is primarily informed by a principal discipline but also draws from insights and methodologies of several other academic disciplines. The areas of labor and gender studies, medical humanities, and critical urban geography have also provided our contributors with alternative and supplemental models to approach the study of Israel-Palestine. This mixed approach reflects the direction of a new generation of young scholars who are broadening their purview to research uncharted territory in the field of Israel-Palestine studies. Indeed, virtually all of our authors are scholars at the beginning stages of their academic careers. They represent an emerging generation of scholars on the subject.

As disciplinary boundaries have been crossed, new themes of inquiry for the study of Israel-Palestine have emerged.[3] This volume captures such themes under the general rubric of interrogating borders: spatial issues in the urban built environment, the intersection of law and space, health and national identity, the employment of temporal borders in nationalist discourse, and the connections between immigration and health. At the same time, the contributions to this volume demonstrate the continued saliency of older themes as they intersect with the newer areas of inquiry we explore. The volume develops these older themes by revisiting ideas about forms of ownership and rights to the land, recasting and analyzing them with evidence from the fields of law and history of science. It continues to explore the role of the state in pursuing its political and demographic interests as well as the resistance to those policies. However, it looks at these phenomena through the windows of spatial relations and reproductive and sexual identity politics. Using heretofore unexplored documents to show such complex dynamics, the book also examines how professionals culturally define themselves vis-à-vis the world community and looks at divisions created and upheld within the communities of Israel-Palestine. Although the contributions deal with new yet broad perspectives, they explore those perspectives primarily through the trajectories of local histories, rather than regional or state histories. Three of our contributions, for example, focus on various aspects in the histories of three major cities: Jerusalem, Nazareth, and Hebron. The examination of local histories deepens our understanding not just of intercommunal relations but also of interspatial relations—that is, we can better discern the connectedness of rural and urban settings in Palestine/Israel, especially how these settings have interacted and mutually shaped each other in various periods. Together, the chapters in this book shift the examination of the history of Israel-Palestine to less-studied but equally politicized arenas in which the social and cultural impact of Israeli-Palestinian conflict can be reevaluated and innovatively assessed.

In compiling this collection, two axes of investigation have emerged in a manner that we did not anticipate. These axes point to the particular importance of two of the primary themes of this volume in a manner that reminds us of how, until the late 1980s, the study of Israel-Palestine was marked by a focus on elites and on the kind of diplomatic and political histories that have tended to reflect and repeat, rather than challenge, the often stereotypical and historically inaccurate accepted narratives of the two sides. The first axis has to do with historical continuity. The chapters in this book, which cover the late Ottoman, Mandate, and post-1948 periods, demonstrate how processes that took shape at the emergence of Zionist and Palestinian nationalisms over a century ago have continued to powerfully influence the dynamics of the two societies and the contemporary conflicts between them. The second deals with the place of the Palestinian citizens of Israel as a boundary, a liminal population through which our dynamics of interest have long been most powerfully expressed. Exploring the historical and contemporary dynamics of a Palestinian community living as citizens in a Jewish state often offers as much, if not more, insight into the core dynamics that simultaneously join and divide Palestinians and Israelis. It also sheds light onto the interface between the more easily categorizable Israeli-Jewish and Palestinian-Arab communities on either side of the internationally recognized border.

REIMAGINING PALESTINIAN AND ISRAELI IDENTITIES WHILE REAPPROACHING THE BORDERS OF SCHOLARSHIP

The chapters that follow focus on three broad themes that are increasingly defining the study of modern Israel-Palestine. These themes form the three major parts of the volume: (1) "Narrating the Past," (2) "Constructing Healthy Identities and Landscapes," and (3) "Shaping Citizens and Space in Israel-Palestine." Each section reapproaches the borders of identity and daily relations as reflected in these selected spheres of interest.

Part I, "Narrating the Past," focuses on the production of narratives in Israel-Palestine and on Arab-Israeli relations. The section focuses particularly on how and why different social actors (especially those usually marginalized from the writing of history) have produced stories about their lives. It also looks at the meaningful material objects left by them. Contributions to this section explore the late Ottoman, Mandate, and post-1948 periods.

The first chapter, Uzi Baram's "Filling a Gap in Time," demonstrates the vitality of socioeconomic development in late Ottoman Palestine through the innovative use of historical archaeology. Drawing on several case studies, Baram's chapter explores how material remains of the later Ottoman period help us reimagine the development of the Palestinian Arab community and its relationship with the emerging Zionist movement in the last decades of Ottoman rule. Through this process, Baram offers a new disciplinary relationship between the fields of historical archaeology, Ottoman studies, and the anthropology of Israel-Palestine.

Michelle Campos's chapter, "Violence, Coexistence, and Memory in Pre-1948 Palestine," complicates our contemporary, assumed divisions and loyalties between Arab and Jew. Campos explores the changing foundations of Zionist identity through the story of one of the most prominent Sephardi families of Palestine in the late Ottoman and Mandate periods, the Chelouche family. Campos's description of Yosef Chelouche's thinking about the violent conflicts of 1921 and 1929 reveals extraordinary insights into the moments when the struggle between conflict and coexistence among

Arabs and Jews was decided for the next century. By focusing on the narrative of a Sephardi businessman, Campos's contribution reapproaches the traditional historiographic communal borders mobilized in the historiography of Israel-Palestine that most often utilize and represent Ashkenazi discourses and those of political elites. Her subject matter also raises the issue of elision as a process of overriding the borders of memory.

Geremy Forman's "Reapproaching the Borders of Nazareth (1948–1956): Israel's Control of an All-Arab City" moves us into a discussion of borders during the post-1948 period. Forman examines the state's military, political, and spatial mechanisms that were used to secure control over the area of Nazareth in Israel's early years of statehood. His chapter reveals how the landscape, development, and demographics of areas like Nazareth in the Galilee are reshaped by ideological conflicts, demographic fragmentation, political initiative, and territorial definitions. All of these factors—along with their unintended consequences—consequently determine the ways in which territories are reshaped, ownership is claimed, and demographic and political control is established and reestablished.

Part II, "Constructing Healthy Identities and Landscapes," takes health and science as areas with which to explore the construction of communal and national identities in Palestinian/Israeli history. The thesis of this section is that both Palestinian Arab and Israeli/Zionist national identities are formulated and contested through the experience of disease and its eradication and treatment. Issues of disease are equally embedded in questions and strategies surrounding professionalism, reproduction, sexuality, and immigration. In addition, the long-standing place of technocracy—the power of scientists to shape Zionist thought and policies from the very start of the enterprise—has profoundly impacted the manner in which scientific knowledge has been used to manipulate and transform the landscape, the resources contained therein, and the bodies of the men and women struggling for rights within the various parts of the country. The contributions in this section specifically examine issues of medical language, reproduction and population control, male sexuality in Palestinian/Israeli society, and the locations of anti-infectious disease campaigns as sites for identity formation and for shaping struggles over resources in Palestine and Israel.

Sandy Sufian explores the debates surrounding the making of a nationalist Hebrew medical terminology during the Mandate period of Palestine. By looking at the role of Hebrew medical terminology in the making of a distinct Hebrew medical profession, Sufian engages with issues of temporal borders, purity of language, communal borders, and professional identity. By investigating how these borders are upheld, negotiated, and crossed, Sufian helps us understand the place of medicine and language in Zionist nationalism. She also examines the creation of new medical knowledge and clinical practice, and the currency of certain medical texts and medical terminology in Palestine at the time, as well as the connection between that medical knowledge and the cultural history of Mandate Palestine.

Nadav Davidovitch, Rhona Seidelman, and Shifra Shvarts's chapter, "Contested Bodies: Medicine, Public Health, and the Mass Immigration to Israel," explores nation building and the way the Ashkenazi Israeli establishment viewed and transformed the bodies of immigrants—both Holocaust survivors and Jewish *olim* [immigrants] from Muslim countries during the 1950s period of immigration. The authors demonstrate how an understanding of the immigrant's body was crucial to the formation of Israeli citizenship, particularly when that body, for health or cultural reasons, did not conform to the Zionist ideal of the new and healthy Jew, free of the (supposed) defects of two millennia of diaspora life. As such, the Israeli government used the diseases that many immigrants brought with them to justify a significant degree of prejudice and institutionalized discrimination. The legacy of that discrimination, and the mistrust it engendered among the Mizrachi Jewish community (Jews from Arab countries) towards the Ashkenazi community, persists to this day.

Sarah Willen's chapter, "Seeing the Holy Land with New Eyes: Undocumented Labor Migration, Reproductive Health, and the Fluctuating Borders of the Israeli National Body," also examines the predicament of the immigrant's body. Yet she explores a very different, more recent group of immigrants arriving in Israel: the hundreds of thousands of guest workers who have come to the state since the start of the Oslo peace process. Generally brought in to replace Palestinian workers, these guest workers—including those from Eastern Europe, Asia, and Africa—remain largely undocumented and "illegal" although their economic role within Israeli society has become extremely critical to its functioning and growth. Willen's research into the struggles of African immigrants to obtain prenatal healthcare demonstrates the fault lines of Israeli identity and the state's relative sense of obligation to all the residents of the country. Her discussion of the boundaries of immigration through the politics of reproduction not only places Israel firmly on the map of worldwide economic transformations that are defining contemporary globalization, but also helps us attenuate the borders between Israeli, Palestinian, and non-Israeli identities.

Daniel Monterescu's chapter, "Masculinity as a Relational Mode: Palestinian Working-Class Gender Ideologies and Categorical Boundaries in a Jewish–Palestinian Arab Mixed Town," moves us from an examination of women's health and identity to an examination of the often competing constructions of masculinity among Palestinian citizens of Israel in the urban setting of Jaffa. His informants reveal the intimate and often paradoxical connections between feelings of political and economic marginalization and the performance of masculinity within that marginalized community. Men within this community are now torn between enforcing traditional masculine roles and recognizing the value of the changes in gender roles that have occurred within the dominant Israeli society and within their communities. These dynamics produce a conflicted masculinity that struggles in vain to retain its position as the sole cultural option for Palestinian men.

Concluding Section 2 is Samer Alatout's chapter entitled, "From Water Abundance to Water Scarcity (1936–1959): A 'Fluid' History of Jewish Subjectivity in Historic Palestine and Israel." Alatout shifts our attention from the healthy human body to a healthy environmental body. By challenging claims of water scarcity in Israel, Alatout shows us that environmental issues and human citizenship are entangled; their definitions and interaction are contingent upon a specific historical juncture in the development of the state. Alatout's tracing of the water scarcity debate in Israel plays with notions of the borders of scientific meaning, their nationalist ramifications, and the management of environmental resources. He shows us that the boundaries between science, technology, and national identity are much more elusive than separate. Alatout demonstrates that human and environmental landscapes are intimately connected.

Part III, "Shaping Citizens and Space in Israel-Palestine," examines the process of urbanization in Israel-Palestine during the last century. The chapters in this section explore how Israeli/Zionist and Palestinian identities and notions of citizenship emerged. They explain how these concepts have been reinterpreted and how they continue to be at the front lines of the struggle over territory, memory, and power. These struggles are reflected in architectural production, urban planning, law, and civil society.

Alona Nitzan-Shiftan begins this section by exploring the role of Israeli architectural discourses in the contest over land around Jerusalem that was conquered during the 1967 war. Nitzan-Shiftan reveals how the lack of preparedness for the conquest of the West Bank and Gaza combined with the lessons of 1948. She shows how a concern to create "facts on the ground" produced an urgent sense of necessity to reclaim the West Bank, particularly around Jerusalem, and give it a sense of architectural unity that was Israeli Jewish yet rooted in the local landscape. The resultant coherent architectural image was ironic and politically charged precisely because, in the words of one official, the "post-1967 architecture of power absorbed the symbols of the conquered rather than those of the conqueror." Nitzan-Shiftan's treatment of these (seeming) contradictions complexifies our understanding of Palestinian-Israeli relations embodied in space and daily living.

Complementing this work for the contemporary period, Tom Abowd examines the politics of monuments in Jerusalem and explores how specific places in this contested city have simultaneously served as sites of remembrance and as locales of historical amnesia. He examines the borders of historical memory. He details how in some emblematic cases appropriated Palestinian properties have been transformed into Israeli national emplacements: places dedicated to the memory of Israeli achievement, sacrifice, or longing. For Abowd, delving into the politics of monuments in Jerusalem necessitates an examination of Israeli national ideology, demonstrating that the two are intertwined. Focusing on the home of the Baramki family of Jerusalem, Abowd looks at the spatial and symbolic transformation of the Baramki home, showing how these changes served the interests and needs of the Israeli state. His contribution illustrates how the articulation of prominent and powerful Israeli narratives—independence, defense, and redemption—have been literally written into a formerly mixed Palestinian-Jewish geography.

Moussa Abou Ramadan's chapter, "Framing the Borders of Justice: Sharia Courts in Israel and the Conflict between Secular Ideology and Islamic Law," moves us from architectural space to legal, rational, cognitive space. Abou Ramadan's chapter discusses the relationship between the sharia courts in Israel and the Israeli State. He examines how the sharia courts employ a rhetoric of autonomy and of the purity of sharia [Islamic law] that ultimately obscures their position as an integral part of the country's legal establishment; it ignores the process of secularization that has affected these courts. Abou Ramadan's research has powerful implications, not only for an understanding of the legal and religious relations between the Jewish state and its Muslim citizens, but also for the role and place of religious courts within societies across the Muslim world.

Finally, LeVine's piece, entitled "Modernity and its Mirror: Three Views of Jewish-Palestinian Interaction in Jaffa and Tel Aviv," points to the permeability of boundaries that have traditionally tried to separate the Palestinian Arab and Jewish communities of Israel-Palestine during the last century. Returning to the space of Jaffa–Tel Aviv explored earlier by Monterescu and Willen, LeVine examines how architecture and urban planning came to be reflected in, and had a mutual influence upon, the cultural production and the material relations between these two communities. The role of modernity has been implicit in these fields and in the evolution of the Jewish and Palestinian Arab nationalist movements and their ongoing conflict. Like Campos's work, LeVine's shows that the often intimate yet paradoxical relations between Jews and Palestinians that broke through the official discourses and politics of separation demonstrate that the past can be read quite differently than before. Such a shift in writing and reading could open up avenues for a future in Israel-Palestine different from the continued conflict and exclusion that is imagined today.

CONCLUSION: AREAS FOR FURTHER RESEARCH

The contributions in this volume reapproach the borders of Zionist, Israeli and Palestinian, and non-Palestinian/Israeli identities and their communal, territorial, nationalist, and religious foundations. As Sarah Willen's contribution reveals, hundreds of thousands of non-Jews and non-Palestinians live today within the borders of Israel as workers, largely undocumented and without regular access to crucial social services. Other residents are only nominal members of the Jewish and Palestinian nations, such as large number of non-Jews who immigrated to Israel from the former Soviet Union, or the much smaller but equally interesting phenomena of Arab migrants from Egypt, Jordan, and beyond who have come to Israel. Many of these immigrants have come to Israel in search of better jobs than they could find at home.

Although this volume only scratches the surface of these borderland identities, it raises the topic as one worthy of more scholarly attention. An equally illuminating series of studies could be comprised solely of research on Russian and Ethiopian immigrants, intermarried couples, or marginalized identities like the disabled or homosexual. An equally valuable set of borderland studies could look at Palestinians returning from the diaspora during the brief honeymoon period that was the early Oslo years (1993–1996) or at Palestinian diaspora communities, whether those languishing in refugee camps in Lebanon or those who have built up more secure lives in Amman or even Paterson, New Jersey. All these groups are reshaping Israeli and Palestinian societies in direct and subtle ways. They are influencing both the way their individual and national pasts are reconstructed and the way their futures are envisioned.

Finally, there are a number of methodologies at the forefront of cutting-edge scholarship on Palestine and Israel that our contributions only touched upon or did not use. Chief among them the Ottoman-era records at the various archives in Turkey and the Islamic/sharia court records [*si-jjil*].[4] Other sources, such as popular cultural productions (literature, poetry, music, theater, and film) or medical and scientific documents, still remain largely unexplored. A failure to utilize rich sources in the field of medicine and science continues to exist despite the fact that scientific ideologies and practices profoundly reshaped the environment of Israel and Palestine before and after 1948. Samer Alatout's and Sandy Sufian's research, presented here and in other venues, clearly demonstrate this point.

Although the contributions in this volume introduce new themes and areas of inquiry, they do not exhaust the possibilities. Our introduction of these themes, however, presents scholars of Palestine and Israel with an important task in the coming years: how to integrate the wealth of data and insights located at the borders of Israeli and Palestinian geographies and identities into our understanding of the histories and present-day dynamics of the two societies. Where do daily developments and relations fit into the wider picture of the politics, economics, culture, and histories of Israel-Palestine? As negotiations toward a final status settlement inch backward and forward toward some sort of territorial compromise (and/or the frustration of a compromise), borders of all kinds (territorial, economic, political, individual, familial and national, social, labor, civic, mental, etc.) and their definitions/scope will be repeatedly raised, reworked, and/or resisted. Similarly to Forman's discussion of the mechanisms of Israeli state control in Nazareth, Amira Hass has noted that the "explicit prohibition regarding entry to the [Jordan] Valley by all Palestinians except a small minority is relatively new. . . . It has involved not a single order published by the media, but rather a series of cumulative prohibitions."[5] Similarly, discussions around Jerusalem's "security fence" or "separation barrier" raise similar questions with regard to the issue of territorial borders. Geoffrey Aronson has commented on the intersection between territorial borders and perceptual ones: "For Palestinians and Israelis who live in nearby West Bank settlements . . . the new border is a constant and inescapable provocation, a mark of their exclusion, and perhaps even an existential threat to their well-being, not only as individuals but also as a social, and in the Palestinians' case, national community."[6] The security fence, Aronson argues, may provide a concrete wall as a tangible mark of a border or separation but it does not provide anything but a *sense* of security as long as its presence is being contested. Indeed, in all of these examples, including the bullets and rockets that continue to criss-cross the Green Line, the need to incorporate borderland geographies and identities, to recognize the daily crossings that occur in the physical, emotional, political, economic, and social lives of Israelis and Palestinians and in their everyday narratives—indeed the need to raise the theme of borders as one to be interrogated at all—has never been more urgent if new and more hopeful futures for the two peoples are to be imagined.

NOTES

1. According to Beshara Doumani, among the most damaging ramifications of the traditional paradigm of treating Arab/Jewish relations in secondary historical texts was the sense that Palestinians had no history outside of their conflict with Jews/Israelis. Enabling such a sentiment was the fact that no body of scholarship existed that accurately described the history of Palestinian society and culture through which such a narrative could be constructed. Furthermore, Israeli scholars Gershon Shafir and Yoav Peled explain that for too long scholarship on Israel has glossed over the "colonial character of the Zionist state and nation-building project," in the process making it more difficult to understand how long-term tensions between the

dialectic of a Jewish yet democratic state impacted the larger conflict with Palestinian Arabs.

2. For more, see the work of scholars such as Salim Tamari, Beshara Doumani,
Gershon Shafir, Zachary Lockman, Ted Swedenberg, Oren Yiftachel, and Dan Rabinowitz.

3. Because this is an interdisciplinary volume, we have made the decision not to
impose a uniform guideline of formatting and citations on contributors. Therefore,
each chapter in this volume will use the style consistent with their discipline: *The
Chicago Manual of Style*, Harvard, or other relevant academic styles.

4. See especially the Baflbakanl archives in Istanbul for Ottoman records. Scholars such as Beshara Doumani, Iris Agmon, Mahmoud Yazbak, and Moussa Abou Ramadan (in this volume) have demonstrated that these archives are among the rich-
est yet most underutilized sources for studying Palestinian Arab, Jewish, Zionist, and
Israeli histories.

5. Ami Isseroff, "Jordan Valley—a Disaster Is Quietly in the Making," Mideast-
Web Middle East Web Log, February 21, 2006, www.mideastweb.org/log/archives/
00000432.htm.

6. Geoffrey Aronson, "Olmert Divides Jerusalem." *Report on Israeli Settlement in
the Occupied Territories: A Special Report of the Foundation for Middle East Peace.* (Foundation for Middle East Peace, 2006), 1. See also p. 6 about the health, religious, cultural, and civic consequences for Palestinians within Jerusalem's new border.

Part I

NARRATING THE PAST

1

Filling a Gap in the Chronology

What Archaeology Is Revealing about the Ottoman Past in Israel

Uzi Baram

INTRODUCTION: A GAP IN TIME

Archaeology in Israel has recovered the dynamics for the spread of humans out of Africa; the rise of agriculture; the development of cities and empires; the developments of Iron Age and classical cultures; the details of Judaism, Christianity, and Islam in the land; and the activities of European crusaders. But at the doorstep of the present "when the modern cultures of the region were in the process of formation . . . the archaeological picture [goes] blank" (Silberman 1989, 232–33). Until the 1980s, the material evidence of the recent past, particularly that of the Ottoman period (1516–1917), was avoided, ignored, or bulldozed away (Baram 2002). Yet the material evidence from the centuries the Ottoman Empire ruled the land that is today Israel has great potential for exposing activities and processes that created the landscape of the twentieth century and for revealing a relatively unknown history in a tangible manner. The successes of archaeology in exposing what happened in history can be found for the recent past as well as the traditional focus on the distant past. An archaeology of Ottoman Palestine has the potential to contribute to scholarship seeking a more dynamic and complicated image of Palestine before the British Mandate. To address that potential, the near absence of such research needs to be examined.

As several scholars have noted (e.g., Silberman 1982, Zerubavel 1995, Abu el-Haj 1998, Benvenisti 2000, Baram 2002, Magness 2003, Yahya 2005), the practice of archaeology has erased evidence, confused chronologies, and muffled interpretations of the millennia of Islamic rule over the eastern Mediterranean, particularly in Israel. This chapter explores the Ottoman period within Israeli archaeology; the practices of and developments in Palestinian archaeology are a project for another contribution. Others (e.g., Silberman 1982) have exposed the histories for archaeology in the Middle East in terms of Western European and North American interests. What is clear from this research is that in Israel, as elsewhere, archaeology is practiced in a political and social context.

This dynamic is, naturally, also true of Palestine. However, no significant monograph has appeared on the history and development of Palestinian archaeology since the 1993 founding of the Department of Antiquities of the Palestine Authority (see Bohannon 2006 for a brief review of developments in the field). Because of the complexity of the histories and the challenges faced by Palestinian archaeology, it demands a separate examination by scholars within the field who have directly participated in the research undertaken by Palestinian archaeologists and their colleagues during the last two decades. This chapter focuses on Israel and Israeli archaeology.

The two archaeologies do share a common legacy. Archaeology in the eastern Mediterranean and Middle East began as a search for the origins of Western civilization and for evidence of Biblical history. In the nineteenth century, Western Europeans and North Americans were searching for evidence of Biblical narratives, for the origins of Western civilization, and for prizes to display in their national museums. During the twentieth century, archaeology became a tool of nation-building, projecting identity deep into the past via the seemingly objective testimony from artifacts and historic sites. This trajectory established questions of identity as the centerpiece of archaeological inquiry. Through excavations that reveal past landscapes and narratives regarding the past, archaeology has constructed notions regarding identity, history, and social relations that are involved in the contemporary discourse on Israel-Palestine. Linking the past to the present, the standard archaeological chronological eras were named for ethnic groups— examples include Israelite, Hellenistic, Hasmonean, and Talmudic—as a means of "commandeering the past" (Lowenthal 1996, 235). The major archaeological chronologies no longer use ethnicity for the Bronze Age and Iron Age but the epochs are still delineated by the same divides; the terminology for chronology is based on materials employed in the epoch (e.g., stone, bronze, iron) but the structures of understandings based on historical ethnic identities remain.

ARCHAEOLOGICAL CHRONOLOGY FOR ISRAEL

Paleolithic	1,500,000–18,500 BP
Epipaleolithic	18,500–12,300 BP
Natufian	10,300–8500 BCE
Neolithic	8500–4500 BCE

Chalcolithic	4500–3600 BCE
Bronze Age	
Early	3600–2000 BCE
Middle	2000–1500 BCE
Late	1500–1200 BCE
Iron Age	1200–586 BCE
Babylonian and Persian	586–332 BCE
Hellenistic	332–63 BCE
Herodian/Early Roman	65 BCE–70 CE
Late Roman	70–324
Byzantine	324–640
Early Islamic Period	
Umayyad Caliphate	661–750
Abbasid Caliphate	750–1258
Crusaders	1099–1291
Late Islamic Period	
Fatimid Caliphate	910–1171
Mamlük Empire	1258–1516
Ottoman Empire	1516–1917

When the Israeli state was young, particularly in the third quarter of the twentieth century, Israelis were famously associated with archaeology. Such leading figures as Yigael Yadin, the excavator of Hazor and Masada, and Moshe Dayan, whose artifact collecting and collections are legendary, were archaeologists, military commanders, and politicians. It is not just such leaders who celebrate archaeology. Israeli folk understandings of the past are intertwined with archaeology (Elon 1994), with excavations affirming "roots in the land" (Zerubavel 1995, 57), as if "digging up the hard earth they were retrieving memory" (Elon 1994, 15). Uncovering the material remains of the past has yielded impressive finds that fill museums with artifacts to display, fill books and magazines with insights, and provide tourists with places to visit and photograph. Archaeology has uncovered and reconstructed considerable amounts of past landscapes for Israel, but the reconstruction of the past has been selective. This chapter focuses on the gap in chronology. The lack of archaeological details on the recent past has contributed to the reification of national/ethnic divides. Filling the gap offers the possibility of retrieving a more complex, fluid, and dynamic set of ethnic identities and relationships for the eastern Mediterranean.

The next section reviews the critiques of the gap in time in order to frame the contributions that are adding an era to the archaeological chronology. With the inclusion of the recent past in archaeological projects, new possibilities are opening up for understanding the past. This is a new endeavor in the history of archaeology.

ARCHAEOLOGY AND SILENCED PERIODS

The historian of archaeology Neil Silberman (1989, 233–34) tells how, in the 1980s, Ottoman-period clay tobacco pipes excavated at Jerusalem's Citadel of David Museum were sold at the gift store. His account exemplifies how artifacts from the upper layers of sites have, until recently, been negated as nonarchaeological (The Citadel of David is a large Ottoman-period military complex at the Jaffa Gate entrance to the Old City of Jerusalem). The archaeological community saw no value in the objects other than as trinkets for tourists.

Traditional archaeological avoidance of the upper levels that contain, in the parlance of the discipline, recent materials, has constructed a chasm between the past and the present. That gap suggests that the later Islamic periods are inferior to earlier, more grandiose epochs. The modern layers, particularly the centuries when the Ottoman Empire ruled the region, are often presented as ephemeral to the history of the land. Most archaeologists leave implicit the notion that the Ottoman past does not need to be explored with archaeology. Site reports might note the existence of late Islamic layers and materials, a development that is encouraging, but analysis is rarely included in publications. Traditionally, most archaeological texts end with the fall of the Byzantine Empire. Even when modern materials are discussed, the interpretations are one-dimensional with descriptions, not explanations.

One of the causes of denial of the recent past for archaeology grows out of the intersection of nationalism and archaeology, a concern that has recently attracted the attention of archaeologists (e.g., Kohl and Fawcett 1995, Díaz-Andreu and Champion 1996). Kohl (1998, 225–26), in a review of the relationship between archaeology and nationalism, locates two trends in the recent literature: a critical evaluation of archaeological data being used for nationalistic purposes and a celebration of indigenous appropriation of archaeology for contesting the dominant narratives of the past. Both inclinations illustrate archaeology's longstanding disciplinary and practical engagement with issues of identity. Conclusions regarding that relationship tend to be cautionary tales about the linear connections created by the manipulation of the past. Research into the nationalistic exploitation of archaeological materials is meant to provide a more self-conscious archaeology, one that recognizes the implications of its finds, interpretations, and unasked questions. A similar dynamic is evident in the tourist appropriation of the past: themes for sites and regions are selected to appeal to tourists. The implications of the intersection of archaeology and tourism include the silencing of particular aspects of the past, stress placed on specific themes, and reduction of complexity into simple narratives (see studies in Rowan and Baram 2004).

Israeli archaeology is often cited as an example of the intersection of nationalism and archaeology (Kohl 1998, 237), but it is not a unique case. It is a useful case study for considering the relationship of identity and the past because archaeology has widespread popularity, there has been large-scale state support for archaeological excavations and reconstruction of ancient sites (specifically for the Iron Age through classic periods), and the archaeology serves to accentuate the notion of the Jewish people returning to their land. For example, in Jerusalem, one of the world's most intensively excavated cities, Abu el-Haj (1998) has shown that archaeology provides the setting for social relations and classifies time periods as the heritage for distinctive groups. While walking around the city, visitors can see heritage based on the excavated components. A landscape has been created for impressing particular themes on inhabitants and tourists. As Palestinian archaeology develops, some strands are constructing a similar nationalist approach, looking to the middle Bronze Age as a contrast to Israeli fixations with the late Bronze/Iron Ages in order to assert an earlier date for Palestinian claims to the land. The competition over the past follows David Lowenthal's (1996) interpretation of heritage as a concern for being first. This approach avoids the complexity of historic context for the peoples who now live in Israel-Palestine. The complex history that produced the present and recent past, that structured social relations and fashioned much of the extant landscape, are left in the shadows.

Remaining from the simplified presentations is a past of Canaanites and Israelites, Hellenistic and Hasmonean, and crusaders and Muslims, binary oppositions that can make the contemporary Israeli-Palestinian conflict seem inevitable. Archaeology has not only been used to support implicit, primordial claims to the land, it has also encouraged singularities of heritage for various time periods. Entire epochs are associated with one ethnic group rather than complexities of social interactions. But archaeology is made by archaeologists. Critical perspectives on the past have been developed to critique assumptions and to build alternative histories, as Schmidt and Patterson (1995) titled their endeavor, *Making Alternative Histories*. The examples provided in this chapter come from archaeological expeditions including the top levels with enough descriptions to allow alternative histories for Israel-Palestine.

CALLS FOR ALTERATIVE ARCHAEOLOGIES

Critiques of Israeli archaeology have ranged from revealing the political nature (e.g., Silberman 1989, Elon 1994) and social use of the past (e.g., Zerubavel 1995, Abu el-Haj 1998) to delegitimating the discipline (e.g., Whitelam 1996). Whitelam's (1996) volume deserves some attention as a critique of Israeli archaeological discourse, with a subtitle *The Silencing of Palestinian History* that implies a concern with Palestinian past. Whitelam seeks to replace the Iron Age Israelites recovered by archaeologists with Palestinians. The replacement of one ethnic group (Israelite) by another (Palestinian) demonstrates a lack of critical understanding of the historical contingency of identity. Positing the Palestinians as an unchanging people who have always been on the land is, to say the least, an outdated conceptualization of peoplehood. The more significant analyses and critiques have opened up alternatives to a narrowly nationalistic archaeology, helping to create approaches to the past that can contribute to bridging the divide between past and present created by nationalism. Such examples came first in the 1980s, when archaeologists such as Albert Glock (1985), Philip Kohl (1989), and Neil Silberman (1989, 228–42) called for expanding archaeology from distant antiquity into the recent past. Bernbeck and Pollock (2005, 31), in a recent critical review of archaeology in the Middle East, note there is still much to do.

The popular image of archaeology tends to focus on excavators recovering a single spectacular find. The endeavor actually requires multiple examples and comparisons to create an understanding of a time period for a particular place. The rationale for archaeological investigations of the Ottoman Empire came from an urge to tell a different story for the history of the region, one that counters the repercussions of colonialism and imperialism. Investigators sought to build up a corpus of archaeological materials that could challenge assumptions about the Ottoman past and bridge the divide between past and present. The advocates for an archaeology of the Ottoman period urged local archaeologists of all nationalities to recognize a shared heritage in the archaeological record of the recent past and to find the commonalities for reconciliation between peoples whose nation-states created distinct and separate pasts. The task for this archaeology centers on rethinking and rediscovering the recent past. Archaeologists can imagine the lives of peoples—both elites and commoners—from the past several centuries from the things they left behind in the archaeological record (see studies in Baram and Carroll 2000).

One locality that has been useful for building an alternative history is Ti'innik, an Ottoman period village on Tell Ta'annek excavated by the American archaeologist Albert Glock (1985, 1994). Glock's 1992 assassination emphasizes the potentially explosive political aspect of this endeavor (Abu el-Haj 1998, 166; Fox 2001). Glock's excavations focused on the Ottoman period village, ethnographic interviews with local Palestinians, inquiries into the documentary record, and a holistic concern for links between contemporary communities and the past (Ziadeh 1995). Glock explicitly sought to train Palestinians in this type of archaeology. Juliana Nairouz's archaeological survey around Ramallah used the methodology of combining archaeological, historical, and ethnographic research to reveal the Palestinian past, particularly through the examination of small stone dwellings called *qusur* (Nairouz 2001).

Within Israel, the archaeological expedition at the top of Tell Yoqne'am recovered and published Ottoman materials (Ben-Tor et al. 1996, Avissar 2005). Other projects have included settlement patterns and ceramic typologies for the middle and late Islamic periods (e.g., Brown 1991, Kareem 2000, Magness 2003). Using the information gained by the expedition at Tell el-Hesi on an Ottoman period cemetery (Toombs 1985, Eakins 1993), Simpson (1995) explored diversity among Muslim burials during the Ottoman period. That analysis is an exception; there is still much to do to integrate these studies since a diversity of approaches has been used to address a range variety of issues and questions (see studies in Baram and Carroll 2000). In the case of Tell Yoqne'am, the interpretation of the artifacts included a critique of historically known events on the ancient hill (Avissar 2005). Thus, the recovery of artifacts is not the key to unlocking the past—artifacts do not speak. Artifacts, architecture, and settlement patterns—the data of archaeological analyses—need theoretical frameworks to bring out their meaning. One means to make the data from the recent past relevant, compelling, and situated in a global context comes from the insights and theories of historical archaeology, an approach developed in North America that has engaged anthropologists, historians, and folklorists and opened up productive lines for investigations of the recent past. Below, I advocate for Ottoman archaeology to engage historical archaeology in order to expose the meaning of the material remains and make them meaningful. I do not advocate historical archaeology as part of an intellectual imperialism from a North American field of study, but as a means to situate the archaeological finds from the Middle East within a global perspective.

UNCOVERING SOCIAL DYNAMICS
FOR THE OTTOMAN PERIOD

Braudel (1972, 13) called the Ottoman Empire "a zone of formidable uncertainty." While some certainty has been created in the last three decades regarding administrative structure and political events during the Ottoman period, there is less information regarding social life, particularly in peripheral areas of the empire like Palestine. Doumani (1992, 6) observes that knowledge on Ottoman Palestine remains "highly uneven." The majority of the people of Ottoman Palestine did not write about their lives, but they did leave traces of their world. The material traces make up the archaeological record and the extant landscape and can contribute to the archival and documentary record as well as provide new insights.

James Deetz (1977) in the classic volume for historical archaeology, *In Small Things Forgotten*, illustrates the insights archaeology can contribute even within historical periods that have plentiful archival sources. From the gravestones, vernacular architecture, and ceramics of the seventeenth and eighteenth centuries in the North American northeast, Deetz is able both to raise social issues and to provide significance for items and peoples that have been "forgotten" within history. In doing so he sustained archaeological research into gender, class, and race and brought forward the lives of African Americans, Asian Americans, Native Americans, men and women, and workers that had been lost in the master narrative of the American story.

Historical archaeology focuses on "the small things forgotten": the objects used in daily life that reveal patterns of culture and social change. Transformations in the structures of daily lives are found in the material culture that people made and used. The small things forgotten of Ottoman Palestine—the excavated artifacts such as clay tobacco pipes, utilitarian pottery, Chinese porcelains, Western European ceramics, and olive presses—can provide information to help rethink the history of the region as well as provide the opportunity to see and feel the things used by people in that past.

Historical archaeology has become a means to explore the material aspects of the modern world and, as Paynter (2000, 201) argues, historical archaeology can "illuminate the complex ways in which state formation, race, class, and gender structure everyday lives and history." The transformations in the daily lives of peoples around the globe are found in archives and other documentary sources but also in the changing material practices of men and women, young and old, as they live their lives. The material record—assemblages of artifacts, architecture, settlement patterns, and other material culture—provides an avenue for conceptualizing change for the people left out of the archives or represented by others in documentary sources.

The changes in the material record reveal the daily lives of people under the dynamics of imperialism, nation-building, gender inequalities, and social transformations. The successes of historical archaeology come from challenging what is taken for granted regarding the past. For the Middle East, a key concern for a historical archaeology would be the assumption that the last several centuries were an unchanging period. The archaeology of the recent past can combat the decline thesis of Ottoman historiography by exposing change during a period of supposed stasis. The decline thesis situates Ottoman rule as despotic and the period of imperial rule as preventing change. It has implications for understanding the development of the post-Ottoman period, facilitating an assumption of separate peoples that mirrors what occurred in the twentieth century. Working with the developing corpus of histories of Ottoman Palestine which frames events, the architectural surveys which record details of construction and style, and the settlement pattern analysis which delineates the presence of towns and villages across the Ottoman centuries, the recovery of Ottoman period artifacts from excavations can answer questions regarding the timing of those transformations and support a rethinking of the divide between peoples in the region. The archaeology of the recent past can work on two levels: providing the details of local histories to illuminate the social aspects of a place and uncovering evidence of broad processes of change to contextualize the development of social relations in the region.

An example of material culture from Ottoman Palestine that illustrates those dual points is clay tobacco pipes. Tobacco pipes were commonly found in orientalist paintings of the Ottoman Empire. They seem to have provided a signifier of the Middle East for Western painters. Exploring the material culture illustrates the potential of historical archaeology to reveal the dynamics for the region during the Ottoman Empire. Tobacco, encountered by Columbus when he reached the Caribbean, rapidly spread through the Old World as an herb smoked with a ceramic pipe. Archaeologists in Israel have uncovered clay tobacco pipes by the hundreds. Clay tobacco pipes are significant on two levels: as evidence of global connections and as indicators of social change, two dimensions of history that can be understood as intertwined.

While archaeologists commonly encountered clay tobacco pipes in excavations, one of the first Israeli archaeological expeditions to publish examples was the 1970s Yoqne'am excavation (Ben-Tor and Rosenthal 1978). But the objects were misidentified as Mamluk devices for hashish, leading to continuing citations that were only recently cleared up. The use of these artifacts correlates to Ottoman control over Palestine. Clay tobacco pipes are now recognized as Ottoman period material culture. The identification is significant since dating the artifacts and the strata in which they are found to the sixteenth century makes it clear that they are not indigenous material culture but part of the global transformations that came after the Columbian voyages (Baram 1999). While neither tobacco nor clay tobacco pipes were indigenous to the Middle East, they did become naturalized as Middle Eastern to the extent that the orientalist descriptions of the people in the empire seemed to require inclusion of pipes.

Tremendous numbers of clay pipe fragments have been recovered by archaeologists. With varied and interesting motifs and designs, the objects have artistic merit but more importantly, they are indicators of social change. Paynter (1988) argues that when archaeologists are confronted with masses of artifacts, social power, social tensions, and social inequalities can be found in the material culture. Paynter uses a Marxian analysis that uses the type of production to analyze artifact assemblages; in doing so, this approach not only returns people to the historic stage, but also illuminates the processes of change in terms of resistance and domination. Paynter's example is glass; examining the variation in attributes of glass bottles (particularly mold seams, which represent different types of production) raises questions regarding the nature of technological change over the nineteenth and early twentieth centuries. A detailed historical examination of glass production brings forward patterns of change in terms of social tensions and labor struggles (Paynter 1988, 420–21). This framework is useful for the clay tobacco pipes of Ottoman Palestine. A close reading of the details of the artifacts (in terms of size, shape, color, and motif) organized by chronology has provided insights into patterns of change for the region (Baram 1996, 134–40). A small number of types of clay tobacco pipes were introduced in the seventeenth century; a wide range of types characterizes eighteenth-century clay tobacco pipes. Significant standardization of the objects started in the middle of the nineteenth century. By the end of the nineteenth century and ending in the early twentieth century, only a few types remained for this class of material culture (Baram 1996, 167–78). This pattern of change in the material culture over the Ottoman centuries intersects with transformations in production, distribution, and consumption. By organizing the clay tobacco pipes by production and chronological typologies, with details in the material culture understood as embodying social meanings and social relationships, the patterns in the objects over the sixteenth through early twentieth centuries are suggestive of social transformations.

"It seems at that the start of the modern era, around the seventeenth and early eighteenth century, these commodities embodied the new, the modern, the rebellion against the social order. But by the end of the nineteenth century and into the early twentieth century, these items became old fashion, the vestiges of an old empire, commodities controlled by Western European powers, items to be replaced by tea, cigarettes, and nationalism, which only further entangled the peoples of the region with global processes of change" (Baram 1999, 148). Since the social changes were an uneven process, impacting urban versus rural areas and coastal versus interior regions differently, the patterns of change are connected to issues of social power on the local level. The distribution of tobacco pipe fragments provides insights into the spatial aspects of those transformations.

Such interpretations of individual classes of artifacts are only one aspect of an archaeology of the Ottoman period. The potential of this historical archaeology revolves around the longer and more complete views in historical social relations that can come from material remains in conjunction with archival resources. At present, the archaeology of the Ottoman period in Israel remains poor both in data and in theory. But this chapter uses three case studies to illustrate the rich potential of this approach to illuminate the complex social history of Ottoman Palestine. The global nature of the historical archaeology framework and its focus on issues of commodity chains, social power, and social divisions as related to capitalist production, distribution, consumption, and discards, open up the artifacts uncovered in sites across the region. Most significantly, with the comparison to other historical archaeological projects, the pathway is explicitly cross-cultural. Many of the artifacts found from the Ottoman period have analogies in the archaeological records from elsewhere. Those commonalities help reveal the interconnections between the peoples of the Ottoman Empire and the rest of modern world system (Orser 1996).

This type of archaeology can be part of a global, anthropological perspective comparing and connecting the processes of change in Palestine to larger social contexts. Events that are considered unique to Israel can be shown to be general processes. For instance, there is the process that Braudel (1972, 66–72) calls the improvement of the plains. In Italy, the conquest of swamps by ditches, canals, and other engineering marvels was a major accomplishment of the sixteenth century. In Anatolia, the seventeenth century witnessed *çiftliks* in newly drained marshes. This conquest sounds surprisingly similar to the Zionist endeavor of draining swamps on the coastal plain into productive farmland. With a comparative perspective, the Zionist endeavor can be seen as part of a larger trend in the Mediterranean, standing in contrast to conventional models that posit a unique immigrant experience/moral paradigm in Ottoman, and then British Mandatory, Palestine. The exploration of the archaeology for Akko, Dayr Hanna, and Ramat Hanadiv is meant to illustrate that point.

EMERGENCE OF MODERNITY AT HISTORIC SITES

Archaeologists recover artifacts and the built environment, evidence of human production and social activities that provides a wealth of insights into human societies and cultural change. For an example of interpreting a place, we turn to Akko (also known as Acre, 'Akka, and Acco). Akko is a mixed town with a Jewish majority and an Arab minority. Using ethnographic research, Torstrick (2000) explores the complicated local dynamic involved in Israeli-Palestinian coexistence in the port city.

The Old City of Akko received World Heritage listing by UNESCO in 2001. More than a millennium ago the port, then known as Acre, was the center of crusader activities; today tourists come to see the recovered crusader city. The crusader remains constitute an underground city; above those layers is the Ottoman city. After the defeat of the crusader kingdom in 1291, the port city was reduced to a village. During the early to mid eighteenth century, the city was built on top of the ruins and fortified; major

trade routes brought goods, specifically cotton and then grain, from northern Palestine and southern Syria. According to Philipp (2001), Akko grew
from a small village into a major Ottoman period port city because rising
Western European needs combined with effective local leadership, first under Zahir al-'Umar and then under Ahmed al-Jazzar. By the late eighteenth
century, Akko was the third-largest city in Syria. Only Damascus and Aleppo
were bigger.

Akko attracted global attention when Napoleon's troops, marching from
Egypt, attacked the city. Its provincial leader, Ahmed al-Jazzar, withstood
the French assault of 1799, leading to Napoleon's retreat and the end of his
quest to conquer the Ottoman Empire. But its history goes beyond that famous battle. For example, the walls around Akko during the Ottoman period endured attacks by more successful invaders. Forty years after
Napoleon, the army of Egypt's Muhammad Ali thrust into Palestine. The attack in 1831 was devastating; the death toll was high and the city lay in ruins for years (Rustum 1926; Divine 1994, 54).

These events led Asad Rustum in 1926 to present questions for study
to the Archaeological Congress of Syria and Palestine. His purpose was
"to place at the disposal of the archaeologist and the historian . . . the
history of the public buildings of Akka and of its fortifications in the
days of Ibrahim Pasha. To do this will be, the author feels, a service to
the few who are interested in the material remains of the modern history
of Syria-Palestine. . . . [The] task will not be fully accomplished until the
expert archaeologist takes the material here presented and verifies it on
the spot" (Rustum 1926, i). In other words, the documents create a landscape that the archaeologist can uncover or disprove. There are differences in perspective between the accounts of Europeans and a material
record reflecting daily activities for the local majority. The ambiguity between the documentary and the material evidence can open up questions
for the city during the Ottoman period that highlight the complexities of
social change for Palestine. Specifically, the issues surrounding the fortifications focus our attention on the rebuilding of Akko during Egyptian
rule in the nineteenth century. There is a continuing debate on the timing for modernity in the region (Ze'evi 2004). The Napoleonic invasion
is one possibility, while some historians posit Egyptian rule as the opening of modernization for the region. If modernization means western-
ization, the key question becomes whether a flow of western goods en-
ters Akko with Egyptian rule. In either case, the archaeological record can
provide insights into the chronological issue and thus the nature of
modernity for the region.

The developing corpus of archaeological materials for Ottoman Akko
(see Stern 1997, Edelstein and Avissar 1997) demonstrates the global context of the material record for Akko before the invasions from Egypt. The

presence of Ottoman tobacco pipes, Ming porcelains, British whitewares, and Çanakkale wares along with the regionally produced ceramic vessels (both Rashia al-Fukhar and Gazaware) illustrate the international context of trade and consumption during the Ottoman period. The presence of foreign-made objects is interesting in terms of broad insights into the commodities that entered Palestine during the Ottoman centuries; precision in chronology allows exploration of whether the Western European goods replaced locally-made material culture (Paynter 1988, 418), examination of what types of objects entered the region at various times, and even investigation into which groups first used certain items. The Chinese porcelains, Iznik wares, and British ceramics were made and distributed to realize a profit; the consumption of those goods occurred within a contingent social context and the uses of such material culture impacted social relations. In broad perspective, a transition is found in the ceramics: Chinese porcelains were replaced by British wares. The shift can be interpreted as part of a larger change; the economic orientation of the region shifted from facing East to facing West, at least for prestige goods.

The relationship between the source of material culture and its use in Ottoman Akko can be seen simply as diffusion. Diffusion implies a passivity on the part of the recipient. Kark (1995) gives examples of the diffusion of Western technology during the nineteenth and twentieth centuries in Palestine: foreign technology for agriculture, industry, and transportation came to Palestine via European agents. Yet when it comes to small things forgotten, like ceramics, consumer choices made by the people at the city's marketplace bring out an entanglement as consumption encourages more distribution and then more production. There is more complexity to the commodity chains that brought objects from one corner of the world to Akko's archaeological record than is implied by diffusionism.

More excavations could continue to bring forward a wider perspective on historic events in Palestine. Typically, Middle Eastern archaeology uses artifacts to support or negate details of the archival record, but the anthropological aspects of the excavations can open up questions regarding the flow of goods and people into Palestine. The information from Akko could open an avenue for rethinking the choices made by the people of the region. Further research is needed to clarify chronology for the different goods, to identify accurately standing structures, and to understand when the people used the commodities and how those activities connect to the construction of the extant landscape. Torstrick (2000, 176) argues that archaeology is being used to hide the city's Arab heritage and to highlight Western European and Jewish aspects of the past. As a place commemorated for its crusader remains, Akko has the potential to reveal the links between invaders and native peoples and to reveal how they built social relations, insights that connect to the contemporary concerns in the mixed city. The period between the commemorated crusader era and the present emphasizes the modernity of social relations and the wide-ranging legacies of invaders and merchants on the region.

EXPRESSIONS OF SOCIAL IDENTITY

As the Akko case indicates, archaeology can reveal social and historical dynamics. For the Ottoman period, another significant question focuses on social identities. Archaeologists focus on ethnic identities, particularly in the intersection of material culture and social identity. The archaeological study of ethnicity is important for Ottoman Palestine. For an example of the complexities involved in associating and analyzing material culture in terms of social identities, we can turn to the central figure of eighteenth-century northern Palestine: Zahir al-'Umar al-Zaydani. Zahir al-'Umar was a tax farmer who gained political control over most of northern Palestine, enforced with Western European support for the cotton production in his polity. His family held sway for several decades until crushed by the Ottoman army in 1776 (Cohen 1973; Joudah 1987; Philipp 2001, 30–48).

Zahir al-'Umar is a significant figure in Palestinian history; some scholars see Zahir al-'Umar as a precursor to Palestinian nationalism (Joudah 1987, 134; Litvak 1994, 40–41). Though mostly overlooked in the histories of the region (Joudah 1987, 16), he was a great builder, with palaces, forts, and fortifications found across northern Palestine: Dayr Hanna, Sepphoris/Zippori, Yoqne'am, Sefar'am, Akko, and Tiberias. Excavations at Tell Yoqne'am uncovered one of Zahir al-'Umar's forts (Ben-Tor et al. 1996).

The British School of Archaeology in Jerusalem has been documenting the standing structures associated with his reign (Petersen 2001). The architectural remains allow exploration of the sociopolitical activities of this rebel against the sultan. For example, in documenting the features of the structures at Dayr Hanna, Edwards et al. (1993) posit a developing regional style in the architecture. Petersen (2001, 132–35) reports on the architectural features of the palace (arches, cross-vaulted ceilings, corbels, and arrow or gun slits), mosque (layers of yellow and black stone, inlaid marble panels decorated with red and chevrons on a white background, and cusped finials in a fleur-de-lis pattern), and fortifications (tall towers and dressed stone exteriors). Edwards et al. (1993, 69) state that the "palace is described by contemporary chroniclers as like a castle from the outside."

While that castlelike structure is accessible to visitors to Dayr Hanna today, it is not commemorated. To commemorate a building associated with Zahir al-'Umar raises questions of what features of the landscape deserve national and tourist attention. Giving attention to material remains intersects with heritage and cultural origins concerns in volatile ways. Khalidi (1997, 177) notes that "one of the most common tropes in treatment of issues related to Palestine is the idea that Palestinian identity, and with it Palestinian nationalism, are ephemeral and of recent origin." The eighteenth-century polity can be seen as the first stirring of national identity and the size of the structure illustrates the polity's strength. Though the Zaydani family-led polity was crushed by the Ottoman military, there are continuities in the material representations across northern Palestine. The later construction projects, which are often described as routine architecture (e.g., Hirschfeld 1995) or as traditional with a negative connotation, can be seen as a positive assertion of tradition—of the ways of construction handed from one generation to the next. Those choices made by the people of the region can support a notion of identity for a people without political independence but with cultural integrity. But those choices were not simple or one-dimensional.

Ottoman architecture, in the empire's periphery, was comprised not of "just one identity, but many" (Schriwer 2002, 215). The complexity of ethnic, class, temporal, and regional diversity is an important insight from the material record. Wobst (1977), in a major contribution to unlocking the meaning of material culture, explained that there are different audiences for material culture, from those most familiar with the person and their messages to more distant viewers and readers of the symbolism. While a European chronicler might have seen the Dayr Hanna structure as a castle, others might have noticed the style of Zahir al-'Umar's grand building as emulating the 'Azm Palace of Damascus (Edwards et al. 1993). The aspect of the meaning of the building provides insights into the sociopolitical competition of the late eighteenth century. The mosque associated with the palace was in the classic Ottoman style except for the minaret, which resembled a church tower. Schriwer (2002) situates architectural studies as a means to recover regional (rather than ethnic) identity for the Ottoman Empire, but the buildings would have been seen by peasants and merchants, Ottoman officials, and the local elite. The architecture indicates wrestling with political economy and illustrates the social changes in Palestine, changes that included Muslims, Christians, and Jews. For Zahir al-'Umar, the Dayr Hanna Palace might have communicated one type of message to kin in Dayr Hanna, other elite at Damascus, and Europeans and provided other messages to the Ottomans, to Jerusalem's elite, and to the peasantry. This example illustrates how archaeology can help uncover a complex genealogy for a particular location or object and how different layers of experience contain different messages for different audiences.

Material identities have social meanings due to their geographic, social, and political context. Material culture in the form of public architecture communicates to diverse audiences. The same theoretical concerns for social identity occur with everyday items. For instance, archaeologists commonly recover sherds from ceramic water vessels called Gazaware (it is as common to recover Gazaware as it is to recover clay tobacco pipes in Ottoman levels). With its black or dark gray slip and gray fabric, the type is readily identifiable and is known to have been used into the early twentieth century. Gazaware is documented in Ottoman archaeological strata from the Negev (Rosen and Goodfriend 1993) to the Carmel Range (Baram 1990). Attempts to locate its production center (assumed to be Gaza) have been unsuccessful (Toombs 1985, 106–7) and even its chronological origins have not been established (Baram 2002, 23). But Gazaware is distinctive and may have played a role in communicating social ties for the people who used the pottery. From Gazaware to elite architecture, the material culture of Palestine suggests the complexity of social expressions of identity over the modern period.

UNCOVERING THE ROOTS OF THE PRESENT

Lockman (1996) argues that the complexity of the relationships between Jews and Arabs in Palestine needs to be included in historical analysis. The context of the actions, activities, and behaviors of people needs to be remembered if we are to understand historical trajectories. Evidence from Ottoman tax lists, rural and urban construction, and changes in consumer patterns illuminate the transformation of Palestine's economies and societies as well as their incorporation into the production and trading networks of the Western world (e.g., Cohen 1989, Doumani 1995). Archaeology offers an additional line of evidence to illuminate the changing social landscape of Palestine. Lockman (1996) focuses on workers, both Arab and Jews, during the British Mandatory period to illustrate the alternative possibilities that existed before the division of Palestine into Israeli and Palestinian components. An earlier period, specifically the initial Zionist settlements, may be more suggestive for recalling the complexities of social relations. The goal is not to classify the endeavor into an historic teleology but to situate the people into large social processes. Excavations at one of these locations offer the opportunity to see similarities between Palestinian peasants and Zionist Jewish workers. The appropriation of their labor has yet to be fully taken up as a project by historians of the region so this example only outlines the labor issues involved in a place where Jewish workers replaced Palestinian ones.

In the 1980s, an archaeological survey of Ramat Hanadiv included the remains of a large standing structure known as Beit Khouri. Beit Khouri is located on Umm el-'Aleq, overlooking the valley which is today called Emec Hanadiv. Umm el-'Aleq (Arabic for "Mother of Leeches") sits toward the southern end of the Carmel Range, separating the coastal plain from the major valleys of northern Israel. Umm el-'Aleq is about 11 square kilometers and is within the present boundaries of Ramat Hanadiv, an Israeli national park near Zichron Ya'acov. Ramat Hanadiv is translated from the Hebrew as "the heights of the benefactor." That benefactor is the baron Edmund de Rothschild, whose financial resources supported many of the early Zionist settlements, and Ramat Hanadiv is dedicated to the baron, his wife, and their memory. The area had a significant Roman occupation but there is no archaeological evidence of significant habitation until the nineteenth century. The name "Mother of Leeches" might explain that gap.

In the early nineteenth century, a small village developed on this property. Hirschfield (2000) lists the travel accounts that cite the small village as having forty-five inhabitants. (The documentary evidence for Umm el-'Aleq includes the 1872 Ottoman registry for the Akko district. In 1875 Victor Guérin mentions it by name. Conder and Kitchener's 1882 report notes destroyed walls. Several European travelers also provide documentary evidence.) He refers to the structures as fieldstones and secondary masonry cemented with mud mortar, the typical style for the period in Palestine. The archaeological evidence is divided into residential and storage areas, comparable to single family domiciles. Recovery of a sheepfold indicates an economy based on herding for this small village. The layout of houses in an oval is known across Palestine, a form usually associated with protecting the properties within the enclosure.

The construction of the farmstead by the family el-Khouri was a significant material event on Umm el-'Aleq. Hirschfeld quotes from E.G. von Mülinen's early twentieth-century visit to Mount Carmel to show that the villagers from Umm el-'Aleq became tenants at the 55- by 47.5-meter farmstead. There were rooms surrounding a courtyard and sheepfolds that indicate some continuity in the economic activities on the hillside.

According to Ma'oz (1968) and Ben-Artzi et al. (1988), changes in Ottoman land laws in the nineteenth century (specifically the Land Code of 1858) led to an accumulation of property by some families. In this case, Khouri, a Christian Arab family from Haifa (Yazbak 1998) gained control of Umm el-'Aleq. To improve the value of the property, a farmstead was built. That farmstead employed the peasants from the earlier village, transforming the peasants into agricultural workers.

When the first groups of Eastern European Jews sought land outside the cities, their agents turned to the large landowners. As Hirschfeld (2000, 349) recounts, in 1913 the Jewish Colonization Association (JCA or ICA) of Baron Rothschild purchased the land. The land connected with the previously purchased land that is now Benjamina. The land was farmed according to the Ottoman requirements of *mahlul* [land deemed by the state to be vacant or unused when it has been fallow for three consecutive years] so that the land would not be given to the central authorities. A granary attests to the success of the farmers from Zikhron Ya'acov and nearby Shuni. In 1919, several Zionist pioneers lived at Beit Khouri. These members of the Third Aliyah changed the name of the region to Ummlaleq [the miserable one] and their diaries include conflicts with Arabs who were evicted, veteran settlers from Shuni, and malaria. They lasted only three months. A new settlement, Tel Tzur, was formed afterward and lasted until 1923. In 1929, officials destroyed the farmstead, possibly due to the presence of squatters using the structure or because of concerns that Palestinians would return to the farmstead.

In 1989, excavations uncovered the Ottoman layers at Umm el-'Aleq. The archaeology was productive, uncovering plentiful ceramics (including Gazaware, clay tobacco pipes, and British whitewares), metal farm implements, some metal jewelry and ornamental beads, animal bones, and architectural features. Adrian Boas (in Hirschfeld 2000) describes the materials in the standard Middle Eastern archaeological manner. Nikki Keddie (1992) critiques archaeological reports for listing artifacts in a manner that is taxing for historians to use. The report for Umm el-'Aleq exemplifies this critique. Looking through the listing of artifacts for the nineteenth-century village, there are descriptions of Gazaware fragments, cooking pans, porcelains, polychrome coffee cups, Ottoman drip-painted wares, Çanakkale, clay tobacco pipe fragments (nineteen described of the twenty-five in a photograph), metal finds (including horseshoes, nails, shears, and scissors), beads, buttons, and bracelets. For the farmstead created in the aftermath of the 1858 land code, the report lists Rashayah el-Fukhar–ware, Gazaware, porcelains, coffee cups, drip-painted wares, Çanakkale, clay tobacco pipes (six described), metal tools and household objects, glass bottles, lamp covers, and ink bottles, as well a varia category that includes a toothbrush, shaving razor, loom weight, glass thermometer, and bracelet fragments. This listing confirms Keddie's observation. There is little in the two descriptions that indicates the significance of these assemblages. But lurking in those lists are the possibilities for revealing what happened at Umm el-'Aleq. First, the ideological assumptions need to be removed. Hannah Hirschfeld (in Hirschfeld 2000, 668) concludes the volume with these lines: "All attempts at settlement in Umm el-'Aleq were in vain, despite the diversity of the people, the many groups, the participants of workers, farmers, and the presence of technological innovations and agricultural experiments." The focus on the Zionist endeavor at the site acts to muffle the history of a potentially important site in Jewish and Palestinian modern history.

There are two descriptive analyses possible for the Ramat Hanadiv materials. First, the presence of British ceramics intermixed with locally produced items illustrates the penetration of the European goods during the nineteenth century. On a simple level, the agricultural production organized by the farmstead went to Europe and the people who lived at the farmstead consumed goods imported from Britain. Secondly, a social transition occurred at the farmstead in the late nineteenth century. In one corner of the farmstead, excavations uncovered a trash pit from the late nineteenth-century/early twentieth-century inhabitants of the site, the Eastern European Jews who replaced the Arab peasants at this farmstead. That replacement came when Baron Rothschild purchased the land from the Effendi Khouri in the 1880s. That Zionist settlement lasted until the 1920s (when the farmstead was demolished).

When we compare the collection of artifacts from the earlier group (the Palestinian peasant workers) to the later group (the Jewish immigrant agricultural laborers), the artifacts associated with the latter group are quite similar to those of the earlier inhabitants, differing mainly in the greater percentage of foreign produced ceramics to locally produced wares. (This analysis is based on Baram 1990 and Boas in Hirschfeld 2000.) Both assemblages contained locally produced items and objects from Western Europe. There was no essential ethnic boundary found between the assemblages. That the people were using similar commodities implies a common material culture for both groups. The commonality is not a similarity in culture, but a common social context for both groups of agricultural workers. The objects used by the people at the farmstead illustrate multilayered connections not only to the global economy but also to the previous inhabitants of the Umm el-'Aleq village.

Many parallels can be drawn between the Arab and Jewish inhabitants of this farmstead. Both were dispossessed peasants (one indigenous, the other from Eastern Europe, though that does not imply the dispossession was the same for both groups) producing crops for export. Production in the region shifted from mulberry trees to wine, an industry that dominates to this day. In both cases, production was export-driven capitalist production. Rothschild made it clear that while he could have chosen any workers for his wine enterprise, he chose Jewish ones (Schama 1978). The transfer of land from Khouri to Rothschild illustrates a pattern found elsewhere in Palestine in which absentee landlords from Haifa, Beirut, or Damascus sold to Rothschild for the Jewish colonies.

Those commonalties are found in the data from the Khouri farmstead, but at present they are merely suggestive. Too little archaeology has been done for the analysis to be definitive. But the interpretation implies the potential to deconstruct the dominant imagery of an eternal Palestinian-Israeli conflict. The material remains offer the possibility for contextualizing Ottoman Palestine within broader global power relations and the expansion of capitalism, alongside the complexities of ethnic interactions in the region over the last century. During the Ottoman centuries, archaeological data can point to the discontinuities and complex interactions among people, the type of interactions that require room for multiple voices.

This conceptualization of the data should not necessarily imply an idyllic period. When combined with the documentary record, ambiguities (Leone 1995) can be located. For example, in the late nineteenth century, Laurence Oliphant, a British observer of the Mount Carmel region, describes a scene between Jewish and Palestinian agricultural workers.

> The experiment of associating Jews and Moslem fellahin in field labor will be an interesting one to watch, and the preliminary discussions on the subject were more picturesque than satisfactory. The meeting took place in the storehouse, where Jews and Arabs squatted promiscuously amid the heaps of grain, and chaffered over the terms of their mutual copartnership. . . .
>
> The discussion was protracted beyond midnight—the native peasants screaming in Arabic, the Romanian Israelites endeavoring to outtalk them in German jargon, the interpreter vainly trying to make himself heard, everybody at cross-purposes because no one was patient enough to listen till another had finished, or modest enough to hear anybody speak but himself. (1887, 11–12)

Oliphant's description of verbal arguing can be read as the start of an essential conflict between the two groups. Yet another reading of the Ottoman period archaeological record of that scene can describe a past in which some Jews and Arabs alike were incorporated into a global division of labor. Ethnicity growing out of class relations in an export-driven agriculture is also found in the interactions on the Carmel.

The archaeological remains point to the commonalities among the peoples at Beit Khouri. One then the other group farmed for the profits of absentee owners, using the same structure as their home and having a common material culture. At present, the peoples of this region have only separate and competing pasts from distant millennia. The archaeology of the recent past offers the potential for finding traces of a common history. Of course, participating in a common history does not imply commonality of interests. However, it is likely that those who perceive a common history are likely to grasp the current conflict in a new and different way.

LONG-TERM GOALS FOR AN ARCHAEOLOGY OF OTTOMAN PALESTINE

This chapter has delineated several types of research questions, each of which exemplifies archaeological insights into the chronology for modernity, the material aspects of identity, and concerns regarding power and the landscape. The excavations at Ramat Hanadiv reveal a dynamic history for Palestinian peasants and early Zionist workers. The archaeological report contains the artifacts from the villagers, the workers at Beit Khouri, and the immigrants from Eastern Europe. But the evidence, as mentioned at the start of the chapter, is muffled. While archaeology has been used for nationalistic purposes across the Middle East, its data has rarely been used to source of modern national/ethnic divides. But as the Ottoman historian Donald Quataert (2000, 172) notes, the "subject of historical intergroup relations in the Ottoman empire looms large because of the many conflicts that plague the lands it once occupied." The excavation's long lists of artifacts and the illustrations of the metal, glass, and ceramic finds fulfill the requirements of archaeology but will not engage the reader to reconstruct the lifeways of the peoples. They do not provide insights into the intergroup relations of this corner of the Ottoman Empire. Yet those workers left small things forgotten, which are archived in archaeological reports and the storerooms of the Israeli Antiquity Authority. The lesson from the archaeology of Akko, Dayr Hanna, and Ramat Hanadiv (the evidence from clay tobacco pipes, Gaza-ware, and architecture) is the complexity of life in the Ottoman period for the peoples of Palestine. There was not a simple divide between the ancestors of Palestinians and the people who settled the places that became the State of Israel. The conflicts are historically conditioned, materially as well as ideologically. Archaeology has been used to locate the material conditions for that history. The evidence has not been consistently presented in that way.

The archaeology of the Ottoman period does not stand alone. The archaeological insights illustrated in this chapter have a dynamic relationship to the new research into archives and their syntheses. The latter is exposing the details of the administration around Jerusalem (e.g., Singer 1994), the political economy of Palestine (e.g., Doumani 1995, Farsoun 1997), as well as architectural studies (Auld and Hillenbrand 2000, Petersen 2001). By uncovering the tactile remnants of the past, archaeology fills a gap not only in chronology, but also in the social analysis of the recent past, especially for the rural areas of Palestine where the majority of the population lived. Tobacco pipes, porcelain coffee cups, and Gazaware were used by people during the Ottoman centuries. They are remains of people making decisions and choosing pathways through the challenges of modernity. Since much of the rural Palestinian past was uprooted with the 1948 war (Khalidi 1992), archaeology is an important means of documenting aspects of that complex history.

The development of Ottoman archaeology comes as archaeology in the Middle East is changing. As Yahya (2005, 71–72) recently noted, Israeli archaeologists are rethinking their approaches to the political and religious influences on archaeology and Palestinian archaeologists are in the process of developing paradigms for their sense of the past. There is a general trend toward a scientific orientation, one that encourages recovering all the materials from the archaeological record rather than from only selected time periods. As more projects are completed that include the recent past, scholars can evaluate whether the archaeology of the Ottoman period contributes a different view on history. There is urgency to the endeavor: archaeological excavations over the last century may have erased the upper strata in the search for the distant past, but development is plowing under sites in both Israel and the emerging state of Palestine at a faster rate than previous archaeologies did. In light of these developments, this chapter ends with a plea for preserving cultural resources from the modern strata: scholars and citizens need to encourage the conservation of the archaeological past in Israel and Palestine before more of the evidence is erased. Conservation of the archaeological record and new ways to investigate the past are interlinked in a move away from the singularity of nationalist-inspired heritage. The archaeological record offers another way of knowing the past, one that can unite divergent views of what constitutes history. Within that history, the archaeological record can explore why people took the actions that produced the present.

REFERENCES

Abu el-Haj, Nadia. 1998. "Translating Truths: Nationalism, the Practice of Archaeology, and the Remaking of Past and Present in Contemporary Jerusalem." *American Ethnologist* 25 (2): 166–88.

Auld, Sylvia and Robert Hillenbrand, eds. 2000. *Ottoman Jerusalem, the Living City: 1517–1917*. London: Altajir World of Islam Trust.

Avissar, Miriam. 2005. *Tel Yoqne'am: Excavations on the Acropolis*. Jerusalem: Israel Antiquities Authority.

Baram, Uzi. 1990. "Excavations at the Khouri Farmstead." In *Ramat Hanadiv Excavations*, ed. Y. Hirschfeld. Jerusalem: Hebrew University Institute of Archaeology.

——. 1996. *Material Culture, Commodities, and Consumption in Palestine, 1500–1900*. Ph.D. diss., University of Massachusetts at Amherst.

——. 1999. "Clay Tobacco Pipes and Coffee Cup Sherds in the Archaeology of the Middle East: Artifacts of Social Tensions from the Ottoman Past." *International Journal of Historical Archaeology* 3 (3): 137–51.

——. 2002. "The Development of Historical Archaeology in Israel: An Overview and Prospects." *Historical Archaeology* 36 (4): 12–29.

Baram, Uzi and Lynda Carroll, eds. 2000. *A Historical Archaeology of the Ottoman Empire: Breaking New Ground*. New York: Plenum/Kluwer Press.

Ben-Artzi, Yossi, Ruth Kark, and Ran Aaronson. 1988. "Khans or Estates? Sites Purchased for Jewish Colonies in Palestine, 1882–1914." *Ha Tsionut* 13: 263–84.

Ben-Tor, Amnon, Miriam Avissar, and Y. Portugal. 1996. *Yoqne'am I: The Late Periods*. Qedem Reports 3. Jerusalem: Hebrew University and the Israel Exploration Society.

Ben-Tor, Amnon and Renate Rosenthal. 1978. "The First Season of Excavations at Tel Yoqne'am 1977: Preliminary Report." *Israel Exploration Journal* 28:57–82.

Benvenisti, Meron. 2000. *Sacred Landscape: The Buried History of the Holy Land since 1948*. Berkeley: University of California Press.

Bernbeck, Rienhard and Susan Pollock. 2005. "A Cultural-Historical Framework." In *Archaeologies of the Middle East: Critical Perspectives*, ed. S. Pollock and R. Bernbeck, 11–40. Malden, MA: Blackwell.

Bohannon, John. 2006. "Palestinian Archaeology Braces for a Storm." *Science* 312 (5772): 352–53.

Braudel, Fernand. 1972. *The Mediterranean and the Mediterranean World in the Age of Philip II*. New York: Harper and Row.

Brown, Robin M. 1991. "Ceramics from the Kerak Plateau." In *Archaeological Survey of the Kerak Plateau*, ed. J. Maxwell Miller, 169–279. Atlanta: Scholars Press.

Cohen, Ammon. 1973. *Palestine in the Eighteenth Century: Patterns of Government and Administration*. Jerusalem: The Magnes Press.

——. 1989. *Economic Life in Ottoman Jerusalem*. Cambridge: Cambridge University Press.

Deetz, James. 1977. *In Small Things Forgotten: The Archaeology of Early American Life*. Garden City, NY: Anchor Press/Doubleday.

Díaz-Andreu, Marguerita and Timothy Champion, eds. 1996. *Nationalism and Archaeology in Europe*. Boulder: Westview Press.

Divine, Donna Robinson. 1994. *Politics and Society in Ottoman Palestine: The Arab Struggle for Survival and Power*. Boulder: Lynne Rienner Publishers.

Doumani, Beshara B. 1992. "Rediscovering Ottoman Palestine: Writing Palestinians into History." *Journal of Palestine Studies* 21 (2): 5–28.

——. 1995. *Rediscovering Palestine: Merchants and Peasants in Jabal Nablus, 1700–1900*. Berkeley: University of California Press.

Eakins, J. Kenneth. 1993. *Tell el-Hesi: the Muslim Cemetery in Field V and VI/IX (Stratum II)*. Vol. 5 of *The Joint Archaeological Expedition to Tell el-Hesi*. Winona Lake, IN: Eisenbrauns.

Edelstein, Gershon and Miriam Avissar. 1997. "A Sounding in Old Acre." *'Atiquot* 31:129–36.

Edwards, Camilla, Karen Livingstone, and Andrew Peterson. 1993. "Dayr Hanna: An Eighteenth Century Fortified Village in Galilee." *Levant* 25:63–92.

Elon, Amos. 1994. "Politics and Archaeology." *The New York Review of Books*, September 22, 14–18.

Farsoun, Samih K. 1997. *Palestine and the Palestinians*. With Christina E. Zacharia. Boulder: Westview Press.

Fox, Edward. 2001. *Sacred Geography: A Tale of Murder and Archaeology in the Holy Land*. New York: Metropolitan Books.

Glock, Albert E. 1985. "Tradition and Change in Two Archaeologies." *American Antiquity* 50 (2): 464–77.

Glock, Albert E. 1994. "Archaeology as Cultural Survival: The Future of the Palestinian Past." *Journal of Palestinian Studies* 23 (3): 70–94.

Hirschfeld, Yizhar. 1995. *The Palestinian Dwelling in the Roman-Byzantine Period*. Jerusalem: Franciscan Printing Press.

Hirschfield, Yizhar, ed. 2000. *Ramat Hanadiv Excavations: Final Report of the 1984–1998 Seasons*. Jerusalem: Israel Exploration Society.

Joudah, Ahmad Hasan. 1987. *Revolt in Palestine in the Eighteenth Century: The Era of Sheykh Zahir al-'Umar.* Princeton, NJ: The Kingston Press.

Kareem, Jum'a Mahmoud H. 2000. *The Settlement Patterns in the Jordan Valley in the Mid to Late Islamic Period.* BAR International Series 877. Oxford: Oxford University Press.

Kark, Ruth. 1995. "The Introduction of Modern Technology into the Holy Land (1800–1914 CE)." In *The Archaeology of Society in the Holy Land,* ed. T.L. Levy, 524–41. New York: Facts on File.

Keddie, Nikki R. 1992. "Material Culture, Technology, and Geography: Toward a Holistic Comparative Study of the Middle East." In *Comparing Muslim Societies: Knowledge and the State in a World Civilization,* ed. Juan Cole, 31–62. Ann Arbor: University of Michigan Press.

Khalidi, Rashid. 1997. *Palestinian Identity: The Construction of Modern National Consciousness.* New York: Columbia University Press.

Khalidi, Walid, ed. 1992. *All that Remains: The Palestinian Villages Occupied and Depopulated by Israel in 1948.* Washington, D.C.: The Institute for Palestinian Studies.

Kohl, Philip L. 1989 "The Material Culture of the Modern Era in the Ancient Orient: Suggestions for Future Work." In *Domination and Resistance,* ed, D. Miller and C. Tilley, 240–45. London: Unwin Hyman.

Kohl, Philip L. 1998 "Nationalism and Archaeology: On the Construction of Nations and the Reconstruction of the Remote Past." *Annual Review of Anthropology* 27: 223–46.

Kohl, Philip L. and Clare Fawcett, eds. 1995. *Nationalism, Politics, and the Practice of Archaeology.* Cambridge: Cambridge University Press.

Leone, Mark P. 1995. "Historical Archaeology of Capitalism." *American Anthropologist* 97 (2): 251–68.

Litvak, Meir. 1994. "A Palestinian Past: National Construction and Reconstruction." *History and Memory* 6 (2): 24–46.

Lockman, Zachary. 1996. *Comrades and Enemies: Arab and Jewish Workers in Palestine, 1906–1948.* Berkeley: University of California Press.

Lowenthal, David. 1996. *Possessed by the Past: The Heritage Crusade and the Spoils of History.* New York: The Free Press.

Magness, Jodi. 2003. *The Archaeology of the Early Islamic Settlement in Palestine.* Winona Lake, IN: Eisenbrauns.

Ma'oz, Moshe. 1968. *Ottoman Reform in Syria and Palestine 1840–1861: The Impact of the Tanzimat on Politics and Society.* London: Oxford University Press.

Nairouz, Juliana K. 2001. *Qusur: the Stone Structures in Historic Palestine; An Ethnoarcheological Study of Qusur in the Village of Al-Mazra'a Al-Sharqiyeh.* Masters thesis, University of Massachusetts at Amherst.

Oliphant, Laurence. 1887. *Haifa or Life in Modern Palestine.* New York: Harper and Brothers.

Orser, Charles E. 1996. *A Historical Archaeology of the Modern World.* New York: Plenum Press.

Paynter, Robert. 1988. "Steps to an Archaeology of Capitalism: Material Change and Class Analysis." In *The Recovery of Meaning,* ed. M. Leone and P. Potter, 407–33. Washington, DC: Smithsonian Institution Press.

Paynter, Robert. 2000. "Historical Archaeology and the Post-Columbian World of North America." *Journal of Archaeological Research* 8 (3): 169–217.

Petersen, Andrew. 2001. *A Gazetteer of Buildings in Muslim Palestine*. Oxford: Oxford University Press.

Philipp, Thomas. 2001. *Acre: The Rise and Fall of a Palestinian City, 1730–1831*. New York: Columbia University Press.

Quataert, Donald. 2000. *The Ottoman Empire, 1700–1922*. New York: Cambridge University Press.

Rosen, Steven A. and Glenn A. Goodfriend. 1993. "An Early Date for Gazaware from the Northern Negev." *Palestine Exploration Quarterly* 125:143–48.

Rowan, Yorke and Uzi Baram, eds. 2004. *Marketing Heritage: Archaeology and the Consumption of the Past*. Walnut Creek: AltaMira.

Rustum, Asad J. 1926. "Notes on Akka and its Defenses under Ibrahim Pasha." Paper prepared for the Archaeological Congress of Syria and Palestine, Beirut.

Said, Edward W. 1979. *The Question of Palestine*. New York: Times Books.

Scham, Sandra and Abel Yahya. 2003. "Heritage and Reconciliation." *Journal of Social Archaeology* 3 (3): 399–415

Schama, Simon. 1978. *Two Rothschilds in the Land of Israel*. New York: Knopf.

Schmidt, Peter R. and Thomas C. Patterson, eds. 1995. *Making Alternative Histories: The Practice of Archaeology and History in Non-Western Settings*. Santa Fe, NM: School of American Research Press.

Schriwer, Charlotte. 2002. "Cultural and Ethnic Identity in the Ottoman Period Architecture of Cyprus, Jordan, and Lebanon." *Levant* 34:197–218.

Silberman, Neil A. 1982. *Digging for God and Country: Exploration, Archeology, and the Secret Struggle for the Holy Land, 1799–1917*. New York: Anchor.

Silberman, Neil A. 1989. *Between Past and Present: Archaeology, Ideology, and Nationalism in the Modern Middle East*. New York: Anchor.

Simpson, St. John. 1995. "Death and Burial in the Late Islamic Middle East: Some Insights from Archaeology and Ethnography." In *The Archaeology of Death in the Ancient Near East*, edited by S. Campbell and A. Green, 240–49. Oxford: Oxbow.

Singer, Amy. 1994. *Palestinian Peasants and Ottoman Officials: Rural Administration around Sixteenth-Century Jerusalem*. Cambridge: Cambridge University Press.

Stern, Edna. 1997. "The Pottery of the Crusader and Ottoman Periods." *'Atiquot* 31:35–70.

Toombs, Lawrence E. 1985. *Tell el-Hesi: Modern Military Trenching and Muslim Cemetery in Field I, Strata I and II*. Volume 2 of *The Joint Archaeological Expedition to Tell el-Hesi*. Waterloo, ON: Wilfrid Laurier University Press.

Torstrick, Rebecca L. 2000. *The Limits of Coexistence: Identity Politics in Israel*. Ann Arbor: University of Michigan Press.

Wachsmann, Shelley and Kurt Raveh. 1984. "In the Footsteps of Napoleon at Tantura, Israel." *Archaeology* September/October, 58–59, 76.

Whitelam, Keith W. 1996. *The Invention of Ancient Israel: The Silencing of Palestinian History*. London: Routledge.

Wobst, H. Martin. 1977. "Stylistic Behavior and Information Sharing." In *For the Director: Research Essays in Honor of James B. Griffin*. Anthropological Papers 61, 317–42. Ann Arbor: University of Michigan Museum of Anthropology.

Yahya, Adel H. 2005. "Archaeology and Nationalism in the Holy Land." In *Archaeologies of the Middle East: Critical Perspectives*, ed. S. Pollock and R. Bernbeck, 66–77. Malden, MA: Blackwell.

Yazbak, Mahmoud. 1998. *Haifa in the Late Ottoman Period, 1864–1914: A Muslim Town in Transition*. Leiden, Netherlands: Brill.

Ze'evi, Dror. 2004. "Back to Napoleon?: Thoughts on the Beginning of the Modern Era in the Middle East." *Mediterranean Historical Review* 19 (1): 73–94.

Zerubavel, Yael. 1995. *Recovered Roots: Collective Memory and the Making of Israeli National Traditions*. Chicago: The University of Chicago Press.

Ziadeh, Ghada. 1995. "Ottoman Ceramics from Ti'innik, Palestine." *Levant* 27:209–45.

2

Remembering Jewish-Arab Contact and Conflict

Michelle Campos

"We read the past differently, see the present differently, dream about the future differently."[1] These are the words of Haim Hanegbi, a long-time opponent of the Jewish settler movement in Hebron, in response to the January 2006 takeover by armed Jewish settlers of an area near the city's vegetable market.[2] Hebron is the city of his grandfathers as well as a place holy to both Muslims and Jews. While the armed settlers claimed that they were simply restoring Jewish land that the city's Muslims had wrongfully taken from the community, Hanegbi saw this as the latest in a series of settler provocations that exploit the past in order to radically transform the future of Hebron.

"Settlers living in the heart of Hebron do not have the right to speak in the name of the old Jewish community," thirty-seven descendants of Hebron Jews—Hanegbi among them—had declared a decade earlier in a paid advertisement published in a leading Israeli newspaper. "These settlers are alien to the way of life of the Hebron Jews, who created over the generations a culture of peace and understanding between peoples and faiths in the city."[3]

The emergence of the Association of Hebron's Descendants and the terms in which it described the legacy of Jewish-Arab relations in Hebron implicitly and publicly challenged the widely accepted Zionist metanarrative that saw Hebron as a central symbol of Jewish persecution at the hands of bloodthirsty Arabs. In 1929, sixty-seven Jews were massacred in Hebron in countrywide clashes, making Hebron a political/national sacred site. Hebron gained this particular status in addition to its traditional status as a place of religious importance.[4]

Within a decade of the 1929 massacre, the tiny Jewish community was evacuated from Hebron. Thereafter, the city took on the symbolic nationalist value of sacred land lost until the Israeli army's "liberation of the biblical lands of Judea and Samaria" (the West Bank) in the 1967 war. The aftermath of the war sparked a messianic settlement drive among Orthodox nationalist Jews who, in addition to their aim of reestablishing the link between the Jewish people and the burial place of the patriarchs and matriarchs, also saw their mission as an act of redemption of the earlier Jewish community. "Not another Tarpat (1929)!" became the settlers' rallying cry as they pushed for the establishment of a strong military and demographic presence in Hebron supported by the army, the state, and public opinion.

By successfully placing the events of 1929 at the center of Hebron's history and using them to legitimize their own presence in the city, the Jewish settlers, argued Hebron descendant Yona Rochlin (of the Mani and Hasson families), "have taken two days and erased 500 years."[5] Yet this process of erasure—whereby the history of Jewish-Arab relations in Palestine is rendered into a simple narrative of persecution and violence—spreads far beyond the tiny group of settlers and their allies. It is intimately linked to the beginning decades of the Zionist project. As we will see, violence and martyrdom for the nation became central tropes in the collective Israeli-Jewish rewriting of prestate Jewish-Arab relations.

Contrary to this narrative of violence and conflict, the memoirs of Yosef Eliyahu Chelouche offer us insight into the ways in which indigenous Palestinian Arabs and Jews inhabited a shared landscape in the late Ottoman period. Chelouche's hope was that his memoirs, "in which I told and described the true and warm treatment of our Muslim neighbors, would awaken those who would deal with the question of relations with the neighbors in a different manner and with different maneuvers, in the manner and maneuver of the locals, who have great experience in neighborly relations, to repair to the extent possible that which is distorted."[6]

Indeed, Chelouche's memoirs show that the border between Palestinian Arabs and Jews in early twentieth-century Palestine was far less rigid and less conflicted than the way it is remembered by the people who employ nationalized histories. I argue that "forgetting" the complex history of social ties and relations between Jews and Arabs in place of "remembering" only moments of violence has served to shape a nationalist collective memory in which the ethos of violent conflict continues to patrol the boundaries of the Israeli-Jewish collectivity and limits the horizons of possibilities for Palestinian-Israeli reconciliation.

YOSEF BEN AHARON/YUSUF IBN HARUN

Yosef Eliyahu was the son of Aharon Chelouche, whose family was from Oran, Algeria, and Sarah, the daughter of Baruch Mazliach from Baghdad.

Chelouche likely spoke Arabic at home, although it seems it was not his father's native North African dialect. Chelouche admitted to not understanding this dialect well as a child so perhaps he spoke his mother's Iraqi Arabic in addition to the local Palestinian dialect. Chelouche's memoirs make clear that being Jewish was a central component of his life experience and of his sense of self. Chelouche's Jewishness was reflected first and foremost in his upbringing and education, but was also reinforced by social ties to other Jews. He repeatedly mentioned his parents' desire to impart their children with a love of Jewish traditions and spirituality and their concern for the small Jewish community in Jaffa was a recurrent motivation. Yosef Eliyahu's father, Aharon, set aside one room in their large house as a prayer room and rented out other rooms to Jewish families in order to facilitate Torah study and prayer. In 1879, Aharon Chelouche brought Rabbi Shlomo Bahbut from Beirut to teach in the Talmud Torah school of the small Jewish community.

A few years later Yosef Eliyahu went to Beirut to study with the Sephardi (word denoting Jews originally from Spain and Portugal) *maskil* [intellectual] Zakai Cohen at his Tiferet Israel boarding school for boys. This school apparently served to educate the Sephardi and Maghrebi [Jews from North Africa] Jewish elite. Two of the sons of Yosef Moyal, another leading Sephardi-Maghrebi figure in Jaffa who had been given the title "Bey," also attended. Chelouche recalled that the Egyptian Karaite Baruch Cohen as well as the future Iraqi finance minister Reuven Yehezkiel Sasson Salah were among his classmates. At school, Chelouche trained in business Arabic, French, and Jewish subjects.

In addition to family and social networks, most of Chelouche's connections in early life from the family compound to the place of worship and education were with other Sephardi and Maghrebi Jews. The Chelouches also had ties with immigrant Ashkenazi Jews who arrived to set up a Zionist infrastructure in the last decades of the nineteenth century, although Ashkenazim were less common in the community. Aharon Chelouche defended the early Bilu settlers (from the first Zionist wave of immigration) from the suspicions of the Sephardi community who thought they were English missionaries rather than fellow Jews. When Menachem Ussishkin arrived from Russia to organize the Jews of Palestine, the elder Chelouche worked with him to convince the Sephardi community to join a general Jewish organization. Furthermore, Avraham Moyal, Yosef Eliyahu's father-in-law, purchased lands for the Russian Zionist organization Hovevei Zion.

For the Chelouches, Zionism was an integral aspect of Judaism, a natural expression of Jewish solidarity, a particular love for the land of Israel [*Eretz-Israel*], and an impetus for progress and development of the country. Though never employed by a Zionist organization or agency, Yosef Chelouche nonetheless was involved in assisting in the creation of the new Hebrew society. He was one of the founding members of the Jewish garden suburb of Tel Aviv and as a builder, businessman, and politician, he was instrumental in its growth throughout the 1920s. Importantly, however, Chelouche did not support the idea of political Zionism. He also did not agree with the xenophobic and ideologically nationalist aspects of Zionism that were, in his mind, dominant among most of the European Jewish immigrant leadership.

Although Chelouche was deeply rooted in the Jaffa Jewish communities, his social horizons were not limited to his co-religionists. The elder Chelouche was a well-off moneychanger and businessman and was friends with the notable Muslims and Christians of Jaffa. The local Ottoman official in Jaffa, the *kaymakam*, would sit in Aharon's office in the afternoons for a coffee, nargila smoke, and leisurely chat.[7] When a Maghrebi Muslim who failed in his attempts to enter into business with the elder Chelouche kidnapped Yosef Eliyahu as a child, the *kaymakam* mobilized a search party for his rescue. According to Chelouche, many locals joined in the search, equally out of distaste for and fear of the kidnapper as out of love and respect for his father. The child was returned unharmed, and the entire town of Jaffa celebrated for two months.[8] Likewise, Chelouche's wedding to Farha, daughter of Avraham Moyal and the niece of Yosef Bek Moyal, was an elaborate affair attended by Jewish and non-Jewish notables of the city alike.[9]

To a large extent, the Chelouche family was no different from the thousands of other Sephardi and Maghrebi Jewish families resident in Palestine for decades, if not centuries. These families spoke Arabic, dressed in the local gallabiyya and fez, and adopted local wedding and funeral customs.[10] Elie Eliachar claimed that many Jerusalemite Arabs learned Ladino from their Sephardi neighbors. He recalls the days when women borrowed food from each other and men relaxed at the public baths, smoking nargileh without regard to religious distinction.[11] The Muslim notable Musa al-'Alami also told of the warm ties his family had with his "foster brother," a tradition that bound children born in the same quarter at the same time. His foster brother was the son of a Jewish grocer down the street from his family's house, and the two families visited and exchanged presents until the 1920s when the altered political situation made such contact costly.[12] In addition to such examples of interaction, notable members of the three religions often served as mediators between rival communities, tribes, or families. According to one account, even the wives of notables intervened to mediate women's quarrels.[13] This social setting makes Chelouche's experiences in many ways rather ordinary.

Like many of the native Jewish inhabitants of the land, Chelouche repeatedly used his connections to local Ottoman officials and Palestinian Muslim and Christian communal leaders for the benefit of the Jewish com-

munity. Yet Chelouche found himself marginalized by the Zionist movement, both as an individual and as a member of the Sephardi-Maghrebi
community. With the arrival of the British to Palestine and the institutionalization and legitimization of the leadership of the tiny Zionist movement
in Palestine, which claimed to represent the Jews of Palestine as a whole, the
Sephardi elite, most of whom had remained outside of the Zionist movement, was marginalized from decision-making positions. Chelouche's integrated position within Palestinian society caused concern for the Zionist
movement. As a result, he and other Sephardi leaders were constantly sus-
pected of dual loyalties.

Throughout his memoirs, Chelouche was sharply critical of the way the
Zionist leadership (which was virtually exclusively Ashkenazi) treated the
local Palestinian Arab inhabitants. He more than once blamed the Zionist
movement for the deterioration in relations between Arabs and Jews and
for endangering the once-native status of Sephardi and Maghrebi Jews in
Palestine. As Chelouche repeatedly bemoaned, "our brothers the new Jews
who come from Europe did not know how to behave with them [the lo-
cals], and because of that their attitude toward us changed."[14] Chelouche
wrote, "our leaders and many of the builders of the *yishuv* who arrived from
exile did not see the great value of relations with the neighbors . . . perhaps
they did not understand . . . and so there is much to blame for the fact that
this question has gotten so complicated and that the question has become
so painful in the *yishuv*. . . . From the first day of Herzl's vision of political
Zionism . . . [they did everything except] for one thing . . . which is to pay
attention to those residents who were already living in the land."[15]

Chelouche blamed the foreign Zionist leadership for their arrogance and
disregard toward the local population, feelings well perceived by the locals.
"What did they [local Palestinians] see in us and in our work from the beginning of our settlement until today? Only cold indifference, deliberate
and demeaning mistreatment, and in addition, they also heard from our
leaders in the Zionist press much nonsense which sometimes harmed us
greatly."[16]

Chelouche argued that the Zionist movement and the Jewish community
in Palestine should look to the Sephardim for a way out of the quagmire of
Jewish-Arab strife in Palestine. Only by returning to the positive history that
had existed between Arabs and Jews in Palestine before the British arrival
would the country be able to reverse the tide of violence and ethno-national
strife.

We, children of the place, know well that it is possible—even very possible—to
forge an attitude of mutual understanding between us and them, we only need
to work tactfully and with a deep psychological understanding. . . . We must
cross the bridge between us and them, because otherwise our work in the

yishuv will be delayed. . . . We, sons of the land, have known this, before the British conquest and soon after it, but our leaders in Berlin and London do not know it, and they did not want to consider our thoughts, since we, sons of the land, thought about this differently, and they always attempted to silence our correct voice in terms of this question like a voice calling in the desert.[17]

In this respect, Chelouche sought to lay claim to ethnic Jewish (Sephardi, Maghrebi) memories, memories that were distinct from, and clearly contradicted, the primary Ashkenazi Zionist narrative at the time. Rather than being a portrait of Jews' social isolation in Palestine as espoused by the Ashkenazi Zionist establishment, Chelouche's memoirs highlighted the degree to which indigenous Jews lived intimately within the broader Palestinian community.

Chelouche was quite cognizant of the ways in which the framework of his lived experiences as an indigenous Jew was being erased from the collective consciousness of the Jewish community in Palestine. He wrote his memoirs to challenge this dual imperative of forgetting and remembering. Chelouche's memoirs are replete with invocations of the various business and social ties he and his family shared with Palestinian Muslims and Christians. These stories were, on the whole, positive and even warm experiences. Above all, Chelouche's narratives of his interreligious relationships center on the recurrent themes of trust, respect, generosity, and a true social contract, all of which he found lacking in numerous interactions with his fellow Jews.

Trust

Chelouche retells several instances that highlight the value of trust in social relationships in late Ottoman Palestine. He relates that his brother Aharon Haim Chelouche began purchasing goods from the Bedouin in the Negev Desert for his business in Gaza. It was his custom to pay the Bedouins and Gazans without counting the money and without getting a receipt; he fully trusted the Arabs to tell him the correct amount.[18] Local customs dictated that the extended family would guarantee one's debts, on pain of humiliation. Chelouche related the custom of sending debtors to a tent on the road with a black flag. This method would expedite the interventions of the debtor's relations in order to preserve the family's honor.

Generosity

The most heart-wrenching passages of Chelouche's memoir center on the kindnesses shown to him in his particular hour of need; men put their own financial and personal security on the line to help Chelouche during the difficult days of World War I. His friend 'Abd al-Rahman al-Taji, a Muslim notable who loaned Chelouche money for his two sons' military exemption tax [*bedel-i askeri*], also gave Chelouche ten sacks of flour and use of his pack camels to sustain his family's exile from Jaffa to Petach Tikva. On another occasion, a friend of Chelouche's father Aharon, Sheikh Ibrahim Samarra from Kufr Danaba near Tulkarm, loaned Yosef Eliyahu 500 gold liras, a tremendous sum at the time. Chelouche's narrative relates that the sheikh felt personally indebted to the Chelouches for a good deed that Aharon had done for him in his youth. Despite that fact, the sheikh's act is considered extraordinary rather than simple reciprocity.

For Chelouche, this generosity and sense of obligation contrasted bitterly with the cold-heartedness of his fellow (Ashkenazi) Jews in Petach Tikva, who left the Jaffa refugees to camp out in the harsh outdoors while they overcharged for rent in their homes.[19] Later, when the running water to the village broke down, the Petach Tikvans pushed the refugees to the back of the line at the water well, helping themselves first. The final straw was when the Petach Tikva leadership expelled the Jaffan refugees from the village, hoping that would satisfy the Ottoman military's demand to evacuate the village.

Chelouche further contrasts this nasty turn of events in Petach Tikva with the kindness and generosity shown to him and the other Jaffan Jewish refugees in their next stop, Kalkilya. Soon after their arrival, Muslim friends of Chelouche helped find apartments for the refugees, settling them throughout the town. When they were later expelled by military order to Kufr Jamal, the Muslim villagers not only gave Yosef Eliyahu and his family exclusive use of the village guesthouse—which meant that the village would have to receive its own guests outdoors—but they also rationed water from the village well equally among the village and refugee families. He remained ever grateful for what he saw as the kindness and generosity with which the villagers treated them in contrast to the parsimoniousness of the Jewish village.

Respect

Throughout the war and despite his status as a penniless refugee, very important people—the local Ottoman military commander, civilian officials, and village elders—showed Chelouche tremendous respect. In return, he honored them through small but important ritualized gestures such as treating guests to cigarettes or sweets. Chelouche's tales of kindness, generosity, and mutual consideration among Muslims were clearly intended to serve a comparative, pedagogical purpose next to his sad, bitter stories of being swindled and betrayed by his fellow Jews. Small betrayals made a strong impression on Chelouche as they violated the norms of social trust that he enjoyed with Palestinian Muslims and Christians. Most painful for Chelouche was the incident of the Jewish family who owned the canteen in Tulkarm (and thus felt threatened by Chelouche's canteen monopoly in Kufr Falama), who slandered Chelouche to the local Ottoman officials. This led to Chelouche's imprisonment on charges of spying. Not only did this Jewish family directly cause Chelouche's imprisonment, they also refused to help him or even display general courtesy toward him or his family. Such shocking behavior pushed the boundaries of Jewish fraternity to their breaking point. Chelouche's time in prison was eased only by his good fortune that one of the Arab officers of the prison had worked in Chelouche's factory before the war. The officer treated him well and with the respect due to an *effendi* from a notable family.

Chelouche's claims of brotherhood with local Palestinian Arabs are heartfelt rather than solely instrumental. Numerous warm exchanges with Christian and Muslim Arabs show that he clearly shared social conventions and social trust with them, virtues that he found astonishingly lacking in his fellow Jews. In many ways, Chelouche clearly felt more at home with his fellow Palestinians than with the European Jews, who repeatedly reminded him of the boundaries between them.

As he narrated numerous examples of strong ties between himself and his Muslim and Christian friends, patrons, and clients, Chelouche also related a few incidents of conflict between Arabs and Jews, which generally revolved around local Palestinian Arab resistance to Zionist land transactions. In the late nineteenth century, a land dispute between Aharon Chelouche, Moyal, and Amzaleg against the Christian Tanus Nassar stretched out thirty years until the deaths of both Moyal and Nassar.[20] Chelouche relayed this conflict without indicating its basis, which may very well have been economic competition. Later, after the founding of Tel Aviv in 1909, conflicts over land grew in the direction of explicit national rivalry. Chelouche tells of one notable who purchased land next to Tel Aviv out of "jealousy and hatred for the Jews" in order to stunt the Jewish neighborhood's growth.[21]

That Jaffa's leaders could have had legitimate concerns about the unending expansion of Tel Aviv (see Mark LeVine's contribution in this volume) does not seem to occur to Chelouche. His view of Palestinian Arab opposition to the Zionist movement was instrumental and in a certain sense, naïve. As a businessman, Chelouche's bottom line was generally measured in economic terms. As a result, he felt the Arab population in Palestine was not sufficiently cognizant or appreciative of the great benefit they were reaping from Jewish immigration and from the developmental aspects of the Zionist project. To Chelouche, there was a basic misunderstanding among Arabs "that [Zionist aims] not only were not opposed to the interests of the Arabs but in fact the opposite, they bring to the Arabs great economic and cultural utility."[22] As a result, he was left decrying the "jealousy and hatred" exhibited by the local Christian Arabs in particular without really acknowledging the political basis of their opposition.

After the Balfour Declaration (November 2, 1917), which supported the establishment of a "Jewish national home" in Palestine, and the beginning of the British Mandate, which sought to institutionalize Zionism in the country, tensions between Jews and Arabs increased. To a large extent, these tensions were between immigrant Jews and Arabs. Chelouche relates his own instrumental role in the tensions, especially as an intermediary between Tel Aviv and the Jaffa Municipal Council during the 1921 riots. Chelouche arrived at the municipality offices hoping to easily secure his friends' assistance in preempting any unrest in Jaffa. Instead, he was surprised to see the Arab municipal officers' anger at the "Bolsheviks from Moscow" who had agitated the local population with their May Day parade. Although he managed to negotiate a peace with Muslim and Christian religious leaders, Chelouche's account of his tense exchange with his lifelong friends is an important marker of his being perceived as dangerously close to being "one of them" more than "one of us." At the narrative's climax, Chelouche relates that one of the Arab notables deplored his audacious request for their intervention, yelling, "If you weren't Yosef Chelouche the son of Aharon Chelouche, I would kill you."[23] That is to say, if he had been simply Yosef ben Aharon Chelouche, a Jew working with the Zionist movement, rather than *also* Yusuf ibn Haroun Chelouche, a Jaffa native with the historical personal networks this implied, he never would have gotten away with such impudence.

In the aftermath of the 1921 riots, Chelouche found increased opposition to the projects emanating from Tel Aviv. Throughout the 1920s, Chelouche's work on the Jaffa municipal council became more constricted. He eventually became isolated from his fellow members on the council. After one particularly divisive debate over whether or not to allow the Tel Aviv municipality to build a road along the coastline (today's Yarkon Street) that would pass by the Hassan Bek Mosque, 'Issa al-'Issa, the Christian editor of the nationalist newspaper *Filastin*, turned to the other council members and said, "Look at Chelouche, may God destroy his home, how loyal he is to Jewish affairs, a French citizen and he sits on both committees in Tel Aviv and Jaffa and he works as a real fiend for the good of the affairs of his nation."[24] Chelouche does not elucidate an answer to al-'Issa's insult in the text, but the hardening boundaries between Arabs and Jews was clear.

MARTYRDOM, VIOLENCE, AND NATIONALISM

The process by which Chelouche's reality of neighborly relations among Jews, Muslims, and Christians in Palestine were "forgotten" on the collective

level is due to the privileging of violence rather than coexistence as the central motif in the history of the country. According to Gyanendra Pandey, "violence . . . becomes a language that constitutes—and reconstitutes—the subject."[25] As Pandey writes about the centrality of violence in the narration of
the partition of South Asia, "nations, and communities that would be nations, seem to deal with the moment of violence in their past (and present)
by the relatively simple stratagem of drawing a neat boundary around themselves, distinguishing sharply between 'us' and 'them,' and pronouncing the
act of violence and act of the other as an act necessitated by a threat to the
self."[26] In the case of the Palestinian-Israeli conflict, this dynamic can be seen
as the marked drawing of boundaries between "Arab" and "Jew" and in the
centrality of violence in narratives of both nations' histories as well as in the
narrative of collective consciousness.[27]

For Israeli Jews, 1929 (known according to the Hebrew year *tarpat*) serves
as an important link in the nationalist construction of Jewish victimization
in Palestine as in Europe. Newspapers referred to the event as a "pogrom,"
to the victims as "sacred martyrs." Hebron became a symbol of both national martyrdom and territorial struggle, taking on a twice-sacred value of
land lost and regained through the sanctification of the martyrs' blood. For
example, the front page of the newspaper *Doar ha-Yom* listed the victims of
the riots under the heading, "Remember O People of Israel [*yizkor 'am Israel*]
Your Sacred and Heroes Who Watered with Their Blood the Soil of the
Homeland" (September 2, 1929). *Davar*, another Hebrew newspaper of the
time, listed the victims under the heading, "Our Martyrs: the Tortured, the
Massacred, and the Dead in Battle for Martyrdom for the Homeland [*kidush
shem ha-moledet*]" (September 2, 1929).[28]

The tropes of martyrdom and national sacrifice that were employed to
commemorate the victims of 1929 were already highly developed within
the Jewish community of Palestine and were extensively used for pedagogical purposes.[29] Already in the years before World War I, the Jewish community in Palestine had begun to recognize Jews killed in clashes with
Arabs as national martyrs. This political process, which was hotly contested
at the time, emerged in the series of memorial [*yizkor*] books published to
honor Jewish guards who had been killed in the second decade of the twentieth century.

In the first memorial book, published in Palestine in 1911, the split between those who commemorated the dead as individuals and those who
wrote hagiographies of the sacred martyrs highlighted differing tensions
within the Jewish community about Jewish nationalism and Jewish-Arab
relations.[30] Within a few years, however, the dominant trend became one of
viewing Jewish nationalism mythologically and of viewing the clash between Arabs and Jews as inevitable. A clear, albeit implicit, assumption was
emerging in the Jewish community that "Jewish settlement in Palestine

would not be able to advance without coming up against and defeating persistent, violent resistance."[31]

Zerubavel (Ya'akov Vitkin), the leading force behind the extremist nationalist strand that was to gain the upper hand by the end of the decade, clarified the didactic purpose of this new focus on martyrdom. "Let the Jewish people remember and know how few among its sons lived a life worthy of the name—and fell in battle. . . . Let the memory of the heroes reach into every Jewish home where the spirit of Exile is felt."[32] In 1916, Zerubavel published a new Yiddish version from the United States that more closely adhered to his own political line; its first printing of 3,500 copies sold out within a few weeks. A second edition edited by the young labor leader (and future prime minister of Israel) David Ben-Gurion sold out 14,000 copies over several months. Ben-Gurion's introduction further highlighted the link between the violent deaths of Jewish youth in Palestine and the national future. "The sweat of those working the fields and the blood of those killed on guard mix together in the stream of new Jewish life. It is this blood which awakens our past, inspires our present and, above all, invigorates our future."[33]

Violence became a central motif in Zionist nationalism, central to the binding of individual to the collective, as well as the past to the future. Today, the Israeli army retroactively recognizes about three dozen Jews killed during the Ottoman period as national martyrs. These people are commemorated annually as part of the official list of War Dead televised on Israeli Memorial Day [*yom ha-zikaron*].[34] Aharon Herschler, killed in his home in Mishkenot Sha'ananim (outside the city walls of Jerusalem) by Arabs from neighboring Silwan in January 1873, has been recognized as the first Israeli national martyr in the Jewish-Arab conflict.

Selecting men and women as official national martyrs for a state that did not even come into existence until fifty to seventy-five years after their deaths contributes to stripping these early clashes between Jews and Arabs of their historical context and infusing them with nationalist purpose. According to the official construction of their memory, these martyrs were not simply victims of Arab mobs (though they were that, too). More importantly, they were upright Jews fighting bravely for their existence on the Land of Israel.[35] The national values (Zionism, land, bravery and self-sacrifice) proved far more important to remember than the actual historical circumstances of the martyrs' death, most of which indicate clearly that their deaths were under far more mundane circumstances such as robbery, "friendly fire," or localized clashes.[36] The last years of Ottoman rule were marked by extensive insecurity on the roads and outside city walls, and a relatively small military presence insufficient for quelling disturbances.[37] These same raids, highway robberies, land disputes, and other clashes were as likely to affect Muslims and Christians as Jews, and were generally not specifically anti-Jewish acts.

It is not coincidental that all of the almost three dozen national martyrs of the Ottoman period were young European immigrants from Russia, Poland, and other parts of Eastern Europe. None of the Sephardi, Maghrebi, or other Middle Eastern Jews who died in this period were celebrated and remembered as national martyrs. Yet the circumstances and outlook of Ashkenazi Jewish life in Palestine became the national template, elevating memories of conflict and violence at the same time that the historical context of that conflict (i.e., why violence affected only some Jews in Palestine, not all) was erased.

Unlike Chelouche and the other members of the indigenous Jewish community in Palestine, many Ashkenazi Jewish immigrants were deeply unfamiliar with and suspicious of the native inhabitants of the land. The large wave of immigration in which these Jewish nationalist socialists arrived in Palestine came on the heels of a series of anti-Jewish pogroms in Russia. Their experiences in Europe colored their experiences and worldviews once in Palestine. Many of the Jewish guards were veterans of Jewish self-defense organizations in Russia.

An ever-present European context has remained in the Israeli imagination. From the beginning of Zionist settlement, Arabs were Cossacks in kaffiyehs; much later, Arabs were equated with Nazis.[38] This application of violence and victimization in Europe to the Palestinian setting was made clear in Zerubavel's *Yizkor* contribution: "Graves there and graves here. . . . Which blood is dearer to [one's spirit]? . . . More people fell there; and here there is only a beginning and only a few."[39]

In response to the European Jewish reality, the motto of the first Jewish defense organizations in Palestine, Bar Giora and Hashomer, was "In blood and fire did Judea fall; in blood and fire shall Judea rise." As a result, the new immigrants had the reputation of being overly aggressive and provocative in their dealings with the locals. Their demands for an all-Hebrew labor force and their derision of local customs exacerbated tensions on the ground.[40] One Zionist official of the period called their opposition to Arab laborers "absurd and dangerous," and warned that their "extremely destructive ideas" would lead to a social struggle in the land.[41] Furthermore, the new immigrants began to arm themselves and dress in Bedouin garb while they patrolled the Jewish colonies day and night, provoking tensions with neighboring Arab villages. Arab villagers filed complaints against these Jewish guards, whom Zionist officials agreed needed to be controlled.[42]

A 1908 article by Ze'ev Smilansky in *ha-Shiloach* cited Arab attacks on Jewish settlements as revenge attacks against individuals who had offended or harmed the attackers rather than attempts to attack the Jewish population at large.[43] Sometimes clashes could be prevented by paying blood money to the relatives of the Arab dead; other times the intervention of the Ottoman government and judiciary could forestall further deterioration.[44] Yet only one official obituary of an early martyr mentioned that his death was connected to the death of an Arab killed by Jews.[45] Instead, the martyrs' heroism and victimhood are simultaneously remembered, whereas the broader circumstances are narrated out.

The process of narrating violence and martyrdom serves the historical purpose of cementing the national community around a unified narrative. At the same time, however, continued commemoration of these deaths today establishes continuity between then and now, linking Aharon Hershler not only to the victims of Hebron 1929, but more importantly to today's soldiers killed in army operations and civilian victims of bus bombings.[46] This narrative also contributes to the establishment and continued relevance of an ethos of conflict, which the Israeli scholars Bar-Tal and Teichman identified as a "prism through which society members construe their reality, collect new information, interpret their experiences, and then make decisions about their course of action."[47] An ethos of conflict is the means by which mainstream Israeli-Jewish society generally identifies with the Israeli collective, absorbs narratives of Jewish and Israeli history, and often processes contemporary events.

From Israeli schoolbooks, to television and cinema, to rhetorical pronouncements on the floor of the Israeli parliament, the language of conflict, violence, and victimization are a central part of both the Israeli public discourse as well as the individual citizens' understanding of reality. Bar-Tal and Teichman's psychological studies of Israeli schoolchildren acutely illustrate this point. The Israeli state and dominant popular culture broadly depict Palestinians and Arabs as "primitive, uncivilized, savage, backward," as well as "murderers, a bloodthirsty mob, treacherous, cowardly, cruel, and wicked."[48] The development, institutionalization, and widespread acceptance of this stereotype have been central to the structural institutionalization of a particular vision of the nation and its history.

This (nationalized) prism simultaneously "serves as fuel to the maintenance of the conflict and to the continuation of violence."[49] That is to say, these cognitive ways of "remembering" the Israeli past, especially the elevation of memories of violence as the core of national history, help continue the national conflict.[50] In many respects, historical narratives are told—and remembered—not in the past tense, but in the metaphysical present.[51] This back and forth between the borders of historical time, along with the centrality of historical narratives of violence and victimization, the continued relevance of the Palestinian-Israeli conflict, and the identification of Palestinians as bloodthirsty terrorists, ensure that the cultural and national continuity of Israeli/Zionist identity is shaped by the ethos of conflict.[52]

NEIGHBORS AND KILLERS, NEIGHBORS AND SAVIORS

With the outbreak of the 1929 riots, Yosef Eliyahu Chelouche found himself in Lebanon for therapeutic rest. While there had been some political unrest around the issue of the Western Wall in the preceding years, the severity of events took him by surprise and left him feeling helpless. "I wanted to run, to fly as if on wings of eagles, to return to the country, but all the roads were closed, there was no exit or entry, and we did not even have clear news of what happened there."[53]

After ensuring that his hometown of Jaffa–Tel Aviv was stable, Chelouche turned to the events that had taken place in Hebron, where dozens of Jews had been killed in their synagogues, homes, and on the street. For the first time, indigenous Sephardi and Mizrachi Jews (Jews from Arab countries) were among those killed in the clashes. The Hebrew press made much of the fact that Hebron's Jews had been killed by their "neighbors." This emphasis made the massacres much more shocking and contributed to legitimizing a final separation between Arabs and Jews in Palestine, irreversibly sharpening the communal border between them.

According to newspaper accounts at the time, the Jews of Hebron had been warned of unrest in Jerusalem, but they were "so certain in the stability of their relations with their Arab neighbors" that they did not imagine there would be trouble in Hebron. Instead, "their neighbors and friends betrayed them."[54] Accounts claimed that before the massacre, "the Arabs threatened the Jews of Hebron, 'We will divvy up your women.'"[55] Another newspaper account claimed, "The Arab homeowners told their Jewish neighbors that today will be the great slaughter." Newspapers and later memorial books relayed that several of the victims drank tea earlier in the morning with so-called friends who turned into their killers by the afternoon.[56]

For Chelouche, the shock of 1929 centered on this image of neighbor killing neighbor. The breakdown of neighborly relations led him to publish "a scream from my wounded heart to my Arab brothers," which appeared in the Damascene newspaper *Alif Baa*, in which he addressed his fellow Palestinians.

> For a neighbor to kill his neighbor—who lives with him in one house or in his neighborhood and took part with him in happiness and sorrow and met him nearly daily in the morning and in the evening in the outlook of peace with neighbors—to kill him in the middle of the day, him and his family, in front of the grave of the father [Abraham] of these two peoples, the Jews and Muslims? Even if we were to suppose that speedy orders incited them to 'holy riots' to kill all the Jews, how then did the murderer not think for a moment that after the massacre and once the country quieted down there would perhaps be

some Jews who remained alive under the protection of God, and how would the murderer meet with those who remained and how could he not be ashamed to look at their faces?[57]

For Chelouche, the riots represented an incomprehensible breakdown in the social order. This order was based on people living next to each other, being invested in each other's lives, and being implicated in a shared social code. When riots broke out in Jaffa on May Day 1921, Chelouche had personally intervened with Muslim and Christian communal leaders to stop the unrest. On his way to the Jaffa municipality, Chelouche was nearly attacked by an Arab youth "from an unknown village," but was saved by a fellow Jaffan who knew Chelouche and ordered the youth to leave him alone, informing him that "he is a son of the land (native)."[58]

Chelouche's appeal to Jaffa's political leadership in 1921 capitalized on this nativism and the goal of preserving peaceful neighborly relations. Even then, it was clear that Chelouche's assumptions of neighborliness were fading from relevance in Palestine. This transformation was due in part to the starkly altered demographics and political landscape in Palestine. By the 1920s, the Zionist movement was transformed from a marginal, tiny segment of the local population to a rapidly growing and deeply institutionalized mainstream. If in the years before World War I the explicitly Zionist immigrant community numbered around 10,000 of the approximately 60,000-strong Jewish community, by the 1922 census there were already 85,000 Jews in Palestine. By 1931, their number had more than doubled to 175,000. Most of this growth was among European Jews who, if not personally involved in the Zionist movement, were at least represented by it to the British Mandatory government.

The makeup of the tiny Jewish community in Hebron had changed as it had throughout the rest of the country. Although there had been a permanent Ashkenazi presence in the city of the patriarchs already in the 1830s, the relative size of that community now grew, as well as the relative importance of Zionism within it.[59] Ashkenazi and Sephardi Jews in Hebron continued to send their children to different schools, pray in different synagogues, live in different houses, and not intermarry.[60] In 1929, the overwhelming majority (four-fifths) of the victims of the massacre were Ashkenazi Jews; some, like the Slonim family, were longtime residents of the town. Many of the victims, however, were yeshiva students from abroad, neither native to the place nor known to the local residents.[61] These yeshiva students commonly had misunderstandings with the locals and engaged in violations of the local cultural code.[62]

A survivor of the massacre, Zemira Mani, highlighted the foreignness of most of the local Ashkenazi community. Mani's granddaughter Noit Geva made a movie based on her grandmother's published account of the massacre,

"What I Saw in Hebron" [*Mah she-raiti be-Hevron*]. The grandmother "said that it all happened because of the Ashkenazim. She apparently was not that well versed in the issue of Zionism. She thought that it all happened because in Hebron, there was an alienated Jewish community that wore *streimels* [hats worn by religious Jews in Europe, usually made of fur], unlike the Sephardi community, which was deeply rooted in the place. And the Sephardim spoke Arabic and dressed like the [Arab] residents. The fact is that the slaughter was mostly directed against the Ashkenazim."[63]

Despite Mani's memory, over a dozen Jews of Sephardi, Maghrebi, or other Eastern descent were killed in Hebron, including home- and shop-owners, artisans, merchants, and the indigent. It is not possible to trace the presence or absence of ties to their neighbors, nor is it possible to understand how or why these Eastern Jews were caught in the cross fire that day. However, it seems clear from the Hebrew press that the Zionist community in Hebron was the intended target.[64]

Sefer Hevron [Book of Hebron], a massive tome published in 1970 by the Committee to Commemorate the Hebron Community, includes lists of Hebron Muslims who saved Jewish individuals and families from massacre, either physically protecting them from their attackers or hiding them in their homes. Perhaps because of this evidence of good neighborliness, Yosef Eliyahu Chelouche did not lose hope that the incitement and madness that had taken over Palestine in those dark days could dissipate. He kept his hope that the brotherly and kind relations between Jews and Arabs could return.

In his discussion of the 1929 riots, Chelouche clearly accepted that the Arab community had a political basis for their opposition to the Balfour Declaration, which set aside Palestine as a future Jewish national home. While he disagreed with Arab sentiment that saw Zionism as a threat, he nonetheless clearly understood that this was a political struggle, not a civilizational, religious, or ethnic struggle, as the Zionist movement often portrayed it.

Despite Chelouche's acknowledgment, 1929 was in fact a turning point in the history of Arab-Jewish relations in Hebron. After the evacuation of the surviving Hebron Jews to Jerusalem, the Hebron Jewish community never regained its former status. Throughout the early 1930s, the rabbinical leadership of Hebron quarreled with the Jewish Agency over the funds needed to repair the old Jewish quarter and to resettle the refugees. The Jewish Agency did not support the idea of rebuilding a mixed city. Rather, it wanted to establish a Jewish fortress completely separate from the Arabs of Hebron. By the outbreak of the 1936 countrywide strike, the remaining Jewish community in Hebron was evacuated, this time permanently. The last Jew in Hebron, Yaakov ben Shalom Ezra, an eighth generation Hebronite and a dairy farmer like his father, remained behind thanks to his friends, who protected him, and to the fact that he blended into the social landscape of the city so much that townsfolk greeted him regularly. Yet he too left on partition day 1947, "never to return."[65]

The year 1929 also represented a turning point in Sephardi imaginings of themselves, as they were now situated squarely within the Jewish and outside the Palestinian collective. Avraham Elmaliach, a journalist in Jerusalem and important Sephardi community leader, saw the 1929 riots as the end of possibilities of Arab-Jewish coexistence.[66] Thereafter Sephardi Jewry would be incorporated into the Zionist narrative as victims and, by extension, as irrevocably part of the Zionist project.

This sentiment is certainly the tone behind a recent rebuttal directed against Haim Hanegbi by an American Jewish organization calling itself the International Sephardic Leadership Council. "Rabbis Bajayo, Franco, and Koenka would be outraged if they knew that descendants of the Jews of Hebron were working with Palestinian Arabs to cede a portion of the Jewish community away from the Jews of Hebron. How grandchildren of the Hebron Jews, a community that suffered such tremendous brutality, could now reward the grandchildren of the Arabs that murdered, amputated, and raped their forefathers, is unconscionable."[67]

This aspect of the narrative—that Hebron's Jews were presumably massacred by their Arab neighbors rather than by complete strangers—has remained at the center of the Israeli collective memory of the event. At the seventy-fifth anniversary commemoration ceremony, one survivor of the massacre, Shlomo Slonim, told the crowd, "I know from the dawn of my childhood what the murderous Arabs are capable of . . . one of the lessons of the massacre, which to my sorrow we have not yet learned, is not to believe and not to trust the promises of the Arabs. The Jews of Hebron believed their Arab neighbors and friends and paid dearly for it; but nonetheless we continue [to believe them] and pay dearly for it both in blood and in money."[68]

The fact that most of Hebron's Jews were in fact saved and spared by their neighbors is an inconvenient reality, better forgotten than remembered.

ARAB JEWS AND THE POLITICS OF MEMORY

By 1948, the Israeli state institutionalized the active political process that has mobilized both Jewish history and Jewish collective memory for the contemporary national struggle.[69] The project of the post-independence Israeli historian, according to then-Minister of Education and Culture Ben Zion Dinur, was precisely to reflect "the [Jewish] people's collective consciousness of its singularity, the singularity of its existence, as one collectivity, which possesses self-essence, distinct from others and unbroken."[70]

Zionist and later Israeli historiography succeeded in depicting the Jewish nation as floating through time and space, whereby the local context of individual Jewish communities was "displaced and rendered meaningless."[71] This process was crucial to the successful rendering of (all) Jews and (all) Arabs as distinct social groups that lived in virtual autonomy from the other, and in essence made Zionism seem like a natural historical development.[72]

From its establishment, the Israeli state has been actively involved in forgetting and making forgotten the non-Jewish past of the land of Israel-Palestine as well as the more recent course of events during the 1948 war in which over 750,000 Palestinians were made refugees from their homeland. This dialectic of remembering and forgetting the 1948 war reflects a reality in which "a complex of official and unofficial Israeli institutions was mobilized to dig a memory hole in which things once known were deposited and rendered unknowable for the vast majority of Israeli Jews."[73] The memories of Palestinian citizens of Israel remain similarly marginalized in the Israeli public sphere. Since they ipso facto contradict the dominant Israeli-Jewish collective memory, they are assumed to be both hostile and incorrect.[74]

This dynamic of organized remembering and forgetting is not unique to the Zionist project or Israeli nationalism, but is rather a common feature of modern nationalist movements and is also strategically employed in modern ethnic conflicts.[75] Mary Layoun writes, "Nationalism lays claim to a privileged narrative perspective on the 'nation' (the 'people[s]') and thus justifies its own capacity to narrate—to organize and link the diverse elements of—the nation . . . That is, the story of a national history, of a past usually identified as continuous and persevering, is told as the legitimation of and precedent for the practices of the national narrative present."[76] State narration often results in the "organized forgetting of subjects," depriving peoples of their memory.[77] For South Asian historian Gyan Pandey, this conquest of memory is another example of the everyday routine violence that is committed by the modern nation-state, the violence that lies inherent in the construction and naturalization of particular categories of thought and in the unity and uniformity in history writing.[78]

The border between individual and collective, lived memories and inherited ones, is constantly being transgressed, as group memberships provide the materials for memory.[79] In other words, memory and history "besiege each other."[80]

The sociologist Yehuda Shenhav has theorized this relationship even further by looking at the case of Israel and its various ethnic Jewish groups. While Zionism posits a conceptual rupture between ethnicity and nationalism, it actually seeks to create itself and imagine its borders through the simultaneous creation and negation of the ethnic groups of which it consists. At the same time that the legacy of colonialism led Zionism to see Mizrachi

Jews as "others" from Europe and as "others" separate from the Zionist movement, Zionist consciousness imagined Mizrachim as part of the homogeneous Zionist community, asking them to cancel their ethnic "otherness" in order to be mobilized for the national project. Mizrachi Jews belonged to the national project (since their religiosity was "remembered") at the same time that they were outside of it (to the extent that their Arabness was half-remembered, half-erased).[81]

The tropes of violence and conflict, though premised on Ashkenazi experiences, were successfully able to penetrate Mizrachi collective consciousness and to slowly replace the memories of the immigrant generation of Middle Eastern Jews with the inherited memories of the state. The teenaged Shenhav, for instance, found himself buying into the "real" history of the Egyptian-born spy Eli Cohen as captured in the bestseller *Our Man in Damascus*, which emphasized the bloodthirstiness of "the Arabs," rather than the personal memories of his grandmother's life in Iraq. Farha, Shenhav's grandmother, considered herself both Jewish and Arab and saw the "uprooting" of 100,000 Iraqi Jews from their home in 1951 as "barbaric" rather than redemptive.[82]

The erasure of Middle Eastern Jewish memory was therefore a necessary precondition both for collapsing Mizrachim into the broader Israeli-Jewish collective and for solidifying the border between Jews and Arabs. This border would be characterized by intractable conflict and bloodshed.

Yosef Eliyahu Chelouche sought to intervene against this process of erasure and reorientation of the border between Arab and Jew. In fact, from the earliest years of the Zionist movement, the Sephardim of the Ottoman Empire had very different experiences and historical trajectories that often butted heads with Zionist policies and aims and officials' understandings of Middle Eastern Jews and their Muslim neighbors.[83] Their criticism was outspoken at times, mildly muted at other moments, yet frequently resulted in the cooptation of Sephardi and Mizrachi memories into the Zionist national ethos.[84] The result of this dynamic is that violence became an inherent part of both the Arab-Israeli conflict and of collective memory. The lachrymose narrative of European Jewish history (the "vale of tears") was transplanted to the Middle East. Whether one remembers coexistence or conflict has direct implications upon one's view of Zionism, the origins of the Arab-Israeli conflict, and the future of the Palestinian-Israeli struggle over the same land.[85] Memoirs such as those of Yosef Eliyahu Chelouche, as well as the writings and historical legacy of other individuals like Yitzhak Shami, Wasif Jawhariyya, Elie Eliachar and Musa al-'Alami, re-open the borders between national groups and national narratives.[86] Indeed, Chelouche vigorously argued against the dominant approach that Arabs "only understand force." Instead, he put forth the surprisingly novel argument that diplomacy, mutual respect, and honor should guide Arab-Jewish relations.

NOTES

The author would like to thank the editors of this volume as well as the participants in the 2005–2006 Cornell Society for the Humanities workshop for their helpful comments on an earlier draft of this chapter. Special thanks are owed to Oren Falk, Baki Tezcan, and Tamir Sorek for their probing insights.

1. Haim Hanegbi, "Get Out of the Shuk" [Tzu li me-ha-shuk], *Musaf Ha-Aretz*, January 20, 2006.

2. A tiny community of 500 guarded by several thousand Israeli soldiers, whose presence in the heart of Hebron keeps the city's 120,000 Muslim residents under curfew at will and whose aggressive behavior regularly earns the opprobrium of human rights organizations. See, for example, www.btselem.org/English/Publications/Summaries/200308_Hebron_Area_H2.asp.

3. *Ha-Aretz*, December 6, 1996. For members of the Association of Hebron Descendants (AHD), the right-wing settlers in Hebron were an obstacle to peace with the Palestinians, particularly acute in the aftermath of the February 1994 massacre of twenty-nine Muslims at prayer in the Tomb of the Patriarchs by a radical Jew from a neighboring settlement. Representatives of the AHD met with the Muslim mayor of Hebron, Mustafa Natsheh, as well as with the Palestinian Authority regional military commander, Jibril Rajoub, sparking outrage among the settlers and their allies.

4. Countrywide, 116 Arabs and 133 Jews were killed. The same wall recognized as sacred in Judaism as the sole retaining wall (the Kotel, or the Western/Wailing Wall) of the Second Temple is revered by Muslims as the site where the prophet Muhammad tied his horse Buraq upon his ascension to heaven. For a good historical account, see Tom Segev, *One Palestine, Complete: Jews and Arabs Under the British Mandate* (New York: Metropolitan Books, 2000).

5. *The Christian Science Monitor*, May 20, 1997.

6. Yosef Eliyahu Chelouche, *Parashat Hayai, 1870–1930* [My life] (Tel Aviv: Stroud, 1930), 366.

7. Ibid., 33.

8. Ibid., 38.

9. According to the family lore, Iskandar 'Awad, the Christian Arab who served as consul of Britain, sent seven carriages for the wedding party's use. Aharon Chelouche, *Mi-galabiyya le-kov'a tembel: Sipurah shel mishpacha* [From Galabiyya to Tembel Hat: The Story of a Family] (Tel Aviv: Bnai Shaul, 1991).

10. Avraham Elmaliach, "Me-hayei ha-Sfardim" [From the Lives of the Sephardim], *ha-Shiloach* 24 (1910). See also Raphael Patai, "Jewish and Arab Folk Culture," in *The Seed of Abraham: Jews and Arabs in Contact and Conflict* (Salt Lake City: University of Utah Press, 1986).

11. Elie Eliachar, *Living With Jews* (London: Weidenfeld, 1983).

12. Musa Alami, *Palestine Is My Country* (New York: Praeger, 1969).

13. Ibid. Alami wrote that the Khalidi family had close ties with the Greek Orthodox community, as the Dajani family did with the Armenians.

14. Chelouche, *Parashat Hayai*, 315.

15. Ibid., 363.

16. Ibid., 365.

17. Ibid., 366.

18. Ibid., 118.

19. Ibid., 226–27.

20. Ibid., 21.

21. Ibid., 149.

22. Ibid., 167.

23. Ibid., 326.

24. Ibid., 345.

25. Gyanendra Pandey, *Remembering Partition: Violence, Nationalism, and History in India* (Cambridge: Cambridge University Press, 2001), 4.

26. Ibid., 177.

27. See also the contributions recently published in Ussama Makdisi and Paul A. Silverstein, eds., *Memory and Violence in the Middle East and North Africa* (Bloomington: Indiana University Press, 2006).

28. Both reprinted in Rehav'am Ze'evi, *Tevach Hevron Tarpat* [The 1929 Hebron massacre] (Jerusalem: Havatzelet, 1994), 8–9. For a discussion of the national value of land and blood, see Sheila Hannah Katz, *Women and Gender in Early Jewish and Palestinian Nationalism* (Gainesville: University of Florida Press, 2003).

29. The work of George Mosse highlighting the sacralization of European soldiers during World War I was an important contribution to this field. At the time, Ottomans killed on behalf of the constitutional revolution of 1908 and 1909, as well as Ottoman soldier citizens killed in its various wars in 1912–1918, were considered martyrs for the Ottoman nation. See Michelle Campos, "A 'Shared Homeland' and Its Boundaries: Empire, Citizenship, and the Origins of Sectarianism in Late Ottoman Palestine, 1908–1913" (Ph.D. diss., Stanford University, 2003), ch. 2. Tamir Sorek argues that a distinct Palestinian martyrology (as opposed to Palestinian support of Ottoman, Arab, or pan-Syrian martyrologies) did not emerge until the 1920s. Tamir Sorek, "The Emergence of a Palestinian National Martyrology," unpublished paper.

30. Jonathan Frankel, "The 'Yizkor' Book of 1911—A Note on National Myths in the Second Aliya," in *Religion, Ideology, and Nationalism in Europe and America: Essays Presented in Honor of Yehoshua Arieli*, ed. Moshe Zimmerman (Jerusalem: Graph Chen, 1986).

31. Ibid., 362.

32. Ibid., 377–78.

33. Ibid., 381–83.

34. According to the Israeli Ministry of Foreign Affairs, the day of remembrance is intended for "recalling and honoring those who fell in the defense of the State of Israel. . . . On Yom Hazikaron the entire nation remembers its debt and expresses eternal gratitude to its sons and daughters who gave their lives for the achievement of the country's independence and its continued existence." www.mfa.gov.il/MFA/History/Modern %20History/Israel%20at%2050/Remembrance%20Day-Independence%20Day %20-%20Selected%20Readin.

35. www.izkor.gov.il/izkor86.asp. This combined victimhood/bravery trope is seen most acutely in the commemoration of Israeli Holocaust and Bravery Day [*Yom ha-Shoah ve-ha-gvurah*]. See Idith Zertal, *Israel's Holocaust and the Politics of Nationhood* (Cambridge: Cambridge University Press, 2005).

36. In the predominant framework, however, the personal has been replaced by the national, and other critical categories are suspended. For a similar critique of the personal being usurped by the "religious lens," see David Nirenberg, *Communities of Violence: Persecution of Minorities in the Middle Ages* (Princeton: Princeton University Press, 1996), 31.

37. Avraham Elmaliach, *Eretz Yisrael ve-Suriya be-Milhemet ha-'Olam ha-Rishona (alef)* [The Land of Israel and Syria during World War I: Part 1] (Jerusalem, 1927) and Avraham Elmaliach, *Eretz Yisrael ve-Suriya be-Milhemet ha-'Olam ha-Rishona (bet)* (Jerusalem, 1928).

38. See Idith Zertal, "From the People's Hall to the Wailing Wall: A Study in Memory, Fear, and War," *Representations* 69 (Winter 2000); and the post-independence movie *Hill 24 Doesn't Answer.*

39. Frankel, "The 'Yizkor' Book of 1911," 362.

40. See Gershon Shafir, *Land, Labor, and the Origins of the Israeli-Palestinian Conflict 1882–1914* (Berkeley: University of California Press, 1996) on Hebrew labor.

41. Report by Dyk, n.d., Central Zionist Archives (CZA), L1/70. Arthur Ruppin, director of the WZO's Palestine Office in Jaffa, also considered Hebrew labor dangerous and sure to bring dire consequences. See Ruppin to Zentralburo, July 28, 1912, CZA, L5/70.

42. Thon to ZAC, August 25, 1913, CZA, Z3/1450.

43. Quoted in Chana Sosevsky, "Attitudes of Zionist Intellectuals to the Arab Population in Palestine As Expressed in the Literature Before the Young Turk Revolution of 1908" (Ph.D. diss., New York University, 1980), 151.

44. Blood money reparations for Arabs killed by Jewish guards were mentioned in a 1911 letter, CZA L2/50I; Memo to ZAC, November 9, 1911, CZA L2/26I; PLDC report, May 25, 1911, CZA L1/97. Formal reconciliations were mentioned in Krause (Sedjera) to Albert Antebi, May 27, 1909, Archives of the Alliance Israelite Universelle Paris (AIU) IX.E.26; Rosenheck (Nazareth) to Franck, March 8, 1910, CZA J15/6343.

45. Revenge killings were mentioned by *ha-'Olam*, May 18, 1909; H. Calmy to President of the Alliance Israélite Universelle, February 15, 1910, CZA, CM434/4; *ha-Herut*, February 18, 1910; *ha-Herut* June 10, 1910; August 1913 letter, CZA L2/26III; Thon to Zionist Zentralburo, August 5, 1913, CZA Z3/1450; Israel State Archives (ISA) 67/peh/415:26.

46. For a discussion of the ways in which the patriotism-sacrifice nexus has been challenged and subverted in popular culture, see Yael Zerubavel, "Patriotic Sacrifice and the Burden of Memory in Israeli Secular National Hebrew Culture," in Makdisi and Silverstein, eds., *Memory and Violence in the Middle East and North Africa.*

47. Daniel Bar-Tal and Yona Teichman, *Stereotypes and Prejudice in Conflict: Representations of Arabs in Israeli Jewish Society* (Cambridge: Cambridge University Press, 2005), 116–21, 124.

48. See also Ruth Firer and Sami Adwan, *The Israeli-Palestinian Conflict in History and Civics Textbooks of Both Nations* (Hannover: Verlag Hahnsche Buchhandlung, 48:2004) and Elie Podeh, "History and Memory in the Israeli Educational System: The Portrayal of the Arab-Israeli Conflict in History Textbooks (1948–2000)," *History and Memory* 12 (June 2000) for an overview of the dominant Zionist narrative in the Israeli educational system, as well as for the language used to describe Palestinian Arabs.

49. Bar-Tal and Teichman, *Stereotypes and Prejudice in Conflict*, 124.

50. A similar phenomenon most likely occurs among the Palestinian Arab population, but this is outside the scope of this chapter.

51. Paul Connerton, *How Societies Remember* (New York: Cambridge University Press, 1989) 43.

52. Eviatar Zerubavel writes that sociobiographical memory is "the mechanism through which we feel pride, pain, or shame with regard to events that happened to our groups before we joined them." We might add to that anger and outrage. Jeffrey K. Olick and Joyce Robbins, "Social Memory Studies: From 'Collective Memory' to the Historical Sociology of Mnemonic Practices," *Annual Review of Sociology* 24 (1998), 123.

53. Chelouche, *Parashat Hayai*, 352.

54. The standard account is "Be-fro'a pra'ot: Megilat ha-damim," which was published in a variety of newspapers and weeklies after the events: *Had-Pe'amim, Dvar ha-Yamim, Dvar ha-Yamim ha-Ele, Ba-Machane, Yerushalayim, Ketuvim, ha-Aretz, Doar ha-Yom, Davar, Kol Israel*. Its centrality in constructing the core of the collective memory of Hebron is evidenced by its duplication in both Oded Avishar, *Sefer Hevron: 'Ir ha-avot ve-yishuvah be-rei ha-dorot* [The book of Hebron: city of the patriarchs and its Jewish community over generations] (Jerusalem: Keter, 1970) and Rehav'am Ze'evi, *Tevach Hevron Tarpat* [The 1929 Hebron massacre] (Jerusalem: Havatzelet, 1994). Tom Segev's recent book on Palestine under the mandate debunks some of the myths perpetuated by the newspaper accounts.

55. "Hazva'a be-hevron," by eyewitnesses, in *Dvar ha-yamim ha-ele*, excerpted from Ze'evi, *Tevach Hevron Tarpat*, 41.

56. Leo Gottesman, *The Martyrs of Hebron: Personal Reminiscences of Some of the Men and Women Who Offered Up Their Lives During the Massacre of August 24, 1929, at Hebron, Palestine and Some of Who Were Spared* (New York, 1930).

57. Chelouche, *Parashat Hayai*, 352–53.

58. Ibid., 325.

59. Although it has been claimed that the Hebron community belonged to the so-called Old Yishuv, and was therefore hostile to the Zionist movement, this is in fact not the case in the yeshiva that was the main target in the riots. Among the photos of the devastation wrought in the synagogue and yeshiva buildings one can see a photo of Theodor Herzl, the father of modern political Zionism, still hanging on the wall. For a representation of how the religious and national aspects were combined in the worldview of the yeshiva, see *Sefer zikaron le-kdoshei yeshivat Hevron 'Kneset Israel' asher nispu al kdushat ha-Shem be-y"Ch Menachem Av Tarpat be-Hevron Eretz Ha-Kodesh* (Jerusalem, 1930) and Gottesman, *The Martyrs of Hebron*.

60. Avishar, *Sefer Hevron*, 172–73.

61. Fifty-four Ashkenazim and thirteen Jews from *'edot ha-Mizrach* (Sephardim, Maghrebim, and Parsim) were killed. See "The Complete List of the Holy of Hebron who were Taken to their Grave on the Night of 20 Av Tarpat," *Jerusalem*, August 29, 1929, which identifies each victim by their profession and ethnicity; they misidentify one Russian Jew as a Sephardi Jew. The newspaper article is preserved in Ze'evi, *Tevach Hevron Tarpat*, 66–69. An additional forty-five Ashkenazim and thirteen Sephardim were injured in the riots and hospitalized in Jerusalem.

62. Gottesman, *The Martyrs of Hebron*.

63. "Hebron Diary," *Ha-Aretz*, July 9, 1999.

64. "Be-fro'a pra'ot: Megilat ha-damim."

65. "The Last One," in Avishar, *Sefer Hevron*.

66. Oral History Project, Institute of Contemporary Jewry, Hebrew University of Jerusalem, "Interview with Avraham Elmaliach," (April 1963).

67. "Statement from the International Sephardic Leadership Council regarding recent claims made by members of the Association of Hebron Descendants," February 2, 2006, www.sephardiccouncil.org/heb.html.

68. *Hevron me-az u-le-tamid: Dvar ha-yishuv* [Hebron always and forever] September 20, 2004.

69. The Israeli sociologist Baruch Kimmerling has accused the Israeli historical and sociological disciplines of being trapped in a "Jewish-Israeli bubble," shaped by the Zionist consensus of the Israeli academy, where scholars have been "mobilized for the collective and give legitimacy to the collective." Baruch Kimmerling, "Be'ayot kontseptualiot be-historiografia shel erets u-va-shnei 'amim" [Conceptual problems in the historiography of a land with two peoples] in *Eretz ahat u-shnei 'amim ba* [One land of two peoples], ed. Danny Ya'akobi (Jerusalem: Magnes Press, 1999). See Yael Zerubavel, *Recovered Roots: Collective Memory and the Making of Israeli National Tradition* (Chicago: University of Chicago Press, 1995) and Nachman Ben-Yehuda, *Masada Myth: Collective Memory and Mythmaking in Israel* (Madison: University of Wisconsin Press, 1995).

70. Yuri Ram, "Zionist Historiography and the Invention of Modern Jewish Nationhood," *History and Memory* 7, no. 1 (June 1995), 14.

71. Gabriel Piterberg, "Domestic Orientalism: The Representation of 'Oriental' Jews in Zionist/Israeli Historiography," *British Journal of Middle Eastern Studies* 23, no. 2 (November 1996), 133.

72. See Beshara Doumani, "Rediscovering Ottoman Palestine: Writing Palestinians into History," *MESA Bulletin* 21, no. 2 (Winter 1992) and Zachary Lockman, "Railway Workers and Relational History: Arabs and Jews in British-Ruled Palestine," *Comparative Studies in Society and History* 35, no. 3 (July 1993) for lucid critiques of the nationalist-framed literature. See also Gershon Shafir, *Land, Labor and the Origins of the Israeli-Palestinian Conflict, 1882–1914* (Berkeley: University of California Press, 1996); Zachary Lockman, *Comrades and Enemies: Arab and Jewish Workers in Palestine, 1906–1948* (Berkeley: University of California Press, 1996); and Salim Tamari, *Jerusalem 1948: The Arab Neighborhoods and Their Fate in the War* (Jerusalem: The Institute for Jerusalem Studies, 1999).

73. Joel Beinin, "Forgetfulness for Memory: The Limits of the New Israeli History," *Journal of Palestine Studies* 34, no. 2 (Winter 2005), 11. I found Beinin's formulation of "forgetfulness for memory" to be stimulating. See also Meron Benvenisti, *Sacred Landscapes: The Buried History of the Holy Land Since 1948* (Berkeley: University of California Press, 2002) and Anita Shapira, "Hirbet Hizah: Between Remembrance and Forgetting," *Jewish Social Studies* 7, no. 1 (Fall 2000).

74. See Shira N. Robinson, "Local Struggle, National Struggle: Palestinian Responses to the Kafr Qasim Massacre and Its Aftermath, 1956–1966," *International Journal of Middle East Studies* 35, no. 3 (2003); Susan Slyomovics, *The Object of Memory: Arab and Jew Narrate the Palestinian Village* (Philadelphia: University of Pennsylvania Press, 1998); and Tamir Sorek, "Cautious Commemoration of a National Mi-

nority: Monuments for Palestinian Martyrs in Israel," (*Comparative Studies in Society and History*, forthcoming).

75. Similar sentiments are expressed by the Turkish scholar Taner Akçam regarding the historical memory of the fate of the Ottoman Empire's Armenian subjects. See Taner Akçam, *From Empire to Republic: Turkish Nationalism and the Armenian Genocide* (London: Zed Books, 2004). Also important is the historical legacy of the Mughal Empire in South Asia vis-à-vis Muslim-Hindu relations. See Sudhir Kakar, *The Colors of Violence: Cultural Identities, Religion, and Conflict* (Chicago: University of Chicago Press, 1996).

76. Mary N. Layoun, *Wedded to the Land? Gender, Boundaries, and Nationalism in Crisis* (Durham, NC: Duke University Press, 2001), 10.

77. Connerton, *How Societies Remember*, 3, 14–15.

78. Gyanendra Pandey, *Routine Violence: Nations, Fragments, Histories* (Stanford: Stanford University Press, 2006), 15.

79. Jeffrey K. Olick, "Collective Memory: The Two Cultures," *Sociological Theory* 17, no. 3 (November 1999), 335, 342.

80. Zerubavel, *Recovered Roots*. See also the discussion in Piterberg, "Domestic Orientalism."

81. Yehuda Shenhav, *Ha-Yehudim he-'Aravim: Leumiut, dat ve-etniut* [The Arab Jews: Nationalism, Religion, and Ethnicity] (Tel Aviv: Am Oved, 2003), 16.

82. Shenhav, *Ha-Yehudim he-'Aravim*, 10–11.

83. See Michelle U. Campos, "Between 'Beloved Ottomania' and 'The Land of Israel': The Struggle Between Ottomanism and Zionism Among Palestine's Sephardi Jews, 1908–1913," *International Journal of Middle East Studies*, November 2005.

84. Gabriel Piterberg makes this argument in his analysis of the movie *A Bowing Palm Tree*, which looks at the uprooting of a Yemenite colony in the 1920s in order to clear out their land for their Ashkenazi neighbors. As Piterberg wrote, the Yemeni community's challenge of the hegemonic (Ashkenazi) Zionist version of history was muted. Rather than countering the validity of the Zionist narrative or viewing themselves as victims of the Zionist project, the Yemeni community instead struggled to be written into the heroic pioneer Zionist narrative. Gabi Piterberg, "Domestic Orientalism."

85. Mark Cohen, a noted historian of the medieval Middle East, has written a lucid critique of these two opposed tropes of either an idyllic golden age or a vale of tears. Mark Cohen, "The Neo-Lachrymose Conception of Jewish-Arab History," *Tikkun* 6, (May 1991–30 June 1991) and Norman Stillman, "Reply to Mark Cohen," *Tikkun* 6, (May 1991–30 June 1991). See also the discussion in Joel Beinin, *The Dispersion of Egyptian Jewry: Culture, Politics, and the Formation of a Modern Diaspora* (Berkeley: University of California Press, 1998).

86. Salim Tamari, "Ishaq Al-Shami and the Predicament of the Arab Jew in Palestine," *Jerusalem Quarterly*, no. 21 (August 2004).

3

Reapproaching the Borders of Nazareth (1948–1956)

Israel's Control of an All-Arab City

Geremy Forman

On the morning of June 17, 1954, a group of Arab villagers affiliated with the pro-government al-Zu'bi clan attacked the six Communist Party members of the Nazareth Municipal Council as they made their way to the municipal building to select a new mayor. That same morning, the Israeli government published an order expropriating 1,200 *dunams* of Arab-owned land in and adjacent to the city for the supposed purpose of constructing district government offices and employee housing.[1] Though the exact timing was coincidental, the two events were related; they both stemmed directly or indirectly from Israeli efforts to maintain state control over Nazareth, which emerged from the 1948 war as the largest and most important Arab center in the country. By examining the state's relationship with Nazareth during the first decade of Israeli statehood,[2] this chapter highlights the relational borders between geographical processes and sociopolitical power relations in a city that has been so central to the political and ideological fabric of Palestinian society within Israel that "if there were no Nazareth, it would have had to have been invented to make Arab politics in Israel unfold."[3]

This formative period in Nazareth-state relations must be understood in the context of Israeli state Judaization strategies during the few decades following 1948. Israeli officials attempted to ensure state control over Arab areas and previous Arab areas with little or no Jewish population by employing a variety of mechanisms. The most blatant of these mechanisms can be roughly classified as military, political, and spatial. In localities completely depopulated during the 1948 war, the primary means for establishing Jewish state control were military and spatial. The Israel Defense Forces (IDF) first expelled or blocked the return of Palestinian inhabitants and then the state expropriated their land and established new Jewish settlements. But in most localities in which a Palestinian population remained after 1948, the Israeli authorities retained the military component long after the war's end in the form of a military government. The military government ruled the bulk of the country's Palestinian population between 1948 and 1966. The military government, in turn, controlled movement, law enforcement, political activity, and resource allocation in order to facilitate Jewish settlement and assist in the manipulation of local government to prevent antigovernment forces from gaining power.

In the case of Nazareth, Israeli officials applied military, political, and spatial mechanisms in cumulative progression during Israel's first decade of statehood in order to enhance state influence over the city, its inhabitants, and the surrounding territory. During this period, they reapproached and redefined the borders of Arab Nazareth in a process that culminated in the establishment and territorial demarcation of a new Jewish urban settlement adjacent to the Arab city. In doing so, they made strategic use of the state's authority to demarcate and redemarcate municipal borders in order to intensify Jewish control of the all-Arab city and surrounding region.

NAZARETH AFTER THE 1948 WAR

Israeli officials regarded Nazareth as a unique and especially sensitive urban area due to its size, its all-Arab population, its religious status throughout the Christian world, and its quickly emerging political dominance among Israel's Palestinian citizens. Despite this uniqueness, and to a large degree because of it, Israeli officials viewed state control of the city as a prerequisite for control of the Arab central Galilee that lay to the north.

Nazareth's population was predominantly Muslim during most of the period following Islam's expansion into Palestine. But by the tail end of Ottoman rule in the late nineteenth century, the town had a sizable Christian majority. During the British Mandate, Nazareth served as district government headquarters, resulting in its rapid expansion into an important urban center with a population of 15,500 people. By the end of the Mandate, the city's demographic makeup began to swing back in favor of its Muslims, who now constituted 40 percent of the population.[4]

The Ottoman Vilayet Municipal Law of 1877 provided Nazareth with its first structure of local government. The law facilitated the installation of an elected municipal council and a government-appointed mayor. This structure, which increased local control over various municipal services, was nonetheless under stringent Ottoman governmental control.[5] Although British Mandate authorities further developed this structure with the Municipal Corporations Ordinance of 1934, local government in Nazareth remained limited by the high commissioner's control of municipal operations.[6] In addition, British Mandate officials structured elected municipal councils in Nazareth (as in other cities in Palestine) to reflect and perpetuate the city's traditional sociopolitical structure based on individual loyalties to familial and religious groupings. At the end of the Mandate, the city's major religious communities (from largest to smallest) were Muslims, Greek Orthodox, Greek Catholics, and Roman Catholics. On this demographic basis, Nazareth's nine-member municipal council included three Muslims, three Orthodox Christians, and three Catholics. Salim Bishara, the city's British-appointed Christian mayor, headed the council.[7]

Although the Palestinian national movement and the Jewish-Arab ethnonational conflict that was intensifying in Palestine affected Nazareth during the Mandate period, its role in the conflict was minor in comparison to other Arab localities in the country.[8] The city's status changed in this respect after the 1948 war, which Israelis refer to in Hebrew as *Milhemet ha-'Atzma'ut* [the War of Independence] and Palestinians refer to in Arabic as *al-Nakba* [the catastrophe]. The war resulted in the establishment of the Jewish State of Israel in most of Mandate Palestine, the flight and expulsion of 80 percent of the Palestinians who had been living in the area incorporated into Israel, the immigration of hundreds of thousands of Jews to the country (see Davidovitch et al. in this volume), and the disappearance of all other major Arab urban centers within its borders. Just before the war, the UN General Assembly called for Palestine's partition into a Jewish state and an Arab state. It allocated Nazareth (and the rest of the central and western Galilee) to the proposed Arab state. With the exception of some Palestinian communists, the Arabs of Palestine and the surrounding countries rejected the concept of partition. Israeli forces conquered the entire Galilee during the ensuing hostilities, placing Nazareth and other Arab regions under military rule.[9] During the war, about one-fifth of the city's population became refugees, while a much larger number of refugees poured into the city. The Nazareth that emerged from the war was transformed. In 1951 the city's population was 20,300, 31 percent greater than it had been before the war. Due primarily to its large refugee population, many city residents were poor, unemployed, and living in substandard conditions.[10]

The state's approach to Nazareth during the 1950s was a function of broader Israeli policy toward the country's Palestinian Arab minority at the time. The authorities regarded Palestinians who remained within Israel's borders after the war as a security threat—a fifth column or a "Trojan horse" of the surrounding Arab countries who would work against the state in the event of another war.[11] Numerous studies have noted prestate Zionist pledges to grant equality to the Arab citizens of a future Jewish state, as well as the commitment of equality contained in Israel's Declaration of Independence.[12] Others have stressed the existence before and after 1948 of

hopes of inducing Palestinian citizens of the Jewish state to leave.[13] These
two approaches—a democratic approach granting Arabs equal rights and an
ethnocentric approach classifying them as undesirable subjects—coexisted
in the pre-1948 ideas of Zionist leaders. After the war, Israel did in fact grant
citizenship, suffrage, and what officials presented theoretically as guaran-
teed equality before the law. Practically, however, it was the other view, the
fifth-column perspective, that shaped Israel's minority policy. As a result,
the provision of equality was extremely limited.[14]

The premise underlying Israel's policy toward its Palestinian citizens during the first few decades of statehood was that the perceived threat they
posed could be held in check through close supervision, a governing system
exerting more control over Palestinian citizens than typical democracy, prevention of the crystallization of a united Arab minority through denominational division, lack of development of the country's Arab economy to ensure Jewish economic dominance, and promotion of Jewish settlement in
predominantly Arab areas.[15] In contrast to the more "benign" policy of social integration and the easing of military government controls that characterized the 1960s, Israel's domestic Arab policy during the 1950s stemmed
from the conviction that expecting Arabs to support the Jewish state was un-
realistic and the hope that many could be compelled to emigrate.[16] It aimed
at maximum surveillance and control by isolating Arabs from the country's
political, administrative, and social systems. During this decade, the state
forced its will on the Arab minority with what Sabri Jiryis describes as "a
clearly aggressive policy of cruelly oppressive measures" including vast land
expropriation, excessive violence, and the repressive policies of the military
government.[17]

Many governmental and quasi-governmental agencies took part in implementing Israel's domestic Arab policy,[18] but the dominant force in
Nazareth as elsewhere was the military government.[19] Most Arab localities
came under military rule toward the end of the 1948 war, and an overall national structure of military government was established in the autumn of
1948. By 1951, officials had structured the military government into three
sectors coinciding with Israel's major concentrations of Palestinian population: the northern sector, which administered the Galilee; the central sector,
which administered the "Triangle" (the area between Megiddo and Kafr
Qasim bordering the Jordanian-controlled West Bank); and the southern
sector, which administered the Negev (see fig. 3.1).[20]

Military governors appointed by the defense minister were granted broad
powers to control movement, institute surveillance, and detain, try, and
punish civilians under the 1945 Mandatory Defense (Emergency) Regulations and subsequent Israeli laws.[21] In July 1949, Prime Minister and Defense Minister David Ben-Gurion dissolved the short-lived Minority Affairs
Ministry and charged the military government with coordinating all gov-

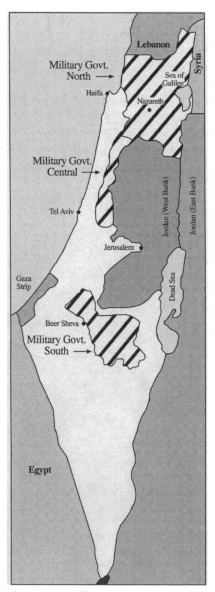

Figure 3.1. Military Government Sectors in Pre-1966 Israel. Courtesy of the Author.

ernment activity in the Arab sector. In 1956 nearly 180,000 of Israel's 200,000 Palestinian citizens (virtually all those not living in "mixed cities") lived under military rule.[22]

But Nazareth was more complicated for Israeli leaders than other Arab localities. On the one hand, officials believed that events in Nazareth would attract international attention due to the city's central position in Christianity. This meant that they were interested in treating residents in a way that appeared fair to outside observers, in order to increase the young country's prestige in the international arena and to prevent interference by the Vatican and overtly Christian countries.[23] On the other hand, officials felt threatened by the city. Not only had 1948 transformed Nazareth into the largest Arab city in the country, with a high concentration of refugees and difficult living conditions, but the city quickly came to exert significant influence on Arab politics in the Galilee and throughout Israel. Officials were also sensitive to the disputed status of the city, which the 1947 UN partition plan allocated, along with the rest of the central and western Galilee, to the future Arab state.[24] For all of these reasons, Israeli civilian and military officials alike came to regard Nazareth as politically volatile, a substantial security threat, and a city to keep under close supervision.[25]

Despite Nazareth's local government infrastructure, the military government alone governed the daily lives of Nazarenes for Israel's first six years of statehood. During this period, officials reapproached the contours of Arab regions and localities on many different levels. The policies they generated aimed to reshape the demographic, economic, geographic, and political boundaries of Israel's Palestinian Arab communities and their relationship with the state and the country's new Jewish majority. As part of this process, Interior Ministry officials slowly began establishing structures of local government in Arab localities. However, they hesitated more in Nazareth, the Arab city with the largest population and one of the oldest municipalities in the country. Some officials feared a major government defeat in Nazareth and the subsequent empowerment of local antigovernment forces. This, they believed, would weaken state control of the city and the Arab Galilee and threaten state security. As we will see, this policy changed in 1953 as pressure mounted in the Knesset.

THE NAZARETH MUNICIPAL ELECTIONS OF 1954

The reinstitutionalization of representative municipal government in Nazareth was accompanied by a shift in government strategy toward manipulating local politics to retain state influence in the city.[26] In the early 1950s, the Israeli Communist Party, Maki, and the left wing Zionist party Mapam (United Workers Party) launched recurring parliamentary attacks on the government for not holding municipal elections in Nazareth.[27] At first, Jewish officials typically justified the absence of elections with security concerns. For instance, when Maki Knesset Member Tawfiq Tubi proposed amending the Municipal Corporations Amendment Bill of 1950 to obligate regular elections in all localities, Zerah Warhaftig of the United Religious Front held that "until we have signed peace treaties with our neighbors, and as long as we have not canceled the state of emergency, it may be impossible to hold elections in certain places." Tubi's amendment was defeated, and the new legislation empowered the interior minister to delay elections at his own discretion.[28]

In August 1950, however, Arab Affairs Advisor Yehoshua Palmon abandoned the security argument in favor of a religious one, a strategic shift with both practical and discursive implications. If elections were held, he argued, they would have to be along denominational lines, as had been the practice during the Mandate, and not between political parties, as was standard practice in the young state of Israel. When addressing the Knesset Interior Affairs Committee on 8 August, he couched this position in respect for the city's unique religious character: "Nazareth is not like other cities in Israel," he explained, "because it is a holy city that, to some degree, belongs to all peoples."[29] But in a letter to Ben-Gurion and Foreign Minister Moshe Sharett the next day, Palmon revealed his true motivation—on the one hand, security concerns no longer justified delaying elections; on the other hand, he held, party-based elections would result in a sweeping victory for Maki, and this had to be prevented. "A communist victory in the Nazareth municipality would have unwelcome reverberations in the Christian world, create and strengthen calls for the internationalization of Jerusalem and possibly Nazareth, and facilitate the crystallization of a provocative anti-Zionist body that will necessarily be anti-Israeli."[30] Palmon's strategy of holding denominational elections to prevent Nazarenes from uniting around Maki and to maintain control over the city is consistent with the findings of political scientist Ian Lustick. Lustick has conceptualized Israel's policy toward its Arab citizens during this period as a "system of control" based on the mutually reinforcing components of "segmentation," "dependence," and "co-optation."[31] Here, attempts to sharpen borders among Nazareth's religious communities, instead of basing elections on political ideology, were directly aimed at fueling already existing segmentation and fragmentation, in order to prevent the crystallization of a united Arab political force in the city. As we will see below, this goal also motivated officials' attempts to shape the governing coalition within the Nazareth municipal council following the 1954 election. Government officials did not adopt this strategy immediately upon its proposal in 1950. They waited three more years, until growing pressure and additional debates on the Knesset floor made the continuation of straight military rule counterproductive.

The government had its own reasons for working to prevent Maki from gaining control of Nazareth's municipal government. Maki was the only non-Zionist Israeli party and the one truly Arab-Jewish party. As a communist party, Maki was hierarchically structured and strictly disciplined, toeing a Soviet line calling for closer Israeli-Soviet relations. However, the anti-nationalist and egalitarian elements of the party's ideological message, in the immediate political context of 1950s Israel, endowed the party with significant Palestinian nationalist appeal despite its predominantly Jewish composition. As a result, it was the most vocal critic of state domestic Arab policy and had already started attracting a significant share of the Arab vote.[32]

In 1954, Maki had marginal influence in the Knesset, holding only 5 of its 120 seats. But it stood to capture much greater influence in Nazareth, which Tubi described at the time as "the nerve center of this oppressed and unjustly treated minority whose rights have been forcefully violated."[33] Based on the party's record in the Knesset and in Nazareth itself, authorities assumed that a Maki-dominated municipal council would tirelessly oppose fundamental components of state policy in the region, such as military government, Arab land expropriation, and discrimination against Palestinian citizens of Israel. In October 1952, Palmon advised Ben-Gurion that Maki would win 50 percent of the vote in Nazareth in the event of party-based municipal elections. Another advisor estimated that it would win even more.[34]

In light of continuing parliamentary pressure, Ben-Gurion instructed a committee of ministers to consider the matter in November 1952.[35] In June 1953, the Ministerial Interior and Services Committee discussed the issue and resolved to hold elections in Nazareth. Palmon continued advocating denominational elections. In a letter coauthored by Shimon

Landman, director of the Interior Ministry's Department of Minorities, Palmon advised that most Nazareth voters presented with denominational lists headed by traditional family leaders would vote for them, and not for political party lists. This, he maintained, was preferable.[36] The issue became even more immediate when, in the midst of demonstrations and a general strike protesting municipal taxes and unemployment, the municipal council that had been appointed by the interior minister three years earlier announced its intention to resign.[37]

The decision to hold elections did not convince all officials that this was the right course of action. In addition to military government personnel who disapproved of the move, some senior officials voiced opposition as well. In August 1953, Warhaftig, now deputy minister of religions, argued that antigovernment opinion in Nazareth would result in victory for the far left. Postal Service Minister Yosef Burg agreed that the time was not right and urged holding off until 1955, when elections were scheduled for other municipalities. In response, Foreign Minister and acting Prime Minister Sharett argued that deciding not to hold elections in the city due to antigovernment sentiment would only exacerbate the problem, and that they should therefore move ahead. On this basis, the government scheduled Nazareth municipal elections for spring 1954 and began practical planning.[38]

According to Palmon and Landman's approach, officials worked to ensure the denominational nature of election lists as a means of counteracting the challenge posed by the reestablishment of local government. This task, however, was not as simple as it had been during the Mandate period. This was because in 1950, Israeli legislators amended the Municipal Corporations Ordinance in accordance with the democratic principles that they strove to implement in the Jewish sector. According to the new legislation, any local resident could submit a list of candidates, regardless of religious affiliation, and the council's constitution would be determined by proportional representation through direct elections.[39] This meant that, in order to implement the strategy of denominational elections, officials had to convince the leaders of national political parties *not* to organize local election lists and at the same time convince the local leaders of Nazareth's religious communities to submit lists of their own. In August 1953, acting Defense Minister Pinhas Lavon further stressed that "in order to prevent a blow to the state" the country's Jewish parties should not even appear on the ballot.[40]

According to the Municipal Corporations Ordinance, the first step in organizing elections was the creation of an election committee. The Interior Ministry appointed members of the Nazareth municipal election committee according to religious affiliation in October 1953. But even before the committee began work, Nazareth denominational leaders started maneuvering to shore up support within their respective communities to ensure that they would in fact receive the votes of their members. Within Nazareth, only Maki opposed the denominational approach, trying in vain to convince local leaders and municipal councilmen to refrain from submitting such lists. Nonetheless, of the eight lists submitted to the election committee during February and March 1954, six were denominational (three Muslim, two Orthodox Christian, and one Catholic) and only two were identified with political parties (one with Maki and one with Mapam).[41] As election day approached, the authorities were dismayed by predictions of a Maki victory despite the denominational nature of the elections and made a last ditch effort to assist the denominational election campaigns. Despite calls by officials to delay or cancel the elections, Sharett and Interior Minister Israel Rokach proceeded according to schedule.[42]

On April 12, 1954, Nazarenes went to the polls. Voter turnout was 83 percent, and the results reflected the authorities' failure to prevent the communists from gaining a foothold on the municipal council. Maki captured 38.4 percent of the vote, becoming the largest municipal faction with six of fifteen seats. The Muslim lists won a total of four seats, the Catholic list won three seats, the Orthodox lists won two seats, and the left wing Zionist party Mapam failed to pass the electoral threshold. Local Maki leaders and supporters celebrated victory in the streets of the city the next day, taking pride in their achievement despite what they described as "the ruling parties' conspiracy to steal the votes of Nazarenes through denominational factionalism."[43]

Officials attributed their defeat to (1) a lack of know-how on the part of the Arab organizers of the denominational campaigns, in contrast to the competent organizing skills of the Maki campaign; (2) growing antigovernment sentiment among Nazarenes and key members of the previous municipal council; (3) the placement of unpopular personalities at the top of some lists; and (4) insufficient involvement by the more experienced Jewish campaigners charged with assisting the denominational campaigns.[44] While the state had lost a critical battle in its struggle for influence on the municipal council, it had not lost the war. Officials now redirected their efforts toward keeping Maki out of the municipal governing coalition.

THE STRUGGLE FOR A COALITION

The 1950 amendment to the Municipal Corporations Ordinance stipulated that each elected municipal council would choose its mayor from among its ranks, rather than continuing the British Mandate practice of having the central government appoint one of the elected councilmen to the post.[45] This new provision made the establishment of municipal government dependent on coalition politics. Within this changed legal context, government representatives began working immediately after the Nazareth elections to unite the nine denominational councilmen into a governing coalition with one mayoral candidate. This proved difficult for a number of reasons. First, the splintered nature of interdenominational politics in Nazareth made many councilmen uncomfortable with the idea of supporting a mayor of a different religion. Ironically, this unintended consequence of the denominational strategy was now an obstacle to achieving government goals. Second, the fact that none of the noncommunist councilmen were subject to a party line made the give-and-take of coalition politics virtually impossible. Third, Maki held six seats, the largest bloc on the council, and was therefore not merely a natural coalition partner but a natural coalition leader. Efforts to create a governing coalition continued for three months and involved numerous meetings between the denominational councilmen and government representatives. These meetings were typically aimed at convincing the councilmen to cede their individual mayoral claims and support one common candidate.

The day after the elections, Shimon Landman, director of the Interior Ministry's Department of Minorities, traveled to Haifa to begin meeting with Nazareth denominational leaders.[46] Landman returned to Jerusalem pessimistic, reporting that the nine non-Maki councilmen were hopelessly divided, with each demanding to be mayor. Later in April, Landman learned that, despite government disapproval and the challenge the party posed to the city's traditional social order, many councilmen appeared to be considering Maki's offer to support a denominational mayoral candidate.[47]

The Municipal Corporations Ordinance specified that choosing a mayor was the elected council's first order of business, to be carried out within fourteen days of official publication of election results.[48] Presumably due to this legal requirement—which meant that the sooner the authorities published election results, the sooner they would have to be ready with an anticommunist coalition—speedy publication of results was not a government priority. Despite calls by Maki leaders to do so earlier, the government waited until May 20, five weeks after the elections, to publish the results.[49] Interior Minister Rokach then stepped up efforts to form a coalition, appointing Deputy District Commissioner and Nazareth election supervisor Moshe Ruah as acting mayor, pending the council's selection of a permanent mayor from among its members. He then summoned Ruah to Jerusalem for consultations. Rokach also invited the denominational councilmen to Jerusalem for talks in late May in order to continue pressuring them to form an anticommunist coalition. Nonetheless, by the time the first council meeting rolled around on June 8, 1954, they were no closer to choosing a joint candidate.

The way the first council meeting played out, and the events that followed, must be understood against a backdrop of officials' growing frustration with their inability to construct an anti-Maki coalition. This frustration induced them to resort to even more blatant manipulation of the political process to prevent Maki from gaining control of local government, to the point of condoning (if not encouraging) the use of violence. Shortly before the first meeting of the council, Landman adopted a strategy of creating provocations aimed at eliciting extreme responses from Maki councilmen and supporters. These responses, he hoped, would justify disbanding the council on the pretext that it was incapable of running city affairs. For instance, Landman recommended appointing Galilee Military Governor Avraham Cohen, instead of Moshe Ruah, as acting mayor. "I proposed charging Lieutenant Colonel Avraham Cohen with this task," reported Landman, "based on the assumption that the Maki faction would refuse to participate in a meeting under his chairmanship and in this way create a situation allowing the Interior Ministry to move in the desired direction."[50] Although Rokach did not adopt this recommendation and instead appointed Ruah, Landman was still able to provoke Maki at the first council meeting by inviting the military governor. In response, Maki councilmen opened the meeting with speeches denouncing the invitation, and this, in turn, enabled Ruah to disband the meeting before the councilmen could even nominate mayoral candidates. He justified this action on the grounds that Maki was using the meeting as a "political platform" instead of tending to council business.[51]

A second council meeting was scheduled for June 17, 1954. Again, Landman was intent upon sabotaging the meeting. On two occasions between the first and second meetings, Landman discussed the situation in Nazareth with Shmuel Divon, the prime minister's Arab affairs advisor, and Lieutenant Colonel Yitzhak Shani, head of the Defense Ministry's Department of Military Government. During these meetings, Landman reported, "I explained the plan of creating obstructions during municipal council meetings in order to have the council disbanded."[52]

It was in this context that things became violent. On the morning of the second council meeting, villagers from the surrounding area attacked the six Maki councilmen. They used rocks and sticks to prevent them from reaching the municipal building. Fu'ad Khuri, head of the city's Maki list, took refuge in a local store long enough to phone Ruah and ask him to delay the meeting and to send help. The others found shelter in the home of Maki councilman Khalil Khuri. The villagers subsequently surrounded the house and pelted it with stones. Next, the group broke into the nearby Maki youth center, destroying musical instruments and furniture and burning documents and books.

Maki and other Arab activists in Israel immediately accused the authorities of involvement in the attack and of employing violence to influence the constitution of the municipal coalition in Nazareth. Leaders of other parties, such as Mapam and the Progressives, were also suspicious of government involvement, but stopped short of making explicit charges. These suspicions were based on a number of factors: (1) the fifty to one hundred villagers involved were Muslims belonging primarily to the progovernment al-Zu'bi clan and had been brought to Nazareth that morning by special transport; (2) as the region was under military rule, it seemed unlikely that so many Palestinians could have entered Nazareth without raising the suspicion of the police or the military government; (3) although the violence lasted for almost two hours, and although Khuri called Ruah for help shortly after it began, the police did not intervene, claiming that they had not received an official complaint (see fig. 3.2).[53]

Other factors also raise suspicions about the authorities' involvement in the events of June 17, 1954. For instance, although Ruah knew that 40 percent of the council was being prevented from attending, he nonetheless opened the meeting and asked for nominations for mayor. As the nine councilmen present constituted a quorum, this gave them an opportunity to elect a mayor without the competition of a Maki-supported candidate. Thus, regardless of whether Ruah himself was involved in initiating the events, he was clearly willing to take advantage of them to achieve government aims. This appears to have gone too far for some denominational councilmen, who suddenly asked to postpone the meeting due to a Christian holiday. Now it was their turn to strategically employ a discourse of religion for political purposes, as Palmon had done almost four years earlier in an early Knesset Interior Affairs Committee discussion on municipal elections in Nazareth. According to an internal military government report, general opinion was "that the holiday was just an excuse and that the religious request was actually an act of solidarity with the elected councilmen who did not have the opportunity to attend the meeting."[54]

All this, in conjunction with additional archival evidence discussed elsewhere,[55] suggests that key officials may have been involved in the attack. It also clearly establishes that some officials condoned the act and worked to take advantage of its results in order to increase government influence in the city. The state's role in this episode, whether instigative or not, is relevant to our discussion for two reasons. First, it indicates the seriousness with which officials viewed the situation in Nazareth and enables us to better understand their state of mind when they called for Jewish settlement and border modification to address the challenge. In this way, it provides helpful insight into officials' subsequent turn to spatial control mechanisms with regard to the city. The episode also sheds new light on what Is-

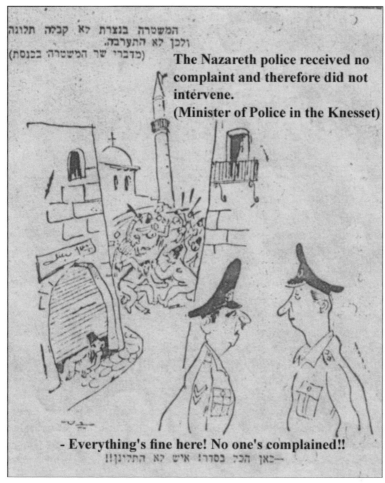

המשטרה בנצרת לא קבלה תלונה
ולכן לא התערבה.
(מדברי שר המשטרה בכנסת)

The Nazareth police received no complaint and therefore did not intervene.
(Minister of Police in the Knesset)

- Everything's fine here! No one's complained!!
כאן הכל בסדר! איש לא התלונן!—

Figure 3.2.   Caricature by Yosef Bass, Ha'aretz, June 25, 1954, 5. Courtesy of Ha'aretz.

raeli officials working in the Arab sector during this period regarded as legitimate modes of operation.

The more time passed after the elections, the more concerned officials became that they would be unable to construct an anticommunist coalition. Despite Maki's dip in popularity among the denominational councilmen after the violence of June 17, Interior Ministry officials were still unable to broker an agreement, especially one that would support the government's preferred mayoral candidate, the Christian Orthodox Amin Jarjura.[56] At the third municipal council meeting on July 1, the only candidate nominated was Maki's Fu'ad Khuri. While none of the denominational councilmen voted for him, they also failed to offer an alternative. "I'm fed up!" Ruah exclaimed soon after the meeting. "I no longer believe any of them! If there is no possibility of imposing our will on them, all our efforts are being wasted. I see no way of bringing the nine to reach an agreement that will solve this troublesome problem."[57]

But government efforts eventually paid off, and the Nazareth Municipal Council chose Jarjura as mayor on July 15, 1954. Jarjura received the support of eight of the council's denominational members, while the other candidate, Ya'kub Farah, also a Christian Orthodox, received his own vote and the six votes of the Maki bloc.[58] Maki remained outside Nazareth's governing coalition for the next twenty years, during which the communists were never able to capture more than 39 percent of the popular vote.[59] Officials, however, did not know at the time how municipal elections in Nazareth would play out in the decades to come. Rather, they were visibly shaken by the events of 1954, understanding that the process could have easily ended in defeat and that state control of Nazareth could not be ensured solely by manipulating local politics. They also believed that Maki would win even more of the vote if elections were held again in the near future. In their eyes, therefore, victory was only temporary.

Based on these impressions, the officials who had been charged with influencing the election and coalition-building process began calling for a spatial strategy for ensuring future state control of Nazareth and the surrounding region—that is, the immediate establishment of a Jewish presence and the introduction of new Jewish-Arab territorial borders in the environs of the city.[60] Although settling Jews at Nazareth had been discussed in theory a number of times prior to the events surrounding the municipal elections of 1954, only then, in light of the potential political threat posed by the Nazareth municipality, did officials regard the idea with practical urgency. As we will see, the authorities had a clear rationale behind this territorial approach.

THE EVOLUTION OF UPPER NAZARETH

After the municipal election debacle, the Israeli government took concrete steps to establish the urban Jewish settlement of Upper Nazareth. The Upper Nazareth plan was part of larger governmental policy of spatial Judaization that dominated state planning at the time. Consistent with sociologist Baruch Kimmerling's findings that the Jewish collective in Palestine (and subsequently Israel) sought territorial control by establishing "presence," "ownership," and "sovereignty,"[61] Israeli officials decided early on to intensify the prestate practice of establishing Jewish settlements in thinly populated and predominantly Arab regions of the country. While Zionist

territorial colonization prior to 1948 had traditionally been based on agricultural settlement, the 1950s and 1960s witnessed the establishment of a
network of towns, as well as a handful of new Jewish cities. The first new
city established in this context was located adjacent to Nazareth. Its aim was
to counterbalance the perceived political and security threats emanating
from Nazareth and to bolster Israeli "sovereignty" in the city and the region.

It appears that General Mordekhai Maklef, head of the IDF General Staff's
Operations Branch and soon to be chief-of-staff, first suggested the establishment of a Jewish presence in Nazareth to Ben-Gurion in November
1951. The idea, which officials raised on a number of occasions over the
next two years, stemmed from their assessment that all-Arab regions of the
country threatened state security and sovereignty, and that the establishment of Jewish settlements (known as "security settlements") in such areas
would solve the problem. In an August 1953 letter to the director of the IDF
Planning Division, IDF Settlement Branch Director Lieutenant Colonel
Aharon Harsina clearly expressed this approach. "[After 1948] it was clear
to us that the war was not over and that we would not be in control of the
country in its entirety until all land within it was settled and cultivated. It
was clear to us that Arabs, from both within the country and across the borders, would invade all areas we neglect, strike footholds, and establish new
roots."[62] A few years later, a government-appointed committee charged with
assessing the need for the continuation of the military government reiter-
ated this approach. "The state cannot maintain its borders by means of the
military alone. Jewish settlement ensures that territory will remain in Israel's possession."[63] On this basis, and in response to the threat officials
perceived as emanating from the Arab central Galilee, the IDF, the Interior
Ministry, and the Jewish Agency began coordinated efforts to Judaize the
Galilee through Jewish settlement in the early 1950s.[64] The idea of Jewish settlement in Nazareth arose as part of this general undertaking. It is
possible that a settlement would have been established there at some
point in the future even if the government had been successful in the
1954 elections.

Nonetheless, as we have seen, Upper Nazareth appears to have been established *when* and *how* it was as a result of state efforts to retain control of
Nazareth in light of the events surrounding its first post-1948 municipal
elections. In fact, when the Ministerial Interior and Services Committee discussed the idea in detail for the first time in late August 1953, they regarded
the establishment of a new Jewish settlement as stemming directly from the
election issue, which the same committee had discussed and decided upon
earlier that summer. It was in this context that officials resolved to augment
the establishment of a Jewish presence in Nazareth by relocating the administrative center of Israel's Northern District to a new Jewish Nazareth;
making it mandatory for government offices and employees to move to the

new settlement; and attracting new services, industries, and settlers.[65] This was a major shift in post-1948 state policy towards the city. "The only chance of making Nazareth a partially Jewish city is by consolidating the [state] institutions there," explained Government Secretary Ze'ev Sharef to the Ministerial Interior and Services Committee in August 1953. "It is a colonizing act with difficulties, but without it we will not be able to Judaize Nazareth."[66]

Subsequent steps taken toward establishing the settlement also coincided with government assessments that Maki could rise to power in Nazareth in the 1954 municipal elections. A special IDF committee was appointed to locate land to expropriate for the project on March 30, 1954, just as government advisors and local military government commanders were concluding that the state had "entered a labyrinth with almost no way out in Nazareth," that Maki was likely to win enough seats to take control of the Municipal Council, and that the elections should therefore be canceled.[67] As Landman explained a few months later, Maki's subsequent electoral victory accelerated the process even further. "The elections in Nazareth not only drew public attention to events in Nazareth and the Arab Galilee and served as a warning of what can be expected in the elections for the third Knesset. It also sparked concern and recurring discussions in the government and the leadership of the two main parties, and led to an acceleration of preparations for a Jewish settlement in Nazareth."[68] On April 27, after two weeks of failed coalition negotiations, Landman urged Rokach to bring the issue of state domestic Arab policy, including settling Jews in the Galilee and in Nazareth, to the cabinet for discussion.[69] Rokach immediately broached the subject with Sharett and the next day submitted a proposal for relocating Northern District headquarters to Nazareth. The plan called for the construction of new government facilities as well as residential units, schools, and stores for Jewish employees and their families.[70]

Like all new settlements, a Jewish presence in Nazareth required land. The legal tool used to appropriate the land was the Land (Acquisition for Public Purposes) Ordinance. This law, which British Mandate authorities originally enacted in 1943, authorized the high commissioner to expropriate any land he deemed necessary or helpful for an aim he defined as a public purpose. In other words, the high commissioner had exclusive authority to decide what constituted a public purpose and what land it required. Post-1948 Israeli law vested this power in the finance minister,[71] who was statutorily responsible for supervising virtually all Israeli land-related legislation enacted during the first decade of Israeli statehood. Based on this authority, the state expropriated 1,200 *dunams* of land in and around Nazareth on June 17, 1954, to lay the territorial foundation for the new Jewish neighborhood.[72] During the months that followed, landowners and municipal councilmen, who organized themselves as the Committee for the Defense of Expropriated Nazareth Land, continued to oppose expropriation, arguing that it was against the city's public interest.[73] Israeli officials, however, consistently portrayed the construction of government offices and employee housing as their true aim. This, they argued, was in the public interest.[74]

The Committee for the Defense of Expropriated Nazareth Land brought the dispute before the Israeli Supreme Court in the spring of 1955.[75] The court rejected the committee's claim that the land had not been expropriated for a bona fide public purpose based on the state's declaration that its sole purpose was to erect government facilities. Here, state officials strategically employed a discourse of public utility based on political and legal considerations, even though their true aim was territorial and demographic. This is confirmed not only by documentation of discussions surrounding the expropriation but by the fact that, as of February 1958, almost four years after the expropriation and more than one year after the first residents had moved to the settlement, the construction of government offices had not even begun. In fact, of the 1,200 *dunams* expropriated in 1954, only 109 *dunams* were actually designated for the construction of government offices.[76] The "public purpose" that served as the pretext for the project in general and the expropriation in particular was a secondary consideration at best, and reached completion only many years later.

With the expansion of its role in plans for Judaization of the Galilee during the second half of 1954, the Defense Ministry set up a Galilee Development Department that dealt with—among other things—the new Jewish settlement.[77] Like Judaization of the Galilee, officials incorporated the Nazareth project into Israel's state planning apparatus. While planners in the mid 1950s classified most of the Arab Galilee as a high priority "development area," they earmarked Nazareth for special development efforts, undoubtedly referring to the work that was already underway.[78] In this way, they set out to reshape the space of Nazareth by setting new priorities for its development.

In March 1956, Mordekhai Alon, coordinator of the Defense Ministry's efforts in the Galilee, was assigned to chair a new four-person interdepartmental committee to coordinate the Nazareth settlement project. The committee consisted of representatives of the Defense Ministry, the Interior Ministry, Amidar (Israel's public-housing company), and the Development Authority (one of Israel's primary landholding agencies). Committee meetings were also attended by representatives of other related government agencies and the military government.[79] The committee regularly discussed all practical details of the undertaking, including infrastructure, services, employment, commercial and industrial development, and municipal status.[80] The first residential units were completed in September 1956, and the first residents moved in towards the end of the year.[81] Alon himself moved to the settlement as the chair of the interdepartmental committee and representative of the Defense Ministry and later served as the head of its local council and, when the settlement subsequently received city municipal status, as its mayor.[82]

Officials initially referred to the new settlement as the Jewish "neighborhood" in Nazareth. Before long, however, they renamed it Kiryat Natzeret (the Nazareth campus), a name undoubtedly originating from the discourse of public utility underlying officials' statements that the land expropriated in 1954 would be used for a campus of government offices. In November 1958, the Government Names Committee within the Prime Minister's Office changed the settlement's name, since it was not yet the site of a large number of government offices, but first and foremost a center of residential and commercial development. The settlement's new name was Natzrat Ilit, or Upper Nazareth.[83]

Like other Jewish settlements in the Galilee, an important aim of Upper Nazareth was to ensure Jewish state control and sovereignty in the region. According to IDF Planning Department Director Yuval Ne'eman, the new settlement would "emphasize and safeguard the Jewish character of the Galilee as a whole, and . . . demonstrate state sovereignty to the Arab population more than any other settlement operation."[84] The new settlement was thus part of broader plans to change territorial, demographic, and political realities in the Galilee in order to reshape Jewish-Arab sociospatial relations in the region. On the local level, Upper Nazareth aimed to address the challenge perceived as emanating from the all-Arab city of Nazareth by changing territorial, demographic, and political realities. It would do this not by achieving a Jewish majority within the city of Nazareth itself but rather by quickly evolving from a neighborhood into a city and eventually overpowering Arab Nazareth numerically, economically, and politically. According to Northern Military Governor Colonel Mikhael Mikhael, the final aim of the settlement was to "swallow up" the Arab city through "growth of the Jewish population around a hard-core group" and "the transfer of the center of gravity of life from Nazareth to the Jewish neighborhood."[85]

As the Arab residents of Nazareth would necessarily oppose this aim, the borders and municipal status of the new settlement were of monumental importance. When Ben-Gurion mentioned the idea in his journal before his temporary retirement in 1953, he took care to emphasize that the Jewish presence must be established not within the borders of the city itself, but rather alongside it, overlooking it from the hills. Ben-Gurion understood that rapid development of such a settlement would require that it be wholly Jewish in population and unburdened by an internal Arab opposition. For this reason, it could not be subordinated to Nazareth municipal jurisdiction. However, little if any attention was paid to municipal status and territorial borders during the project's early stages, when Sharett was prime minister, Lavon was defense minister, and Rokach was interior minister. As a result, 590 of the 1,200 *dunams* initially expropriated for the project were located within Nazareth municipal borders, as were all the buildings in the first phase of construction.[86] Soon after returning to power, Ben-Gurion clarified the issue of municipal status to his new interior minister, Israel Bar-Yehuda, in February 1956. "Clearly," explained Ben-Gurion, "the Jewish locality, which will have a minority status with relation to the Arab locality of Nazareth for quite some time, should not be part of the Nazareth municipality, just as Ahuzat Bayit [the beginning of Tel Aviv] was not part of Jaffa."[87] According to Colonel Mikhael, Nazareth and Upper Nazareth could be merged into one municipal framework only after the Jewish population had substantially grown and the center of public life had moved from Arab Nazareth to Jewish Nazareth.[88] Until then, he regarded separate territorial borders (denoting both jurisdictional and demographic boundaries) and an independent municipal status as critical preconditions for the settlement to achieve its overall aim of achieving state control through Jewish dominance.

During the first half of 1956, Ben-Gurion, Interior Minister Bar-Yehuda, and officials of the IDF and the Defense Ministry acknowledged the importance of removing the new neighborhood from within Nazareth municipal borders and endowing it with a municipal status of its own.[89] This was necessary, officials again argued, to ensure that the Nazareth municipality would be unable to hinder the quick development of the new Jewish neighborhood.[90] In exchange, government officials proposed compensating Nazareth by placing alternative land adjacent to the city under its jurisdiction.[91] The matter was referred for decision to the Knesset Defense and Foreign Affairs Committee, which, out of concern for possible political ramifications, decided to wait for the conclusion of the UN General Assembly then in session.[92]

In the meantime, officials supervising the project noted growing difficulties stemming from attempts by the Nazareth municipality to carry out its legally prescribed functions vis-à-vis the neighborhood. In one instance, the municipality called for the fiscal assessment of the new residential units for taxation purposes. In another instance, a local security guard expelled an Arab municipal council member attempting to tour the Jewish neighborhood. Officials were also concerned that allowing the municipality to remain legally responsible for granting private building permits for the new settlement would hinder its development, as would claims by some local Arab leaders that the city's six thousand Palestinian refugees deserved housing no less than new Jewish immigrants.[93] As a result, officials increased their pressure on Bar-Yehuda to remove the neighborhood from Nazareth municipal borders as soon as possible.

After investigating a number of legal options, Bar-Yehuda began consultations for modifying Nazareth's municipal borders, a process that by law required the creation of a specially established committee to research the issue and recommend a new demarcation. Despite the urgency with which officials perceived the process, it took almost two years, until March 1959, for the government to approve this step.[94] The subsequent appointment of a borders committee was delayed as well, this time to prevent the eruption of local Arab opposition before the parliamentary elections of 1959. Work resumed in early 1960, immediately after the elections. The government officially proclaimed Nazareth's new borders in December 1960 and endowed Upper Nazareth with the municipal status of local council in July 1961.[95] This officially removed the new Jewish settlement from the jurisdiction of the Arab municipality and legally normalized the direct manner in which central government officials, under the direction of the Defense Ministry, had been developing the settlement from the outset.

The gradual process of establishing and developing Upper Nazareth as a separate municipal entity adjacent to the Arab municipality supports political geographer Oren Yiftachel's assessment that Israeli spatial planning in the Galilee during this period was aimed primarily at controlling the Arab population and preventing it from threatening Jewish settlement, state sovereignty, and territorial integrity.[96] In the case of Nazareth and Upper Nazareth, the demarcation and redemarcation of municipal borders served government strategies for reshaping sociospatial power relations in both the short term and the long term. In the short term, the removal of Upper Nazareth from Nazareth's municipal borders enabled officials to circumvent local Arab opposition to the development of the new urban settlement. In the long term, endowing the new settlement with municipal borders, independent municipal status, and the status of Northern District capital facilitated state efforts to transform Jewish-Arab demographic, economic, and political relations in Nazareth and the rest of the central Galilee.

CONCLUSION

During the first few decades of Israeli statehood, officials reapproached, reassessed, and redemarcated territorial borders between Jews and Arabs throughout the country, applying a variety of policies within the geographical units that resulted. The ultimate aim of these policies was to ensure the stability, security, and sovereignty of Israel as a Jewish state, which usually involved weakening Arab localities and their residents in a variety of ways. In the case of Nazareth, the decision to reshape the territorial contours of the city was not immediate, and officials initially relied on military and political mechanisms to achieve their goals. However, faced with the seemingly insurmountable difficulties that emerged from the 1954 municipal elections, they changed their approach to the city and instead called for the immediate establishment of a Jewish settlement alongside the Arab city. The redemarcation of municipal borders was a precondition for ensuring the new settlement's rapid development. The redemarcation emerges as a vital component of state efforts to transform interethnic power relations in the region.

The case of Nazareth provides a glimpse of the decisive role that Jewish-Arab sociopolitical power relations played in shaping the post-1948 historical geography of Israel. It also demonstrates the close connection among borders of territory, jurisdiction, and identity and their malleability in contexts of sociopolitical change. The establishment of Upper Nazareth was part of a broader process of Jewish settlement that went on for years. During the decades that followed 1948, Israeli authorities attempted to achieve a dominant Jewish spatial presence throughout all parts of the country by establishing hundreds of Jewish settlements, with an emphasis on thinly populated regions and regions populated primarily by Palestinians. Although Upper Nazareth did not remain an all-Jewish locality for long and although it is not clear if officials were successful in reducing the threat they believed that Nazareth posed,[97] it is clear that the settlement was part of a broader process of Judaization. This strategy served as a central component of Israeli policy in the Galilee and other predominantly Arab regions under Israeli control for decades to come.

Interestingly, recent steps undertaken by the Israeli government indicate that, after more than fifty years of this approach, some senior officials have concluded that Jewish settlement is *not* always the key to Israeli control and sovereignty. Nonetheless, the 2005 evacuation of settlements from the Gaza Strip and a small portion of the northern West Bank reflect that today, as much as ever, Israel continues to reapproach and redemarcate its territorial and demographic borders with an eye toward ensuring future Jewish state control and sovereignty over as much of the territory under its control as possible.

NOTES

1. Aviel, "Hitparuyot bi-rehovot Natzeret," *Ha'aretz*, June 18, 1954; see the expropriation order in *Yalkut ha-Pirsumim* 356 (June 17, 1954): 1284.

2. Little scholarship has thus far been produced about post-1948 Nazareth. The few works that have been published to date are more anthropological, geographical, and sociological than historical, and none adequately explore the first decade of Israeli rule. See Chad Emmet, *Beyond the Basilica: Christians and Muslims in Nazareth*

(Chicago: University of Chicago Press, 1995); Raphael Israeli, *Green Crescent over Nazareth: The Displacement of Christians by Muslims in the Holy Land* (London: Frank Cass, 2002). Falah, "Land Fragmentation and Spatial Control in the Nazareth Metropolitan Area;" *The Professional Geographer* 44, no. 1: 30–44; Dan Rabinowitz, *Overlooking Nazareth: The Ethnography of Exclusion in the Galilee* (New York: Cambridge University Press, 1997); Henry Rosenfeld, "Nazareth and Upper Nazareth in the Political Economy of Israel," in *Arab-Jewish Relations in Israel*, ed. John Hoffman et al. (Bristol: Wyndham Hall Press, 1988); Uri Stendall, "Natzeret ka-yom: Kavin le-hitpatehut ha-ir (1948–1981)" (Nazareth Today: Directions of the City's Development [1948–1981]), *Kardom: Du-yarhon li-yedi'at ha-aretz* 4, no. 19 (1982): 46–52. A similar lacuna exists in the historiography of Arab cities in Israel-Palestine in general. This is problematic for three reasons. First, it limits our ability to understand the processes and events that have shaped these localities to the present. Second, it renders these important centers of Palestinian society within Israel misleadingly silent and absent from the country's historiography and historical geography. Third, it deprives social scientists of an updated historical foundation for developing and corroborating their theories about societal phenomena and change.

3. Israeli, *Green Crescent over Nazareth*, 37.

4. Emmett, *Beyond the Basilica*, 17–45; Alexander Schölch, *Palestine in Transformation, 1856–1882* (Washington, DC: Institute for Palestine Studies, 1993), 146–7; Charles Kamen, "After the Catastrophe I: The Arabs in Israel, 1948–51," *Middle Eastern Studies* 23, no. 4 (1987): 465.

5. Carter Findley, "The Evolution of the System of Provincial Administration. As Viewed from the Center," in *Palestine in the Late Ottoman Period: Political, Social, and Economic Transformation*, ed. David Kushner (Jerusalem: Yad Ben-Zvi, 1986), 14; Government of Palestine, *A Survey of Palestine* (Washington, DC: Institute of Palestine Studies, 1991 [first published in 1946]), 128–36.

6. "Municipal Corporations Ordinance, 1934," in *Laws of Palestine, 1934–1935*, ed. Leon Rotenberg (Tel Aviv: Shoshani, 1936), 361–400; Government of Palestine, *A Survey of Palestine*, 128–36; Majid al-Haj and Henry Rosenfeld, *Arab Local Government in Israel* (Boulder: Westview Press, 1990); Ylana Miller, *Government and Society in Rural Palestine* (Austin: University of Texas Press, 1985), 43–46.

7. Emmett, *Beyond the Basilica*, 73; Palmon to Ben-Gurion and Sharett, 9 August 1950, Ben Gurion Archive, Sde-Boker (hereafter BGA), Correspondences; David Ben-Gurion, entry of 19 October 1952, BGA, Ben-Gurion's Full Journal (hereafter BGJ). Salim Bishara served as mayor from 1924 until he left Nazareth during the war, on May 10, 1948. He was replaced by Yusef al-Fahum, who remained mayor after Israel's conquest of the city in July 1948. He held this position until the municipal elections of 1954, in which he refused to participate. Interior Ministry's Department of Minorities (hereafter IMDM), report on Nazareth municipal government, undated, Israel State Archives, Jerusalem (hereafter ISA) (50) 1904-gimel/16; Adib Abu-Rahmun, interviewed by the author, September 2, 2004.

8. Emmett, *Beyond the Basilica*, 39–40; IMDM, report on Nazareth municipal government.

9. Benny Morris, *The Birth of the Palestinian Refugee Problem, 1949–1996* (New York: Cambridge University Press, 1987); Joel Beinin, *Was the Red Flag Flying There?*

Marxist Politics and the Arab-Israeli Conflict in Egypt and Israel, 1948–1965 (Berkeley: University of California Press, 1990), 43–55.

10. Kamen, "After the Catastrophe I," 465, and Charles Kamen "After the Catastrophe II: The Arabs in Israel, 1948–1951," *Middle Eastern Studies* 24, no. 1 (1988): 77–78.

11. Uzi Benziman and 'Atallah Mansur, *Dayarei mishneh—Aravei Yisrael: Ma'amadam veha-mediniyut klapeihem* (Subtenants—The Arabs of Israel: Their Status and the Policy towards Them) (Jerusalem: Keter, 1992), 11–23; Sabri Jiryis, *The Arabs in Israel* (New York: Monthly Review Press), 49; Don Peretz, *Israel and the Palestine Arabs* (Washington, DC: Middle East Institute, 1958), 94; Report of the Committee to Examine the Affairs of the Military Government, February 24, 1956, ISA (130) 2401-htz/20; "The Absorption of Arab Refugees into Israel from the Security Point of View: Appreciation of the Situation," 1949, Israel Defense Forces Archive, Tel-Hashomer (hereafter IDFA) 488/55–168.

12. Benziman and Mansur, *Dayarei Mishneh*, 11–14; Peretz, *Israel and the Palestine Arabs*, 93–94; Sarah Ozacky-Lazar, "Hitgabshut yahasei ha-gomlin bein yehudim le-medinat Yisrael: Ha-asur he-rishon, 1948–1958" (The Crystallization of Mutual Relations between Jews and Arabs in the State of Israel: The First Decade, 1948–1958) (Ph.D. diss., University of Haifa, 1996), 48; Yossi Katz, *Medinah ba-derekh: Ha-tokhniyot le-halukat Eretz Israel ule-hakamat medinah yehudit* (A State in the Making: Zionist Plans for the Partition of Palestine and the Establishment of a Jewish State) (Jerusalem: Magnes Press, 2000), 86–104; David Kretzmer, *The Legal Status of the Arabs in Israel* (Boulder: Westview Press, 1990), 1; Ilan Pappé, "An Uneasy Coexistence: Arabs and Jews in the First Decade of Statehood," in *Israel: The First Decade of Independence*, ed. S. Ilan Troen and Noah Lucas (Albany: SUNY Press, 1995).

13. Morris, *The Birth of the Palestinian Refugee Problem*, 134–38; Nur Masalha, *Expulsion of the Palestinians: The Concept of "Transfer" in Zionist Political Thought, 1882–1948* (Washington, DC: Institute for Palestine Studies, 1992); Nur Masalha, *A Land without a People: Israel, Transfer and the Palestinians, 1949–1996* (London: Faber and Faber, 1997); Yair Bauml, "Yahaso shel ha-mimsad ha-yisraeli la-aravin be-Yisrael: Mediniyut, ekronot u-fe'ulot: Ha-asur ha-sheni, 1959–1968" (The Attitude of the Israeli Establishment to the Arabs in Israel: Policy, Principles, and Activities: The Second Decade, 1959–1968) (Ph.D. diss., University of Haifa, 2002), 61–63.

14. Kretzmer, *The Legal Status of the Arabs in Israel*, 4.

15. Bauml, "Yahaso shel ha-mimsad," 67–86; Benziman and Mansur, *Dayarei mishneh*, 22.

16. Bauml, "Yahaso shel ha-mimsad," 62–63, 107–8; Benziman and Mansur, *Dayarei mishneh*, 71, 73.

17. Bauml, "Yahaso shel ha-mimsad," 62–63, 107–8; Benziman and Mansur, *Dayarei mishneh*, 61, 71, 73; Jiryis, *The Arabs in Israel*, 27–28, 41, 137–57; Geremy Forman and Alexandre Kedar, "From Arab Land to 'Israel Lands': The Legal Dispossession of the Palestinians Displaced by Israel in the Wake of 1948," *Environment and Planning D: Society and Space* 22, no. 6 (2004).

18. Such as the General Security Services, the police force, the Office of the Arab Affairs Advisor, the Interior Ministry's Department of Minorities, individual Arab affairs advisors within state agencies, and the Arab Section of the Histadrut.

19. Bauml, "Yahaso shel ha-mimsad," j.

20. Benziman and Mansur, *Dayarei mishneh*, 33; Ian Lustick, *Arabs in the Jewish State: Israel's Control of a National Minority* (Austin: University of Texas Press, 1980), 53; Ozacky-Lazar, "Hitgabshut yahasei ha-gomlin," 71; Report of the Committee to Examine the Affairs of the Military Government, February 24, 1956; Menachem Hofnung, *Yisrael: Bitahon ha-medinah mul shilton ha-hok* (Israel: Security Needs vs. the Rule of Law) (Jerusalem: Nevo, 1991), 150.

21. Hofnung, *Yisrael*, 76–79.

22. Benziman and Mansur, *Dayarei mishneh*, 34, 37–38, 110; Peretz, *Israel and the Palestine Arabs*, 95.

23. Morris, *The Birth of the Palestinian Refugee Problem*, 201–3. Also see Moshe Sharett's comments at the August 5, 1953 meeting of the Ministerial Interior and Services Committee, ISA (77) 308-alef/6.

24. Ben-Gurion, journal entry of 14 December 1949, BGA BGJ.

25. Kamen, "After the Catastrophe II," 77; Jacob Landau, *The Arabs in Israel: A Political Study* (London: Oxford University Press, 1969), 179; Report on the Nazareth and District Military Government for 17 July–17 October 1948, ISA (130) 2564-htz/11.

26. For a discussion of state influence on local government in a different Arab locality in Israel during the same general period, see: Sa'di, "Control and Resistance."

27. *Divrei ha-Knesset* (Knesset record), 3 (17 January 1950): 550–51; 5 (29 June 1950): 1965–67; 11 (5 March 1952): 1529–32; 14 (16 June 1953): 1622; 14 (29 July 1953): 2067–68.

28. "Hok le-tikun pekudat ha-iriyot, 1950" [Municipal Corporation Ordinance Amendment, 1950], *Sefer ha-Hukim* 31 (26 January 1950): 41–64, quote on 42 (section 8B).

29. Minutes of Knesset Internal Affairs Committee, 8 August 1950, ISA (60) 24-kaf/13.

30. Palmon to Ben-Gurion and Sharett, August 9, 1950, BGA Correspondences.

31. Lustick, *Arabs in the Jewish State*, 70–77.

32. During the five years preceding 1948, communists in Palestine had been split along ethnonational lines between the Palestine Communist Party (Jewish) and the National Liberation League (Arab). Soviet endorsement of the 1947 UN partition plan, and the eventual acceptance by the Palestinian Arab communists remaining in Israel of their minority status, facilitated reunification in the form of Maki in October 1948. Soviet support for Israeli statehood and the fact that most Palestinian leaders were now refugees in other countries meant that the communists remained the single prestate Arab party operating among the country's Palestinian citizens after 1948. Ilana Kaufman, *Arab National Communism in the Jewish State* (Gainesville: University of Florida, 1997), 23–36, 43–44, 80–81; Beinin, *Was the Red Flag Flying There?* 40–55; Landau, *The Arabs in Israel*, 78–92; Dunia Habib Nahas, *The Israeli Communist Party* (London: Croom Helm, 1976), 31–48; George Karzum, *al-Hizb al-Shuyu'i al-Isra'ili bayn al-Tanaqud wa-al-Mumarisa* (The Israeli Communist Party: Between Internal Conflict and Work in Practice) (Jerusalem: Manshurat al-sha'la, 1993), 9–14, 201–3.

33. "Kalimat khassa ila al-Nasira al-hamra', allati satadhull hamra'" [Special words for Nazareth which is red and will stay red], *al-Ittihad*, August 12, 1955, 2.

34. Ben-Gurion, journal entry of 19 October 1952, BGA BGJ.

35. Government decision 102, November 30, 1952, ISA (43) 5439-gimel/ 1494.

36. Palmon and Landman to government secretary, 9 July 1953, ISA (43) 5439-gimel/1494.

37. Moyal to defense minister, 16 July 1953, ISA (43) 5439-gimel/1494; Palmon to government secretary, 23 July 1953, ISA (43) 5439-gim/1494; Lt. Col. Cohen to Military Government Department, ISA (43) 5439-gim/1494; *Divrei ha-Knesset* 14 (29 July 1953): 2067–68.

38. Minutes of Ministerial Interior and Services Committee, 5 August 1953, ISA (77) 308-alef/6.

39. See sections 19–39 of "Hok le-tikun pekudat ha-iriyot, 1950."

40. Minutes of Ministerial Interior and Services Committee, August 5, 1953, ISA (77) 308-alef/6.

41. Yitzhak Segev, "Bhirot le-iriyat Natzeret" [Nazareth municipal elections] (11 October 1953) and "Erev ha-bhirot le-iriyat Natzeret" [On the eve of the Nazareth municipal elections] (4 and 22 February 1954), ISA (79) 164-lamed/6; "Qawa'im al-murashshahin li-intikhabat baldiyat al-Nasira li-yawm 12/4/1954" [Lists of candidates for the Nazareth municipal elections of 12/4/1954], Tawfiq Ziyad Center, Nazareth.

42. Cohen to prime minister, March 31, 1954, ISA (43) 5439-gimel/1494; IMDM, report for April 1954, ISA (50) 1904-gimel/16.

43. "Bi al-zagharid wa bi al-raqs al-sha'bi istaqbalat al-Nasira al-qa'ima al-shuyu'iyya" [With folk-dancing and cries of joy, Nazareth celebrates the victory of the communist list], *al-Ittihad*, April 16, 1954, 1.

44. Shimon Landman, "Le-totza'ot ha-behirot be-Natzeret ve-harkavat ha-ko'alitziyah" [Results of the Nazareth elections and building a coalition], April 14, 1954, ISA (50) 1904-gimel/16; Moshe Ruah, "Skirah legabei totza'ot ha-bhirot be-Natzeret" [Survey of the Nazareth election results], May 4, 1954, ISA (50) 1904-gimel/16; Cohen to prime minister, March 31, 1954, ISA (43) 5439-gimel/1494.

45. See section 50 of Municipal Corporations Ordinance, 1934 and "Hok le-tikun pekudat ha-iriyot, 1950."

46. Landman, "Le-totza'ot ha-behirot be-Natzeret."

47. Ibid.; Shimon Landman, "Pe'ulot hasbarah leshem gibush ha-ko'alitziyah be-iriyat Natzeret" [Information campaign for forming a coalition in Nazareth municipality], April 27, 1954, ISA (50) 1904-gimel/16; "Ko'alitziyah katolim-Maki be-Natzeret?" [A Catholic-Maki coalition in Nazareth?], *Ha'aretz*, May 4, 1954, 4.

48. See sections 8E, 35, and 50A of "Hok le-tikun pekudat ha-iriyot, 1950."

49. Al-Qasem to interior minister, 25 April 1954, ISA (50) 1904-gimel/16; Khuri to interior minister, 17 May 1954 ISA (50) 1904-gim/16; *Yalkut ha-Pirsumim* 349 (20 May 1954): 986.

50. IMDM report for May–June 1954, July 13, 1954, ISA (50) 1904-gimel/16.

51. Minutes of first Nazareth Municipal Council meeting, June 9, 1954, ISA (43) 5439-gimel/1494; "Mahalakh ha-yeshivah ha-rishonah shel ha-nivharim la-mo'etzah" [The first meeting of elected councilmen], June 9, 1954, ISA (43) 5439-gimel/1494.

52. IMDM report for May–June 1954, July 13, 1954, ISA (50) 1904-gimel/16.

53. Maki Local Council of Nazareth, "Kahal Natzeret lo yarsheh bi-shfikhat damei netzigeiha ha-ne'emanim" [The public of Nazareth will not allow the blood of its loyal representatives to be spilled], June 17, 1954, ISA (43) 5439-gimel/1494; Koussa to Knesset chairman, June 18, 1954, ISA (74) 8002-gimel/20; *Divrei ha-Knesset* 16 (21 June 1954): 1974–82; Rozen to Sharett, June 22, 1954, ISA (43) 5439-gimel/1494; Brook to mailing list, August 9, 1954, ISA (79) 164-lamed/6.

54. Shafan to Military Government Department, "Hitparuyot be-Natzeret" [Riots in Nazareth], June 18, 1954, ISA (43) 5439-gimel/1494.

55. For a detailed discussion of evidence pointing to the possibility of state involvement in the attack, see Geremy Forman, "Military Rule, Political Manipulation, and Jewish Settlement: Israeli Mechanisms for Controlling Nazareth in the 1950s," *Journal of Israeli History* 25(2): 335–59.

56. Meeting record, June 22, 1954, ISA (50) 1904-gimel/16; Landman to Moyal, June 29, 1954, ISA (50) 1904-gimel/16; Ruah to Landman, July 1, 1954, ISA (50) 1904-gimel/16; IMDM report for May–June 1954, July 13, 1954, ISA (50) 1904-gimel/16.

57. Ruah to Landman, July 2, 1954, ISA (50) 1904-gimel/16.

58. Yitzhak Segev, "Behirot le-rosh iriyat Natzeret" [Elections for the mayor of Nazareth], July 15, 1954, ISA (79) 164-lamed/6.

59. Communist Party election results (1954–1986), Tawfiq Ziyad Center, Nazareth.

60. IMDM report for May–June 1954, July 13, 1954, ISA (50) 1904-gimel/16.

61. Baruch Kimmerling, *Zionism and Territory: The Socio-Territorial Dimensions of Zionist Politics* (Berkeley: Institute of International Studies, 1983), 26–30.

62. Harsina to Ne'eman, August 12, 1953, IDF 157/59-146.

63. Ratner Commission report, appendix: "Hityashvut bithonit ve-she'elat ha-karka'ot" [Security settlement and the land question], February 24, 1956, ISA (130) 2401-htz/20.

64. Yuval Ne'eman, "Be'ayat pituah ha-Galil" [The problem of developing the Galilee], December 1954, IDF 72/70 – 649; Harsina to Northern Command and director of Department of Military Government, May 3, 1953, IDF 756/61–79; Kahana, "Taktzir al ha-hitpathut ha-yehudit shel ha-Galil ha-Ma'aravi" [A survey of Jewish development in the Western Galilee], August 17, 1954, ISA (56) 2761-gimel/14; Harsina to Department of Military Government, June 3, 1953, IDF 756/61–79; Aharon Harsina, "Yihud ha-Galil" [Judaization of the Galilee], February 2, 1954, IDF 756/61–79; Ben-Gurion, journal entry of March 16, 1954, BGA BGJ; A. Kerin, "Yihud ha-Galil" [Judaization of the Galilee], November 30, 1954, IDF 72/70-649.

65. Ben-Gurion, journal entries for November 11, 1951, February 12, 1953, and March 4, 1953, BGA BGJ; Haim Israeli, "Al Mordekhai Alon zal," June 26, 1994, Nazareth Ilit Municipal Archive, booklet in memory of Mordekhai Alon.

66. Ministerial Interior and Services Committee minutes, August 30, 1953, ISA (77) 308-alef/6.

67. Tzadok to mailing list, March 30, 1954, Nazareth Ilit Municipal Archive; Cohen to Prime Minister, March 31, 1954.

68. Landman to Moyal, June 29, 1954, ISA (50) 1904-gimel/16.

69. Landman, "Pe'ulot hasbarah."

70. Rokah to Sharett, April 28, 1954, ISA (43) 5439-gimel/1494.

71. Yifat Holzman-Gazit, "Dinei hafka'at mekarke'in Bi-shnot ha-hamishim bi-re'i ha-ideologiyah ha-tziyonit shel klitat aliyah ve-khinyan prat" (Land Expropriation Law in the 1950s, in the Zionist Ideological Mirror of Immigrant Absorption and Private Property), in *Mekarke'in be-Yisra'el: Bein ha-prati li-le'umi*, ed. Hanokh Dagan (Tel-Aviv: University of Tel-Aviv, 1999), 223–24.

72. *Yalkut ha-Pirsumim* 356 (17 June 1954): 1284; Yitzhak Oded, "Land Losses among Israel's Arab Villagers," *New Outlook* 7, no. 7 (September 1964): 23; Hanna Nakkarah, untitled manuscript (1982), 112–16.

73. Nazareth Municipal Council minutes, October 2, 1954, ISA (56) 2215-gimel/2 (alef-dalet-mem/235); Committee for the Defense of Expropriated Nazareth Land to mailing list, December 18, 1954, ISA (56) 2215-gimel/2 (alef-dalet-mem/235).

74. Knesset Committee's Public Complaints Subcommittee minutes, January 3, 1955, ISA (56) 2215-gimel/2; Minutes of meeting between minister of agriculture and Committee for the Defense of Expropriated Nazareth Land, February 21, 1955, ISA (43) 5439-gimel/1494.

75. HCJ 30/55, *Piskei din shel beit ha-mishpat ha-elyon le-Yisrael* [Decisions of the Israeli Supreme Court], 11 (1955): 83.

76. Mordekhai Alon, "Ha-tokhniyot le-fituah Natzeret" [Plans for the development of Nazareth], November 30, 1955, 72/70–651; Report of the Interdepartmental Committee for Moving Northern District Government Offices to Nazareth, February 14, 1958, ISA (43) 5439-gimel/1494; Alon to Bar-Yehuda, July 10, 1956, ISA (50) 2625-gimel/56; Nakkarah, untitled manuscript, 115.

77. Alon, "Ha-tokhniyot le-fituah Natzeret"; Israeli, "Al Mordekhai Alon zal."

78. Amihai to Brutzkus, April 28, 1955, ISA (56) 2761-gimel/14; Divon to government secretary, undated (late 1955 or early 1956), ISA (56) 2761-gimel/14; map of development areas, ISA (56) 2761-gimel/14.

79. Zelinger to Alon, Neufeld, Yanai, and Tamir, March 16, 1956, IDF 72/70–651.

80. Summaries of the Interdepartmental Nazareth Coordination Committee, 1956–1958, IDFA 72/70–651.

81. Summary of the Interdepartmental Nazareth Coordination Committee, October 22, 1956, IDF 72/70–651; Dekel to Peres, November 22, 1956, ISA (43) 5439-gimel/1494; "Ra'iti shamati" [I saw it and heard it], *Ha'aretz*, July 24, 1957.

82. Nazareth Ilit Municipality, *Nazareth Ilit* (1998): 14–16.

83. Eshel to Navon, November 30, 1958, BGA Correspondences.

84. Ne'eman, "Be'ayat pituah ha-Galil."

85. Ben-Gurion to Bar-Yehuda, February 20, 1956, ISA (50) 2625-gim/56; Mikhael to mailing list, April 20, 1956, IDF 70/72-651; Alon, "Ha-tokhniyot le-fituah ha-Galil."

86. Ben-Gurion, journal entries for November 11, 1951 and February 12, 1953, BGA BGJ; Alon to Bar-Yehuda, July 10, 1956, ISA (50) 2625-gimel/56.

87. Ben-Gurion to Bar-Yehuda, February 20, 1956, ISA (50) 2625-gimel/56.

88. Mikhael to mailing list, April 20, 1956, IDF 70/72-651.

89. Ben-Gurion to Bar-Yehuda, February 20, 1956; interior minister's secretary to Prime Minister's Office, April 11, 1956, ISA (43) 5439-gimel/1494; Mikhael to mailing

list, April 20, 1956; Divon to Prime Minister's Office, April 26, 1956, IDF 72/
70–651.

90. Mikhael to mailing list, April 20, 1956.

91. Alon to Bar-Yehuda, July 10, 1956, and Ben-Gurion to Bar-Yehuda, February
20, 1956, ISA (50) 2625-gimel/56; Natan to Shaham, Harsina, Dekel, and Alon,
April 25, 1956, ISA (43) 5439-gimel/1494.

92. Minutes of the Committee on Security and Political Problems in Nazareth,
July 6, 1956; Dekel to Peres, December 26, 1956, ISA (43) 5439-gimel/1494.

93. Summary of the Interdepartmental Nazareth Coordination Committee, February 11, 1957, IDF 72/70–651; Pavel to Bar-Yehuda, February 14, 1957, IDF 72/
72–651; Gevirtz to director-general, August 1, 1957, ISA (50) 2625-gimel/56.

94. Pavel to director-general, September 1957, ISA (50) 3961-gimel/1; Bar-
Yehuda to Landman, November 28, 1957, ISA (50) 3961-gimel/1; Gevirtz to Landman, June 4, 1958, ISA (50) 2625-gimel/56; Bar-Yehuda to Ben-Gurion, January 5,
1959, ISA (50) 3961-gimel/1; Bar-Yehuda to Ben-Gurion, February 4, 1959, ISA
(43) 5439-gim/1494; government secretary to Bar-Yehuda, March 30, 1959, ISA
(43) 5439-gimel/1494.

95. Gevirtz to deputy director-general for local government, May 10, 1959, ISA
(50) 2625-gimel/56; Gevirtz to director-general of Interior Ministry, January 5,
1960, ISA (50) 2625-gimel/56; Gevirtz to Kalfon, June 28, 1960, ISA (50) 2625-
gimel/56; Gevirtz to director-general of Interior Ministry, January 5, 1960, ISA (50)
2625-gimel/56; Gevirtz to Kalfon, June 28, 1960, ISA (50) 2625-gimel/56; *Kovetz
ha-Takanot* 1073 (1 December 1960): 397–98; *Kovetz ha-Takanot* 1178 (20 July
1961): 2437–2438. A local council was only established in 1963. The borders between Nazareth and Upper Nazareth were repeatedly modified in subsequent years.

96. Oren Yiftachel, "The Internal Frontier": Territorial Control and Ethnic Relations in Israel," in *Ethnic Frontiers and Peripheries: Landscapes of Development and Inequality in Israel*, ed. Oren Yiftachel and Avinoam Meir (Boulder: Westview Press,
1998), 46–49, 63.

97. Rabinowitz, *Overlooking Nazareth*, 7.

Part II

CONSTRUCTING HEALTHY IDENTITIES AND LANDSCAPES

4

Defining National Medical Borders

Medical Terminology and the Making of Hebrew Medicine

Sandy Sufian

INTRODUCTION

From 1927 to 1948, the Jewish medical profession in Palestine started a project to construct a distinctly Hebrew medicine.[1] This national medicine was intended to merge extant scientific and medical knowledge and practice with Zionist ideology and goals. A major effort within the "Hebrew medicine" endeavor was the creation of a modern Hebrew medical terminology, the words of which would embody those nationalist goals and ideals.

The project to create a set of Hebrew medical terms must be situated within the general effort to revive the Hebrew language and to rehabilitate the diaspora Jewish immigrants in Palestine before and during the Mandate period (1920–1947). Zionist leaders and ideologues considered both of these initiatives as ways to promote national revival through the healing of the Jewish nation and of Palestine as a land.[2] Revitalizing the Jewish nation and the land of *Eretz Israel* [the Land of Israel, the Holy Land] was a response to European anti-Semitic claims that Jews were diseased and unproductive, effeminate and weak. Zionists tried to "cure" the Jewish people of this alleged condition by creating the conditions for a physical and mental conversion whereby in Palestine a new "Hebrew man" would be born, healthy in body and mind.

The specific use of the term "Hebrew" in the phrase "Hebrew man" refers as well to the revival of Hebrew as a national language in Zionism. Doctors writing in Zionist health documents before and during the Mandate period considered the acquisition of the Hebrew language as one of the ways to become physically and mentally healthy.[3] To them, using modern Hebrew was a means to improve one's psychological well-being, to connect with one's nation, and to purify one's soul.[4]

The process of creating a Hebrew medicine involved debates about the nature, form, uniqueness, and types of acceptable and forbidden procedures for Jewish physicians in Palestine to undertake during this time. Such debates were repeated in other areas of living in the *Yishuv* (the Jewish community in Palestine), although they were adapted to the particular dynamics of the field. The creation of Hebrew labor, Hebrew art, Hebrew literature, and Hebrew medicine were all instances of the larger phenomenon to produce a distinct Hebrew culture in Palestine that would provide proof that Jews could "normalize" to become a legitimate and accepted nation in the world.[5] The Hebrew medical terminology project was a professional example of this broader process.

In this contribution, I argue that the project of constructing a Hebrew medical terminology involved the formation and navigation of borders of professional, national, and communal identities. These included Jew/European non-Jew, Jew/Arab, Sephardi Jew/Ashkenazi Jew, and Zionist Jew/Diaspora Jew. Physicians had diverse opinions about the meaning of these boundaries, where to draw them, and how to uphold them. The question of geographical (East/West) and temporal borders (imagined past, present, and future) overlapped with concerns about the borders of identity, most notably in many physicians' desire to revive the Hebrew spirit and body and create an "authentic" Hebrew medical culture based in Semitic roots. This occurred alongside a concomitant desire to deeply engage with the advances of Western science.

By upholding its distinctly national character, doctors saw medical terminology work as a way to distinguish the Jewish medical profession and its clinical practice from other medical communities in Palestine and from European medicine. Even though medical developments in Europe served as the primary basis of knowledge for the medical community in Palestine—and perhaps precisely because of this great influence—Hebraist physicians wanted Hebrew medicine to become a contrast to medicine as practiced in the diaspora (Europe). Yet terminology activists simultaneously saw the project as a way to enter into international scientific discussions, demonstrate their ideals and knowledge, and prove their contribution on and with their own terms. The gravitation toward engagement in the international medical arena while building and maintaining a particularistic national approach existed within a historical context in which central European medical circles were increasingly shutting their doors to Jews.[6] Together, the foundation and negotiation of such communal and ideological distinctions reflect the important place science and medicine played in constructing a new, healthy Zionist national identity and culture, one that expressed and promoted Zionist nationalist agendas in Palestine.[7]

CREATING A HEALTHY NATIONAL MEDICAL TERMINOLOGY

The revival of the Hebrew language had its roots in the Jewish Enlighten-ment movement and resembled a phenomenon in nineteenth-century Eu-ropean nationalism of standardizing language through the creation of printed literature and dictionaries.[8] Within this context, Zionist Hebrew ed-ucators in Palestine wished to supplant other languages spoken in the *Yishuv* [Jewish community in Palestine] for they considered Hebrew the au-thentic and ancient language of the Jewish people.[9] Their efforts were part of a well-known struggle over the revival of the Hebrew language in the *Yishuv* beginning with the second wave of Jewish immigration (1904–1914), known as *tehiyat ha-lashon* or *tehiyat ha-ivrit*. This campaign to revive the language/Hebrew, called the language wars, began at the Tech-nion Institute in Haifa (the first institution of higher learning in the *Yishuv* with a focus on technology/engineering) in 1913–1914 when Hebrew edu-cators fought to make Hebrew the sole language of instruction instead of the dominant German. The drive to adopt Hebrew as the sole pedagogical language was particularly fierce for the fields of science and medicine; the absence of Hebrew textbooks for scientific subjects made it difficult for He-brew to compete with European languages during this time.[10] Promoters of Hebrew won the language battle in 1914, at which point the *Yishuv* adopted Hebrew as the exclusive language of school instruction. Postponed by World War I, the Technion finally opened in 1924 as an all-Hebrew institu-tion. However, debates surrounding the use of Hebrew as the single lan-guage in schools continued throughout the Mandate period, gaining special attention during the fifth wave of immigration when the threat of German reappeared in the 1930s with an influx of German Jews who were fleeing Hitler's Germany to Palestine.[11]

The push to use Hebrew was part of the Zionist movement's ideology of ridding Jews of all symbols and practices of diaspora life. It was also a prac-tical measure to unify the various Jewish communities who immigrated to Palestine with their different European languages and dialects. Hebrew ac-tivists also sought to bridge the language gap between Ashkenazi and Sephardi Jews (who spoke Ladino or Arabic) to create a more unified Jew-ish community in Palestine.[12] The question of reviving the Hebrew lan-guage, according to Yael Zerubavel, "became a crucial factor in the con-struction of a new national culture."[13] The evolving national culture, which developed during the Mandate period, ultimately translated into the basis for the national state established in 1948. State leaders continued to believe that having a single, primary language was central for state-building and sustenance. Speaking, writing, and reading Hebrew therefore connoted a desire and attempt to become a healthy Jew in mind, spirit, and body in Palestine and to become a full citizen in Israel.

Before and during the Mandate period, the promotion of Hebrew as the single national language extended beyond Zionist educational and literary circles to other Jewish professional communities in Palestine. These groups often overlapped. In the field of medicine, activist physicians wanted to create a Hebrew medical dictionary to advance the daily use of Hebrew by clinicians instead of their native Yiddish or German. In the late 1920s, these Jewish physicians began again to discuss making science instruction fully operative in Hebrew. They understood science, like education, as a central component of a unified Zionist culture and as a vital arena for embodying Zionist ideals of European rationality, progress, and innovation (as opposed to degeneracy, considered inherent in the state of exile, the diaspora). The conversation about whether or not it was possible to create a solid base of Hebrew medical terms that Jewish physicians and residents would write and speak would last until the late 1930s, with remnants even in the early 1940s.[14]

Not surprisingly, Jewish physicians actively involved in the medical terminology project were often Hebraists or Hebrew writers. Dr. Aaron Mazie, a physician who settled in Palestine in 1888 and served as head of the internal medicine department of the Bikur Cholim hospital from 1902 until his death in 1930, was the central figure in writing the first and largest Hebrew medical dictionary. He was also the editor of the medical journal *HaRefu'ah*, a publication of the Hebrew Physicians' Association of Palestine. Mazie's dictionary was entitled *Book of Terminology of the Medical and Natural Sciences* and consisted of 790 double-sided pages.[15] The dictionary was the culmination of forty years of gathering material for a compendium of Hebrew medical terms. Dr. Shaul Tchernichovsky (1875–1943), a famous Hebrew poet and a pediatrician in the Tel Aviv municipal schools (1930s), edited and completed Mazie's dictionary, publishing it in Jerusalem in 1934, after Mazie passed away. Tchernichovsky was one of the most prominent coiners of new words in Hebrew and invoked them in his poetry during this time.[16] According to the Jewish physicians' journal, approximately 1,500 Jewish doctors were using Mazie's dictionary by 1937.[17] One year earlier, Dr. L. M. Herbert wrote a review of Mazie's dictionary, stating that Mazie exemplified one of the most significant figures in the revival of "our language" and that the editor was "beloved to our generation." Despite the book's value, the author noted that most Hebrew newspapers in Palestine, except for those of a scientific nature, did not mention the dictionary's publication: "It's a criminal offense against our nation to pass over this dictionary in silence when it is necessary to proclaim it to the nation." The dictionary's relative lack of exposure was due in part to the fact that many visitors to Palestine and other interested parties living in the country could not afford its sixteen-dollar price tag. Dr. Herbert suggested giving it out for free to honored guests in order to expose the world to the dictionary and to the Jewish medical profession's accomplishment.[18] Zionist physicians of the time believed that conveying Zionist medical activities to the world medical community was crucial because they thought positive contributions would secure them a legitimate place as respected, professional citizens within the boundaries of a "normal" nation, rather in than in an abnormal state of being in the Jewish diaspora.[19] Jewish physicians believed that engaging in medicine in the Holy Land, while advancing medicine and scientific discovery worldwide, would aid the process of normalization and validity to which Zionism aspired. As Dr. Shalom Cohen wrote, "It is a fact that the Hebrew nation can live a normal life, to develop its special genius and to fulfill its historic role only in Eretz Israel."[20] Ironically, they sought to achieve acceptance by the international medical community through a particularization of language and sometimes of practice; these Hebraist physicians built distinct professional borders by using a language foreign doctors would not understand as a way to attain scientific prestige and impart seriousness to their project. They believed that having a language that fully functioned in professional spheres was an emblem of national progress and professional and cultural authenticity.[21] This dual attitude within the Zionist medical profession—wanting to be fully integrated into the international medical community on equal footing yet also bolstering the particularities and nationalist character of its work—permeated the medical terminology project throughout its evolution.[22] Although these attitudes are seemingly contradictory, physicians do not seem to have viewed them as mutually exclusive.

Dialogue about Hebrew medical terms continued after the publication of Mazie's dictionary. The main Hebrew medical journal dealing with the topic of Hebrew medical terminology, *HaRofe HaIvri* [The Hebrew Doctor], consistently dedicated a section of its publications to discussions about Hebrew medical terms and Hebrew medicine. Even before the section's publication, Dr. Rafael Ben Dov indicated that he agreed with another doctor, Shimon Meklar, that the choice of words should be an exercise shared between the editorship and readership of *HaRofe HaIvri*. Both doctors believed that a section on terminology should be set up in the journal. "The question of a Hebrew medical terminology is not only a 'literary controversy' but a practical question that requires heavy consideration and serious attention to its resolution."[23] Solving the question of terminology, Ben Dov thought, would help bring order to the Hebrew literary-medical profession. There was no time to waste.

Upon initiating its terminology column, called the Section for Determining Medical Terms [*Mador lekvi'at munachim refui'im*], *HaRofe HaIvri* reappraised earlier choices found in Mazie's work and tried to systematize a logic for creating new terms. According to a physician writing in *HaRofe HaIvri*, Mazie's dictionary was not a "holy book" (not sacred) and therefore could be revised for the needs of the future and adapted with new medical knowledge.[24] Terminology, in other words, should be adaptable and responsive to the state of medical knowledge and to anticipated needs; it was not, and should not be, a timeless collection of words. Even the Hebrew Language Committee (of which Mazie was at one point president) stated that Mazie's dictionary was not the "final seal on medical terms . . . the lexicography of medicine is still a tender plant . . . and will need to develop in the coming generations."[25] The Hebrew Language Committee [*Va'ad Ha-Lashon Ha'Ivrit*], founded in 1890 by Eliezer Ben-Yehuda, coined new terms and determined the proper pronunciation and spelling for modern Hebrew.[26] It began its standardizing activities in earnest during the Mandatory period after the British rulers officially recognized Hebrew as one of the official languages of Palestine in 1921. The Committee published the quarterly journal *Leshonenu* [Our Tongue/Language] beginning in 1928 and was responsible for publishing many specialized dictionaries.[27] Notwithstanding the Committee's observation about Mazie's dictionary, Chaim Nachman Bialik, a central literary figure of the *Yishuv* and member of the Language Committee, added that Mazie's work was the most comprehensive and most important compilation of medical terms to date.[28] Indeed, Ben-Yehuda, who led the project to revive the Hebrew language as a modern spoken language, integrated some of Mazie's medical terms into his general dictionary with Mazie's permission.[29]

The Central Committee of the Hebrew Physicians' Society in Palestine and the Special Council on Language made the final decisions about which terms to use for the revised and expanded set of medical terms.[30] The process leading to those final decisions can be found, in part, in the pages of the physicians' journal *HaRofe HaIvri* [The Hebrew Doctor]. Additions, deletions, and discussion of other lexicons made up the lively pages of *HaRofe HaIvri*. Doctors like Dr. Israel Givner, Dr. Samuel Boorstein (orthopedic surgeon, member of the board of directors of the American Jewish Physician's Committee, and member of Hebrew Speaking Physicians' Society),[31] Dr. L. M. Herbert, and Dr. Alter Alexander Fried took an active part in adding new words and in debating the methodology of choosing appropriate terms.[32]

COMMUNAL IDENTITIES, TEMPORAL BORDERS, AND THE PURITY OF LANGUAGE

Many of these physicians took a very strict approach to the addition of terms, limiting all new medical terms to those derived from Jewish sources to ensure the purity of the language. Other physicians, however, took a more lax approach, allowing the integration of transliterations of widely used foreign medical terms. As Dr. Tchernichovsky indicated in one of his commentaries, the latter approach acknowledged that immigrant physicians and their patients would continue to speak in more than one language as they assimilated into an evolving Hebrew culture in Palestine.[33] It may also have reflected a more pragmatic realization that participation in world medical debates would require the occasional use of foreign words in certain venues.

This dual approach toward word choice in medical circles echoed a larger literary argument between the "conservationists and the innovationists."[34] Some people wanted to recover and redefine words from the Bible and other Jewish sources while others preferred to adopt foreign words. The division reflected not only differential attitudes toward the diaspora but also about Zionism's relationship to the Jewish past and a national future. As in other nationalist projects, many Zionist physicians involved in this project wanted to establish continuity with a Jewish past by deliberately appropriating medical terms from the Hebrew Bible, the Talmud, and even sometimes from Ibn Sina's *Qanun*, a definitive Arabic medical text that was translated into Hebrew in the late fifteenth century.[35] It is possible that the *Qanun* was acceptable to these particular physicians not only because of its historical, authoritative status but also because Jewish philosophers in the Middle Ages wrote in Arabic and deeply engaged with Islamic philosophers. Arabic is a Semitic language like Hebrew and therefore related to Jews' Semitic roots.

Dr. A. A. Goldin was among those engaged in the project who found no value in using Talmudic terms.[36] In contrast, Dr. Asher Goldstein argued, "culture means tradition;" that continuity with the past was important to preserve. "We don't need to sacrifice the altar of the past and of tradition for scientific grammar and brevity."[37] Since language reflected the nation for Goldstein, even medical words had to be steeped in tradition in order for a national culture to evolve in the present and future.

Responding to a call for an "open stage" in the journal *HaRofe HaIvri*, Dr. A. Shimoni-Melkar of Kfar Yarkona took a middle stance, suggesting that the ends of foreign words could be used for clarity but should be adapted to sound more like Hebrew so that they would not "grate on our ears." So, for instance, he proposed that terms with the Latin ending -*itis* (denoting an infection of some kind) should be changed to -*it*. Looking to the example of other languages like Russian and French, Melkar believed that Jewish doctors could elect to take only a part of the ending. Appendicitis, therefore, could change to appenditzit in Hebrew; the letter "tet" would change to "tav" in the process. Arthritis would become *artrit*, otitis would become *otit*, and the like.[38] Dr. Levi from Chicago entered the debate about the ending -*itis* five years later in 1938, suggesting that words ending in -*itis* in foreign languages should have their equivalent in Hebrew with the addition of *char-*

instead of -*it*. This prefix would come from the Hebrew *chara* or *charar*, meaning burn. The author noted that in Aramaic and Arabic, related Semitic languages, the words *harara* mean "fever and inflammation" and so the addition of *har* would make readers, speakers, and listeners aware from the beginning about what kind of disease they were discussing. A skin infection would therefore be *char-or* instead of the foreign word "dermatitis." The related words for such infections would sound more authentic to Hebrew linguistic roots rather than borrowed from Greek or Latin. In this sense, we can see that terminology activists prioritized issues of authenticity in the new nation's language by prioritizing its grammatical rules and tendencies, its sounds, and its local context in the ongoing "game of words."[39]

Discussions about specific word choices also reveal the evolution of Hebrew medical terminology. For instance, one of Herbert's articles in *HaRofe HaIvri* notes that the word *hatkiv* was out of use in Palestine; in fact, the word was *titkivit* until Dr. Mazie himself suggested *lavlav*, the word for pancreas. According to Herbert, Mazie "took the word from the [Jewish] nation and not from the Arabic greats, and perhaps saw in his choice a chance to remember the ancient national Hebrew that had disappeared."[40] To Herbert, Mazie was recovering the Jewish past only, not borrowing from Arabic history. Shlomo [Solomon] Rabinovitz also appropriated the past for present use in order to claim authority, long-term rootedness, and legitimacy for the project and to promote the consideration of ancient and medieval Hebrew terms. "Even in Talmudic times, a Hebrew medical terminology existed."[41]

The maneuver to reiterate the boundary between Jewish history and Arab history (although these boundaries were much more fluid during the height of Arabic medieval medicine), to claim a preexisting terminology, and to resurrect a nostalgic ancient Jewish past for present purposes is clearly seen here as a way to revitalize and perhaps purify the Jewish nation and to uphold its communal and national borders. This kind of maneuver, appropriating the past to enable future progress, was a common move made in nationalist movements during the time, not only in the Zionist movement. The Zionist movement deeply engaged in an ideological movement in time. It upheld borders of identities in its language, its sentiments toward Palestine/Eretz Israel, and in its goal toward establishing national autonomy there.

In addition to concerns about recovering a Jewish past and recognizing Arabic influences, debates about word choice often reflected larger attitudes about the contemporary symbolic import between East and West. In addition to excluding German, Russian, French, or English terms, one physician practicing in Tel Aviv, Dr. Goldenstein, advised against using Arabic terms. His strict stance conflicted with other Hebraist doctors mentioned above, who accepted the use of texts like Ibn Sina's *Qanun* as a source of terms. For

Goldenstein, common Semitic roots were not enough. Goldenstein echoed the previous sentiments of Jacob Fishman, a member of the Hebrew Language Committee in 1910, who wrote, "despite the fact that the Arabic language is our sister language in the family of Semitic languages, it has no foundation in our psyche."[42] Goldenstein's words reflected Zionist notions of progress and Western rationality that the Jewish physicians wanted to bring to Palestine: "It is important to note, that our haste to bring the two communities [Arab and Jewish] closer doesn't mean that we should *cross over the border* [my italics] and damage our scientific position. Our goal is to bring the West . . . to the East and not to totally settle in the East in terms of our spirit."[43] For Goldenstein, although using Arabic sources might help in the Jews' spiritual return to the East, it could, more importantly, hinder realizing the enlightened Western goals of the *Yishuv*. The latter, to him, was a more imperative charge. Dr. Goldenstein's words mark his clear intention that the medical dictionary project, and the Hebrew medicine endeavor at large, should build and uphold communal borders in the medical and scientific fields in Palestine. Bringing the "rationality" and scientific advances of the West to the East was a goal of this project; the specifics on how to fulfill that goal were subject to debate.

The issue of East/West and communal borders did not only refer to Arab and Jew but also to the divide within the *Yishuv* between Ashkenazi and Sephardic Jews. Despite a general desire to bring Western advances to the East, some Hebraist physicians considered the authentic character of their terminology project, consistent with an Eastern setting, as essential. Since many of the physicians engaged in general discussions about the revival of the Hebrew language, they also felt that medical terminology had to be consistent with the standardization and general rules of the larger Hebrew language project. Many physicians therefore made strong appeals to consult with the general Hebrew Language Committee to ensure that proper grammar, pronunciation, and a Sephardi accent over an Ashkenazi one was used. The Sephardi accent was considered more authentic since it belonged to those Jews who never left the Middle East after the destruction of the Second Temple in 70 CE (or those who had roots in Spain and the Mediterranean.) As a result, it was closer to Arabic pronunciation and farther from the Ashkenazi diaspora experience.

Since biblical and rabbinic Hebrew lacked certain words about concrete objects and nature, Hebraist physicians of this school of thought took pains to research and identify possible words in the sources that could be adapted and invented for modern use.[44] The pages of *HaRofe HaIvri* contained energetic debates centering around which words would convey the meaning of the disease or symptom in the clearest and most succinct way. Most physicians stressed consistency with the rules of the Hebrew language and with the meaning of the term because creators felt word choice reflected and would enhance nationalist goals.[45] Even for those physicians who accepted foreign terms, transliterated terms had to be consistent with general Hebrew grammar.

Returning to the evolution of words, we also learn that the word for arthritis evolved in a short time. As Dr. Dubnow explained, at first the word was translated as *daleket haperek* [infection of the joint]. Dr. A. Goldenstein preferred the Maimonidian term and so changed it to *daleket prekit*. Dr. Goldin then decided that the term was too long and shortened it to *delekperek*. In 1928, Dr. Dubnow suggested the term *pereket*. That term was eventually accepted for a time but was then Dr. Levi challenged it yet again. We should remember that Levi felt that all infection terms with the Latin *-itis* should have the prefix *char-*, so for him arthritis should turn into the Hebrew *chorperek*. Dr. Dubnow noted that this continual back-and-forth about the word arthritis was entirely unnecessary and that one could not understand Dr. Levi's new word unless one clearly knew his meaning/connotation of *char-*. What if a person doesn't think of *char-* as meaning inflammation but rather as literal burning? In other words, Dubnow asked the rhetorical question: What makes Levi's word better than the ones before it?[46] These kinds of questions reveal the process by which physicians created, challenged, and finally either rejected or accepted new words. Such processes and decisions were not incidental; Hebraist physicians deliberately made each decision about the assimilation of words with the conscious assumption that medical language had a part to play in the physical and mental transformation of Jewish identity in Palestine.

Other debates surrounding word choice and word endings were rather technical and arduous. Such efforts in addressing the issue, however, reveal the ongoing debate and deep investment physicians showed in choosing words for a Hebrew medical terminology. Dr. Herbert, for instance, commented on the suggested introduction of new words for terms like *gonorrhea, benign, heartburn,* and *malignant*. Dr. Alter-Alexander Fried, who emphasized the importance of etymology[47] and suggested the alterations to which Dr. Herbert referred, wanted to change the word *gonorrhea* (pronounced in Hebrew the same way) to *raatan*. Rav Shimon Ben Gamliel used the word *raatan* in the Talmud as a skin disease like boils, so its use for the sexually transmitted disease could be considered confusing. Because of this, Fried's suggestion was not wholly accepted. Fried also wanted to change common words already in use, like *bish* or *bimme'ir* (for the English word *malignant*) to *meriri*. Herbert felt that most of Dr. Fried's suggestions were weak and would not be accepted.[48]

L. M. Herbert also critiqued elements of Tchernichovsky's rendering of medical terminology. This particular exchange with Shaul Tchernichovsky centered on the length of medical terms, the use of consistent suffixes, and the comprehensiveness of Mazie's dictionary. It also inadvertently raised the issue of audience. Tchernichovsky wrote a seven-page rebuttal to Dr. Herbert's critique of Mazie's dictionary and of the selection of certain anatomical terms. In his rebuttal, Tchernichovsky explained how and why certain phrases or words were chosen and why they could or could not be shortened. He revealed that he and Mazie consulted existing foreign language medical terminologies (German, English, and Russian) and weighed their methods when choosing new Hebrew terms. He argued that the Hebrew dictionary was the most exhaustive of all of them. Tchernichovsky, the doctor and poet, explained that he and his critic had different goals in mind for the terminology project: Dr. Herbert "dreamt" of highly specific, professional terminology that only doctors would use, while Dr. Tchernichovsky wanted a vocabulary that could be used and understood by both doctors and patients that was clear, precise, and in good Hebrew. He argued, "There will be phrases that doctors will always use in their foreign tongue;" it's more important that the term be understood by the patient.[49] A lack of verbiage in Hebrew, he explained, hampered the creation of "pretty" terms with consistent suffixes (like the Latin ending *-itis* as mentioned above). The effort to force such suffixes onto Hebrew roots, in his view, was not worth it.[50] Tchernichovsky stressed practicality: "In Eretz Israel we use terms for [daily] practice, and the ear absorbs the purity of the sounds!"[51] Tchernichovsky clearly took offense to Herbert's critique, as Herbert subsequently apologized for any impression the poet may have had that he underrated the seriousness and consideration put into the dictionary project and underappreciated the extent of its importance. He emphasized his deep admiration of Mazie's dictionary, including Tchernichovsky's input, and its significance for the medical profession. He also noted that his suggestions were just alternative submissions in the current process of developing the terminology. Despite these praises, Herbert asked why translations of terms were given as lengthy explanations. "What we want in a dictionary is translation not explanation, we are doctors, [and] I presume that we understand international [medical] terms."[52] But Herbert had answered his own question earlier in the piece; he highlighted the fact that Dr. Tchernichovsky's rebuttal disclosed a heretofore unrevealed intention: that the dictionary was in fact not only meant for doctors but also for a general audience.[53] In other words, Mazie's project of creating a Hebrew medical dictionary was thought of as not only a scholarly endeavor but as a public contribution—it was not intended only for the medical profession but to influence the national identities of all Jews in Palestine. The dictionary was intended then as a national dictionary, one that would translate into the general sphere of new Hebrew usage and that would shape Hebrew culture. Medical science, it can therefore be suggested, was considered vital not only for the profession itself but for all the people and for the nation's health.

Supplementing the belief that healing the body and mind could be achieved through public health projects in the Jewish sector, the proponents of a medical language believed that using Hebrew in their daily clinical practice was yet another way to heal oneself and one's patient of an exilic state; in other words, Hebrew itself had healing properties and could be coupled with the therapeutic effects of medical treatment. Like the healing power of words in magical charms and other folkloric medicine, Hebrew could be employed here to cure and transform the Jew. The rational methods of Western science and healing power of language do not seem to clash here; both contribute to the renaissance of the Jewish nation. In fact, Dr. L. M. Herbert wrote that the goal of a Hebrew medical language *and* of Hebrew medicine [*HaRefuah haEretz-Israelit*] was "part of the renewal of our life, as a way to sacrifice ourselves and to consecrate our lives; this is only a small angle in the larger project of establishing our renewal. This is [was] our contribution to the pioneering project for our independent life that is being formed on the land of our forefathers. . . . [This is our] participation in the realization of an ideal of generations!"[54] Using Hebrew in clinical practice would show the physicians' professional allegiance and national loyalty to the emerging Zionist homeland. It would reinforce the new national language and would manifest the importance of medicine and science for achieving a strong Jewish nation.

Given the fact that words were chosen with such care, it is rather ironic that there seems, in the end, to have been no systematic way of choosing words. However, choices were not random. Three sources generally determined the choice of new medical terms: (1) terms that were already in use by the ancients; (2) terms that literary/medical figures chose during the Mandate period (criteria unknown); (3) terms that were more or less translated from internationally recognized medical terms but complied with general Hebrew grammar.[55] These general rules and sources resulted in a relatively cohesive Hebrew medical terminology by the end of the Mandate period. Of course, as with every language, activist physicians continued to introduce new medical terms after the Mandate period as new medical technology and knowledge evolved.

A WINDING ROAD: THE ADOPTION OF MEDICAL TERMS

Just as the "emergence of Hebrew as the *Yishuv*'s national language was a complex process that entailed a struggle on both ideological and practical grounds,"[56] so too was the project of instituting a Hebrew medical terminology. To be sure, the process of consolidating and fully implementing the use of Hebrew medical terms was a choppy one. This uneven path mirrored a larger pattern seen in Zionists' adoption or rejection of foreign cultural influences on their road to put an "end to diglossia" (the use of two or more languages simultaneously in a society) in the *Yishuv*.[57]

At first, many physicians did not widely use the new words found in these dictionaries and disparate lists in daily practice. In fact, implementation of a Hebrew medicine was not immediately nor perhaps ever fully successful; only a minority of doctors in Palestine who were active in the terminology endeavor readily took up the use of these words. Most others, at least initially, resisted. As Liora Halperin has observed about the broader attempt to integrate Hebrew in all aspects of the *Yishuv*, "Despite fervent advocacy on behalf of a unique and unified Hebrew culture . . . the border regions of language could never be and were never walled off by concrete barriers."[58] For most practicing Jewish physicians in Palestine during the Mandate period, the borders between languages remained fluid.

The dispute about the absolute use of Hebrew versus partial or no use of Hebrew became exacerbated in 1933, a year in which large numbers of doctors emigrated from Germany and other parts of Europe to Palestine due to the rise of the Nazi regime. This immigration made German doctors an ethnic majority of Jewish doctors in Palestine during the 1930s. Speaking to this point, Dr. Shapira wrote a piece from Metulla in *HaRofe HaIvri* in 1933 describing his frustration concerning the refusal of German Jewish doctors to use Hebrew in their medical practice and their persistence in using German in the hallways of the hospitals, in correspondences with other doctors, and in describing the natural history of disease to their patients. To his dismay and with "public outrage," he noted that only a small number of the numerous Jewish doctors in *Eretz Israel* wrote in medical Hebrew and that number was continually decreasing. "The scorn [by German doctors in Palestine] of our language from their side crosses every boundary."[59] Although he recognized that doctors remaining in the diaspora (e.g., United States) might not use Hebrew in their daily practice, he still expressed a desire for them to study Hebrew medical terminology in their spare time and understand its content. "But in Eretz Israel, the place of our language's renaissance, it's a necessity that doctors will assimilate medical language and terms not only as theory but in their everyday work."[60] It is possible that he differentiated these two types of doctors (those in Palestine and those in the diaspora) and their obligations toward Hebrew terminology because those in the diaspora could never achieve full health of mind and soul unless they physically left the diaspora. Studying Hebrew medical terms could at least prepare them for this transformation of their soul once they got to Palestine. Shapira called for American Jewish doctors to take the issue to Hadassah Medical Organization—one of the main medical institutions in Palestine sponsored by American Zionists at the time—and demand with administrative and moral pressure that doctors in Palestine speak Hebrew and pass a Hebrew test in order to practice medicine there. According to

Shapira, a doctor who didn't pass the test should lose his or her position.[61] Shapira wrote that Hadassah was compelled to do this because it was not just a philanthropic organization but a medical *national* institution and therefore must take steps to solidify the use of Hebrew as a national medical language. Comparing the medical profession to other professional groups in Palestine, Shapira argued that just like German Jewish lawyers, Jewish doctors should have to pass a Hebrew test to become licensed.

In contrast, Dr. Rafael Ben Dov's position on this matter was attenuated. He recognized that decisions about terminology and usage couldn't just be made by the staff of *HaRofe HaIvri* and be expected to be used at once. Terms had to be practical for the readership; they had to be easy to remember, easy to pronounce, and easy to construct sentences with.[62] Ben Dov, like Tchernichovsky and others, understood that the expansion and consolidation of a Hebrew medical terminology occurred not only on paper but had to occur consensually in practice through the efforts of doctors, nurses, pharmacists, and patients. The adoption process would take time. In the meantime, clear communication needed to be upheld as it was vital for a positive doctor-patient relationship.

NEGOTIATING AND BUILDING BORDERS: SIMILAR MEDICAL PROJECTS WITHIN THE ZIONIST MEDICAL COMMUNITY AND PALESTINIAN ARAB MEDICAL COMMUNITY

Despite attempts to uphold boundaries between Hebrew medicine and diaspora medicine, the project for a national medical terminology extended beyond the Jewish medical community in Palestine. As we saw with Dr. Levi's comments, the Society of Hebrew Speaking Physicians in New York and other Jewish doctors from across America contributed to the effort and debates occurring between the two communities.[63] Perhaps Hebraist physicians considered the boundary between America and the *Yishuv* as more fluid than other boundaries (i.e., Europe) or at least more easily passable for the project's purposes, for the relationship had a longstanding precedent in wider health affairs. The American Jewish medical community was very active in Zionist medical affairs in Palestine, starting with the American Zionist Medical Unit during World War I and the establishment of Nathan Straus Health Centers. This involvement continued Hadassah Medical Organization's vast healthcare delivery system in Palestine throughout the Mandate period. Much financial and technical assistance for medical affairs in the *Yishuv* came from America. It is within this context that American Jewish physicians became involved in the medical terminology project.

American Jewish physicians' involvements in conversations about Hebrew medical terminology are reflected in the pages of *HaRofe HaIvri*. In fact, the journal had two editions, one American and the other Palestinian, although both were published in Hebrew. The American edition sometimes had articles written in English. Sometimes American authors would be published in the Palestinian edition and vice versa. A concerted exchange did take place.

Two prominent physicians in the *Yishuv*, Dr. Julius Kleeberg and Dr. Aryeh Feigenbaum, also encouraged the foundation of a distinct Hebrew medicine—but not necessarily the exclusive use of Hebrew—in their publication of the *Folia Medica Orientalia* in the 1930s. These editors intended the *Folia* to be a high-standard Middle East medical journal which would "show the international character of medicine, transcending all boundaries and to establish Israel as a recognized center of modern scientific research."[64] Despite its lofty mission, consistent with those physicians of the terminology project, Dr. Shapira criticized the *Folia* for upholding the "purity of foreign languages" and for not insisting upon the use of Hebrew.[65] However, elsewhere in *HaRofe HaIvri* Dr. Herbert noted that Feigenbaum, an ophthalmologist, was an important contributor and creator of many medical terms and expressions in Hebrew. Dr. Malchi's medical dictionary was yet another Hebrew medical dictionary mentioned in historical documents, but it is not clear if it bore the same recognition by professionals as Mazie's dictionary.

Medical texts published in Hebrew included Dr. Feigenbaum's book *The Eye* as well as Dr. Gruenfeld's book on hygiene. Dr. Levinson's *Child Care* was a text for nurses studying in Hadassah's nursing school. Kupat Holim [the Sick Fund] printed a calendar for mothers in Hebrew that showed them how to care for their children in the national language.[66]

The popular medical journal *HaRefuah* [Medicine], served as another testament to the use of Hebrew in medical circles and reemphasized the borders between an abject diasporic condition of identity and a healthy national identity in Palestine. It also distinguished the particularistic character of the Hebrew medical profession as opposed to their European Western colleagues. As editors of *HaRefuah*, the quarterly journal for the Hebrew Medical Society in Palestine, wrote, "For all of our work in the Diaspora it only had individual value and not national value. Of all the stones that we added to the palace of general medical science [in the Diaspora], no national-Hebrew character was attributed to them. Only when we build our future here in Palestine will there be double and lasting value: national, and individual together." Also, "our magazine has another important field of work—it must adapt our renascent Hebrew to medical use, providing it with all the theoretical and practical terminology. We must revive old terms and invent many new ones."[67]

Besides research and publications, performing procedures like autopsies appeared critical in discussions about the nature of Hebrew medicine since the procedure went against Jewish religious law, but was considered an important part of Western medical practice. It seems from available evidence that medical leaders allowed autopsies in cases where the cause of death needed to be known. Autopsies were not allowed for simple anatomy lessons. In the latter case, the borders between European and Hebrew medical professions could fracture; Zionist medical texts would assimilate knowledge from other parts of the world.

As Jewish activist doctors tried to define the etymological borders of new Hebrew medical terms, a national project for creating a medical terminology took place in the Palestinian Arab medical community. Palestinian Arab doctors took part in creating a Palestinian Arab medical dictionary and a "Palestinian medicine" during the Mandate period. It is unknown whether this effort occurred concomitantly with, predated, or postdated the Hebrew one. It is likely that earlier debates about the reform and modernization of Arabic (especially in the sciences) occurring in the late nineteenth and early twentieth centuries and concurrent languages projects at the Arabic Language Academy in Cairo influenced the Palestinian project.[68] Unfortunately, a detailed history of the Palestinian Arab medical terminology project is hard to reconstruct because surviving materials, mostly in the *Palestinian Arab Medical Journal* [al-Majala al-tabiyya al filastiniyya al Arabia] exist only from 1945–1948. The Palestine Arab Medical Association (PAMA) initiated this medical journal in Jerusalem and held their first congress in June 1945.[69] Its editorial board included Dr. M. T. Dajani, Dr V. Kalbian, Dr. I. Hajjar, Dr. I. George, Dr. T. Canaan, and Dr. P. Freij.[70] The *Palestinian Arab Medical Journal* dealt with various clinical and pharmaceutical questions, kept track of the whereabouts and training of different Palestinian doctors, and presented historical essays on medieval Arab medicine, appropriating it for Palestinian nationalist purposes. It discussed various medical activities across the country.[71]

Like their Jewish counterparts, the editors and authors of *Al-Majala al-tabiyya* tried to use distinct Arabic words instead of transliterations from the Latin, English, or German texts. Articles in the journal dealing with Palestinian medicine similarly look to an Arab past to define a national present and hopeful future. They focus on Palestinian medicine's "glorious roots" during the heyday of Islamic medicine and how Arab philosophers and physicians formed the basis for modern-day medicine. Unlike many physicians involved in the Hebrew project, the Palestinian Arab endeavor raised the Arab medical greats as heroes and forerunners of modern medicine. The journal's purpose, according to Dr. Mahmud Dajani, leader of the Palestine Arab Medical Association, was to help Palestinian Arab doctors "fulfill the national message towards their nation and homeland," to reflect the "renaissance of Arab physicians," and to maintain intellectual linkages with other physicians in the Arab world.[72] In a reply from the president of the Physicians' Society in Iraq, Dr. Hashim Watra added that the journal would serve as part of the "renaissance of science and nationalism in the beloved Arab Palestine."[73] Just like the Hebrew project, the Palestinian Arabic medicine would revive the Palestinian nation and be a basis for a strong future.

It must be noted that these sentiments found their place in the *Palestinian Arab Medical Journal* at about the same time that professional competition between the Arab and Jewish medical sectors increased.[74] Even though Jewish and Arab doctors regularly worked together in government hospitals, by the end of the Mandate period, the Palestine Arab Medical Association (PAMA) advocated ethnic separation of staff and patients in medical services.[75] The PAMA protested against the disproportionate number of licensed Jewish doctors in the country and the unfair professional competition this posed for Palestinian Arab physicians, particularly since Jewish patients did not equally consult Arab physicians. Drs. Dajani and Canaan noted that their association aimed to promote a scenario where "the Arabs [will] run all the medical services catering to the Arabs."[76]

Such economic and professional conflicts cast into relief the ideological and practical importance of each group's medical terminology project during this decade. The Palestinian Arab project took place amid a widespread push for medical and linguistic reform in the Arab world during the interwar period. But within the particular context of Palestine, Palestinian Arab physicians' belief in using medicine and science to revive the nation was also a way to make Palestine able to survive and overcome what was seen as the incursion of the Zionist project at large and its medical activities in particular. Using Arabic words certainly helped fulfill that goal; Arabic medical terminology played a role in the larger attempt to recapture professional dominance and to help define their own national medical borders.

Like the Zionist project, the Arabic medical project revealed the role of science and medical knowledge in displaying one's allegiance to and professional contribution to the Palestinian nation. In an era of extremely contested claims over the land and over professional turf, such expressions of loyalty through science and medicine on both sides, Palestinian Arab and Jewish, cannot be underestimated.

CONCLUSION

For Zionist physicians to use medical knowledge and practice medicine meant that it had not only to be consistent with nationalist agendas, but that it had to be expressed, as much as possible, in the national language. The project to create a Hebrew medical terminology was part of the larger endeavor of reviving both the written and spoken Hebrew language. Hebrew physicians regarded the use of Hebrew as a way to heal the Jews of their degenerate, exilic state and to help them become rehabilitated as a nation in

Palestine. They believed that language and medicine could merge to physically and intellectually heal the Jewish nation and to create healthy identities.

The creation of a medical terminology therefore marks another step within a particular professional sphere in the emergence of what Benjamin Harshav calls the "base language" of the *Yishuv*. By looking at the professional sphere, rather than purely at the political or diplomatic sphere as done by scholars in the past, we can better understand how medicine was imbricated in the crossing of intellectual, linguistic, communal, nationalist, and temporal borders; how it contributed to the establishment of new borders; and how medicine and science advanced the larger Zionist national project of creating healthy identities. Although the project was not immediately accepted by all, in time many of the words began to be used in daily clinical practice by physicians and in everyday parlance by Jews in the country. Discussions about word choice not only involved issues of grammar, religious-historical precedence, and departure or adherence to foreign terms but raised the question of intracommunal borders between Ashkenazi and Sephardic Jews. Attempts to capture and consolidate an "authentic" culture were bound up with these debates.

Depending upon the variety of opinions involved, the project for a national professional terminology crossed or upheld intercommunal borders. Some doctors' calls to exclude German, Russian, Latin, or French terms were meant to distinguish the Hebrew medical community from other European medical communities. An insistence by some Zionist physicians upon Hebrew terms and not Arabic ones promoted the idea of a pure Hebrew medicine based on either ancient or modern Jewish achievements. For other physicians, allowing terms used in Ibn Sina's *Qanun* or other Arabic texts only furthered the Semitic character of the project and its claim of authenticity.

On the other hand, the Palestinian Arab community also engaged in establishing Arabic medical terms for the same purpose and consolidated its own Arab medical professional community. Reviving the great Arab doctors of medieval times as paragons in theory while calling for separation of Jewish and Arab healthcare on the ground helped further Arab medical affairs at the end of British rule. While they upheld the symbolic import and prestige of each community's professional sector, professional medical terms set forth in each national language also further defined the medical communal borders between the Arab and Jewish communities in Palestine during this time.

Both terminology projects—Zionist and Palestinian Arab—show that medicine and medical knowledge were inextricably tied to the two nationalist projects and reflected and solidified national ideologies. Physicians utilized language to invoke a connection to an authentic past, create present practices, and signify potential healthy and productive futures.

Many changes to Hebrew medical terminology have occurred since the Mandate period as new medical technologies and etiologies have emerged.

These changes, however, did not dilute the connections initially made between medical science and practice, culture (literary or otherwise), and national identity during the Mandate period. Physicians deemed medical words during this time of intense nationalist drive as just as important as medicine itself in the cure of the pathologies the words described.

NOTES

Unless otherwise noted, the *HaRofe HaIvri* volumes cited are the Palestine editions.

1. It is unclear why Jewish physicians started this project in 1927, but it is perhaps related to the establishment of the Hebrew University of Jerusalem in 1925 and an increasing need for academic texts and medical language.

2. For a full discussion of this idea, see Sandy Sufian, *Healing the Land and the Nation: Malaria and the Zionist Project in Mandatory Palestine, 1920–1948* (Chicago: University of Chicago Press, 2007), ch. 1.

3. Georges Canguilhem, *The Normal and the Pathological* (New York: Zone Books, 1991), 43, 91, 100–1; Ludwig Fleck, *Genesis and Development of a Scientific Fact* (Chicago: University of Chicago Press, 1979), 37; John Efron, *Defenders of Race: Jewish Doctors and Race Science in Fin-de-siecle Europe* (New Haven: Yale University Press, 1994), 138; Lennard Davis, "Constructing Normalcy" in *The Disability Studies Reader* (Routledge: New York, 1997), 9–28.

4. For more on language and its connection to the spirit of the nation, see writings of H. N. Bialik. One example is Chaim Nachman Bialik, "Al umah ve-lashon," *Devarim she'be'al peh* (Tel Aviv: Devir, 1935), 16.

5. Liora Halperin, "Other Tongues: the Place of 'Lo'azit' in Hebrew Culture" (unpublished paper, 2006), 15. Thank you to Liora Halperin for raising this point.

6. This may in part (but not wholly) explain the dynamic of attraction toward European medicine alongside the encouragement of a national medicine.

7. Sandy Sufian, *Healing the Land and the Nation: Malaria and the Zionist Project in Mandate Palestine 1920–1948* (Chicago: University of Chicago Press, 2007).

8. Specifically in the Eastern European enlightenment and the strand of cultural Zionism that emerged from it. Chaim Rabin, "The National Idea and the Revival of Hebrew" in *Essential Papers of Zionism*, eds. Yehuda Reinharz and Anita Shapira (New York University Press: New York, 1996), 749.

9. Even Zohar, "Emergence of a Native Hebrew Culture," *Essential Papers in Zionism*, 730.

10. The Teachers' Association [*Histadrut HaMorim*] and teachers of the Hilfsverein schools led the campaign to make Hebrew the sole language of instruction in the Yishuv. The German Hilfsverein der deutschen Juden was founded in 1901 to spread enlightenment ideas in the Middle East and Eastern Europe. See Liora Halperin, "Other Tongues: The Place of 'Lo'azit' in Hebrew Culture" (unpublished paper, 2006), 1; *Encyclopedia of Zionism and Israel*, ed. Raphael Patai (New York: Herzl Press, 1971), s.v. "language war."

11. Liora Halperin, "Other Tongues: The Place of 'Lo'azit' in Hebrew Culture" (unpublished paper, 2006), footnote 1.

12. As part of the rejection of diaspora life, Zionist Labor leaders pressed Jewish immigrants to adopt a new kind of lifestyle of farming and closeness to the land; to engage in what Labor Zionists referred to as Hebrew labor. Zionist ideologues and leaders like A. D. Gordon believed that working the land (as opposed to alienation from the land in the diaspora), like speaking the national language, would purify the soul and spirit of the Jew.

13. Yael Zerubavel, *Recovered Roots Collective Memory and the Making of Israeli National Tradition* (Chicago: University of Chicago Press, 1995), 80.

14. The question is still asked in 1933 by Dr. A. A. Goldin of New York in *HaRofe HaIvri* [The Hebrew Doctor] 2 (1933): 106.

15. Dr. A. I. Levi, "Ha'arot lemunachim refuiim," *HaRofe HaIvri* 1 (1937): 153; Z. Shneour, "Passing of a Literary Figure: In Memory of Saul Tchernichovsky," *HaRofe HaIvri* 1 (1944): 174.

16. Shlonski was another. See Raphael Patai, ed., *Encyclopedia of Zionism and Israel* (New York: McGraw-Hill, 1971), 773–1136. See also Benjamin Harshav, *Language in Time of Revolution* (Berkeley: University of California Press, 1993), 97, 106.

17. Dr. Herbert, "Sfat Harefuah shelanu," *HaRofe HaIvri* 1 (1937): 161; Dr. A. I. Levi, "Munachim refuiim," *HaRofe HaIvri* American Edition 2 (1938): 94.

18. Dr. L. M. Herbert, "Book Reviews: The Book of Terms for Medicine and Natural Sciences," *HaRofe HaIvri* 1 (1936): 228.

19. For more on this topic, see Sandy Sufian, "Colonial Malariology: Medical Borders and the Sharing of Scientific Knowledge in Mandatory Palestine," *Science in Context* 19 (3): 381–400.

20. Shalom Cohen, "Rofim yehudim chalutzim betnu'at haZionit," *HaRofe HaIvri* 1 (1945): 68.

21. The notion of authenticity itself implies inclusion and exclusion.

22. This tension is echoed in malaria work as well. See Sandy Sufian, "Colonial Malariology," 381–400. Thank you to Liora Halperin for pointing this out.

23. Dr. Rafael Ben Dov, "Bikoret Sefer 'HaRefuah' haEretzIsraelit," *HaRofe HaIvri* 2 (1933): 134.

24. Herbert, "Sfat Harefuah," 162.

25. Dr. A. I. Levi, "Ha'arot," *HaRofe HaIvri* 1 (1937): 153.

26. After a short cessation of activities, the Teacher's Association reorganized the language committee in 1904.

27. *Encyclopedia of Zionism and Israel*, ed. Raphel Patai (New York: Herzl Press, 1971), s.v. "Hebrew Language Academy."

28. As quoted in Dr. Herbert, "Book Reviews," 238.

29. Herbert, "Mesaviv," 77.

30. Dr. Ben-Ami, Dr. Ben-Ra'anan, Dr. Halprin, Dr. Tchernichovsky, Dr. Matman, Dr. R. A. Friedman, and Dr. Shechter were actively involved. Dr. Asher Goldenstein, "al Haterminologia harefuit ha'Ivrit HaChadasha" *HaRofe HaIvri* 1 (1938): 88.

31. The American Jewish Physicians' Committee was the forerunner of the American Friends of Hebrew University. They funded the first medical sciences laboratory at the Hebrew University of Jerusalem in the 1920s.

32. Such support by American physicians like Samuel Boorstein fits into the wider context of medical assistance and involvement of American Jews in establish-

ing Jewish medical institutions and doing medical work in Palestine, most notably done by Hadassah Medical Organization.

33. Shaul Tchernichovsky, "LeBekirat al hamilon harofei shel Dr. Mazie-Tzerni-chovsky Medor lekviat munachim rofeiim," *HaRofe HaIvri* 1 (1938): 69.

34. Terms used by Dr. A. A. Goldin, "Alhabikoret shel Dr. A. A. Fried, a'havaker' hadikan," *HaRofe HaIvri* 2 (1939): 66, 71.

35. See Eric Hosbawm and Terence Ranger, *Invention of Tradition* (Cambridge: Cambridge University Press, 1992); Kitab al-Qanun [the Medical Code]: five books that contained whole of medical science—Hippocrates, Galen, Alexandrian physicians, etc. The Qanun became the authoritative text on medicine until as late as the nineteenth century. See Roy Porter, *Greatest Benefit to Mankind: A Medical History of Humanity* (New York: W. W. Norton, 1997), 98–99; Encarta Encyclopedia, "Avicenna."

36. Dr. Asher Goldstein, "Al HaLashon herefuit haIvrit ha'atida," *HaRofe HaIvri* 1 (1941): 87–88.

37. Dr. Asher Goldstein, "Al Terminology harefuit haIvrit hachadasha," *HaRofe HaIvri* 1 (1938): 89–90.

38. Dr. A. Shimoni-Melkar, "Bimah Hofshit," *HaRofe HaIvri* 1 (1933): 193.

39. Phrase used by Dr. Levi, "Munachim," 86.

40. Herbert, "Mesaviv," 77.

41. Shlomo Rabinovitz, "Ha'arot leterminologia harefuit haivrit," *HaRofe HaIvri*. 1 (1938): 110.

42. As quoted in Yasir Suleiman, *A War of Words: Language and Conflict in the Middle East* (Cambridge: Cambridge University Press, 2004), 140.

43. Dr. Asher Goldenstein, "Al Harefuah ve hamunachim ha'ivriim," *HaRofe HaIvri* 1 (1927): 18.

44. This happened as well in the general Hebrew revival. See Benjamin Harshav, *Language in Time of Revolution* (Berkeley: University of California Press, 1993), 83.

45. Dr. A. I. Levi, "Munachim refuiim," *HaRofe HaIvri* 1 (1938): 83.

46. Dr. Aaron Dubnow, "Al Hamunchaim lemineyhem," *HaRofe HaIvri* 1 (1938): 106.

47. Dr. Alter-Alexander Fried, "Lashon refuah or refuya," *HaRofe HaIvri* 1 (1938): 93.

48. Herbert, "Mesaviv," 82.

49. xxii Shaul Tchernichovsky, "LeBekirat al hamilon," 69.

50. Ibid., 71–72.

51. Ibid., 68–74, especially 71.

52. Dr. L. M. Herbert, "Mesaviv lekvi'at munachim refuiim," *HaRofe HaIvri* 1 (1938): 77.

53. Ibid.,75–76.

54. Dr. L. M. Herbert, "Sfat harefuah shelanu," *HaRofe HaIvri* 1 (1937): 161.

55. Dr. Aaron Dubnow, "Al Hamunachim lemineyhem," *HaRofe HaIvri* 1 (1938): 105.

56. Zerubavel, *Recovered Roots*, 30.

57. Israel Bartal, "From Traditional Bilingualism to National Monolingualism," in *Hebrew in Ashkenaz*, ed. Lewish Glinert (New York: Oxford University Press, 1993), 146 as quoted in Liora Halperin, "Other Tongues: the Place of 'Lo'azit' in Hebrew Culture" (unpublished paper, 2006), 7.

58. Halperin, 10.

59. Dr. L. Shapira, "Munachim refuiim be Ivrit: lehalacha o lema'ase?" [Medical terms in Hebrew: for theory or practice?], *HaRofe HaIvri* 1 (1933): 190.

60. Ibid.

61. Ibid.

62. "HaRefuah haEretz Israeli," general survey, *HaRofe HaIvri* 2 (1933): 134; also Dr. Matamon, *HaRofe HaIvri* 1 (1940): 81.

63. No title. Description of Jewish doctors and their achievements. *HaRofe HaIvri* 2 (1946): 155–75.

64. Phillip Karger, *Recollections of a Medical Doctor in Jerusalem: from Professor Julius J. Kleeberg's Notebooks 1930–1988* (EK Medical Library, 1992), 54–55.

65. Shapira, "Munachim refuiim beIvrit," *HaRofe HaIvri* 1 (1933): 191.

66. Dr. A. I. Levi, "Ha'arot munachim," *HaRofe HaIvri* 1(1937): 153.

67. "Magamatenu" [Our Aim], *HaRefuah* 1.1 (March–May/June 1924): 3; M. Shechter, "Medical Literature in Palestine," *HaRefuah* 1.1 (March–May/June 1924): 166.

68. Thank you to Liora Halperin for alerting me to these Arabic projects. See Muhammed Rashad Hamzawi, *L'academie de langue arabe du Caire, histoire et oevre* (Tunis: University of Tunis, 1975); Yasir Suleiman, *The Arabic Language and National Identity: A Study in Ideology* (Edinburgh: Edinburgh University Press, 2003), 103–4, 179–80, 187. Zionist Hebraists and physicians engaged in the same type of debates about borrowing words, the connection between language and nationalism, the connection between language and modernization, etc. as Arabists had done since the late Ottoman period. Yasir Suleiman, *A War of Words: Language and Conflict in the Middle East*, Cambridge Middle East Studies 19 (Cambridge: Cambridge University Press, 2004), 41–48.

69. An article in *Filastin* on February 3, 1946 entitled "al-Jam'aia al'tabia al-'arabia: majalaha al-jedida wa ba'd anba'ha," advertised the publication of the Palestine Arab Medical Journal and noted the various activities of different doctors. *Filastin* 29 (February 3, 1946), 285; for more on PAMA see Sandy Sufian, *Healing the Land and the Nation: Malaria and the Zionist Project in Mandatory Palestine, 1920–1948* (Chicago: University of Chicago Press, 2007).

70. *Al-majala a-tabia al-'arabia al-filastiniyya* [Journal of the Palestine Arab Medical Association] 1 (November 1945). Ein Kerem Medical Library.

71. *Al-majala a-tabia al-'arabia al-filastiniyya*, vols. 1–3. Jerusalem, Ein Kerem Medical Library.

72. Dr. Dajani, "Kalimat," *Majala al jamia a-tabia al-'arabia al filistaniyya* 1 (1945): 1.

73. Dr. Watra, "Kalimat," *Majala al jamia a-tabia al-'arabia al filistaniyya* 1 (1945): 4.

74. Letter from S. Qasem, Secretary-General of Arab T. U. Congress in Palestine to Director, Department of Public Health. October 21, 1947. ISA 1597/60/28/S as in Karakara's appendix, 338.

75. The Palestine Arab Medical Association served as a liaison between the government and the Arab medical professional community. As part of the Arab Medical Congress in Palestine, the association pressed for an increase in the health budget in order to finance more sanitation, build more hospitals and clinics across the country, raise health institutions' standards, and secure free and adequate medical treatment for the poor. In the 1940s, some of the same doctors who had worked to-

ward medical professional cooperation at the beginning of the Mandate were now expressing their dissatisfaction with the lack of governmental medical services for the Arab population, their strong political opposition toward the Zionist project and with that, the unfair competition that Jewish doctors posed to Arab doctors in the professional market. This separation began with the 1936 Revolt when Arab patients stopped going to Jewish doctors in Jerusalem out of fear. Before the revolt in areas throughout Palestine, Jewish doctors were known to set up practice in Arab areas, both to alleviate some professional competition and also to serve underserved areas. *Survey of Palestine*, vol. 2, 614; Interview with Amin al-Khatib, July 18, 1996, Jerusalem.

76. The association wrote to the government in 1947 that it had received protests from the Arab public concerning the employment of Jewish doctors in government hospitals. Letter from Drs. Dajani and Canaan on behalf of the Palestine Arab Medical Association to the director of medical services, August 2 and 10, 1947. ISA M325/32/45 in Karakara's appendix 336. In another document, Dr. Canaan disputed the need for a Hebrew medical school, commented on the disproportionate number of Jewish doctors in the country, and noted that they were taking business away from Arab doctors. Indeed, by 1946, the ratio of Jewish to Arab doctors was approximately nine to one. The chief secretary was notified of this issue; see letter from the director of medical services to the chief secretary, August 18, 1947. ISA M1597/60/28/5; Palestine Arab Medical Association, *The Hygienic and Sanitary Conditions of the Arabs of Palestine.* March 1946, 14–15; *Survey of Palestine*, vol. 2, 614.

5

Contested Bodies

Medicine, Public Health, and the Mass Immigration to Israel

Nadav Davidovitch, Rhona Seidelman, and Shifra Shvarts

INTRODUCTION

The period of mass immigration to Israel in the 1950s was a period filled with drama. It was a multifaceted time; a time when the ingathering of peoples from dozens of different countries took place against the backdrop of war. It was a time when refugees, new immigrants, "landed" immigrants, and native-born Israeli Jews encountered one another. Scholars have generally accepted the years of the mass immigration to the State of Israel to be from 1948 to 1956, for after 1956 there was a significant decline in the number of immigrants. Scholars tend to give the first three years much more attention than the remaining years because this period marked a time when the Jewish population of Israel, which had numbered around 650,000 people, absorbed about another 700,000 immigrants.[1] For the immigrants, the 1950s was a time of separation from their homes, of change from the familiar to the strange, of uprooting, relocation, and of the hope for the growth of new attachments and roots.[2] For some, immigration was an act inspired by a return to the Holy Land, infused with messianic significance. For others, immigration to Israel was an act of nationalism; an identification with, and desire to be a part of, the political Zionist movement. For still others, moving to Israel was a last resort, a result of having no other potential asylum. All immigrants, whatever the meaning of their migration, coped with adjusting their hopes and expectations to the harsh reality of foreignness and reconstruction in Israel.

The 1950s brought excitement to Jews already living in Israel[3] as they realized and constructed a sovereign Jewish state. But this excitement was mixed with a fear of how the new immigrants, in their foreignness, might

121

alter the ideal state that the earlier Zionist pioneers had hoped to create. Official Israeli state policy during the 1950s was therefore characterized as a melting pot of policies, which government officials tried to achieve through education, medicine, language, religious practice, and culture. Like the goals of the government before the period of statehood, the goal of these mechanisms was to transform immigrants from diaspora Jews into Israelis.[4]

As in other immigration scenarios, this task of transformation was not a process of simple top-to-bottom indoctrination. Newcomers and veterans struggled, negotiated, and resisted in their interactions with others and with Israeli policies on an everyday basis.

As part of the Israeli melting pot philosophy and policy, medical and public health measures crossed from the curative and preventive spheres into the social sphere. Israeli policymakers and physicians approached migrants' bodies as entities to be cleaned and acculturated.[5] Confident in the justice and necessity of their science, health care workers' approaches to immigrants' bodies were acts that were often foreign and traumatic to the immigrants, who came from different cultures and medical traditions.

Although unique in many ways, the Israeli health care system of the 1950s functioned within a larger global context of body politics, nation building, and immigration. Like other countries, Israel developed a system of border control and infectious disease notification, which included quarantine stations (for people and goods) and immigrant inspection. The uniqueness of this system's development lay in its inheritance from the British Mandate administration and the Zionist public health system, both of which had already been formed before the establishment of the Israeli state. Similar to the establishment of other international health regimes in industrialized countries and in the postcolonial context, Israeli public health operated within a discourse and practice of nation building. Public health measures implicitly adhered to the idea that scientific progress should overcome all obstacles. Those who didn't comply with its main human and environmental tenets would need to be "civilized" and tamed. Because of this, public health reformers of this era targeted immigrants as a special population for public health surveillance. As a result, this population was in constant conflict with the Israeli establishment.

For instance, public health practices such as vaccinating or irradiating children took place within the broader context of antagonism about differential perceptions of health and illness and of the care of children. Discord also surrounded questions about the limits of the state's involvement in the private sphere. In particular, the practices of vaccination or ringworm irradiation were, in the final analysis, a struggle over "the body of the child" played out through the injection of vaccines into the bodies of the young and through the irradiation scalps against a fungal disease.

Although traditional accounts of this period claim that no widespread or organized resistance by immigrants to public health measures took place, historical source material shows that many cases of opposition did in fact occur. Vaccination, medical selection, and mass ringworm treatment (particularly for children, who were the primary target of the public health programs) constituted special areas of concern in which resistance was evident. It is from an examination of these particular public health measures that we can learn how Israeli state power was exercised on immigrants and their bodies and how immigrants responded to that state power.[6] As we will see, such an examination illustrates that immigrant health is an extremely useful category through which to explore the larger construction of Israeli national identity. Historians have long sought to make sense of the spectacular, if contested, consolidation and legitimization of modern states' attempts to regulate and discipline bodies and minds. Only relatively recently, however, have new studies begun to point out the significant role of science and medicine in shaping national identity and in playing a role in nation building, particularly for immigrant nations. Despite the ubiquitous racial rhetoric of "hygiene" and "cleansing" in most medical immigration policies of the past hundred years, the exclusionary impulse of certain immigration policies has had a long tense history alongside inclusionary policies regarding workforce or culture. This contribution will investigate the Israeli medical establishment's immigrant absorption policy during the mass immigration in the 1950s to detail such regulation and opposition. We argue that the process of establishing an idea of Israeli citizenship, so central to the immigration and absorption process and to the public at large, involved the formation and destruction of conceptual borders. These borders entailed distinctions about human immigrant bodies: the normal or healthy body and the pathological or primitive body.

CONTEXT: NATION BUILDING AND THE IMMIGRANT BODY

With the end of the British Mandatory government in 1947, the newly independent State of Israel worked to crystallize governmental institutions and to implement democratic rule. It worked to gain international recognition for its existence while fighting a war with neighboring countries.[7] Domestically, the new state engaged in a process of understanding and formulating its own concept of citizenship. State officials grappled with several issues. Should the state be open to all Jews, even those who did not conform to the Zionist paradigm of being healthy and strong? What place did non-Europeans have in a nationalist movement founded on European values? Could religion play a part within a larger political framework of avowed state secularism? How could cultural differences be a part of a model of conformity? In other words, how would the borders of citizenship be defined?

Though not new questions for Zionist Jewish society in the land, the founding of the Israeli state forced a conceptual and practical change that effected a new definition of Israeli citizenship and altered functioning of formal institutions. The reverberations of the Holocaust took place amidst these vast changes in nation building and self-definition. Soon after the end of the 1948 war, Israeli society engaged in a concerted act of understanding of the Holocaust, which, in turn, facilitated a process of transforming and traumatizing Jewish collective consciousness and identity. Public events in Israel that symbolized this process were the debate over reparations from Germany and the Kasztner trial.[8]

The question of how to reconcile Zionist ideology about the body with the reality of the immigrant Holocaust survivors' bodies posed a particular problem in the process of collectively coping with the Holocaust. In Zionist thought, life in the diaspora had caused the Jew to undergo a process of physical and psychical degeneration.[9] The return of the Jewish people to the Land of Israel was, in Zionist ideology, considered curative both for the Jews and for the land because it afforded Jews the opportunity to become industrious and active in physical labor.[10] This self-image extended to notions of the new Israeli after statehood. The new Israeli was supposed to be healthy and robust, representing success in having left illness and weakness behind in the European diaspora.[11] Yet the arrival of Holocaust survivors, Jews who were physically and emotionally weary, to the shores of Israel put the Zionists in a position in which they had to confront their own demons.[12] These immigrants, arriving by the thousands, were flesh and blood reminders of the reality from which Zionist leaders, ideologues, and activists tried to distance themselves: that the "weak" and "diminished" diaspora Jew is, in fact, an indissoluble part of the "strong" and "healthy" Israeli.

The large numbers of Holocaust survivors suffering from various physical and mental problems who came to Israel after the establishment of the state raised a troubling question about the borders of Israeli citizenship and the standards of migration. Survivors coming from displaced persons (DPs) camps in Europe suffered from various chronic diseases ranging from tuberculosis to mental illnesses. Their arrival initiated a debate on unlimited migration, a policy that would put demands on the new country's already strained resources. In addition, many people in Israeli society expressed suspicion toward the survivors, which did not help simplify the absorption process. The change in the demography of migration to Israel from Holocaust survivors to Jews from Arab countries (*Mizrachim* in Hebrew) added to these already existing tensions. Such intensification can be seen in the veteran Israelis' perceptions and receptions of the immigrants from North African and Asian countries.[13]

Studies conducted on the topic of Jewish emigration from Arab countries reveal themes of xenophobia, classism, racism, and disgust among the Israeli public. Indeed, most scholars agree that the Ashkenazi establishment feared that North African Jews in general (particularly those of Moroccan extraction) would threaten the quality of the population and culture with what leaders called "Levantinization."[14] In general, the establishment felt that the borders erected during the prestate era between the "civilized" body and the local, backward "oriental" body were being transgressed. The Jews coming from Arab countries threatened the concept of the "new Jew's" body as designated in Zionist ideology: healthy, civilized, and free from infectious diseases. Diseases caused by social conditions like trachoma and ringworm were much more prevalent in immigrants coming from Arab countries and were considered particularly dangerous. Such public health threats not only shaped perceptions and images of the Israeli physical body, but shook the very foundation of Israeli citizenship as it was being forged in this primordial stage of the state.

One of the most thought-provoking studies on the topic of Mizrachi immigration to Israel is Orit Rozin's discussion. Rozin's research, which focuses on the predominance of images of physical disgust within Ashkenazi descriptions of "Oriental" immigrants, focuses on the central role perceptions of health played in framing feelings of disdain toward the immigrants.

> It was already in Yemen that the potential immigrants were described as having no knowledge of personal hygiene. North African immigrants were also described as being unfamiliar with basic hygiene. The idea that immigrants from Islamic countries didn't maintain any hygienic practices, didn't know how to use the bathroom and were unable to keep their bodies and household utensils clean, was very common amongst the native-born Israeli Jews. As a result, the absorption workers (mostly women), volunteers and female soldiers invested great efforts in changing the new immigrants' habits while they were staying in immigrant camps and *ma'abarot* [temporary housing settlements]. The health services were to impart the immigrants with knowledge of hygienic practices once they moved into permanent housing.[15]

Discussions like Rozin's emphasize how the perception of the immigrants' otherness stemmed largely from concepts of health, ill health, filth, and the ideal or "chosen" body.[16] These perceptions had an important influence on the process taking place in Israeli society in which new ideals of citizenship were being forged. This process involved the formation and destruction of borders: borders between the normal, healthy, or civilized body and the pathological, ill, or primitive body. The movement of immigrants, health care workers, real diseases, and ideas further complicated these border dynamics. Thus, medical and public health images and practices informed boundaries of inclusion and exclusion in the definition of Israeli citizenship.

CONTEXT: MEDICAL SCIENCE, ZIONIST IDEOLOGY, AND IMMIGRATION

Western medical science predominantly influenced medical practices of the Israeli health care system during the mass immigration. These Western medical traditions, however, took on a unique twist in Israel, where all aspects of life were infused with Zionist ideological principles. To be sure, science, technology, medicine, and public health played central roles in Zionist thought. They were fields of knowledge that created the ideal Zionist state and were related to other "discourses of development" (agriculture, architecture, and urban planning) that sought to modernize the land and the people as a necessary condition for the realization of a modern Jewish homeland in the Land of Israel. These fields drew on the wellsprings of American and European influences but also arose, at least in part, from the Zionist establishment's concept of creating a "new man."[17]

Health care services in the Jewish *Yishuv*[18] had their roots in European and American concepts of medicine and public health as well as Jewish traditions of *bikur holim* and *linat tzedek*.[19] In the mid-nineteenth century, philanthropists Moses Montefiore and Baron Edmond de Rothschild brought Jewish doctors who were born and trained in Europe to Palestine. These physicians took the place previously held by traditional healers. Later, in what is known as the Fifth Aliyah, numerous German physicians settled in the Jewish *Yishuv* in Palestine, thus significantly contributing to the persistence of European-trained health care workers. The American approach to medical practice gained a strong foothold in Palestine through the works of Hadassah, the philanthropical Women's Zionist Organization of America. Hadassah first began its work in medicine and public health in Palestine in the early twentieth century.[20]

One cannot understand the roots of immigration policy during the mass immigration without taking into consideration the strong public health traditions, such as health education and the promotion of physical exercise, which existed in Zionist ideology years before the 1950s. Medical practitioners adapted these traditions, imported from Europe and the United States, to the local context of Palestine and put them into practice well before the establishment of the Jewish state in 1948.

As in other places around the world, eugenics theory played an important role in the consolidation of Zionist public health discourse and practice. It had a significant impact upon immigration policies both in the pre- and post-state eras.[21] A eugenic outlook became intertwined with colonialist practices that presented the white/European body as the right model.[22] With its European foundations and aspirations to forge a "New Jew," Zionist ideology fit in well with this approach.[23]

In the state period, public health policy toward immigrants in Israel was founded on a belief that public health measures, based in earlier eugenic thought, could serve as a vehicle for shaping a person who would be healthy in body and soul. Leaders deemed this public health approach as an important goal not only on the level of individual health but also on the level of national health. Various authorities often described immigrants as "passive raw material" that could be molded through health education programs.

Immigrants, however, possessed a world outlook on health and illness that was not always in keeping with the outlook of the absorbing society. Within a larger context of negotiating the borders of Israeli citizenship, they resisted and negotiated the public health measures imposed upon them. While good intentions on the part of the health care system indeed brought about a significant improvement in health indices such as infant and maternal mortality, infectious disease incidence, and mortality, these positive transformations also came with a complex social cost.

REGULATION/SELECTION

Medical selection of immigrants was one of the ways in which borders were destroyed and constructed in terms of health. The issue of medical selection during the 1950s is not a cut-and-dried scenario of necessity/philosophy leading to policy leading to implementation. It was an issue that, from the start, challenged the fundamental ethos of the Jewish state by raising the question of entitlement. Such discriminatory sentiments persist to this very day. Within Zionist thought, unregulated *aliyah* [immigration to Israel]— open-door acceptance of all Jews to the Land of Israel—is a powerful philosophy. Yet the Right of Return, the right of every Jew to claim and be a part of the Land of Israel, is challenged by a tenet central to political Zionism: building an ideal society.

Each of the five major waves of *aliyot* before the Israeli state's establishment had been both limited in scope and strongly ideological. While the Zionist movement has always been made up of various branches (e.g., Religious Zionism, Cultural Zionism, and Labor Zionism), a common thread between these various ideological approaches was the drive to establish and build an ideal society.[24] In spite of the ideal of unfettered *aliyah*, implementation of an ideal society necessitated regulation to ensure that only those subscribing to and capable of implementing nationalist philosophies were included. Before the State, British authorities who ruled over Palestine complicated this process by capping the number of Jewish immigrants allowed into the country. In addition, they relegated responsibility for selection of immigrant candidates to the Jewish Agency.[25]

With this authority, the Jewish Agency implemented a selection policy based upon medical fitness. They argued that immigration numbers were extremely limited and Zionist leaders needed to ensure that those coming could handle the work required. They were careful that the limited number of immigration certificates allotted to them by the British would not be wasted on someone physically incapable of contributing.

When the country moved from a state of British rule to sovereign Jewish rule in 1948, the issue of medical selection took on a different meaning. With statehood, claims about immigration limitations on the Jewish community imposed by a foreign ruler were no longer applicable. Limitations on immigration to the Land of Israel were now imposed on Jews, by Jews. As in most nation-states, immigrants were not allowed to freely come to Israel wherever or whenever they chose. The Law of Return, passed unanimously in the Knesset (the Israeli Parliament) in 1950, includes among its stipulations that an individual could be prevented from immigrating "if the Minister of Interior was convinced that the applicant . . . was liable to endanger the public health or the security of the state."[26] This law is the principal document that frames the nature of immigration regulation in Israel.

Although medical selection was a central issue of debate among Israeli policy makers in the 1950s, such debate largely remained on theoretical level. The number of people actually denied entry because of medical reasons was minimal. In cases where illness was found, the carrier was treated abroad or, if that was impossible, she or he was isolated in Israel until proper treatment was received. Here, the inclusion of immigrants was given priority, despite a rhetoric of exclusionary practices as exemplified in medical examination practices.[27]

The significance of the medical selection issue for understanding the boundaries of citizenship primarily lies in the debate itself. The philosophy of medical selection underscores the traditionally held perception of immigrants as carriers not only of infectious diseases, but also of dangerous political ideas that could destabilize social order. The line between the biological and the social in contemporary discussion of immigration was easily transgressed.[28] Throughout the course of the twentieth century, questions of health and immigration gained an increasingly firm hold on the process of receiving immigrants from various countries. These questions were often fuelled by a prevalent fear of the foreigner.[29] In more than one case, medicine served as a roadblock for preventing the entrance of certain immigrants. In the final analysis in Israel during the 1950s, however, medicine served more as an assimilation tool for immigrants into local society. It served as a litmus test about the apprehensions of the absorbing society rather than being a real practical threat to immigration.[30]

VACCINATION

While vaccination controversies certainly had their internal medical logic, they must be analytically situated within the broader context of creating and contesting borders of Israeli citizenship. For example, several studies on antivaccination movements in England and the United States examine the issue of vaccinations in the context of democracy and citizenship. How, these studies ask, should the state intervene in the lives of its citizens? How can the state inculcate practices that it deems for the greater public good? Can a government claim custodianship over the bodies of its citizens in the first place? While one does not find a coherent mass movement of antivaccinationists during this period of mass immigration to Israel, the interaction between immigrants and public health officials during the vaccination campaigns played an important role in the broader process of creating Israeli citizens.

Immigrant camps established abroad constituted the first site for engaging in public health work that would lead to healthy citizenship. This public health work included giving vaccinations. According to camp physicians' letters and reports, vaccine shortages, long distances between the camps and medical supply facilities, and improper conditions for the transportation of the vaccines caused a multitude of problems. Further, staff had to deal with cases of side effects from vaccinations, particularly local skin infections.[31] These difficulties delayed full implementation of the vaccination program as planned by the Israeli Immigrant Medical Services.

Although vaccinations were given to all Israelis, newcomers and veterans alike, archival material indicates that the Israeli government emphasized achieving a high level of coverage among immigrants. The immigrants were supposed to be vaccinated during their sojourn in *machanot ma'avar* [processing camps] prior to embarking for Israel, but there were cases in which vaccinations were carried out on the actual ships going to Israel. Still, most vaccinations were administered only in Israel, either because of a loss of records or a failure to vaccinate immigrants abroad because of shortages.[32]

The smallpox vaccine was one of the most important vaccines administered. Because there was no international medical consensus on the technique for smallpox vaccination, Israeli practitioners utilized various means of introducing the vaccine. These ranged from a single prick or a series of pricks to peeling off a small piece of skin to introduce the vaccine. These methods sometimes caused infection or created a large and ugly scar.[33] In all cases, the sign that the vaccine had "taken" was the appearance of a scab a week after administration. There was no technique for measuring the level of antibodies, nor was there any other procedure for determining whether the level of immunity was high enough to protect subjects against the outbreak of disease. Consequently, children who received vaccines had to be brought to the doctor by their mothers to have the scar examined. Testimonies indicate that the scarring process was considered ugly, particularly in the case of girls.[34] Bandaging the vaccination area was forbidden and mothers were instructed not to wash their children for three days after vaccination. The vaccination area then had to be kept dry for a week. At the end of the seven-day period, a medical practitioner would examine the child to see if the vaccine had taken or not. If it had failed, the child had to be revaccinated.[35] In the years 1949, 1950, and 1953, following word of an outbreak of smallpox in neighboring countries, the Israeli media announced mass vaccination campaigns, urging individuals to be vaccinated.[36]

The scarring process produced by smallpox vaccination was not merely a necessary nuisance. The vaccination was a symbolic historic reminder of vaccination campaigns conducted during colonialism.[37] Immigrants also saw it as another ritual in the trying route to citizenship. Thus, the scar represented a state-imposed mark on its citizens, most of them newly arrived immigrant adults and children. Alternative methods of scarification, such as the possibility of vaccinating girls under the knee if the mother demanded this for cosmetic reasons, represented a part of a negotiation process on how citizens' bodies should be marked as potential healthy bodies.

Another important vaccine targeted at immigrants was the typhoid vaccine. Typhoid fever is an infectious disease that causes diarrhea. For tourists and immigrants, vaccination against typhoid was already common during the period of British rule over Palestine. The typhoid vaccine, however, did not enjoy the same obligatory statutory status as the smallpox vaccination. Also, the entire population was not a target of this vaccine. It was primarily given to new immigrants and soldiers.[38] In addition, the typhoid vaccine's utility and efficacy were subject to controversy. Many physicians argued that vaccination could not replace good hygienic practices such as washing hands and washing fruit. Doctors felt that vaccination, in essence, could undercut such broader hygiene campaigns. In contrast, the smallpox vaccine would not have the same effect, since the disease was a contagious disease not tied to personal hygiene.

Despite the debate over its utility, many medical practitioners and policy makers viewed vaccination of immigrants against typhoid as important, and so it remained a component in the Israeli health care program until the mid 1950s.[39] To achieve full immunity against typhoid required a series of three vaccinations. The follow-up on this procedure was therefore difficult to administer in conditions that prevailed in Israel in the 1950s. Furthermore, vaccinations could not be fully given outside Israel. Indeed, completing the series of vaccinations on time once the people had already arrived was problematic. Reports by epidemiologists reveal that the range of coverage against typhoid was 55 percent. This number is considered low. It could not provide full protection for the entire population in the case of an outbreak of typhoid. This fact made the vaccination program all the more controversial.[40]

Study of the typhoid vaccination program raises questions about the use of invasive, painful, and costly procedures. These procedures were difficult to administer effectively and doctors questioned their efficacy. In contrast, officials within the Israeli health care system possessed a greater consensus with regard to the smallpox vaccine. Nevertheless, the procedure was difficult and drawn out for the recipients.

RINGWORM MASS IRRADIATION

Ringworm of the scalp is a fungal disease caused by various *Tinea* species, affecting mainly children and young adults.[41] The disease has been known for centuries and has been usually related to other "loathsome" diseases such as trachoma, parasitic infections, and venereal diseases. These repellent diseases could have serious consequences for their carriers. The U.S. government defined "loathsome" diseases as part of Category A diseases, with the consequent ramification of denied entrance to the United States during that country's mass immigration at the turn of the twentieth century.[42] Physicians, nurses, educators, and other public health personnel included "loathsome" diseases in the hygienic programs developed mainly in Europe and the North America.

Between 1949 and 1960, several tens of thousands of immigrants to Israel (many of whom were North African) were irradiated against ringworm of the scalp.[43] At the time, this medical procedure was a recognized, mainstream medical treatment. Yet the Israeli case is unique due to the program's scale and scope. According to the official narrative about ringworm, the Israeli story was one of success. Ringworm and other infectious disease rates declined relatively rapidly after the program's implementation.[44]

But the consequences were severe. Several decades after the x-ray treatment, irradiated immigrants developed complications ranging from ugly scars to life-threatening complications such as meningioma and thyroid cancers.[45] In 1994, the Israeli state enacted a compensation law that established a bureaucratic apparatus of committees to evaluate the damages and claims.

From the turn of the twentieth century, with the discovery of x-rays and their growing use in medical diagnosis and treatment, various medical authors praised the use of scalp irradiation to combat and treat ringworm. Although the consequences of x-ray irradiation, including the development of various malignancies, were gradually discovered, ringworm irradiation was still considered throughout the world to be a mainstream scientific treatment until the late 1950s.

It is important to reconstruct the mundane practicalities of ringworm irradiation. The x-ray irradiation was actually the easy part of the treatment. The therapy included cutting the person's hair to a length of 0.5 cm to allow for several consecutive irradiation treatments of the scalp. A temporary sterile cap was put on for eighteen to twenty-one days. Subsequently, hot wax was put on the head and immediately removed after the wax had hardened, leading to complete epilation of the hair.

Most of the children irradiated recall this painful part of the treatment. Irradiation itself, which carried the long-term consequences, is a fainter memory. Doctors often recalled some of the children (most of the treated patients were young children) for a second and even third course of treatment because of relapses. This public health program, in its physical and social aspects, had traumatic consequences for the immigrants' children and their families. These traumas influenced their overall feelings about their encounter with the Israeli state as represented by its public health system.

Ringworm irradiation in Israel did not start in the 1950s. The Zionist movement and British government conducted ringworm irradiations in a very efficient manner during the pre-state era, but after the establishment of the Israeli state, the scale of the campaign changed dramatically. Screening and treatment of ringworm were already initiated in camps in the immigrants' countries of origin. Despite the fact that immigrants were gathered in temporary processing camps prior to their arrival, and therefore were a captive audience, the medical checkups or full treatment were often impossible.

The immigrants themselves did not view medical examinations in a positive light. Some Holocaust survivors sought to avoid medical examinations because they triggered memories of medical "selections" in the concentration camps. Many immigrants tried to escape medical examinations, even sending others to be examined in their stead out of fear that their immigration would be delayed should some medical problem be discovered.[46] These gaps in medical screening and categorization resulted in the adoption of a policy by which additional medical inspections and classifications would be carried out in the *Shaar Haaliya* [Gate of Immigration] processing camp upon an immigrant's arrival in Israel. Even after leaving the camp, children all over the country who had been diagnosed with ringworm were sent to *Shaar Haaliya* (and later, to centers in Tel Aviv and Nazareth) to receive the full treatment. Medical practitioners would take the children from their parents, shave their heads, and treat them for several days to several weeks. They would then return the children to their families. The children's treatment continued even after returning to their parents. They had to be isolated until deemed no longer infected. They had to wear a hat which, because it was noticeable, imparted physical and emotional consequences.

ISOLATION AND TREATMENT: THE SHAAR HAALIYA CAMP

The practices at Shaar Haaliya represent a physical manifestation of Israel's melting pot policy. The literal translation of Shaar Haaliya signifies a passageway, a threshold for the immigrant's transformation into an *oleh* [immigrant]. The camp's name embodies the idea of passing the border from immigrant to citizen. Physically, Shaar Haaliya was the first home of thousands of new immigrants in Israel. Bureaucratically, it was a place of registration where the immigrants were first officially inscribed as Israelis militarily, socially, and medically. Symbolically, it was the starting point for shedding the body of the diaspora Jew and becoming an Israeli.

Located off the shore of Haifa in what had previously been British army barracks, Shaar Haaliya was the largest immigration camp of the mass immigration. Over 300,000 of the approximately 700,000 immigrants in this period passed through its gates.[47] Dr. Giora Josephtal, head of the Jewish Agency's Immigration Department, had encouraged the Israeli government to establish large quarters to enable the more efficient processing of immigrants. Shaar Haaliya was thus opened in 1949 with the aim of providing a contained environment to ensure that before being absorbed into Israeli society, immigrants would undergo final medical examinations and be registered for military and social purposes.[48] To prevent people from leaving before the process was complete, the camp was surrounded by barbed wire and overseen by a police force. Such conditions were built despite concerns that Shaar Haaliya would resemble a concentration camp.[49]

The initial plans for Shaar Haaliya to process 5,000 people before the next 5,000 people arrived three days later quickly fell through. Very soon after its implementation in 1949, a huge backlog of thousands of people overflowed the camp quarters. The environment was cramped, uncomfortable, and unsanitary. A shortage of health care staff, both physicians and nurses, translated into extreme pressure for those who worked there.[50] Often, no common language existed between the immigrants and the camp personnel. Few ways existed to bridge the huge chasms that lay between the numerous different ethnic groups and their respective cultures.

The role of the health care services in Shaar Haaliya focused on the examination and vaccination of immigrants and, when deemed necessary, treatment and isolation. Within several days, every immigrant underwent a complete physical examination, including an exam by a dermatologist (with emphasis on diagnosis of venereal diseases, leprosy, and ringworm) and an ophthalmologist (with emphasis on diagnosis of trachoma and other contagious eye ailments). Those immigrants found to be ill were isolated on the premises or taken to Ramban Hospital in Haifa.[51]

Yehuda Weissberger described the atmosphere of mistrust among parents whose children were taken by the medical personnel for examination or treatment. "We were strangers in their eyes, and they did not believe us. Their past experience had taught them to not even trust Jews . . . the fear in their eyes was clear. When we were finally given a child or a sick baby, we were witnesses to many difficult scenes. The parents were overcome with despair, as though they were parting with their children forever."[52]

There were various stages in Shaar Haaliya's function. From 1949–1950, while state policy demanded absorption of newcomers in immigrant camps, Shaar Haaliya served as the largest immigrant processing camp. People in this processing camp lived there and received all social services from the state. While the government's intention was that people would stay in Shaar Haaliya for only a few days, cases of families living there for months on end existed. Due to the high cost of maintaining state support for immigrant camps, alongside a concern that immigrants had no incentive to become independent, the Israeli government changed its absorption policy in 1950 to one of *ma'abarot*. *Ma'abarot* were temporary housing settlements near large, established municipal centers. Underlying the *ma'abarot* idea was the principle that the state would provide only housing for the immigrants. The government would not be responsible for food, work, etc. Despite this change in policy, it was not until around 1953 that the population of Shaar Haaliya was significantly reduced.[53] From 1952–1956, the government no longer housed new immigrants in Shaar Haaliya. Instead, Shaar Haakiya served as the largest center for ringworm irradiation. In all of these various stages, the constant factor was that Shaar Haaliya was an isolated environment, physically segregating immigrants apart from others. Its primary function was to heal the immigrants in a space separate from non-immigrant Israeli society. In this way, the interplay between inclusionary and exclusionary borders becomes clear: immigrants' bodies were to be healed outside of the body politic and accepted only once they were made healthy.

NEGOTIATION AND RESISTANCE

Written and oral testimony supplementing Ministry of Health documents further reveals the complex reality regarding the Israeli medical establishment's acceptance of immigrants. A harsh picture emerges from various doctors and nurses who visited immigrants' camps. Sanitary conditions were dismal; piles of trash and open sewage were common.[54] Statistics reflected the poor sanitary and other dangerous conditions: high infant mortality levels spiraled, peaking at 157 deaths per 1,000 live births among residents of the *ma'abarot*. All these facts generated harsh criticism; *ma'abarot* were certainly not places for healing.[55]

Public health officials encountered grave difficulties when trying to implement preventive medicine policies, including vaccination. Although practitioners were instructed to record vaccinations on immigrants' registration cards and in clinic logs, in practice, they did not always to do, resulting in records that were often inaccurate or lost. Such failures led to needless revaccination. Dr. Chaim Sheba, deputy general of the Ministry of Health in 1951, underscored the severity of the situation when, in a meeting with the Coordination Institute on July 11, 1951, he suggested that food ration stamps be given to immigrants on the condition that they are able to substantiate that they had been vaccinated.[56]

In the first conference of Sick Fund pediatricians held in Natanya, doctors passed a resolution that called upon the Ministry of Education to demand that every child entering kindergarten present a document certifying that the youngster had received a diphtheria shot.[57] Solutions such as these, which made preventive medicine (whether through vaccination or medication) a precondition for receiving another "service" provided to Israeli citizens (like education), were considered legitimate in the eyes of many doctors.

A nurse who worked in the *ma'abarot* in the 1950s expressed this same attitude. She spoke of the "impossibility" of explaining to immigrants what was going on and why. "The vaccinations were not known to the majority of immigrants and their objection to vaccination was strident at times and a source of great frustration to the nurse. One could compare the attempt to explain and convince the immigrants of the need for vaccination to an attempt to explain to an infant the meaning of treatment with DDT or vaccination against smallpox."[58]

Medical staff of the period repeated this motif: that there was no sense in explaining the meaning of various medical procedures to immigrants due to their mental and spiritual "limitations." Underlying this perception was the belief that medical personnel could make patriarchal decisions on health issues in light of the preferential knowledge they held. Yet such knowledge was strongly anchored in perceptions about what constituted a healthy body versus a sick body. It was also implicitly anchored in ideas about how immigrants' bodies should be transformed and should be integrated into the body politic of the new state. The "wardenship" over the bodies of inhabitants of Israel in the 1950s, a peak period of nation building, fits into what anthropologist Meira Weiss labels "the culture of the Chosen Body"; that is, the very culture that sought to create an Israeli collective identity.[59] But these medical perceptions did not always sit easily with the absorbed. This clash in perceptions about illness, health, and the body caused great tension and clashes.

In response to the official public health policy, immigrants developed their own public health perceptions. This development did not necessarily mean automatic rejection or resistance by immigrants. Most of the time immigrants complied with and accepted public health measures. They often assumed that these practices would improve their health or would even help them achieve a quicker assimilation into the Israeli society. Hastening the absorption process would allow them to cross the border faster on their way to becoming Israeli citizens.

From time to time, however, various public health practices provoked strong resistance. Mass vaccination, treatment for ringworm, and other preventive medicine measures could trigger opposition and dissent. Usually these events were not remarkable. Such micro-resistance, which mostly surfaced on a local level, occurred at moments of interaction between public health personnel and the immigrants. At these moments, newcomers had their opportunity, though limited and sometimes problematic, to maneuver and negotiate with the establishment. Of course, not all immigrants reacted in the same manner, for they were all very different. Similarly, the agents operating in the public health realm came from various professions and traditions—physicians, nurses, social workers, etc. Many of the professionals were once immigrants themselves. While these negotiations about the body (and caring for it) helped to forge a new Israeli identity, some unresolved tensions relating to the health realm have continued to haunt Israeli society.

CONCLUSION: CONTESTED BODIES

The previous discussion eases an understanding of the testimony of Phyllis Palgi, the first anthropologist to work with the Ministry of Health in 1953. Palgi conveyed her impressions of a visit she conducted with public health nurses in one of the then-new settlements made up of immigrants from the Atlas Mountains of Morocco. She related how the immigrants threw stones at the nurses who had come to vaccinate their children. Common rumor held that the nurses had come to put "tainted blood" in the bodies of their children.[60]

Rumors of inoculating contaminated blood and abuse of medical power against vulnerable populations such as immigrants was not just the province of health issues in the 1950s in Israel. Various anthropological studies demonstrate that similar rumors have occurred among immigrant populations in other countries such as Australia, Canada, and the United States.

This phenomenon is usually labeled "medical gossip."[61] According to Manderson and Allotey, medical gossip among immigrant groups serves a number of objectives. While in the short term such rumors create conflict with the local health system, in the long run the system internalizes criticism and opens up opportunities to improve communication between medical staff and immigrants. Better communication can be achieved by bringing in cultural facilitators who often come in contact with immigrant populations on one hand and the medical system on the other. Such tension can thus ultimately lead to better understanding. It is, however, important to keep in mind that medical gossip, and the tension it reflects, point to unequal power relationships. It often intends to resist attempts by the state to model the bodies of immigrants. Often this struggle is carried out vis-à-vis control over the bodies of children. Children's health programs (and resistance to them) often constitute another component in negotiating borders of citizenship, this time of the future generation.

Most recently, the control of the Israeli state of the 1950s over the bodies of immigrant children was questioned in a significant, pervasive, and fateful manner. During the period of immigrant encampments of "tent cities" (the period that preceded the *ma'abarot*) with their "enhanced housing" of wooden shacks and tin huts, all infants were transferred to children's houses shortly after their arrival. This area was almost off-limits to parents and the babies were left under the exclusive care of the children's house personnel. Through strict enforcement of limited visiting rights to feeding and nursing times, there was what Weiss referred to as a state "mastery over the bodies of children."[62] From their moment of their arrival, therefore, the same children symbolized very different things to parents and to medical teams. In some cases where parents went to the children's house, they were told that their infant had been transferred to a hospital based on the evaluation of the medical staff. This decision was made without consulting the parents. To travel to a hospital from these tent encampments or from a *ma'abara* was an extremely complex journey under the conditions of the 1950s. Nevertheless, doctors and nurses have testified that there were cases where parents made the effort to visit their children in the hospital only to be told that their child had died. Without going into contemporary controversy over the disappearance of a certain number of Yemenite children during this period,[63] there is no question that these children, and the authority taken by the medical system over their bodies, constituted a defining issue in the clash between immigrants and the state.[64]

Children have constituted a core axis in Zionist perceptions of the rebirth of the Hebrew nation in its homeland. Yet these immigrant children were viewed very differently. It is easy to imagine that the high incidence of illness and death only amplified parents' sense of need to protect their children in every way possible. The medical establishment was often perceived as an assistive and beneficial agency, but reciprocal relations were very complex and contrary to the perception among the absorbing society. Overall, immigrants did not play a solely passive role.

For a variety of reasons, some of which have been detailed here, immigrant populations have been one of the key groups that public health personnel in various countries have focused upon. Arrival in a new country, a process that included medical examination in most cases, provided an opportunity to decide who could belong and who should be excluded. The perception that immigrants as a group were less healthy than the local population served as the justification for many inflexible policies with regard to preventive medicine, including the adoption of mass treatments of various kinds.

Public health programs, as part of a broader system of regulations that govern care of infants, hygiene, and health, are part of the mechanism through which countries "supervise the bodies of their citizens." The use of state authority and power is all the more amplified when it is applied to weaker or marginalized elements in the population.

The use of state authority is not clear-cut. It is usually a process of struggle and resistance. It is a negotiation process that determines the borders of citizenship while defining the relationships between the state and various components of its society. In the case of Israel, the health domain served as an important field for the playing out of conflicts and negotiations over how the boundaries of "normal" and "proper" bodies should be developed and absorbed in the new society. These contested immigrant bodies varied from Holocaust survivors arriving from displaced persons camps in Europe, to "Oriental" Jews coming from Arab countries. Yet all were involved in the intricate process of crossing the border between immigrant and citizen.

NOTES

Reprinted with permission from *Hagar: Studies in Culture, Polity and Identities* 6, no. 2 (2006): 35–58.

1. For exact numbers on the mass immigration, see Dvora Hacohen, *Immigrants in Turmoil* [in Hebrew] (Jerusalem: Yad Yitzhak Ben Tzvi, 1994) and Moshe Lissak, *The Mass Immigration in the Fifties: The Failure of the Melting Pot Policy* [in Hebrew] (Jerusalem: Bialik Institute, 1999).

2. Oscar Handlin, *The Uprooted: The Epic Story of the Great Migrations that made the American People*, 2nd enlarged ed. (Boston: Little, Brown and Company, 1973).

3. Definition of the terms *native* or *immigrant* is a challenge when used in the context of Israel, particularly in this period. In her book *Israel in the Great Wave of*

Immigration, 1948–1953 (Tel Aviv: Yad Yitzhak Ben Tzvi, 1996), Dalia Ofer addresses the subjectivity of this concept whereby people who had arrived in 1946–1947 were considered "veterans," whereas those who came after 1948 were "immigrants."

4. On the concept of the melting pot, see Moshe Lissak, *The Mass Immigration in the Fifties*; Zvi Zameret, *Across a Narrow Bridge: Shaping the Education System During the Great Aliya* [in Hebrew] (Sde Boker: Ben Gurion University of the Negev Press, 1997).

5. See also Nadav Davidovich and Shifra Shvarts, "Health and Hegemony: Preventive Medicine, Immigration, and the Israeli Melting Pot," *Israel Studies* 9 (2004): 150–79.

6. A similar analysis of micro-resistance related to the settlement policy of the newcomers in the 1950s can be found in Adriana Kemp, "Nedidat Amim oh ha'Be'era ha'Gdola: Shlita Medinatit ve'Hitnagdut ba'Sfar ha'Israeli," in *Mizrachim in Israel: A Critical Observation Into Israel's Ethnicity*, ed. Hannan Hever, Yehouda Shenhav, and Pnina Motzafi-Haller [in Hebrew] (Tel Aviv: Van Leer Jerusalem Institute and Hakibbutz Hameuchad Publishing House, 2002), 36–65.

7. For the political, social, economic, and military dimensions involved in Israel's establishment see: S. Ilan Troen and Noah Lucas, *Israel: The First Decade of Independence* (Albany: State University of New York Press, 1995).

8. The trial of Malkiel Gruenwald, which has come to be known as the Kasztner trial, took place in Jerusalem in 1954. Gruenwald was sued for libel after having publicly accused Israel (Rudolf) Kasztner, a Hungarian Holocaust survivor and Mapai party member, of having collaborated with the Nazis. The proceedings of the trial turned on Kasztner, with the judge famously declaring that he "had sold his soul to the devil." Yechiam Weitz, "Mapai and the 'Kastner Trial,'" in *Israel: The First Decade of Independence*, ed. Troen and Lucas; Yechiam Weitz, "The Holocaust on Trial: The Impact of the Kasztner and Eichmann Trials on Israeli Society," *Israel Studies* 1 (1996).

9. Zeev Tzahor, "Ben-Gurion's Attitude toward the *Gola* [Diaspora] and Aliyah," in *Ingathering of Exiles: Aliya to the Land of Israel, Myth and Reality*, ed. Dvora Hacohen [in Hebrew] (Jerusalem: Zalman Shazar Center for Jewish History, 1998), 132.

10. Shlomo Avineri, *The Making of Modern Zionism: The Intellectual Origins of the Jewish State* (New York: Basic Books Inc., 1981), 154.

11. Meira Weiss, *The Chosen Body* (Stanford, CA: Stanford University Press, 2002). Weiss' *The Chosen Body* offers an analysis of the construction of the perceived ideal Israeli body: healthy, powerful, Jewish Ashkenazi, and male—largely in defiance of the perception of the diaspora Jew.

12. Hanna Yablonka, *Survivors of the Holocaust* (London: Macmillan Press Ltd., 1999). On the politics of Holocaust memory, including of its survivors, see Idith Zertal, *Israel's Holocaust and the Politics of Nationhood* (Cambridge: Cambridge University Press, 2005).

13. Yaron Tsur, "Carnival Fears: Moroccan Immigrants and the Ethnic Problem in the Young State of Israel," *Journal of Israeli History* 18 (1997); Moshe Lissak, "The Demographic-Social Revolution in Israel in the 1950s: The Absorption of the Great Aliyah," *Journal of Israeli History* 22 (2003): 1–31.

14. See Haim Malka, *The Selection: Selection and Discrimination in the Aliya and Absorption of Moroccan and North African Jewry, 1948–1956* [in Hebrew] (Tel Aviv: Tal, 1998); Avi Picard, "Immigration, Health and Social Control: Medical Aspects of the Policy Governing Aliyah from Morocco and Tunisia, 1951–1954," *Journal of Israeli History* 22 (2003): 32–60; Shifra Shvarts, Nadav Davidovitch, Avishay Goldberg, and Rhona Seidelman, "Medical Selection and the Debate over Mass Immigration in the New State of Israel," *Canadian Bulletin of Medical History* 22 (2005): 5–34.

15. Orit Rozin, "Terms of Disgust: Hygiene and Parenthood of Immigrants from Moslem Countries as Viewed by Veteran Israelis in the 1950s," *Iyunim Bitkumat Israel* 12 (2002): 199 (our translation from Hebrew).

16. Rozin's theory is substantiated by Meira Weiss's work on the missing Yemenite children.The missing Yemenite children issue refers to Yemenite children who disappeared from immigration and transit camps from 1948–1954. Several families of the missing children accused the state and state personnel of kidnapping their children. Yair Sheleg, "Panel on Yemenite Children Rejects Conspiracy Theory," *Haaretz*, May 23, 2004. See also Meira Weiss, "The Immigrating Body and the Body Politic: The 'Yemenite Children Affair' and Body Commodification in Israel," *Body and Society* 7 (2001): 2–3.

17. See also Rina Peled, *"The New Man" of the Zionist Revolution: Hashomer Hatzair and Its European Roots* [in Hebrew] (Tel Aviv: Am Oved, 2002).

18. *Yishuv*, literally translated as settlement or community, is the term used to refer to the Jewish community in Palestine prior to the establishment of the state of Israel.

19. *Linat Tzedek* is a tradition of nighttime watch over the ill to ensure that they are not alone, while *bikur holim* is the charitable act of visiting the ill. To understand how these traditions were incorporated in Jewish health care in Palestine, see Shifra Shvarts, *The Workers' Health Fund in Eretz Israel: Kupat Holim, 1911–1937*. (Rochester, NY: University of Rochester Press, 2002).

20. For the history of the first Jewish doctors and hospitals in Jerusalem, see Shifra Shvarts, "Hospital Wars" [in Hebrew] *Et Mol*, 27 (2), 2001/2. For the history of Hadassah involvement in Israeli health care, see Shifra Shvarts and T. Brown, "Kupat Holim, Dr. Isaac Max Rubinow, and the American Zionist Medical Unit's Experiment to Establish Health Care Services in Palestine 1918–1923," *Bulletin of the History of Medicine* 72 (1) (1998): 28–46.

21. On eugenics, see Daniel Kevles, *In the Name of Eugenics: Genetics and the Uses of Human Heredity* (New York: Knopf, 1985). For a recent analysis of eugenics in the United States and its influences after World War II, see Alexandra Minna Stern, *Eugenic Nation: Faults and Frontiers of Better Breeding in Modern America* (Berkeley: University of California Press, 2005).

22. See Warwick Anderson, *The Cultivation of Whiteness* (New York: Basic Books, 2003).

23. On eugenic thinking and Zionist ideology, see Raphael Falk, "Zionism and the Biology of the Jews," *Science in Context* 11 (1998): 587–607; John Efron, *Defenders of the Race: Jewish Doctors and Race Science in Fin-de-Siècle Europe* (New Haven, CT: Yale University Press, 1993).

24. This humanistic, egalitarian welfare state is represented in Herzl's utopia by the motto "Liberalism, Tolerance, Love of Mankind!" Theodor Herzl, *Altneuland: Old-New Land*, trans. Paula Arnold) (Haifa: Haifa Publishing Company, 1960), 109.

25. For a detailed discussion on the medical selection debate during the British Mandate in Palestine, see Nadav Davidovitch and Shifra Shvarts, "Health and Zionist Ideology: Medical Selection of Jewish European Immigrants to Palestine," in *Facing Illness in Troubled Times. Health in Europe in the Interwar Years, 1918–1939*, ed. Iris Borowy and Wolf D. Gruner (Berlin: Peter Lang Verlag, 2005), 293–308.

26. David Shachar. *Regime and the State of Israel* (Tel Aviv: Yasod, 1993), 126.

27. See Amy L. Fairchild, *Science at the Borders: Immigrant Medical Inspection and the Shaping of the Modern Industrial Labor Force* (Baltimore and London: Johns Hopkins University Press, 2003).

28. In the Israeli context, this blurred line between the biological and social that shaped medical selection policy is particularly significant in the discussion surrounding immigrants from Arab countries. Varying positions exist among scholars on the extent to which those immigrants from Arab countries were more discriminated against than others. It is a complex and important issue that is currently being explored and debated in Israeli scholarly discourse. For some of the writing dealing with the various aspects of this issue, see the aforementioned works: Haim Malka, *The Selection: Selection and Discrimination in the Aliya and Absorption of Moroccan and North African Jewry, 1948–1956* [in Hebrew] (Tel Aviv: Tal, 1998); Avi Picard, "Immigration, Health, and Social Control: Medical Aspects of the Policy Governing Aliyah from Morocco and Tunisia, 1951–1954," *Journal of Israeli History* 22 (2003): 32–60; Shifra Shvarts, Nadav Davidovitch, Avishay Goldberg, and Rhona Seidelman, "Medical Selection and the Debate over Mass Immigration in the New State of Israel," *Canadian Bulletin of Medical History* 22 (2005): 5–34.

29. Another interpretation views immigrant medical selection in the framework of disabilities studies. See Douglas Baynton, "Disability and the Justification of Inequality in American History," in *The New Disability History: American Perspectives*, ed. Paul Longmore and Lauri Umansky (New York: New York University Press, 2001).

30. Alan M. Kraut, *Silent Travellers: Germs, Genes, and the Immigrant Menace* (Baltimore, MD and London: The Johns Hopkins University Press, 1994); Howard Markel, *Quarantine! East European Jewish Immigrants and the New York City Epidemics of 1892* (Baltimore and London: The Johns Hopkins University Press, 1997).

31. Memorandum on a visit to Eden June 18–September 16, 1949, Ministry of Health, September 20, 1949, Labor and Pioneer Archive, Levon Institute, IV 104-81, portfolio #17.

32. Dr. Y. Shapira to Dr. Yekutiel, *Harkavat Abaabuot le-Olim Chadashim* [Smallpox vaccination for new immigrants], January 24, 1956, State Archive, 2/13/ Gimel/5084 – Beit.

33. Essentially, smallpox vaccination techniques have not changed since that period. This issue reemerged recently when the Israeli Ministry of Health decided to vaccinate against smallpox the "first responders" in a case of a bioterrorist attack.

34. Interview with B.S., a doctor who practiced at the time and worked in immigrant camps in the 1950s. The physician said that at times they vaccinated girls under

the nipple for cosmetic reasons, to hide the scar. No sign of this as a method was found in contemporary medical textbooks, but the medical literature of the period mentioned the possibility of vaccinating girls under the knee, should the mother demand this for cosmetic reasons. The authors usually do not recommend these methods due to the pain and sensitivity involved. See: *Merck Manuel of Diagnosis and Therapy* (Rahway, NJ: Merck & Co., Inc., 1950), 680–1.

35. A. Kleinberg, *Horaot le-Chisun ke-Neged Abaabuot* [Instruction for vaccination against smallpox), IDF Archives and the Ministry of Defense, 110-648/53, 1950.

36. See, for instance, the letter classified "secret—very urgent" from Dr. Fritz Yekutiel, *Peulot Mini'a neged Aba'abuot Shchorot* [Preventive measures against smallpox], September 21, 1953, State Archives, Beit-5084/13/Gimel.

37. See, for example, David Arnold, *Colonizing the Body: State Medicine and Epidemic Disease in Nineteenth Century India* (Berkeley: University of California Press, 1993); Stree P, Chowdhury AMR, and Pilar Ramos-Jimenez, "Patterns of Vaccination Acceptance," *Social Science & Medicine* 49 (1999): 1705–16.

38. For information on the degree of public response to calls for vaccination against typhus, see "Horaot Chisun Chova neged Typhoid: Kshaim be-Peilut Tavruah be-Rachavei ha-Aretz" [Instructions for compulsory vaccination against typhoid: difficulties in sanitation activities throughout the country], *Haaretz* April 9, 1952: "Last year's attempt to reach the public to vaccinate via propaganda failed in essence. Last year only 200 souls received the required vaccination, at least 2/3 of them schoolchildren and youth, that is the response among adults was almost nil." The article underscored that the primary danger was tied to "mass immigration and our economic straits."

39. On the controversy over typhoid vaccination versus hygiene, see *Hygiene and Health* 1 (1940): 8–9.

40. In 1954, the Epidemiology Department of the Ministry of Health recommended that only school-age children receive the vaccination. See letter from Dr. F. Yekutiel to the director general, Ministry of Health, State Archives, 4520-2/5/4/Gimel. In 1957, typhoid vaccinations were removed from the vaccination program in the schools.

41. On the ringworm affair, see also Baruch Modan and Shlomit Peri, "Gormei Sikun ve'Gormei Pitsui: Medini'ut Ha'Memshala mul Mukranei Gazezet" [Risk factors and compensation factors: governmental policy toward ringworm irradiated patients) in *Moral Dilemmas in Medicine*, ed. Raphael Cohen-Almagor [in Hebrew] (Tel Aviv: Van Leer Jerusalem Institute, Hakibbutz Hameuchad Publishing House, 2002), 388–411.

42. Alan M. Kraut, *Silent Travelers: Germs, Genes, and the Immigrant Menace* (New York: Basic Books, 1994); Fairchild, *Science at the Borders*.

43. The exact number of irradiated children is unknown. It is clear that previous estimations, which put the numbers close to 20,000 based mainly on epidemiological investigations of Prof. Baruch Modan, were too conservative.

44. Theodore Grushka, *Health Services in Israel: A Ten Year Survey, 1948–1958* (Jerusalem: Ministry of Health, 1959).

45. Baruch Modan, a public health physician and epidemiologist, was the main whistle blower regarding the consequences of the mass ringworm irradiations. He published through the years several articles on the subject that were substantial in

the enactment of the compensation law. See Baruch Modan, Hannah Mart, Dikla Baidatz, Ruth Steinitz, and Sheldon G. Levin, "Radiation-Induced Head and Neck Tumours," *Lancet* 303 (1974): 277–79; B. Modan, E. Ron, and A. Werner. "Thyroid Cancer Following Scalp Irradiation," *Radiology* 123 (1977): 741–44; E. Ron, B. Modan, D. Preston, E. Alfandary, M. Stovall, and J. D. Boice Jr. "Thyroid Neoplasia following Low-dose Radiation in Childhood," *Radiation Research* 120 (1989): 516–31.

46. See Davidovitch and Shvarts, *Health and Hegemony.*

47. Yehuda Weisberger, *Shaar Ha'aliya: The Diary of the Mass Aliya, 1947–1957* (Jersualem: World Zionist Organization, 1986).

48. Ibid., 70

49. Ibid., 71.

50. Ibid., 70.

51. Avraham Sternberg, *A People is Absorbed* [in Hebrew] (Tel Aviv: Kibbutz Hameuhad Press, 1973), 123.

52. Yehuda Weisberger, *Shaar Ha'aliya,* 88 (our translation of excerpt).

53. Ibid., 107.

54. Dvora Hacohen, *Olim be-Saara* [Immigrants in turmoil], 264–66.

55. On the state of infants in the transit camps, see also Sternberg, *be-Hikalet Am* [A people is absorbed], 38–68; "Controversy over infant mortality in Israel," *Briut Hatzibur,* September–October 1958, pp. 16-19, see also the letter from Dr. Towstein to Dr. Lotan, on the health status of infants in the transit camps, July 16, 1952, State Archives, 188/7/Gimel/4265. For another document that describes conditions in the *ma'abarot* from the perspective of doctors who served there, see Dr. Emanuel Margalit and Dr. Betzalel Pinchas, *Hirhurim al ha-Sherut ha-Refui ba-Ma'abarot* [Reflections on medical service in the *ma'abarot*], n.d, State Archives, 4265/188/7/ Gimel.

56. Meeting of the Coordination Institute, July 11, 1951, Dr. Chaim Sheba, State Archives, 4250-2/6/4/Gimel.

57. "The sum total of problems in medical assistance and preventive [medicine] which exacerbated with the closing down of the immigrants camps and transfer of the inhabitants to *ma'abarot* and immigrant neighborhoods throughout the country—was discussed in the first conference of Sick Fund pediatricians that opened on Friday at the retreat facility in Netanya. Participants and lectures did not limit themselves to a professional-medical discussion but dealt with the problems of the immigrant child from a social standpoint, *for social problems become medical problems, as well.*" (italics added by N.D. and S.S.), *Haaretz,* 1950.

58. Hannah Rosental Munk, "The Response of Public Health Nursing to Mass Immigration in Israel 1948—1958," (Ph.D. diss., Columbia University, 1979), 232.

59. See Meira Weiss, "The Immigrating Body and the Body Politic: The 'Yemenite Children Affair' and Body Commodification in Israel," *Body and Society* 7 (2001): 93–109.

60. See: Phyllis Palgi, "How It All Began . . . A Personal Saga," *Practicing Anthropology* 15 (1993): 5–8.

61. See Lenore Manderson and Pascale Allotey, "Storytelling, Marginality, and Community in Australia: How Immigrants Position Their Difference in Health Care Setting," *Medical Anthropology* 22 (2003): 1–21.

62. Weiss, "Immigrating Body and the Body Politic," 98.

63. Recently the third report on the missing Yemenite children was published. One of the core issues is the subject of the infant houses and transfer of sick infants to hospitals.

64. The health system was not the only one tied to this struggle. Other systems such as the educational system, the army, and other social institutions constituted additional challenges in the "remolding" of the identity of the immigrants.

6

Seeing the "Holy Land" with New Eyes

Undocumented Labor Migration, Reproductive Health, and the Fluctuating Borders of the Israeli National Body

Sarah S. Willen

While Israel aims to be a Jewish state with a Jewish demographic majority, it became home in just one short decade—during the 1990s and early 2000s—to an estimated two hundred thousand non-Jewish transnational migrant workers from countries as diverse as Nigeria, the Philippines, Columbia, and the Ukraine. As a result, by 2000 Israel ranked among the industrialized countries most heavily dependent on transnational labor.[1] About half of these new arrivals were defined by the Israeli state as documented, or "legal," and half as undocumented or "illegal."[2] Between sixty and eighty thousand of these migrants, most of them "illegal," settled in the Tel Aviv metropolitan area. While Israel eagerly welcomes immigrants of Jewish descent, non-Jewish arrivals are generally viewed as a threat to the security and integrity of the Israeli state and Israeli society. As such, these new arrivals have evoked an array of complicated and ambivalent but increasingly antagonistic attitudes. In particular, issues of transnational migrants' biological reproduction—including first, bureaucratic dilemmas created by the birth of non-Jewish, noncitizen children in Israel and second, the potential demographic impact of these trends on the Israeli national body—have become matters of discussion and concern among Israeli policy makers, in the courts, and within the media. This chapter analyzes the politics of undocumented migrants' reproduction in Israel as well as the role of reproductive health concerns in migrants' lives. Not only does it provide an opportunity to examine Israel and the Israeli/Palestinian conflict through new eyes—that is, those of undocumented transnational migrant workers in Tel Aviv—but it also has implications for research on parallel concerns in other migration contexts.

The findings presented here illustrate many of the various, and at times contradictory, ways in which Israeli institutions and individuals have imagined, engaged, and responded to illegal labor migration and illegal migrants in the shadow of the state's and society's explicit, deeply entrenched commitment to remaining a "Jewish state." As the chapter illustrates, and as several recent studies corroborate, matters of biological reproduction, reproductive health, and demography in Israel are deeply embedded within highly charged ideological conversations about the nature and substance of the Israeli national body.[3] In other words, reproduction is always political within the territory of Israel-Palestine, and this preexisting ideological matrix has a significant impact on Israeli policies toward pregnant migrants and their offspring. At the same time, the chapter also sheds light on how this array of contradictory attitudes, policies, and practices has created both complicated practical challenges in undocumented pregnant migrants' lives and complicated challenges for local migrant aid organizations that advocate on their behalf.

Overall, the chapter examines undocumented migration to Israel from a reproductive health angle. It considers the specific forms of reproductive health care open to undocumented pregnant migrants, the organizations involved in the struggle to achieve access, and the link between these organizations' localized successes and their flexible, creative approaches to advocacy and activism. The analysis is part of a larger study of how "migrant illegality" is both configured and experienced in Israel.[4] In order to shed light on the relationship between local configurations and lived experience, I include several ethnographic vignettes that illustrate first, how migrant illegality shapes and constrains undocumented women's access to reproductive health care in Tel Aviv, and second, how women have experienced this particular health need in light of existing constraints.

The structure of the chapter is as follows. I begin with an overview of the research methods and ethnographic setting of my research, followed by a brief discussion of how both transnational migrant workers and Palestinians fit into Israel's larger "biopolitics of otherness." I then turn to issues of undocumented migration and health to consider first, illegality as a health condition; second, undocumented migrants' paradoxical exclusion from most of the Israeli health care system and inclusion in the reproductive health domain; and third, explanations for this apparent paradox in light of Israeli nationalism, political progressivism in Tel Aviv, and civil society activism. The next section tells the story of Priscilla, a Ghanaian wife, mother, and undocumented migrant worker who gained firsthand experience with both the benefits of and the contradictions embedded in this constellation of Israeli policies. In conclusion, I reflect upon the importance of analyzing local configurations and experiences of migrant illegality through the prism of local biopolitics of otherness both in Israel and more broadly.

RESEARCH METHODS

Between September 2000 and June 2004, I conducted twenty-six non-consecutive months of ethnographic fieldwork in the southern neighborhoods of Tel Aviv. Research focused on two communities of undocumented, English-speaking, Christian migrants: first, the community of Filipinos, most of whom came to Israel to work as elder care providers on a legal basis and later lost their legal status; and second, the community of West Africans, primarily Nigerians and Ghanaians, most of whom arrived in Israel as tourists or religious pilgrims intending to overstay their visas and seek work.[5] I was able to meet members of both communities through participant observation at several local migrant advocacy organizations. These included one Israeli nongovernment organization (NGO), the Open Clinic for Migrant Workers run by Physicians for Human Rights–Israel (PHR); and one municipal organization, the Mesila Aid and Information Center for the Foreign Community of Tel Aviv–Jaffa. Volunteering at these migrant aid organizations provided a way to meet illegal migrants and set the study into motion. Moreover, it also enabled me to explore the migrant advocacy community itself as an additional complementary site for research and analysis.

As scholars of transnational migration have demonstrated in other contexts, ethnographic research on pregnancy, fertility decision making, and reproductive health can help elucidate the larger issues shaping the political climate and daily life struggles for illegal migrants.[6] Since these were among my primary areas of inquiry, many of the migrants I met were pregnant women or new mothers. I accompanied a subset of these women in their efforts to obtain reproductive health care including abortions, prenatal checkups, diagnostic tests, and for three women, labor and delivery in Israeli hospitals. I also accompanied women and their babies to checkups at municipal Mother-Child Health (MCH) Centers; participated in the home, family, and community lives of key research participants; and attended community activities including church services, life-cycle events, and community meetings. At the PHR Open Clinic, I distributed a self-administered English-language survey to a multinational convenience sample of 170 patients. Of the patients surveyed, twenty-nine had children born in Israel.

AN UNHEALTHY CONTEXT: SOUTH TEL AVIV, CAPITAL OF THE FOREIGN WORKERS

The setting for my research was an area described as Israel's "capital of the foreign workers,"[7] the cluster of neighborhoods spanning South Tel Aviv and nearby Jaffa, which was annexed to the Tel Aviv municipality in 1950.[8]

Disparities between the wealthiest and the poorest economic strata in Israel are among the highest in the world,[9] and illegal migrants in Tel Aviv regularly bear witness to these opposing poles of the Israeli socioeconomic spectrum: one pole in their South Tel Aviv neighborhoods of residence, and the other in the northern parts of the city and its wealthier suburbs, where they travel each day to earn a living cleaning Israeli homes and offices. South Tel Aviv is characterized by poverty, unemployment, crumbling buildings, ethnic tensions, irregular trash pickups, petty crime, fundamentalist Jewish proselytizing, and the occasional shouting match in the streets; indeed, this area of the city constitutes a fascinating world unto itself. These are the strained and stressed neighborhoods, already systematically underserved and politically underrepresented, into which 60,000 to 80,000 mostly illegal migrant workers arrived between the mid-1990s and early 2000s. By the end of that period, they constituted a full quarter of the city's population.[10] For most, getting settled meant carving out lives that straddled these grittier urban spaces and the spacious, clean, well-manicured neighborhoods inhabited by the middle- and upper-class employers whose homes and offices they worked hard to keep clean and well-manicured. At the same time, the rapid arrival of so sizable and so diverse a population changed the local "ethnoscape"[11] in multiple ways, not only by introducing new people, languages, ideas, and forms of religious and cultural expression, but also by creating new points of articulation between this locus in Israeli space and other loci across the globe.

While undocumented migrants were excluded from Israel in multiple tangible and intangible ways from the moment they arrived, these powerful exclusionary trends have had a much more direct and palpable impact since the initiation of a resource-intensive mass deportation campaign in 2002, as elaborated in the coming section.

ILLEGALITY IN ISRAEL

For a brief moment, lasting just over a decade, it gradually began to appear that Israel—for reasons completely unrelated, at least on the surface, to the conflict between the Israelis and the Palestinians—might become something radically different from the longstanding vision upon which it was established. It appeared that the state, designed in explicit terms as a homeland for the Jewish people, was en route to becoming unexpectedly multicultural, "multiracial," and multiethnic. Even as the borders of the Israeli social body were expanding—or so it seemed in a purely demographic sense—this sort of radical national makeover remained virtually unfathomable to most Israelis regardless of their ethnic origin, political commitments, or religious affiliation (or lack thereof). Not surprisingly, the issue of transnational migrants' biological reproduction began functioning as an occasional lightning rod for citizens' and policy makers' anxieties about the political impact of transnational migration on the body of the Israeli nation. Former Interior Minister Eli Yishai, for instance, voiced these anxieties in stark terms when he declared that "they have to be deported before they become pregnant."[12]

Despite policy makers' aggressive language, hundreds and then thousands of transnational migrants concentrated primarily in the Tel Aviv metropolitan area had, in fact, begun giving birth to children in Israel. The potential social implications of this demographic shift were held in check by a wide array of exclusionary policies and practices, including migrants' exclusion from the national health care system.[13] However, as more and more children were born to undocumented migrant parents in Tel Aviv, a variety of Israeli activists and advocates mobilized to combat undocumented pregnant women's lack of access to affordable, accessible prenatal and delivery care. So, too, did members of the diverse Israeli migrant advocacy community—including allies at the municipal level—fighting to increase the social welfare, health care, and educational opportunities available to undocumented women's Israeli-born offspring. Following long, and at times deeply discouraging struggles, these combined NGO and municipal advocacy efforts did yield an array of meaningful results: subsidized prenatal care for migrant women as well as full labor and delivery coverage, subsidized childhood immunizations and development checkups, health insurance for children, access to municipal preschools, and integration into area elementary and high schools.[14]

These inclusionary trends, however, have been paralleled by increasingly aggressive exclusionary trends. Throughout the 1990s, illegal migrant workers (and, to a large extent, their legal counterparts as well) were excluded and, as human rights organizations have consistently argued, exploited in numerous ways.[15] Then in 2002, a mass deportation campaign initiated under the government of Prime Minister Ariel Sharon ratcheted things up to an entirely new level of intensity. The ostensible aim of the campaign has been to minimize the number of undocumented migrant workers in the labor force with the goal of reducing Israeli unemployment. In practice, the campaign has sought to discursively reframe undocumented migrants as a threat to the (Jewish) body of the nation and, by the same token, as criminals who must be expelled from Israeli space. This ideologically charged, resource-intensive campaign has made explicit the degree to which non-Jewish migrant workers—unlike *olim chadashim*, or authorized Jewish immigrants who arrive under the Law of Return—are unwelcome in Israel. So, too, has it rendered them vulnerable to intimidation, humiliation, spontaneous arrest, and even violence in the form of police brutality.[16]

The impact of the mass deportations on the local labor market appears limited[17] for three key reasons. First, the government has continued authorizing visas for new groups of "legal" workers in a number of labor sectors. Second, the widespread patterns by which large numbers of "legal" workers lose their documentation status and join the ranks of illegal persist. Third, labor sectors dominated by migrant workers have become both economically devalued and socially stigmatized, perhaps even more so than when they were filled by Palestinians from the occupied territories.[18] Yet the local economy has become dependent on cheap labor, there are no signs that Palestinians will be invited to work in Israel again in the near future, and employers cannot easily afford to pay more expensive Israeli workers. Nor are Israelis—despite painfully high rates of unemployment following the collapse of the local high-tech bubble of the 1990s and the economic downturn related, in part, to the Second Intifada—eager to replace them. Neither are they obligated to do so, at least for the moment, since unemployed Israeli workers maintain the option of collecting unemployment benefits.

In this context, "being illegal" in Israel has come to entail a substantial measure of indeterminacy, anxiety, and fear. Not only has the deportation campaign wreaked havoc on individual migrants' everyday lives, but it has also had a devastating effect on Tel Aviv's undocumented migrant communities more generally. In its first year, the campaign spurred the collapse and disintegration of these communities' existing social and institutional infrastructures. The overall impact on the strongest, most well organized communities has been devastating. According to a 2003 report released by the Mesila Aid and Information Center, which was established in 1999 by Tel Aviv Mayor Ron Huldai in quiet contravention of the national government's exclusionary agenda,[19] the deportation campaign rapidly reduced the migrant population of Tel Aviv "from a strong community of capable individuals with educational backgrounds and personal strengths that managed, over a period of years, to create pivotal community aid and welfare organizations and even channel its energies into social, cultural, and religious organizations, into a dwindling, hunted, frightened community that lives day-to-day, on borrowed time, and whose members are unable to assist or cooperate with one another."[20]

Thus a major rift has divided the state-sponsored, nationally broadcast messages of aggressive xenophobia, on one hand, and the much more subtle inclusionary trends mentioned above, on the other hand. This rift illustrates the dynamic, evolving, and even paradoxical heterogeneity of policy and practice vis-à-vis transnational labor migrants in Israel.[21] This heterogeneous policy environment frames the present article, which examines a curious paradox within Israel's social welfare system: undocumented pregnant women's formal entitlement to subsidized prenatal care and free labor and delivery coverage despite increasingly aggressive state policies. On one hand, illegal migrants are imagined as outsiders even to the point of being described as a demographic threat to the long-term integrity and security of the Israeli state. As such, they are roundly excluded from nearly all aspects of the state's nationalized health care and social welfare system. At the same time, however, undocumented pregnant women are eligible for most forms of state-subsidized pregnancy and delivery care. Analysis of this curious situation raises a number of important questions regarding the political economy of illegal migrants' access to reproductive health care and other forms of health care more generally.

The ongoing tension between these inclusionary and exclusionary trends also hints at a space ripe for ethnographic investigation and analysis in Israel and in other host countries. As I have argued elsewhere, "migrant illegality" is a juridicial, sociopolitical, and—no less importantly—phenomenological condition generated in the context of nation-states' efforts to demarcate, surveil, and defend the boundaries of the collective.[22] It is important to note that for many migrants, being illegal yields important positive consequences including, for instance, the ability to work, and earn, within a First World labor market (albeit at its lowest rungs). So, too, does illegal labor migration generate opportunities for social and economic mobility.[23] Still, on an everyday basis, the negative consequences of "being illegal" tend to outweigh the positive. These negative consequences stem not only from structural barriers to inclusion and integration, but also from the complex array of limitations, concerns, and constraints that influence migrants' everyday experiences of being illegal more generally. This article brings an ethnographic lens to the three dimensions of illegality noted above—the juridical, the sociopolitical, and the experiential—as well as the relationships among them. Put differently, the chapter asks, "What material, bureaucratic, sociological, and phenomenological consequences does classification as an illegal migrant in Israel entail?"

TRANSNATIONAL LABOR MIGRATION
AND THE ISRAEL-PALESTINE CONFLICT

One cannot speak about labor migration to Israel without reference to the Palestinians, their (former) role in the Israeli labor market, or the ways in which the population of approximately 200,000 transnational migrant workers both did and did not come to replace these other, similarly mobile, similarly vulnerable noncitizen workers in the wake of the First Intifada. In some labor sectors, low-wage Palestinian workers were replaced en masse with legal workers from Romania, Bulgaria, Turkey, China (in construction), and Thailand (in agriculture) beginning in 1993 and in increasing numbers throughout the rest of the decade. Many of these legal workers stayed on in Israel illegally after their visas expired. (Other migrants—including West Africans and Filipinos—worked in sectors Palestinians had not previously occupied, such as housecleaning and eldercare).

The presence of this new alternative labor force of cheap and exploitable workers signaled to Israeli employers, and to the Israeli state, that the labor market could manage just fine without Palestinians. In fact, as Israeli sociologists Raijman and Kemp have demonstrated,[24] during the First Intifada some Israeli politicians regarded the recruitment of foreign labor as both a political tool—that is, to prove to Palestinians that they were replaceable—and a form of collective punishment.

From the perspective of Israeli employers, the Israeli state, and Israeli popular opinion, the decision to close Palestinians out of their former jobs in Israel and replace them with transnational migrant workers has generally been regarded as expedient and prudent. The high price for Palestinian workers, families, and communities, however, has received virtually no attention in Israel. Given the heavy dependence of the Palestinian economy on jobs across the Green Line, from 1967 until the mid-1990s, this reconfiguration of the labor market has left tens of thousands of Palestinian families bereft of their breadwinning relatives' hard-earned wages, and the resulting economic consequences have been devastating for Palestinian families and communities. The resulting rise in poverty must be counted among the factors contributing to the political unrest of the early-to-mid 2000s.

At the same time, transnational migrants' arrival has also strengthened broader neoliberal trends within Israeli society, including the growing gap between the highest and lowest wage earners, the disintegration of long-standing national commitments to the social rights of workers, and the disintegration of broader protections associated with the increasingly weakened Israeli welfare state. As Raijman and Kemp explain in a passage worth quoting at length,

> the recruitment of labor migrants was an expression of and a catalyst for the inauguration of a new chapter in the society and the economy of Israel, which passed from the "old" regime, based on collectivist and Keynesian principles, to a neo-liberal socio-economic regime (Shalev 2000; Shafir and Peled 2002; Filc 2004). In this new regime, based on the ethos of liberalization, deregulation, privatization, and casualization of labor, the non-citizen labor migrants became a test case in a wide-ranging social experiment that did not stop at the boundaries of citizenship. The essence of this experiment is the increasing encroachment upon the welfare state by the welfare state (Jessop 1994). Within this context, labor migrants fulfill the central role that states commonly assign to them: a bargaining chip for the enfeeblement of the local workers and the banishment of "weak" workers from the world of work (Gottlieb 2002). As in other advanced capitalist states, in Israel, too, labor migrants have become, unwillingly, a means of turning labor into a rare resource, and of making workers a cheap commodity.[25]

Thus two groups of non-Jewish, noncitizen workers—Palestinians on one hand, and transnational migrant workers on the other—have been relegated to different but not unrelated positions within what can be described as Israel's "biopolitics of otherness."[26] Throughout the history of modern Israel but especially since the outbreak of the First Intifada, Palestinian workers have been collectively constructed as a threat to Israeli security. The transnational migrants who arrived in their stead, in contrast, have largely been constructed—rightly or wrongly—as politically neutral in relation to the simmering conflict despite their cultural, linguistic, and racial/ethnic foreignness.[27] Importantly, however, migrants' purported neutrality has not garnered them any greater welcome into the Israeli social body or body politic than their Palestinian predecessors. While initially perceived as nonthreatening to the state's material security, they have sometimes been constructed as a threat to its "demographic security."[28] Following the initiation of the mass deportation campaign, transnational migrants were no longer portrayed as benign, albeit excluded, others; instead, they have been reimagined as wanted criminals whose presence and everyday social and economic activities threaten the security and integrity of the Israeli state and nation as well as the security and stability of its economy.

More than any other single factor, the state's willingness to pursue and expel undocumented migrants with violence has marked a turning point in Israel's treatment of transnational migrant workers. Despite substantial differences between the particular kind of security threats ostensibly posed by Palestinians on one hand and transnational migrant workers on the other, there are important similarities in the ways in which these two groups are portrayed, and treated, by the Israeli state. This is particularly true since the initiation of the mass deportation campaign in 2002. At that point in time, the escalation of the Israeli state's deportation efforts transformed state practices of quiet othering and exclusion into a much more aggressive atmosphere of rapidly escalating criminalization and expulsion. Designed to operate "like a military campaign,"[29] the campaign relies on a constellation of techniques ranging from intimidation and coercion to the persistent threat—and at times, the material reality—of physical violence and police brutality. These techniques include: (1) biosocial profiling;[30] (2) a propaganda campaign designed to mobilize public support and cooperation in implementing the mass deportations; (3) an information hotline that some citizens have used to "snitch" on undocumented migrants; (4) police informers, including migrants as well as Israelis; (5) systematic arrest and deportation of known community leaders; (6) a "voluntary departure" campaign that provided subsidized plane tickets to departing migrant families; (7) police surveillance of public and private areas; (8) the surreptitious marking of apartment doors in preparation for late night arrests; (9) arrests and deportations, some of which involve humiliation and psychological violence; (10) use of physical violence in the course of arrest; and (11) a generalized failure to investigate or punish police brutality.[31] While the ideological underpinnings of the earlier phase can be understood in terms of local ethnonational ideologies of membership and belonging (and their inverses), we cannot understand this second, considerably more violent phase without taking into consideration how the Israeli state has conceptualized and treated its other others—or, some might contend, its "real" others: Palestinians living under Israeli occupation in the West Bank and Gaza.

Thus the deportation campaign, like Israel's policies of occupation in the West Bank and Gaza, highlights Israel's readiness to protect what it defines as state security through governmental techniques and practices that would be deemed unacceptable and, in some cases, illegal were they wielded against ratified Israeli-Jewish citizens. Important differences notwithstanding, the psychological, symbolic, and physical violence of the recent deportation campaign demonstrate how Palestinians and transnational migrants have been systematically excluded, othered, and at times criminalized by the Israeli state in similar ways. In some respects, these patterns of exclusion accord with what political theorist Giorgio Agamben has characterized as an originary distinction between valued "politicized life" and disvalued "bare life"[32] that maps to the distinction between citizen and noncitizen and between what he calls "interiorized" versus "detritus humanity."[33]

It is thus crucial to point out that from every possible angle of reflection and analysis, Israel's encounter with undocumented labor migration is inflected with the political framing, the naturalized ideological positions, and the rhetorical and practical residues of the struggle over Israel-Palestine. Israel's experience of existential insecurity and perpetual anxiety has profoundly influenced how it, as a state and a society, has constructed, imagined, and treated undocumented migrant workers. More fundamentally, this insecurity and anxiety are among the factors that prompted many transnational migrants' arrival in the first place. We will return to these considerations in the chapter's conclusion.

ILLEGALITY: A HEALTH CONDITION

Even during the heyday of the migrant communities in Tel Aviv (i.e., before the initiation of the mass deportation campaign in 2002) Israel's systematic policies of exclusion bore significant, generally negative ramifications for this population's ability to obtain needed health care.[34] Under the 1994 National Health Insurance Law, all Israeli citizens and permanent residents are entitled to comprehensive health coverage through the country's national health care system, which is administered via four separate nonprofit HMOs or "sick funds" [*Kupot Cholim*]. Transnational economic migrant workers, however—including both documented and undocumented migrants—are formally excluded from that system. While employers are required by law to ensure that their non-Israeli employees, including illegal employees, have private health insurance, the rapid growth of the resource-poor, volunteer-run Physicians for Human Rights (PHR) Open Clinic—which held over 10,000 patient files, primarily for illegal migrants, as of 2004—attests to the failure of this arrangement. Virtually no employers ask their illegal employees for proof of insurance, and given the overwhelming lack of enforcement, few employers are even aware that such an obligation exists.

Until 1998, when PHR established its Open Clinic in Tel Aviv, illegal migrant workers had virtually no consistent access to any form of health care unless they could afford services in the private health care market, where the price of one day's hospitalization is roughly equivalent to most workers' monthly wages. While they can receive emergency treatment in Israeli public hospitals, and while hospitals do not report illegal patients to the authorities, many migrants nonetheless avoid seeking care for fear of arrest.[35] Moreover, emergency care is not free, and migrant patients—or Israeli "Good Samaritan" escorts—may be required to guarantee payment before care is provided.

The PHR Open Clinic for Migrant Workers

I was first guided toward the Open Clinic in the late summer of 2000, when my research was in its earliest stages and when Tel Aviv's diverse population of illegal migrants still lived under the radar of public consciousness and public discourse.[36] It was Matabisi Lukumu, a young Congolese man and author of the first graduate thesis on migrant labor in Israel,[37] who handed me a golden thread during an afternoon conversation in the Congolese Embassy offices in North Tel Aviv. "You may be interested in knowing about the clinic for migrant workers in South Tel Aviv," he told me. "Here's the address."

The following day I wandered around, map in hand, searching for the clinic in a South Tel Aviv neighborhood I could barely locate since I had never before had occasion to visit. Among the blocks of ground-floor shops and industrial workspaces topped by crumbling three- and four-story apartment buildings, I finally reached my destination—and I was completely unprepared for what awaited me.

The clinic's green-on-white storefront sign was clear enough: OPEN CLINIC, it declared in bold capital letters. Outside the clinic, housed in a small storefront preceded by a narrow stoop, I found a long line of people—among them South Americans, Eastern Europeans, West Africans, and others—standing, sitting, or leaning on the railing, all waiting for a chance to enter and consult with a doctor. I loitered a bit among the patients gathered outside, then tentatively tried striking up a conversation with Solomon, a Nigerian man waiting in line. He had lived in Israel for five years, he explained; he earned his living polishing floors; and he had a Nigerian girl-friend who soon planned to leave Israel for Dublin, Ireland.[38] In fact, Solomon's narrative-on-the-fly hit upon most of the themes I would eventually pursue throughout the protracted, painstaking work of ethnography in the years that followed, for they were among his most immediate and most pressing concerns: straining physical labor, a tenuous conjugal tie, a health emergency, and a subsequent financial crisis. The occasional sympathetic Is-raeli individual as a foil to unsympathetic systems. Marriage as a strategy for accessing mobility and membership despite rigid, bureaucratically fortified nation-state boundaries.

After a brief conversation with Solomon, I managed to introduce myself to the clinic's director and declare my interest in volunteering regularly and on a long-term basis—either until I had completed my research or until the organization kicked me out. With those words and the acceptance they met, my work had begun. By the time PHR *was* ready to consider kicking me out (and for one brief moment late in my fieldwork, they were),[39] two years had passed, and the thread of my volunteer work was deeply woven into the fab-ric of the clinic, which relocated twice and experienced two changes in in-stitutional leadership in the period during which I conducted my research. It is this form of engaged, long-term participant observation that helped generate the ethnographic findings presented here.

Illegality and the Emergence of a Two-Tiered Medical System

Since its establishment in 1998, the Open Clinic has been a crucial re-source for migrants in Tel Aviv and, simultaneously, a key advocate for in-stitutional change and policy reform. In addition to the services its vol-unteer medical staff provide at the clinic and, not infrequently, in their own offices, several limited forms of state-sponsored care have become available, or more readily available, largely through the efforts of PHR.[40] These include: (1) free treatment for some infectious diseases, including tuberculosis and sexually transmitted diseases (for all)[41] and HIV (for pregnant women, to prevent mother-to-child transmission);[42] (2) early childhood immunizations and child development checkups at neighbor-hood MCH centers; and (3) comprehensive health care for children of mi-grant workers through an experimental arrangement with one of the ma-jor sick funds.[43]

Although these exceptional forms of state-sponsored care are available in theory, substantial barriers impede access. These range from language barri-ers, prohibitive costs, and transportation problems to continued (albeit ungrounded) fears that contact with health care providers might result in arrest and deportation.[44] With the notable exception of the Open Clinic's services, therefore, most basic forms of curative and preventive care remain unavailable. Outside of Tel Aviv, even these services are often inaccessible.[45]

Israeli physicians Meltzer and Elkayam have noted a disturbing consequence of transnational migrants' formal and systematic exclusion from most branches of the Israeli health care system.[46] While keenly aware of the burden undocumented migration has created for the already financially strapped Israeli national health care system (primarily through the provision of costly emergency care), the authors criticize what they perceive to be the emergence of a two-tiered medical system in Israel.[47] Under present circumstances, physicians are under pressure to provide what the authors describe as substandard care to migrant patients lacking health coverage. According to Meltzer and Elkayam, "in public hospitals in Israel, in a system that explicitly strives for excellence, equality, and upholding international standards, a substandard, parallel health arrangement has been created for illegal migrant workers. The practical and moral significance of this situation is varied: a hospitalization system that can simultaneously include two tiers of care can also include additional levels—medicine for the poor, for criminals, etc."[48] The apparent emergence of a two-tiered medical system, which implies a frightening pattern in which forms of human life are ranked and effectively treated as more or less valuable, is far from being an exclusively unique Israeli phenomenon; indeed, it has strong parallels in a number of Western European countries and in North America.[49] (To be sure, such patterns of ranking are deployed not only to distinguish citizens from noncitizens, but also—especially in states where health care distribution is determined according to neoliberal economic principles—to differentiate richer from poorer potential "consumers" of health care.)[50]

ILLEGALITY, PREGNANCY, AND DELIVERY: THE REPRODUCTIVE PARADOX

Reproductive and infant health stand as notable, and in many ways surprising, exceptions to this general state of affairs. In Israel, three forms of state-sponsored services are available to undocumented migrants in this health care domain: (1) subsidized prenatal care at municipally operated Mother-Child Health (MCH) Centers [*Tipat Chalav*] through an arrangement with the Ministry of Health (MOH); (2) full labor and delivery coverage at Israeli public hospitals if appropriate advance arrangements have been made; and (3) early childhood immunizations and checkups. Amina's story illustrates one pathway by which many pregnant migrants become aware of this patchwork array of policies and practices.

Amina's Pursuit of Prenatal Care

Amina, a Nigerian woman in her early thirties, met her husband Naanah Kofi, a Ghanaian man in his late thirties, at the evangelical church they both attended in South Tel Aviv, just a block away from the city's central bus station. Both came to Israel on an undocumented basis with the goal of working and earning money, some to save and some to remit home to kin. Eventually the couple moved in together, and Amina became pregnant. Interested in obtaining prenatal care but unable to pay a private Israeli doctor, Amina followed a friend's advice and began making monthly trips to East Jerusalem, over an hour's journey each way across the invisible but tangible border between Israel and Palestine, to consult a Palestinian physician known within the West African community in Tel Aviv to provide prenatal care at low rates.

During Amina's second trimester, the doctor recommended an advanced sonogram he lacked the technology to provide and referred her to the sole medical facility in Tel Aviv fully accessible to migrant workers: the low-tech, volunteer-run PHR Open Clinic. The clinic itself—equipped with little more than a few donated examination tables, a used EKG machine, an ill-stocked medicine cabinet containing first aid supplies, and a limited supply of donated medications—could not perform the diagnostic test Amina needed. Through the creative resourcefulness of the clinic's administrative staff, however, Amina was able to obtain the sonogram at an affordable rate through an informal price reduction agreement between PHR and a local public hospital.

In addition to the sonogram, Amina's visit to the Open Clinic also linked her into the web of reproductive and infant health services for which, to her great surprise, she was eligible. First, clinic staff explained she could obtain state subsidized prenatal care at a municipally run MCH center in her neighborhood instead of traveling to East Jerusalem each month. There she could obtain a full course of prenatal checkups for a one-time fee of less than US$100. (Importantly, however, this fee would not include any diagnostic tests—i.e., sonograms or labwork—although discounts on some tests are available at local labs and hospitals through PHR.) Second, they explained that since she was working regularly, her employer could register her with the National Insurance Institute (NII) to receive free hospitalization and delivery coverage and even a small delivery grant following the baby's birth. Finally, she was advised to return to the MCH center after her delivery to register the infant for subsidized immunizations and development checkups.

Undocumented Migrants' Access to Prenatal Care: Theory vs. Reality

Many illegal migrant women who are aware of the MCH option, including Amina, nonetheless prefer to consult private doctors for prenatal care, as both my narrative findings and the small survey I conducted at the Open Clinic suggest. Of the twenty-nine survey respondents who were parents to children born in Israel, only 7 percent (2) indicated that they or their spouses had received prenatal care at a local MCH center, whereas 90 percent (26) had visited private physicians, including Israeli doctors who accepted migrant patients on a discounted basis in Tel Aviv (18) and/or Palestinian doctors in East Jerusalem (8).

While some women may avoid MCH centers for fear of contact with the authorities, it appears there are other strong deterrents as well: the lack of ultrasound machines (necessary to determine the gender of a fetus), the added cost of laboratory and other diagnostic tests, and overall inconvenience (since appointments are infrequently available and, even then, only at certain MCH centers and only on weekday mornings). When a more desirable alternative became available during my stint as a volunteer at the Open Clinic, already low levels of interest in the MCH prenatal care option further dwindled. The new alternative: an obstetrician and PHR member opened his clinic to migrant patients one evening per week and charged a nominal fee. His appointment book filled up rapidly and he often stayed late seeing additional patients. For pregnant migrants, most of them working women, the option of seeing a private doctor in the evening (like the PHR physician) or on Saturday morning (like the Palestinian physician Amina visited in East Jerusalem) was far more convenient.

While illegal pregnant migrants' theoretical eligibility for state-subsidized prenatal care would seem to highlight a fascinating paradox in the Israeli legal and policy environment, the possibility is effectively moot since first, so few women exercise this option, and second, the care available excludes basic diagnostic testing and, as PHR insists, is therefore inadequate by normative Western biomedical standards.[51]

Creative NGO Advocacy: Establishing Undocumented Migrants' Right to Free Hospital Delivery

When it comes to labor and delivery, however, the situation is quite different. While women have the theoretical option of delivering in Palestinian hospitals in East Jerusalem or (at least until the outbreak of the Second Intifada and the resulting closures imposed by the Israeli army) in the nearby Palestinian cities of Bethlehem or Ramallah for relatively low fees, most prefer to deliver in Tel Aviv closer to home, friends, and family. For thousands of women, a loophole in the National Insurance Institute (NII) regulations enabling illegal migrants to obtain full hospital delivery coverage has made this possible.

The legal grounding for this coverage was established in the late 1990s by two established Israeli human rights NGOs that expanded their missions to include migrant advocacy: first, PHR, and second, the workers' advocacy organization Kav La'Oved [the Workers' Hotline]. Staff at these two organizations read the Israeli labor laws and NII regulations closely and concluded that, at least according to one possible interpretation, working women as well as spouses of working men are eligible for hospital delivery benefits regardless of citizenship or legal status.[52] Migrant workers cannot, however, register themselves; only an Israeli employer can register them by completing a simple form and paying the biannual NII tax, amounting to 2 percent of a worker's wages.

Without delay, the two organizations divided the labor and began testing this interpretation. Kav La'Oved primarily focused on the legal issues while PHR publicized the arrangement to patients and fielded procedural questions. PHR began circulating flyers, in both Hebrew and English, that explained to migrants and their employers exactly how to register with the NII. While many employers were reluctant to register their employees, primarily for fear they might be punished or fined for employing an illegal worker, growing numbers of employers did agree. To the NGOs' surprise, NII complied not only by covering the cost of hospital deliveries, but also by providing registered women with the NII "delivery grant" regularly issued to Israeli new mothers. Since the NII provision still offered nothing in the way of prenatal care services, Open Clinic staff and volunteers cobbled together the rough package of reproductive health services offered to Amina during her visit. Fifty-nine percent of the seventeen parents I surveyed had registered with NII. Utilization of the third form of available care—MCH childhood immunizations and child development checkups—was notably higher; seventy-six percent of the twenty-two parents surveyed had used these services.

In a moment, we will explore the impact of this patchwork assortment of policies and practices, and the impact of illegal status more broadly, in the life of Priscilla, a Ghanaian woman, wife, and mother who lives in Israel as an illegal economic migrant. First, however, it is important to consider how the highly politicized and deeply ideological nature of reproduction in Israel shapes both migrants' paradoxical exclusion from Israeli society and their inclusion within these branches of the national health care system.

ILLEGALITY AND BODILY TRANSGRESSION: REPRODUCTION, NATIONALISM, AND THE BOUNDARIES OF THE ISRAELI BODY POLITIC

As indicated earlier, the Israeli government has no interest in encouraging transnational migrants to settle permanently or start families in Israel. To the contrary, some Israeli politicians have described these migrant communities as a "time bomb" waiting to explode. How, then, can we explain the availability of these subsidized—or even free—health care services to pregnant illegal migrants and their infant children? Four key factors come into play: first, historic Israeli pronatalism and, in particular, the institutional environment it has generated; second, the political character of Tel Aviv, the country's largest and most politically "progressive" urban center; third, the support of certain officials within the national MOH and public health departments;[53] and fourth, the ongoing and concerted efforts of left-leaning Tel Aviv–based advocacy NGOs. Together, these factors pose an important set of counterweights to prevailing government attitudes and policies.

First, as Kahn and Kanaaneh, among others, have demonstrated, demography and reproduction have played a central role, as Kanaaneh explains, in "thinking, creating, and sustaining the Israeli nation-state."[54] Kahn further points out that "the imperative to reproduce has [for Israeli Jews] deep political and historical roots," involving powerful and compelling religious, sociocultural, and emotional motives.[55] These have included first, a desire to counterbalance the perceived demographic threat represented by Palestinian and Arab birthrates, and second, at least in earlier historical periods, a desire to produce soldiers to defend the state—desires Kanaaneh has analyzed in their Palestinian inverse. A third implicit motivation is the desire to "replace" the six million Jews killed during the *Shoah*, or Holocaust.[56]

For Israeli Jews, then, demography is by no means a dry academic issue; instead, it is a prominent concern that is almost always linked to politics, history, and memory and framed in ideologically charged discourses of nationalism and collective survival. These motivations, it is important to point out, are far more than simply sociocultural tropes; throughout Israel's history, pronatalist policies and laws have been actively promoted by the state and its institutions. Two practical consequences of this overall pronatalist orientation are the Heroine Awards, which were granted in the 1950s to women who bore ten or more children, and current laws granting financial benefits to families "blessed with children."[57]

Significantly, institutionalized Israeli pronatalism is, as Kanaaneh points out, a "selective pronatalism" aimed an ensuring a Jewish majority and, as its apologists explain, ensuring Israel's continued existence as a "Jewish state."[58] Israel has a long history of waging political battles in demographic terms. In the 1980s, for instance, the MOH was eager to provide family planning services in Arab but not Jewish communities, and in some Arab communities, family planning has been available even when other forms of health care are not.[59] Moreover, the country's demographic anxieties are a frequent topic of discussion in the mainstream Israeli media.

In this atmosphere, how can we explain illegal migrants' eligibility for the forms of care delineated above? First, despite Israel's "demographic anxiety" and "selective pronatalism," certain factors have constrained the translation of this controversial, though by no means unique, agenda into practice. These include the state's socialist history, its democratic foundations, and substantial degrees of political, professional, and ideological heterogeneity both within and among successive governments, the MOH, Tel Aviv municipal authorities, and other relevant institutions.[60] A second and related factor is the engagement and support of several high-ranking, albeit institutionally constrained, officials in various branches of the MOH.[61]

A third key reason for migrants' access to subsidized reproductive and infant health care is the distinctive political and ideological atmosphere of Tel Aviv. Unlike municipalities elsewhere in the country, key officials in Tel Aviv, reflecting the city's relatively liberal and progressive character relative to other Israeli cities, have taken a firm position in favor of prenatal health care for undocumented migrants along with the limited array of other health and social services described earlier.[62] In Israel, the Tel Aviv municipality is the only branch of state power to view illegal economic migration as a predictable outcome of contemporary global processes. It is also the only state agency to employ discourses of humanitarianism, human rights, and institutional responsibility rather than promulgating populist constructions of illegal migration as a danger to the state. This explicit contradiction between the policies and practices of the Tel Aviv municipality and those of the Israeli state constitutes one of the most intriguing aspects of Israeli's encounter with transnational labor migration.[63]

Perhaps the most significant proximate factor explaining illegal migrants' access to reproductive and infant health care is the ongoing advocacy work of the two NGOs mentioned earlier: Kav La'Oved and PHR. Priscilla's story, to which we now turn, offers considerable ethnographic insight into how illegal pregnant women negotiate this complicated policy environment and, at the same time, into how NGOs work with migrants in their ongoing efforts to monitor, interpret, and, when they deem necessary, challenge existing policies and practices.

PRISCILLA'S STORY

When Priscilla traveled to Israel from Ghana in 1995 to join Maxwell, her husband of six years, they had not seen one another for more than half of their years of marriage. During their separation, Maxwell had worked abroad, first in Germany and later at a large beachfront hotel in the southern Israeli city of Eilat, and remitted some of his earnings home regularly. Like her husband before her, Priscilla came to Israel with a short-term tourist visa, and like him, she came to work. Upon her arrival, Maxwell found her a job on the hotel's housecleaning staff, and each of their incomes vastly exceeded any potential combined income they might have earned at home in Ghana. After several years, the couple moved northward to Tel Aviv to join that city's larger and institutionally more developed West African community.

During their first years in the Tel Aviv area, Priscilla and Maxwell found housecleaning jobs through Ghanaian friends and acquaintances. Although they were able to manage financially, Priscilla had much to say about the experiential consequences of being illegal in Israel. In particular, she found it "very, very difficult" to be black in a country where nearly everyone looks either European or Middle Eastern. "We are suffering because of this color," Priscilla told me. "Wherever you go you are suffering. Nobody cares about you." "Do you think Israelis treat black people differently from other people?" I asked her. While she had already described to me the occasional kindnesses shown to her and her husband by a handful of Israelis, her overall assessment was unequivocal. "They hate us," she declared. "They don't respect us at all. If you are going somewhere they say 'kushi,' 'kushi,' 'kushi.' You know what this means? Like if an American man says 'nigger.' You see?" I knew perfectly well what she meant, and I could hear the humiliation and anger in her voice as she spit into the air a hurtful word that had often been spit out at her.

Priscilla's painful experiences of racism were inseparable from her experiences of illegality, particularly after the family's move to Tel Aviv. As the number of arrests and deportations gradually rose, Priscilla and Maxwell became increasingly aware of the need to live clandestinely and, as much as possible, invisibly. For a Ghanaian couple living in Israel, this was clearly impossible. Already constrained by political exclusion, social marginality, and racism, Priscilla explained how the increasing criminalization of illegal migrants in Tel Aviv crept into her own, and her husband's, most private thoughts, dreams (and nightmares), and prayers. "I pray, I pray in the night, at one o'clock," she explained. "I pray a lot. Because you know, we are here, and we don't have anyone to help us, only God. . . . And God is a good Father. When you talk to him, he hears you and answers you." Weighed down in multiple political, social, and practical "arenas of constraint,"[64] prayer—at home and in church, on Saturday mornings and late at night in bed—gave Priscilla hope.

Pregnancies and Predicaments

Although earning money was Priscilla's primary motive for joining her husband in Israel, it was not the only one. Thankful to be reunited with her husband after such a long separation, she also hoped—and expected—to start a family. Her first pregnancy, during their time in Eilat, ended in the eighth month when she realized the fetus had stopped moving and sought help at a public hospital, where a doctor performed an operation to "take it out." Not only was this late-term miscarriage physically and emotionally draining for Priscilla, who lived far from any of the female relatives and friends who might have offered support in those trying times, but it was also a major financial blow, costing the couple several thousand dollars of their hard-earned savings.

Two years later, she became pregnant again and gave birth to a healthy baby boy via caesarean section, again in an Eilat hospital. In addition to the considerable physical and emotional strain of her two difficult pregnancies, the new medical bills associated with her second delivery also created considerable financial strain. Not long after their move to Tel Aviv, the couple made a difficult decision: to send their son "home" to Ghana. Like many other migrant parents in Israel—especially those from Ghana, Nigeria, and the Philippines—Priscilla and Maxwell felt their family would be better off with their child in relatives' care while they continued to work in Israel and send home money regularly. Caring for him on a regular basis, Priscilla explained, would have constrained their ability to earn money to support him both now and in the future. They found a Ghanaian woman with plans to return home and asked her to take their son with her. For a fee, the woman traveled with the baby, with the hospital release papers from his birth, and with Priscilla's passport, which Priscilla later declared "lost" upon requesting its replacement at the Ghanaian embassy. Although she misses her son very much, she did not want him to grow up in Israel.

Not long after Priscilla and Maxwell had bid farewell to their small son, Priscilla became pregnant for a third time. Again, she was simultaneously happy and concerned. The earlier pregnancies had taken a severe toll on her physical and mental health, and again she feared for her baby's health and for her own. For a while, she continued working without telling her employers she was pregnant. "If I stop," she would tell herself, "I can't eat." Eventually, however, she and Maxwell decided she should stop working for the duration of the pregnancy.

In Eilat, Priscilla had not known where to go for affordable prenatal care. In Tel Aviv, however, she had met many pregnant African women and new mothers, and they had much advice to offer. While she knew of the Open Clinic, most of her Ghanaian friends, like the Nigerian friends advising Amina, suggested she consult a Palestinian "private doctor" in East Jerusalem. Following their advice, she made Saturday morning trips to do so throughout her third pregnancy.

While Priscilla did not want to deliver her baby in Jerusalem, she and her husband could not afford a third expensive stay in an Israeli hospital. They were thus elated to learn through friends that hospital delivery coverage was available through NII. In theory, a single employer paying NII taxes would have been sufficient to ensure Priscilla's delivery coverage, and that em-

ployer could have been either her own or her husband's. These details, however, were unclear from the flyers they had picked up at the Open Clinic, so
she and Maxwell posed their request to all of their current and recent employers. Like many other Israeli employers of illegal domestic workers, most
refused.

Only two of the couple's employers, Edna and Penina, agreed. Edna, who
liked Priscilla very much, was more than happy to oblige. She completed
the NII form with her own name and Priscilla's—thereby taking the risk of
formally declaring Priscilla as her employee—and submitted the payment
to NII. Maxwell's employer Penina, in contrast, agreed to register only if he
paid the premium himself. Eager to avoid any more costly medical bills, he
readily agreed to her conditions. Each week, Penina withheld a full 50 percent of his earnings rather than the minimal 2 percent NII required and
which, moreover, Penina herself was legally required to pay. Politically constrained by his illegal status and socially constrained in his interactions
with Penina, whom he simply could not afford to lose as an employer,
Maxwell kept silent.

Fighting for Rights

As though Penina's exploitation and deceit were not enough, the couple
encountered an even greater difficulty after the birth of their second son at
a Tel Aviv public hospital, again via a painful caesarean section. Since migrants' access to reproductive health services relies on a patchwork of policies and arrangements rather than any single policy or law, the risk always
exists that services might be cut off without notice. This nearly happened
after NII had covered illegal migrants' delivery costs for several years. Unfortunately for Priscilla, her NII claim crossed their desk at precisely that
moment.

Although Edna (happily) and Penina (grudgingly) had followed PHR's
instructions, the NII, citing Priscilla's expired visa, now refused to pay the
hospital bills. Still weak from her third surgery, Priscilla was furious. "I
said what? It's not fair! Why are you saying now 'you must bring a visa'?
Why did my employer come and make *Bituakh Leumi* [NII] for me? You
didn't ask my employer, 'that woman working for you, does she have a
visa?'"

Furious she was being cheated and unable to pay the bill on her own,
Priscilla followed a friend's recommendation and took her case to a place
she described to me as "human rights": the Kav La'Oved workers' advocacy
organization, located in an office building near the central bus station in
South Tel Aviv. There, she finally felt someone was listening to her. "I explained everything to them. They said no, it's not fair. They told me, "If the
government says—the *government* says—this is a *new law*, then they can't do

anything about it. But if the *manager* says this is the new law . . . you have
to fight with them.'"

Fully prepared to fight, Priscilla agreed to return to the NII office with a
lawyer from Kav La'Oved. She did fight, and they won. Apparently, the local NII manager had made an independent decision—to deny delivery coverage to illegal migrant women for whom NII premiums had been paid—
in contravention of national NII policy. In the end, Priscilla's bill was paid,
and she happily accepted a check for the delivery grant as well.

Yet the struggle waged on pregnant migrants' behalf by Kav La'Oved and
their NGO partners, including PHR and a third organization called the Association for Civil Rights in Israel (ACRI), was far from over. Soon after
Priscilla's run-in with NII, a parliamentary effort sought to legislate the NII
loophole out of existence. The coordinated legal and political efforts of this
NGO coalition prevented the attempt from succeeding. Following a lengthy
lobbying and negotiation process, an agreement was reached whereby migrants would be ineligible for the cash benefits NII provides Israeli
women—i.e., compensation for maternity leave (which, in any event, few
migrant women had sought to claim)—while the substantially more important benefit, free hospital delivery, would be preserved along with the
delivery grant.

Through lobbying and case-by-case advocacy for women like Priscilla, Israeli NGOs like Kav La'Oved, PHR, and ACRI—in a rapidly changing and,
in many respects, hostile policy environment—have helped hundreds, if
not thousands, of illegal migrant families gain access to much-needed
health care services. Overall, Israel's pronatalist climate and the migrant-
friendly policies of the Tel Aviv municipality have played important roles in
facilitating access to reproductive and infant health care services. The most
important legwork, however, has been performed by the creative, persevering NGO community of migrant advocates, whose petitions on migrants'
behalf are grounded in international human rights legislation, in a philosophy of humanitarianism and, no less, in an understanding of the larger
political economic processes that generate illegal labor migration in the
first place. Even so, their reach and their capabilities are limited.

CONCLUSION

The chapter has attempted to shed light on how local configurations of migrant illegality shape migrants' experiences of everyday life in contemporary
Israel. As proposed earlier, and as I elaborate elsewhere,[65] illegality is three-
dimensional: it is a form of political status, a social condition, and a mode
of being in the world. Research on the condition of migrant illegality in Israel and elsewhere requires a research methodology attentive to all three of

these dimensions. Put differently, it requires an approach attentive not only to how illegality is *configured* in ideological, political, and bureaucratic terms, but also to how it is *experienced* in phenomenological terms.

These three dimensions of migrant illegality do not, as we have seen, take shape in a vacuum; rather, they are informed by considerations and constraints at multiple levels of political, economic, and social reality. By engaging all three dimensions, this article has sought to show how local ideologies and local politics have contributed to the emergence of a heterogeneous and contradictory policy environment with significant implications for individual migrants' lived experience. Israeli institutions and individuals have imagined, engaged, and responded to illegal labor migration, and to illegal migrants' biological reproduction, in varied and contradictory ways. These diverse responses have been influenced by a wide array of factors, among them economic concerns, demographic anxieties, geopolitical considerations, and commitments to humanitarianism and human rights. All of these responses, however, have evolved in the shadow of the state's and society's explicit, deeply entrenched commitment to remaining a "Jewish state."

In conclusion, I would like to comment briefly on two of the chapter's broader implications for research on undocumented transnational migration, on Israel-Palestine, and on the lived implications of local biopolitics of otherness. First, although Israeli nationalist ideology is alternately celebrated and maligned as distinctive and unique, it is important to note that this particular commitment—to preserve the integrity of an imagined national body—bears striking parallels in many other industrialized host countries. The vigorous anti-immigration sentiment that emerged in the United States in the mid-2000s, for instance, has been fueled not only by economic considerations associated with the structure of the U.S. labor market, but also by fears of losing a core sense of Americanness through the arrival of "foreign" bodies, languages, and cultural influences.[66] One prominent item on the anti-immigrant agenda in the United States involves a proposal to revoke a fundamental cornerstone of the United States citizenship regime: birthright citizenship, the automatic right to citizenship for all individuals born in the United States. The impetus to eliminate this right stems from the veiled eugenic notion that foreign bodies—especially Mexican bodies—threaten the broader social body and body politic in both physical and moral terms. While the anti-immigrant movement in the United States is largely a movement of the right, a similar proposal to revoke birthright citizenship in Ireland recently met with success in a nationwide referendum. There, the government succeeded in mobilizing overwhelming public support from both right and left by using a similar logic—that is, by constructing citizenship as a moral regime and casting the local population of largely nonwhite foreign nationals and their fetuses as inherently transgressive and immoral.[67] In Israel, there is no discussion of revoking birthright citizenship for Israeli-born children of transnational migrants, for no such entitlement has ever existed. Instead, undocumented migrants' biological reproduction is discussed, debated, and politicized in other ways. As Priscilla's and Amina's stories illustrate, the political nature of reproduction within Israel affects the everyday lives of pregnant undocumented migrants and their offspring in multiple and often profound ways.

Yet, as we have seen, the politicization of reproduction does not necessarily lead to a unified constellation of policies and practices. Nor does it necessarily imply that Israel's determination to remain a Jewish state with a Jewish demographic majority will necessarily result in the automatic exclusion of non-Jews—even illegal Christian residents from countries as far away as Ghana and Nigeria—from the state's well-developed array of reproductive and child health care services. Instead, fears of losing a "Jewish demographic majority" coexist with strong tendencies toward ideological as well as institutionalized pronatalism. So, too, does the xenophobia of right-wing politicians coexist with the humanitarian universalism of migrant advocates within the Tel Aviv municipality and the local NGO community alike. Indeed, it is precisely these tensions—between competing ideologies of reproduction and conflicting visions of the ideal Israeli national body—that have produced the paradoxical array of conflicting policies described here, in which some branches of state power remain concerned with the health and well-being of some undocumented migrants and their offspring even as others round migrants up by the thousands, warehouse them in specially adapted prison facilities, and ship them homeward either at their own expense or at the expense of the state. Contradictory policy environments like this one, and their lived implications, merit investigation in other migration settings as well.

My second concluding comment pertains to the impact of this local biopolitics of otherness on the construction and treatment of undocumented men and women and their offspring. Despite substantial differences between the particular kind of security threats ostensibly posed by Palestinians and transnational migrant workers, there are important similarities in how these two groups are portrayed and treated by the Israeli state. This is particularly true since the initiation of the mass deportation campaign in 2002. Although the arrival of these new others is predicated upon a variety of macro-level, regional, and local processes, migrant workers' exclusion and dehumanization in Israel is influenced by the state's ideological and practical treatment of Palestinians, who are already well-integrated into local biopolitical regimes of ideology and governance. Frequently, such forms of exclusion compromise individuals' and groups' fundamental humanity by rendering them vulnerable to forms of treatment that would be judged explicitly unacceptable and, in many cases, patently illegal were they applied to ratified citizens. Yet both Palestinians' and migrant workers' otherness is frequently understood as immutable—as being literally written on their bodies—and in both cases these forms of presumed primordial difference have become justification for, and legitimation of, the use of state-sponsored physical violence against them.[68]

In Israel, as in other purportedly democratic states, the quick and ungrounded use of violence against *citizens* is universally condemned and violated. Moreover, citizens possess the political rights and, at least in theory, the social and political means to seek justice and compensation via mechanisms of the legal process. *Noncitizens*, on the other hand, are not only more susceptible to such quick and ungrounded uses of state violence, but they also lack the political capacity to use normative measures of legal redress even if they are formally entitled to do so. Their vulnerability, "abjectivity,"[69] and speechlessness make such attempts extremely difficult. Even under such adverse circumstances, however, dissenting political views and small groups of counterhegemonic local voices, like those of PHR, Kav La'Oved, ACRI, and Mesila, support disempowered noncitizens in their efforts to be subjects rather than simply objects. These groups' capacities for agency, and their everyday lived experience, merit careful ethnographic investigation as windows onto some of the disturbing human consequences of nation-state building and maintenance, not only in Israel-Palestine but in every society that divides human beings into what Agamben characterizes as "interiorized" and "detritus humanity."[70]

ACKNOWLEDGMENTS

This chapter, adapted from an article that appeared in the *Journal of Middle East Women's Studies* (2005: 1, 2), is part of a doctoral study supported by Fulbright-Hays, the National Science Foundation (No. 0135425), the Social Science Research Council, the Wenner Gren Foundation, the Lady Davis Trust at the Hebrew University of Jerusalem, and the Department of Anthropology and Center for Health, Culture, and Society at Emory University. Any opinions, findings, conclusions, or recommendations expressed are those of the author and do not necessarily reflect the views of funding agencies. Portions of the article were presented at the annual meeting of the Society for Medical Anthropology (Dallas, TX, 2004) and the Association for Israel Studies (Jerusalem, Israel, 2004). An earlier version was awarded the Rudolph Virchow Prize from the Society for Medical Anthropology's Critical Anthropology of Health Caucus. The author is grateful to Rami Adout, Peter Brown, Erin Finley, Marcia Inhorn, Carol Kleiner Willen, Mark LeVine, Sandy Sufian, and an anonymous JMEWS reviewer for their helpful feedback on earlier drafts.

NOTES

1. Adriana Kemp and Rebeca Raijman, *"Foreign Workers" in Israel* (Tel Aviv: Adva Center, 2003).

2. Henceforth I will use these terms interchangeably and without the problematizing quotation marks for ease of reading, but they are implicit throughout.

3. Susan Martha Kahn, *Reproducing Jews: A Cultural Account of Assisted Conception in Israel* (Durham, NC: Duke University Press, 2000); Rhoda Kanaaneh, *Birthing the Nation: Strategies of Palestinian Women in Israel* (Berkeley: University of California Press, 2002).

4. Sarah S. Willen, "'No Person is Illegal'? Configurations and Experiences of 'Illegality' among Undocumented West African and Filipino Migrant Workers in Tel Aviv, Israel" (Ph.D. diss., Emory University, 2006); Sarah S. Willen, "'Illegality,' Mass Deportation, and the Threat of Violent Arrest: Structural Violence and Social Suffering in the Lives of Undocumented Migrant Workers in Israel," in *Trauma and Memory: Reading, Healing, and Making Law*, ed. A. Sarat, M. Alberstein, and N. Davidovitch (Palo Alto, CA: Stanford University Press, forthcoming); Sarah S. Willen, "Toward a Criminal Phenomenology of 'Illegality': State Power, Criminalization, and Abjectivity among Undocumented Migrant Workers in Tel Aviv, Israel," *International Migration* (forthcoming 2007).

5. I chose to concentrate on, and to a certain extent compare, the undocumented Filipino and West African communities for several reasons. First, these constituted two of the three largest and most institutionally well-organized undocumented communities in Tel Aviv (with the large South American population constituting the third; see Adriana Kemp and Rebeca Raijman, "Christian Zionists in the Holy Land: Evangelical Churches, Labor Migrants, and the Jewish State," *Identities—Global Studies in Culture and Power* 10 (2003): 3, 295–318; Adriana Kemp et al. "Contesting the Limits of Political Participation: Latinos and Black African Migrant Workers in Israel," *Ethnic and Racial Studies* 23 (2000): 1, 94–119; Adriana Kemp et al. "'Making it' in Israel? Latino Undocumented Migrant Workers in the Holy Land," *Estudios Interdisciplinarios de America Latina y el Caribe* 11 (2000): 2, 113–36). Second, these two groups filled a single labor niche in Israel while at the same time constituting two separate cultural and religious communities. Third, members of the two groups tended to arrive via two different migration pathways. Nearly all West Africans tend to arrive via the "tourist loophole" (Sarah S. Willen, "Perspectives on Transnational Labor Migration in Israel," *Revue Européene des Migrations Internationales* 19 (2003): 3, 243–62) in Israel's otherwise strict migration regime and overstay their visas, as explained above. On the other hand, the vast majority of Filipinos living "illegally" in Israel, like Filipinos in numerous other countries (see citations later in paragraph), are legally recruited in the Philippines to fill a specific labor need in the host society, in this case elder care, and later lose or relinquish their legal status. (Abigail B. Bakan and Daiva Stasiulis, *Not One of the Family: Foreign Domestic Workers in Canada* (Toronto: University of Toronto Press, 1997); Rhacel Salazar Parreñas, *Servants of Globalization: Women, Migration, and Domestic Work* (Stanford: Stanford University Press, 2001); Rhacel Salazar Parreñas, "The Care Crisis in the Philippines: Children and Transnational Families in the New Global Economy," in *Global*

Woman: Nannies, Maids and Sex Workers in the New Economy, ed. B. Ehrenreich and A. R. Hochschild (New York: Metropolitan Books, 2003).

6. Heide Castañeda, "Citizenship, Rights, and Ambiguity: Undocumented Migrant Workers and Access to Health Services in Berlin, Germany and Tel Aviv, Israel," in *Transnational Migration to Israel in Global Comparative Context*, ed. Sarah S. Willen (Lanham, MD: Lexington Books, forthcoming 2007); Leo R. Chavez, "A Glass Half Empty: Latina Reproduction and Public Discourse," *Human Organization* 63 (2004): 2, 173–88; Leo R. Chavez, Wayne A. Cornelius, and O. W. Jones, "Utilization of Health Services by Mexican Immigrant Women in San Diego," *Women and Health* 11 (1986): 3–20; Carolyn Sargent and Dennis Cordell, "Polygamy, Disrupted Reproduction, and the State: Malian Migrants in Paris, France," *Social Science and Medicine* 56 (2003): 1961–1972; Anwen Tormey, "'Everyone with Eyes Can See the Problem': Moral Citizens and the Space of Irish Nationhood," in "'Illegal' and 'Irregular' Migrants' Lived Experience of Law and State Power," ed. Sarah S. Willen, special issue, *International Migration* (forthcoming 2007).

7. Ayoob Kara, "Comments" (speech to the joint session of the Special Parliamentary Committee on the Problem of Foreign Workers and the Immigration and Absorption Committee in recognition of International Migrants' Day. December 18, 2001).

8. Daniel Monterescu, "Spatial Relationality: Ethnic Relations and Urban Space in Jewish-Arab Mixed Towns, 1948–2004" (Ph.D. diss., University of Chicago, 2004).

9. Smeeding 1998, quoted in Ichiro Kawachi and Bruce Kennedy, *The Health of Nations: Why Inequality is Harmful to Your Health* (New York: New Press, 2002).

10. Itim (news service), "Foreign Workers Make up ¼ of Tel Aviv's Population," *Haaretz* [online], June 10, 2003. Accessed on December 12, 2006, www.haaretz.com.

11. Arjun Appadurai, *Modernity at Large: Cultural Dimensions of Globalization* (Minneapolis: University of Minnesota Press, 1996).

12. Quoted in Adriana Kemp, "Labour Migration and Racialisation: Labour Market Mechanisms and Labour Migration Control Policies in Israel," *Social Identities* 10 (2004): 2, 267–92, 284.

13. Rami Adout, *Aggressively Passive: The State of Health of Migrant Workers in Israel* (Tel Aviv: Physicians for Human Rights Israel, 2002); Dani Filc and Nadav Davidovitch, "Health Care as a National Right? The Development of Health Care Services for Migrant Workers in Israel," *Social Theory and Health* 15 (2005): 1–14; Mordechai Fried, "The Israeli Health Care System's Treatment of Migrant Workers," [in Hebrew] *HaRefuah* 142 (2003): 430–32; Eyal Meltzer and Uri Elkayam, "Medical Care for Undocumented Migrant Workers in Public Hospitals: The Urgent Need for a Solution," [in Hebrew] *HaRefuah* 142 (2003): 6, 402–4.

14. In 2006, following a long struggle by local human rights organizations, the Israeli government approved a one-time arrangement according to which a small group of migrant workers' children meeting a strict set of eligibility criteria were granted Israeli citizenship and their parents were granted permanent residence status.

15. See, for instance, Kav La'Oved Workers' Hotline and Hotline for Migrant Workers, *Immigration Administration or Expulsion Unit?* (Tel Aviv: 2003).

16. Willen, "'Illegality,' Mass Deportation and the Threat of Violent Arrest."

17. See, for instance Ruth Sinai, "NPOs Accuse Immigration Police of Brutality, Human Rights Violations," *Haaretz* [online], May 20, 2003. Accessed on December 12, 2006, www.haaretz.com.

18. Transnational migrant workers have replaced Palestinian workers in the labor sectors within which they predominated before the First Intifada, such as construction, agriculture, and restaurant work. Other sectors, such as elder care and housecleaning, were not previously occupied by Palestinian workers but rather expanded in the 1990s with the arrival of large cadres of migrants willing to work for below minimum wage.

19. See Michael Alexander, "Local Migrant Policies in a Guestworker Regime: The Case of Tel Aviv," in *Transnational Migration to Israel in Global Comparative Context*, ed. Sarah S. Willen (Lanham, MD: Lexington Books, forthcoming 2007); Adriana Kemp and Rebeca Raijman, "'Tel Aviv is Not Foreign to You': Urban Incorporation Policy on Labor Migrants in Israel," *International Migration Review* 38 (2004): 1, 26–51.

20. Mesila Aid and Information Center for the Foreign Community of Tel Aviv-Yafo, *Annual Report 2003* (Tel Aviv: 2004), 23.

21. Alexander, "Local Migrant Policies in a Guestworker Regime"; Zeev Rosenhek, "Migration Regimes, Intra-State Conflicts, and the Politics of Exclusion and Inclusion: Migrant Workers in the Israeli Welfare State," *Social Problems* 47 (2000): 1, 49–67.

22. Willen, "'No Person is Illegal?'"; Willen, "'Illegality,' Mass Deportation and the Threat of Violent Arrest Sarah S. Willen, "Citizens, Real Others, and Other Others: The Biopolitics of Otherness and the Deportation of Undocumented Migrant Workers from Tel Aviv, Israel," in *Deported: Removal and the Regulation of Human Mobility*, ed. Nicholas de Genova and Nathalie Peutz (forthcoming)."

23. Barbara Ehrenreich and Arlie Russell Hochschild, *Global Woman: Nannies, Maids, and Sex Workers in the New Economy* (New York: Metropolitan Books, 2003); Michele Ruth Gamburd, *The Kitchen Spoon's Handle: Transnationalism and Sri Lanka's Migrant Housemaids* (Ithaca, NY: Cornell University Press, 2000); E. Georges, "Gender, Class and Migration in the Dominican Republic: Women's Experiences in a Transnational Community," in *Towards a Transnational Perspective on Migration*, ed. N. Glick Schiller, L. Basch, and C. Blanc-Szanton (New York: New York Academy of Sciences Press, 1992); Parreñas, *Servants of Globalization*.

24. Raijman and Kemp, "Labor Migration, Managing the Ethno-National Conflict, and Client Politics in Israel," in *Transnational Migration to Israel in Global Comparative Context*, ed. Sarah S. Willen (Lanham, MD: Lexington, forthcoming 2007).

25. Ibid.

26. Cf. Willen, "Citizens, Real Others, and Other Others"; Didier Fassin, "The Biopolitics of Otherness: Undocumented Foreigners and Racial Discrimination in French Public Debate," *Anthropology Today* 17 (2001): 1, 3–7.

27. In fact, there is some evidence that transnational migrant communities in Tel Aviv have tended toward the right wing of the Israeli political spectrum (Nurit Wuhrgaft, "If Foreign Workers Voted, the Right would get a Boost," *Haaretz* [online], April 14, 2002. Accessed on December 12, 2006, www.haaretz.com). Factors contributing to such positions are varied but include Christian Zionist sentiment, fear of or antipathy toward Muslims on the basis of local conflicts in migrants' home

countries (including the Philippines and Nigeria), and admiration for Israel's strong government and, in particular, its strong military.

28. Zeev Rosenhek, "Challenging Exclusionary Migration Regimes: Labor Migration in Israel in Comparative Perspective," in *Transnational Migration to Israel in Global Comparative Context*, ed. Sarah S. Willen (Lanham, MD: Lexington Books, forthcoming 2007).

29. National police chief Shlomo Aharonishky, cited in Vered Levy-Barzilai, "Unpromised Land," *Haaretz* [online], June 5, 2003. Accessed on December 12, 2006, www.haaretz.com.

30. Ronen Shamir, "Without Borders? Notes on Globalization as a Mobility Regime," *Sociological Theory* 23 (2005): 2, 197–217.

31. Willen, "'Illegality,' Mass Deportation and the Threat of Violent Arrest."

32. Giorgio Agamben, *Homo Sacer: Sovereign Power and Bare Life*, trans. Daniel Heller-Roazen (Palo Alto, CA: Stanford University Press, 1998).

33. For more detailed consideration of this point see Willen, "Citizens, Real Others, and Other Others."

34. Adout, *Aggressively Passive*; Nadav Davidovitch and Dani Filc, "Rights, Citizenship and the National State: Migrant Worker Health Policies in Comparative Perspective," in *Transnational Migration to Israel in Global Comparative Perspective*, ed. Sarah S. Willen (Lanham, MD: Lexington Books, forthcoming 2007); Filc and Davidovitch, "Health Care as a National Right?"; Fried, "The Israeli Health Care System's Treatment of Migrant Workers"; Meltzer and Elkayam, "Medical Care for Undocumented Migrant Workers in Public Hospitals." For more on undocumented migrants and healthcare in Israel and, by comparison, in Western Europe, see Sarah S. Willen, "'Illegal' Migration as a New Global Health Challenge: Israeli Perspective and European Comparisons," (master's thesis, Emory University, 2006).

35. This Israeli policy differs starkly from the policy in Germany, for instance, where hospital personnel are bound by a "duty to denounce" undocumented patients to the immigration authorities (Castañeda, "Citizenship, Rights, and Ambiguity"; Davidovitch and Filc, "Rights, Citizenship and the National State").

36. The main exception to this rule was a newspaper series by journalist Einat Fishbein called "The New Tel Avivians," which appeared in the weekly Tel Aviv newspaper *Ha'Ir*.

37. Lukumu earned a degree in public policy in 1997 from Tel Aviv University before joining the staff of the Congolese Embassy.

38. Later in my field research, I learned that African women typically left Israel for Dublin if they were pregnant. Were they to give birth on Irish soil, their children would have been entitled to Irish—and European Union—citizenship under a policy that has since been revoked following a national referendum on the issue (Tormey. "Everyone with Eyes Can See the Problem"; see also the conclusion to this chapter).

39. The eventual source of tension related to the classic dilemma of critical activist anthropology. After attending staff meetings for over a year and doing my best to be little more than a "fly on the wall," at a certain point I chose to express my views on several procedural and administrative issues (as opposed to political or social issues). My comments were not well received by a prominent member of the organizational staff who, incidentally, has since left the organization.

40. Adout, *Aggressively Passive*; Fried, "The Israeli Health Care System's Treatment of Migrant Workers"; Alex Leventhal, Itzhak Berlovitch, and Daniel Shem-Tov, "Migrant Workers: Developments in the Approach of the Israeli Ministry of Health," [in Hebrew] *HaRefuah* 142 (2003): 632–35.

41. Given the highly infectious nature of TB and STDs and the dangers they pose to public health, treatment is universally available, at least in theory. It is not, however, universally accessible.

42. Leventhal at al., "Migrant Workers." See also Anat Rosenthal, "Battling for Survival, Battling for Moral Clarity: 'Illegality' and Illness in the Everyday Struggles of Undocumented HIV+ Women Migrant Workers in Tel Aviv," in "'Illegal' and 'Irregular' Migrants' Experiences of Law and State Power," ed. Sarah S. Willen, *International Migration*, special issue (forthcoming 2007).

43. According to this provisional arrangement, parents pay monthly premiums for child health services equivalent to the care Israeli children receive. Following an initial rush to register, however, only a small number of parents, mostly parents of children with chronic illnesses, have consistently maintained their children's coverage.

44. Adout, *Aggressively Passive*.

45. Little is known about migrants' health care utilization patterns beyond the Tel Aviv area, but it seems likely that most consult private doctors for high fees, visit emergency rooms in dire cases, or simply go without medical care.

46. Meltzer and Elkayam, "Medical Care for Undocumented Migrant Workers in Public Hospitals."

47. Important studies have argued that the Israeli health care system, although grounded in the principles of socialized medicine, is already multiply tiered with differential patterns of access and affordability for Jewish and Arab citizens, Ashkenazim and Mizrachim, and wealthier and poorer Israelis. See Nadav Davidovitch and Tali Margalit, "Public Health, Law, and Traumatic Collective Experience: The Case of Mass Ringworm Irridiations," in *Trauma and Memory: Reading, Healing, and Making Law*, ed. N. Davidovitch, M. Alberstein, and A. Sarat (Palo Alto, CA: Stanford University Press, forthcoming); Dani Filc, "Post-Fordism's Contradictory Trends: The Case of the Israeli Health Care System," *Journal of Social Policy* 33 (2004): 417–36; Nira Reiss, *The Health Care of the Arabs in Israel* (Boulder, CO: Westview Press, 1991). So, too, have Palestinians working in Israel for Israeli employers long been excluded from the system (with a handful of exceptions). From a broader political economy of health perspective, the exclusion of noncitizen migrant workers involves yet another axis of exclusion within an already stratified health care system rather than a new phenomenon signifying a simple two-tier system of access and affordability.

48. 403–40; original translation

49. See T. Braun and W. Würflinger, *Access to Medical Care for Undocumented Migrants in Germany* (Berlin: PICUM, 2001); PICUM, ed. *Book of Solidarity—Volume 1: Providing Assistance to Undocumented Migrants in Belgium, Germany, the Netherlands, and the UK*, (Antwerp: De Wrikker, 2002); PICUM, ed. *Book of Solidarity—Volume 2: Providing Assistance to Undocumented Migrants in France, Spain and Italy*, (Antwerp: De Wrikkler, 2003); Román Romero-Ortuño, "Access to Health Care for Illegal Immigrants in the EU: Should We Be Concerned?" *European Journal of Health Law* 11 (2004): 3, 245–72; as well as Willen, "Illegal Migration as a New Global Health Challenge."

50. This pattern is especially evident in the United States, but see Filc 2004 for an examination of increasing neoliberal pressures on the Israeli health care system. So, too, does it shape the distribution of health care resources on a global level; that is, between richer and poorer countries and world regions.

51. Adout, personal communication.

52. Palestinian women from the Occupied Territories, however, are explicitly excluded (Adout, personal communication).

53. Leventhal et al, "Migrant Workers."

54. Kahn, *Reproducing Jews*; Kanaaneh, *Birthing the Nation*, 23.

55. Kahn, *Reproducing Jews*, 3.

56. Ibid., 23.

57. Kahn, *Reproducing Jews*; Kanaaneh, *Birthing the Nation*; Nira Yuval-Davis, "The Jewish Collectivity" in *Women in the Middle East*, ed. M. Salman (London: Zed Books, 1987).

58. Kanaaneh, *Birthing the Nation*.

59. Ibid., 37.

60. Rosenhek, "Migration Regimes, Intra-State Conflicts, and the Politics of Exclusion and Inclusion"; Adout, personal communication.

61. Leventhal et al, "Migrant Workers."

62. MCH infant care is also available, at least in theory, in West Jerusalem (Leventhal et al, "Migrant Workers").

63. Alexander, "Local Migrant Policies"; Kemp and Raijman, "'Foreigners' in the Jewish State: The New Politics of Labor Migration to Israel," [in Hebrew] *Sotziologia Yisraelit* 3 (2000): 1, 79–110; Willen, "Perspectives on Transnational Labor Migration in Israel."

64. Marcia C. Inhorn, *Local Babies, Global Science: Gender, Religion and In Vitro Fertilization in Egypt* (New York: Routledge, 2003).

65. Willen, "Towards a Critical Phenomenology."

66. The irony of such assertions is clearly lost on these contemporary anti-immigrationists. Given the United States' complex immigration history as well as its long-term commitment to "melting pot" and then "salad bowl" approaches to multiculturalism, it is difficult to argue that the United States possesses any sort of homogeneous core identity that might now be in danger of disappearing.

67. Tormey, "Everyone with Eyes."

68. For more on this issue, see Willen, "Citizens, Real Others, and Other Others."

69. Willen, "Towards a Critical Phenomenology."

70. Agamben, *Homo Sacer*.

7

Masculinity as a Relational Mode

Palestinian Gender Ideologies and Working-Class Boundaries in an Ethnically Mixed Town

Daniel Monterescu

THE PROBLEM: DEFINING
THE BOUNDARIES OF MASCULINITY

"You want to know what Arab masculinity is?" Khaled, an old Palestinian friend of mine from Jaffa, said to me, "read the first 40 pages of *Bayn al-qas-rayn* [Palace Walk] by Naguib Mahfouz." The excerpt below describes the life of Amina, the mother of the family, and clarifies what Khaled meant (Mahfouz 1990, 4; emphasis added):

> It had occurred to her once, during the first year she lived with him, to venture a polite objection to his repeated nights out. His response had been to seize her by the ears and tell her peremptorily in a loud voice, "I'm a man. I'm the one who commands and forbids. I will not accept any criticism of my behavior. All I ask of you is to obey me. Don't force me to discipline you." She learned from this, and from the other lessons that followed, to adapt to everything, even living with the jinn, in order to escape the glare of his wrathful eye. It was her duty to obey him without reservation or condition. She yielded so wholeheartedly that she even disliked blaming him privately for his nights out. She became convinced that true manliness, tyranny, and staying out till after midnight were *common characteristics of a single entity*.

For Khaled, as for many Palestinian men in Jaffa, though by no means all, the definition of proper masculinity is constructed as a "single entity" that is premised on unchallenged patriarchal masculinity. Yet in the conflict-ual and fragmented social reality of Jaffa, masculine domination is constantly challenged by women seeking to undermine it. The intervention of state institutions and the erosive urban influence of Jaffa's mixed border-land also challenge Palestinian masculine domination.

Khaled's reference to a well-known text in Arab literature creates a parallel between the literary text and a social reality in Jaffa. His choice is intended originally to glorify and neatly define the authority of Arab masculinity. Notwithstanding Khaled's intention, further reading of the novel reveals an unexpected similarity between the real-life story of Palestinian men in Jaffa and the fictional account of Ahmad 'Abd al-Jawwad. It becomes even more complex than what Khaled intended: the book questions the simple notion of the all-powerful patriarch. The father, who at the beginning of the trilogy assumes the role of the undisputed ruler of all around him, is later revealed in all his fragility. Professor Sasson Somekh, a literature scholar and a friend of Mahfouz, writes, "Sooner or later we discover that the man's might is not infinite, he tries to lock the doors of his house against social changes, but without much success. He has a growing feeling that time has betrayed him, that time means decay and death. The powerful man whom we saw at the beginning becomes towards the end a pitiful creature stumbling towards his death . . . a king whose throne has been dragged from under him and his people scattered in all directions" (Somekh 1981, 377).

This parallel between the novel and social reality is further substantiated when we explore popular perceptions of time. As in Mahfouz's trilogy, many men in Jaffa, particularly those of the working class, feel betrayed and even outrun by time. They respond with sayings such as *al-dunya akhir zaman* [this is the end of world]. These phrases reflect both utter despair and resignation. They express the feelings of the men of Jaffa with regard to their social universe and their collective self-image.

"Time," it is often said, "runs too fast, just like the wind." The use of this eschatological image of the end of days is not fortuitous. In popular and canonical Islam, the signs that herald the coming of the Day of Judgment [Asharat al-Sa'a] are characterized by disruption of the world order. Somekh (37) argues, "Social time changes the styles and rhythms of life in 'Abd al-Jawwad's family circle and in society as a whole. The patriarchal family structure gives way—slowly and with a violent struggle—to a less rigid structure." Disrupted time here functions as a metaphor for men's difficulties in coping with rapid social changes.

The ideology of masculinity in Jaffa is deeply embedded in the local sociohistorical context. The ideology of masculinity described here is not just a vanishing "survival" of a "traditional" culture; it is largely an ongoing reaction by many working-class Palestinian men to their social predicament. In the context of a Jewish-Arab mixed town, this ideology constitutes a coping strategy that attempts to stabilize conflictual gender relations and consolidate them around a traditional and agreed-upon patriarchal "essence."

Understanding the cultural complexity of masculinity as a field of social relations and cultural meanings helps us understand the changing world of Palestinian men in Jaffa (Bourdieu 1990, 1997). While the literature on Mediterranean masculinities has often simplified masculinity within the constraints of the honor/shame complex (Gilmore 1990), I point to the internal conflict within this cultural system (Monterescu 2006). I analyze the Palestinian "crisis of masculinity" as a neopatriarchal outcome of a historically and sociologically specific cultural and political context as opposed to one about Palestinian "traditionalism" vs. Israeli "modernism"(Shokeid 1997, Sharabi 1988).

THE CHANGING PATRIARCHAL ORDER IN JAFFA: AN ETHNOGRAPHY OF MASCULINITY IN CRISIS

There are two opposing cultural trends in Jaffa that exist against a background of the changing structure of the Arab family and the status of men and women: the crumbling of the patriarchal systems of control and the desperate attempt to cling to a core of "tradition" and conservatism. Male actors, who are the subject of this study, are perceived in Jaffa as guardians of the normative moral system. They position themselves at the forefront of a cultural confrontation, which the tense political context only serves to aggravate.

Opposing Processes: the Loosening and Tightening of Patriarchal Order

As told by its men, the social history of Jaffa is predicated on the collapse of the values, norms, and practices that constituted the framework of the old social order in the pre-Nakba "days of the Arabs" [*Ayyam al-'Arab*]. The political, social, and cultural fragility of the Arab community in Jaffa (Monterescu 2006) have left the Jaffans more exposed to global, Western, and Jewish Israeli cultural intrusions. The presence of a Jewish majority in Jaffa and the growth of gentrified mixed neighborhoods generated a confrontation between lifestyles. It led to a weakening of the old patriarchal social order. This uneven social encounter combined with complex relations with state institutions pits Jewish and Palestinian cultural patterns against each other at all levels of social interaction. Jaffa has been strongly affected by the cultural presence of Tel Aviv as a self-defined modern, secular, and today globalizing city. Since 1948, a new reality has increasingly led to a change in styles of dress, models of parent-child relations, marital relations, patterns of recreation, and intergender relations. These changes have challenged existing norms and undermined the patriarchal authority of the Palestinian man.

Several opposing examples, drawn from my fieldwork, illustrate these processes:

September 16, 1998. Today I went to Sami's Ful and Falafel restaurant in Jerusalem Boulevard. I ate breakfast there and we talked. We got on to the subject of women and the difference between Jewish and Arab women in Jaffa (translated from Arabic):

> Today they are all the same . . . the world today has turned upside down, the man cleans, washes dishes, holds the children, and takes care of them. The influence comes from the Israeli culture [*al-hadara al-Isra'iliyye*]. The Arab women learn from the Jewish women, and even the law is on the women's side [*al-qanun li-saleh al-mara*]. In this country the woman rules the men [*Ha-dole khallat al-mara tuhkum al-'alam*]. If I curse her [*basibha*] she can complain to the police and certainly if I hit her. In the West Bank, when someone hits his wife she goes to her father for two days and then comes back home [*btihrad*], here she goes to the police.

At this point his wife's cousin, who helps him in the restaurant, joined in the conversation and said proudly:

> Once my husband cursed me and I put him in jail [*habasto*]. He cursed many times so I called the police. I telephoned, they came at once and said to him either you go into the Abu-Kbir jail for 48 hours or you pay bail and stay out of the house for three days. He called his friend, who paid the bail, and didn't come into the house for three days. And since then he speaks nicely to me and doesn't do anything wrong.

Sami turned to me and said, invoking a proverb usually used at the beginning of a marriage, when the hierarchy between the couple has not yet been established:

> There is a proverb that says 'hit the cat, the bride will be afraid' [*udrub el-bissa bitkhaf al-'arussa*] Today, the woman kills the cat and the man is afraid of her [*al-yom al-mara btidhbah al-bisse wa-zalame bikhaf minha*].

The second example is the story of many women in Jaffa who can be seen wearing very revealing clothes but are often exposed to constant manifestations of patriarchal domination, violence, and oppression. For instance, from July 1996 on, the Tel Aviv weekly *Ha'ir* published articles reporting on the case of J.K., wife of the principal of a local elementary school in Jaffa (see particularly January 24, 1997, January 30, 1998 and February 27, 1998). Parallel with the reign of violence that he maintained in the school, Saleh K. used to beat his wife, was unfaithful to her, and humiliated her in public. He did all of these acts while still enjoying great popularity among men in Jaffa. When I asked Kifah, manager of the car wash I used to visit frequently, what he thought of Saleh K., he said in an amused tone, "Clinton screws around, so why shouldn't Saleh?" (This occurred at the time of the scandal over Clinton's affair with Monica Lewinsky). He added, "Saleh is a good guy and a strong man, people like him in Jaffa." J.K. herself testified that she was the object of public condemnation in Jaffa and that half of the teachers in the school where she taught did not speak to her because she dared to make the case public.

An initial explanation of this case can be drawn from Miriam Mer'i's analysis (1989, see also Shokeid 1997):

> Palestinian men, the family breadwinners, were forced to turn to the Jewish labor market, and were thus exposed to a different lifestyle from what they had known hitherto. On the one hand they acquired 'modern' behaviors and skills, and on the other hand they saw the modern lifestyle as a threat to the only sure thing that was left to them. The Palestinian man's lack of security in the ability to support his family, his exposure to the alien culture and his encounters with Jewish women whose behavior was alien to him—all these threatened the national identity and status of the Palestinian man. He reacted by tightening his control of his wife and thus tied himself even more to tradition. The control of women became a measure by which Arab society's ability to preserve its uniqueness was judged.

This dual coping strategy is characteristic of the Jaffa context. It reflects the heart of the gender predicament of men in Jaffa: the fact that these men feel trapped between conflicting and unsatisfactory cultural options. The first story above is a story that could not have been heard twenty or thirty years ago.[1] The new pattern of relationships is the product of the intervention of the welfare state, which has undermined the structure of authority in the extended patriarchal family. Above all, the story teaches us about a perceived utopian gender perception, the social order that existed before "the world turned upside down" for men like Sami. It also gives us insight into a nostalgia for the dominant centrality of the imagined male identity. This perception of a stable gender hierarchy can no longer be sustained under contemporary conditions, not only because of intervention by state institutions, but also because of the cultural conflict between the Jewish majority and the Arab minority in an ethnically mixed town.

With its expressions of patriarchal violence, the second story can be interpreted as emblematic of the same problematic attitude of Palestinian men who feel that their symbolic and real authority has been taken from them by the state institutions and changing circumstances. These men are sometimes perceived as less "manly," even compared to, and in the eyes of, women. "The women in Jaffa," Sami's wife told me after the conversation with her husband, "are more manly than the men [*arjal min a-zlam*]—they work and support the family." She added scornfully, "The men are all either drug addicts or spend their time in cafes, gambling and playing games. Women can manage without men—men can't [without women]."

The Effect of Welfare State Institutions

The patriarchal order in Jaffa, which preserves and sanctifies the centrality of what we can term hegemonic masculinity (that is, a type of patriarchal practice that is accepted by the majority of Palestinian men and women, backed by enough coercion on the part of men to ensure those who disagree with it cannot challenge its core beliefs or practices), has become weaker over the years since 1948. At the same time, this patriarchal system has created new oppressive practices to sustain itself and survive. Such social and cultural processes have generated what many people in Jaffa perceive as egoistic individualism. "Today nothing shakes people out of their indifference. Siblings no longer help each other, wives don't obey their husbands [*kul wahad bhalo*]—it's everyone for himself."

State institutions, particularly Israeli law, are largely responsible for this change. Polygamy, which served as a powerful control mechanism over women, is forbidden by Israeli law. Muslim citizens of Israel are subject to this polygamy law, even though the shari'a courts have limited legal autonomy. Their limited autonomy was further restricted in the wake of the 2001 amendment which allows Muslim citizens to choose between religious and civil family courts. Harsh sentences imposed for "honor killing" have resulted in its practical disappearance in Jaffa. Changes in child allowance regulations, laws decreeing obligatory education, and housing assistance for widows and divorced women are all examples of the impact of the modern welfare state on the structure of power in the Arab family. Women have joined the labor market in increasingly large numbers. They accumulate cultural and economic capital, which then expands their authority in the family and relieves them of their traditional dependence on men. The following passage from my field log illustrates the effect of housing assistance for divorced women in Jaffa:

April 13, 1998: Today I met with Osama. We spoke about my progress with my work and I told him that I am examining the impact of the state institutions on men's status.
  Osama: The impact is enormous. Take, for example, divorced women. Usually women who get divorced go home to their father or to an older brother. In Jaffa there is a new phenomenon of divorced women renting apartments alone, and then because they have no money they receive housing assistance [*siyu'a diyur*]. Amal, my neighbor, got divorced and went to live with her mother, but they didn't get on well because she is too free according to her mother. So she went to live with her brother, at first with her eldest brother Khader, and there too she quarreled with him and his wife and moved to Hussein, the brother

who is less strict [*himesh*] and more forgiving, but there is no room for everyone in his place. She applied to National Security [*bituah leumi*] and now she receives monthly housing assistance. She moved into a rented apartment and she is now going out with another man with whom she had an '*urfi* wedding [conducted by a civil lawyer].

I asked: Why not an official wedding?

Osama: Her family is very angry. The whole story of the wedding and the contract is just to shut them up, so that her ex-husband will not take custody over the child. Nobody considers it a real wedding, but this is a new thing that Arab women have learned from the Jews.

On the link between the patriarchal family and the state institutions, Nadia Hilu, an experienced social worker in Jaffa, writes in her research on juvenile delinquency (1992):

> The encounter with Israeli society in Jaffa and with its modern economic patterns undermined the patriarchal concept of the family and of the father's sole responsibility; and thus family relations were also undermined, diminishing the father's authority to supervise the younger generation. The prevalent family model among Jaffa Arabs is that of a nuclear family in which the father's status is weakened. Due to the changes that have occurred in his environment and living conditions, he is no longer capable of fulfilling the traditional functions that he performed in the past in terms of mutual responsibility, financial care and social security. Today these functions are more and more filled and organized by institutional bodies.

The Effect of the Urban Context

Palestinians in Jaffa live in a dynamic urban space in which there is both convergence and separation of social worlds (Monterescu and Rabinovitz, 2007). This context is manifested externally in the daily contact between Jews and Arabs and internally between Christians and Muslims and between religious and nonreligious. All of these relations take place in the constant presence of crime, prostitution, and drugs. This urban context has led to a dual confrontation with the cultural alternative represented by its Jewish neighbors. Thus, cross-communal interactions are seen as the cause of social change. "The contact with Jewish society in Jaffa led to a change in the attitudes of the Palestinian men and more openness regarding the status of women, but to a certain extent it also caused the men to entrench themselves in their traditional beliefs out of fear that improvement of women's status might be a threat to their honor" (Hilu 1992, 112).

The erosive effect of the "next-door neighbor's customs," together with the impact of state institutions, stripped away the taken-for-granted guise of the Arab patriarchal social order. Moreover, a struggle is taking place between rival cultural forces within the Arab community (among others, Islamic and liberal-secular Arab forces). These forces contribute to the disintegration of what Alfred Schutz called the cultural "scheme of reference" (Schutz 1964, 97). For example, I witnessed an embarrassing situation in the home of a friend when his father asked his sister not to go out with her new fiancée. He was referring to the Arab tradition that the engaged couple must stay in the parents' home for their entertainment and must not go out without a chaperone. Despite his insistence, the father had great difficulty establishing grounds for his argument by finding a relevant reference group. When he explained his refusal by saying that *in Jaffa* it is not customary to behave that way, the daughter answered that many do. She cited names to prove it. When he expanded the reference group and told her that *Muslims* don't go out together before their wedding, the daughter mentioned the name of her cousin, a young man who is active in the Islamic Movement in Jaffa and goes out with his fiancé. Finally, as a last attempt the father resorted to the *village code* of the village from which he came (a village in the Galilee), but this code is not an effective rhetorical tool in Jaffa, as it is regarded as outdated, provincial, and irrelevant. For lack of choice and firm cultural ground to stand on, the father gave in and permitted the young couple to go out alone for the evening.

As these cases show, the incompatibility between the conservative norms and the changing reality creates constant frustrations and fear of the erosion of patriarchal power. Added to this incapability is the drug problem, a severe social problem in Jaffa that damages man's authority: "Drugs turn men into nonmen," said a former addict. He confessed that his wife had to undertake the "masculine" roles and even threw him out of the house when he harassed the children. All of these conditions, in addition to the weak social control and the absence of a social elite to lead the community, underlie a general sense of a "crisis of masculinity" (Sa'ar and Yahia-Younes 2006).

THE DIALECTIC OF PATRIARCHY: IS THERE A REAL IMPROVEMENT IN WOMEN'S STATUS?

Working-class Palestinian men in Jaffa facing this cultural crisis react in two ways: a desperate and sometimes violent attempt to preserve the patriarchal order combined with reinforcement of an ideology of mythic masculinity (as seen in Khaled's reference to Mahfouz). Sociologist Majid El-Haj insightfully remarks (1989): "It is enough to sit in a café and hear men boasting that they are the masters in their homes or others who emphasize that full understanding [*tafahum*] prevails between them and their wives, to understand that both of these are struggling to defend themselves against public opinion which complains that the woman "wears the trousers" [*btilbas al-bantalon*] in their homes."

By interpreting these societal changes and narratives of patriarchal crisis, can we deduce that there has been an improvement in the status of Arab women? On this seemingly simple question, women in Jaffa are divided. On the one hand, the argument is heard that "the status of women, particularly in the family, is much stronger than is reflected in the ideology" (Hilu 1992, 12). Data are put forward to point to processes of feminization and the growing power of women, especially in the spheres of work and education. On the other hand, many women with whom I talked expressed severe dissatisfaction with the gender situation in Jaffa. The common complaint is that the intergender power relations are too extreme. "In Jaffa there are either weak men and then there are prostitutes and adultery, or very tough and violent men." Educated women who adopt the discourse of modernization speak in terms of distorted modernity that breaks up the old order without being able to replace it with a new order that is really egalitarian. The local profits gained by the women are perceived as just one side of the "patriarchal bargain" (Kandiyoti 1991) and not as a real process of emancipation. In this light, it seems that the weakened status of men in Jaffa often has an adverse effect on the family but does not necessarily strengthen women's status. In the social field, which is not a zero sum game, both sides can lose.

THE MAP OF MASCULINITY [RUJULE]: SUBORDINATE IDENTITIES

Al-nisa' haba'il al-shaytan [women are the devil's traps] *Al-janna taht aqdam al-ummahat* [Paradise is under the feet of mothers]

Life in an Israeli reality, which involves many contacts with the state authorities and with the local Jewish "other," leads to intense cultural struggles for Arab Jaffans. One of the expressions of this for Palestinian men is constant preoccupation with sexual borders in general and with the boundaries of masculinity in particular. This preoccupation reflects two major dilemmas in the collective identity of men in Jaffa: the struggle of being a national-cultural minority in a Jewish state, and the struggle with a changing patriarchal order. A gendered expression of these dilemmas constitutes one of the main cultural struggles in the social world of Jaffa men: the question as to what is proper Arab/Palestinian masculinity.

From this discourse, a cultural map of masculinity emerges as an imaginary polygon with the proper category of masculinity at its center (see fig. 7.1). The cultural types (Simmel 1971) of the woman (Bourdieu 1990, 1997); the homosexual (Tapinc 1990); the Western or, specifically, Jewish man (Kressel 1996); and the failed man (Connell 1995) constitute its vertices. The vertices

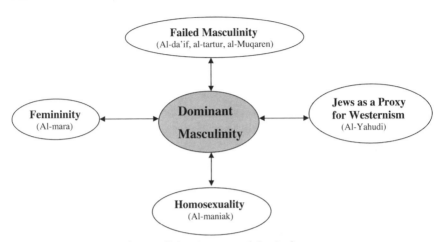

Figure 7.1. The Map of Masculinity. Courtesy of the Author.

of the polygon serve as symbolic referential axes, from and to which one measures the appropriate cultural distance.

This polygon represents the range of gender identities in Jaffa and the social and symbolic relations that constitute the category of proper hegemonic masculinity vis-à-vis subordinate categories (Connell 1996). This layout defines a field of power that places masculinity at its center as a relational unit, distinct from the other categories in form and content. According to this formulation, masculinity as a cultural language and a social order positions the threatening "other" in relation to itself. At the same time, it translates questions of collective identity into terms of body and sexuality. Alternative symbolic registers such as the language of femininity, languages of improper Arab masculinity, and the language of Western masculinity threaten the hegemonic code and are therefore excluded and marginalized.

The Woman [*Al-mara*]

"The most important thing in being an Arab man," said Khaled, "is that people should not think that you are like a woman." Indeed, the world of images of the men in Jaffa constitutes a cultural space with borders defined mainly in terms of negation: the symbolic negation of femininity. Conversely, femininity is the victim of this negative construction, which defines it as lacking "masculine" characteristics. As Brandes (1981) has argued, one of the enigmas of Mediterranean masculine discourse is that despite their social and economic advantage, men describe the relationship between the sexes in terms of perpetual conflict and thus feel threatened by women. Paradoxically, the masculine ideology reverses the actual state of affairs: women are portrayed as dangerous and powerful, while men are portrayed as victims who are forced to suffer the results of their caprices and desires.

The Moral Dichotomy Between the Sexes: Woman and the Devil

The first stage in analyzing the working-class male gender ideology in Jaffa entails an understanding of the basic moral dichotomy whereby men believe that they are inherently "better" than women. As Fatima Mernissi has famously shown, the sexuality of the Muslim Arab woman is perceived as active and thus dangerous to the man (Mernissi 1975, 11). In this context men often cite (mostly jokingly but sometimes also seriously) a saying attributed to the Prophet Muhammad, claiming that it is forbidden to leave a man and a woman alone in a room because "the third one present with them is always the tempting devil" [*thalathuhuma al-shaytan*]. The woman is presented as an extreme antithesis of the man's moral characteristics. She exploits her beauty and power over men; she is lustful, impulsive, and liable to seduce men who are forbidden to her. Just because the woman is expected to control her desires, she is perceived as man's Achilles' heel. "Her beauty is destructive to her and to me," I was told by an informant who had recently married a woman who is regarded as very beautiful: "You must not have a beautiful wife—that is a sickness [*marad*], it is the same as an ugly wife, only worse. With an ugly wife, you will not want to be at home. With a beautiful wife, you will not want to go out. You will be obsessed, you will go out and come back after fifteen minutes to see if she is still at home. A man needs an average woman."

In view of these perceptions, it is clear why, when cases of infidelity become public in Jaffa, men are forgiving toward the man, who is considered not able to resist the temptation. Women, on the other hand, are the targets of harsh criticism. This criticism often comes from other women, ranging from minor comments such as "Why didn't she restrain herself?" to calls to teach them a lesson: "Those whores should have acid poured over them; that would teach them!"[2] These fears constitute a discourse based on metaphors of war and rivalry between men and women, as well as war between men and their peers. "Your cousin can steal your wife—you have to be careful. Someone who has a piece of meat should keep it in the refrigerator, for fear that the dogs may come and eat it [*illi 'indo shaqfet lahmeh, uhuttha bi-tallaje, ahsan ma yiju al-klab yuntushuha*]!"

This gender discourse is replete with contradictions—tolerance of the weakness of men as an abstract category, and fear of falling victim to the weakness of concrete men. Men cope with this tension by casting wholesale blame on the woman even when they themselves are the seducers. In legal terminology, it may be said that although the man is sometimes perceived as *responsible* for the seduction, it is always the woman who is deemed *guilty* of it. One interlocutor boasted to me, describing how he had seduced the young wife of his childhood friend. He at once added contemptuously, "Trust me with everything, except with women [*aminni 'a-kul ishi, te'amin-nish 'a-bint*]." These working-class men picture women as a threat to their rational judgment. A woman is wily, intriguing, plotting to enslave the man and cheat him of his manhood, as in the proverb, "Women's tricks overcome men's tricks [*kayd al-nisa' ghalab kayd al-rijal*]." Moreover, because of her power and cunning, the stereotypical woman is attracted to the rich and powerful. A forty-five-year-old merchant told me the following story that describes woman's materialism. "Once there was a very rich man who was blind in one eye [*a'war*]. As a bachelor, he was very popular and in the end he married a beautiful woman. After a few years, he went through a hard time and lost all his money. When he became poor his wife came to him one day and asked him in surprise, 'What, are you half-blind?'"

In contrast to woman's impulsiveness and irrationality, which endanger the honor of the family, man is constructed as superior to woman but at the same time weaker and victim to her vices. It is precisely this construction of their weakness that justifies patriarchal domination in men's eyes, because the source of their weakness is women. "Woman," goes the popular saying, "has long hair and a small brain [*sha'r tawil wa-'aql zghir*]." Therefore man, who is more moderate, rational, and responsible, has to act without consulting her in order to subordinate her to the normative social rules and guard the family honor (Hassan 1991, Ghanem 1995).[3] This subordination is ultimately embodied in the role of the mother.

Woman as Mother: Paradise on Earth

"Your mother, then your mother, and only then your father," states the popular saying that expresses the centrality of the mother.[4] Upon becoming a mother, the single woman's inferior cultural status suddenly changes. The woman is transformed from the personification of potential evil into the paragon of *hanan*: humanity, tenderness, warmth, affection. In the words of the proverb, "Paradise is under the feet of mothers."[5] This dual image of woman reflects the divided image of the Palestinian man himself. He has an ambivalent relationship with his mother, with the domestic sphere identified with her, and with womanhood in general.

Arab culture's reduction of woman to overflowing sexuality appears in reverse in another reduction that identifies woman with her offspring: a male child who will ensure that the boundaries of the social order are preserved.

A woman who bears a son wins vast esteem and gratitude from the father. The father's status undergoes a substantial change, expressed in the change of his name-identity from his own first name to "father of" his firstborn son.[6] "I don't know what I would do if my mother hit my father," said an informant, describing the special status of the mother in Arab society, "but I would definitely protect my mother if she was beaten." As Bouhdiba (1985) has eloquently shown, the mythical link between the son and his mother, known in Islamic tradition as the "uterine link" [*silat al-rahm*], is a central component of the masculine ethos. This link also changes in the course of the life cycle, becoming a source of tension and conflicts between the growing youth and codes of masculinity. The mother's cultural status as an essential part of the category of femininity constitutes a split discourse with contradictions that reflect the ambivalent essence of masculinity itself.

The Failed Man

As Mosher has argued, masculinity and femininity are opposites as words. As theoretical concepts, however, they are not always logical opposites. Masculinity can be opposed not only to femininity but also to childishness, homosexuality, cowardice, weakness, and sentimentality (Mosher 1991). These opposites construct different modes of masculinity as inferior and delineate the borders of dominant and desired forms of masculinity (Connell 1996).

The group of "failed men" denotes men who have not adequately internalized the code of dominant masculinity; they have stumbled and revealed one of the stigmatized masculine characteristics. These are divided into three types: the weak man, the cuckold [*muqaren*], and the man who does not control his wife and daughters [*tartur*].

The Weak Man [al-da'if]

The following story demonstrates the status of a man whose socialization to dominant masculinity was inadequate because he publicly expressed emotions that are regarded as manifestations of weakness. Tha'ir, a young man who had been engaged to be married for about a year, was disappointed with his fiancé. She did not try hard enough, didn't dress up for him, and was not willing to go out with him, although her sister did go out with her fiancée. Following his threats to break off the engagement, they went to the Islamic shari'a court for arbitration. Instead of reaching an agreement in court, she publicly enumerated his faults and even laughed when the judge rebuked him for slouching in his seat during the hearing. Out of humiliation, Tha'ir burst out in front of those present, accused her of being cold to him and even wept tears of frustration. Later, he explained to me, "My nerves can't stand it, I always cry [*bathamalesh al-'asab, daiman badamme'*]." This public manifestation of weakness naturally worked against him both in his relations with his fiancé and with her family. In a telephone conversation with her afterwards, she said to him, "You are not a man, you're like a woman. Someone who cries and weeps is not a man."

This story illustrates the rigidity of the masculine code and the woman's role in reproducing it. Tha'ir's fiancé, as the female victim of the patriarchal regime of cultural domination, has internalized the code and is not prepared to forgive any deviation from it.

The Cuckold [al-muqaren]

One of the most severe infringements of the code of masculinity is loss of control, the ultimate expression of which is the wife's infidelity (see Cutileiro 1971, 99; Brandes 1981; Mernissi 1976). A wife's infidelity threatens the good name of the whole family but the main injury is to the betrayed husband who has "grown horns" and has failed to restrain his wife's sexuality. He has failed to restrict her desires to their bedroom. The stigma of the cuckold is attached only to men who are aware of their wife's infidelity and continue to live with her. Public opinion, therefore, is the decisive factor, as a social worker in Jaffa said to me:

> Most cases of infidelity that are not made public and remain within the family end with reconciliation. Violence, divorce, or murder only occur when all of Jaffa knows about it and then the man has no choice. For example, last month there was a case when someone's mother discovered that his wife was cheating on him with his brother. On the spot he and her brothers threatened to kill her and she went to the battered women's shelter. But after I spoke to them, they took her back and they went on living together on condition that they would wipe the slate clean and if there was another incident they would get divorced.

The sense of social anomie in Jaffa, accompanied by an alarmed discourse on the increasing number of cases of infidelity, attests to men's anxiety. Many men call for severe punishment for unfaithful wives, like "throwing acid in their faces" in order to teach them a lesson. The code of feminine purity and modesty is constantly deteriorating in the view of working-class men in Jaffa hence their growing fear of being stigmatized as cuckolds.

Male infidelity, on the other hand, meets with understanding and even admiration. According to Hussam, who married recently:

> A man who has a lot of women is regarded—even by Arab women in Jaffa—as a real man, not stupid or a fool. A girl doesn't respect a man who goes out with

her for the first time because he has no experience. It seems strange but that's the way it is; the man is just the opposite—only if it's not for marriage can she fool around. If a woman is unfaithful to her husband and people know about it and he doesn't divorce her, then she despises him and society despises him. The image of the unfaithful husband is not damaged, on the contrary, everyone admires him—he's a man!

The Tartur

If the daughter errs, according to masculine ideology, the family and the man at its head will pay a heavier social price than she does.[7] It is therefore the men's duty to control their wives and daughters. Failure to control the woman is given the epithet *tartara*. The failed man in this case is the *tartur*. A female informant, a clerk in the civil service, explicated:

> A tartur is a mother's boy, but that's not all. There used to be a punishment imposed by the market inspector on a vendor who was caught cheating. They would humiliate him with a punishment called *tajris*—making him wear a high hat like a clown's cap, called a tartur, dressing him in rags and bells and sending him round the market for everybody to laugh at him.
>
> A *tartur* has no opinion of his own, and the woman rules and does whatever she wants: "Go! Go! Go! Come! Come! Come! [*ruh! ruh! ruh! Ta'! Ta'! Ta'!*]."
> A *tartur* is a weak man who wears the apron at home [*bilbas al-tannura*].

The fear of women taking control is manifested in the masculine discourse in the myriad epithets labeling women who are liable to turn the man into a tartur. The range of epithets goes from *qawiyye*; strong, assertive, sharp and appreciated for her quick wits [*pilpel*]; through a girl who behaves like a man [*zay hassan sabi*]; to the *mdakara* or the *mara mzambara*—the virile, impertinent woman of whom they say in popular masculine discourse that "*zamburha atwal min lsanha*"—her clitoris is longer than her tongue, so much that it seems like a penis.[8]

The Homosexual [al-maniak]

One of the primary ways male sexuality is expressed in the Middle East is through a cultural configuration of sex, power, and the binary between being sexually active and passive. This configuration maps the body and defines some organs as active and masculine and others as passive and feminine. It attributes to bodies and organs honor/shame and status/stigma, respectively. This process of defining male power through the body helps to establish the alternatives to masculinity as inferior. According to the language of images of the men in Jaffa, a strong man is a man "with balls." ("That judge," said a petty criminal I know, "has balls this big [*bedato hal-qade*].") A weak man who spends too much time at home with the women is a *mekasses*, that is, has a female sexual organ.

The main metaphoric pivot defining the power structure in masculine sexual discourse revolves around the symbol of the anus. This discourse marks the Arab homosexual, the *maniak*, as the ultimate expression of the "failed man" (see Bowman 1996). As opposed to the "man," who is active in the public sphere and in sexual activity, the maniak is passive in anal sex (*"bokol ftizo* [eats in his ass]"), and is perceived as a stigmatic hybrid between a man and a woman (Lancaster 1988; Tapinc 1990). Hence the popular saying: "Fuck a stone but don't fuck a man [*Nik hajar wala tnik dakar*]."

The case of Sami-Samantha, a Jaffan homosexual who chose not to surrender to the heterosexual order and left Jaffa for Tel Aviv and later Berlin, is a good example of how the maniak functions within the larger Jaffan society in surprising ways (cf. Monterescu 1998).

> Samantha is the trade name of Sami, a declared homosexual from Jaffa, who decided to leave town and take up a career as a drag queen in Tel Aviv. One typical response to Samantha is given by 'Adel, a garage worker aged 30, who explains that, "there can be no worse disaster for an Arab family than to discover that their son is a homosexual. They think that the chain has been broken. It is broken because he will not have children. It's a disaster. . . . Even Muslim Sheiks will tell [the man's] father that they don't want this creature—*it's not a person, it's a UFO*. Men are afraid even to exchange a word with him and certainly not to touch him."

Interestingly, Sami himself paints a less harsh picture. He explains:

> Although there is a taboo on this subject in Arab society, I have not encountered so many problems. But I am an exceptional case. Perhaps because I grew up in Jaffa, which is more modern and open to the west. . . . Arab society, which is mainly Muslim, is very conservative, and there is total prohibition of this subject in Islam. It is not accepted at all. . . . Today I am cut off from the Arab community, I don't live in such a closed society, first of all because I am part of Tel Aviv, my life is in Tel Aviv. I come from Jaffa but my family has not ostracized me. It was still very hard for them to accept it, but they somehow came to terms with the fact that I am their son and there is no need to talk about it any more.

At first glance, the motifs that emerge from these testimonies—dehumanization ("it's not a person, it's a UFO"), disgust, ostracism, power, and hierarchy—call for the reading of the maniak as the ultimate social "other." This interpretation perceives the homosexual as a "disturbance" to the social order (Gluzman 1998), similar to what anthropologist Mary Douglas calls a "contaminating person" (Douglas 1969, 113): "A contaminating person is always wrong. He has developed an aberrant condition or crossed some line he shouldn't have crossed, and this crossing creates danger for someone." The "failed man" and above all the maniak cross the border between masculinity and femininity, between inside and outside, between permitted and forbidden in a way that is perceived by their environment as violation of a taboo. This crossing deprives the maniak of his humanity, and in the end may force him to leave the collective.

In my opinion, closer scrutiny (particularly of Salim's evidence) presents a completely different picture of the place and status of homosexuality in Arab society. The maniak maintains close interaction with the dominant masculinity category and in fact forms a vital link in the gender chain and the map of masculinity in Jaffa. The honor of the macho male [*rijjal*] and the stigma of the maniak are two sides of the same cultural coin. The rijjal and the maniak are both necessary for the dynamic definition of each other. If the category of maniak did not exist, it would have to be invented.

The maniak, therefore, is also defined by his *participation* in the active sexual framework of "proper" men. In contrast, the Western homosexual is merely defined by his *exclusion* from the framework of sexual practices of heterosexual men. In the Arab gender system, the main distinction is between active masculine "giving" and passive feminine "receiving." Maniaks are thus feminine men who are used by other men. The maniak's passive surrender to the sexual desires of other men defines his status and stigmatizes him. Somebody using a maniak thereby acquires a status of cultural maleness. When someone serves as a maniak he wastes his masculinity (the same logic of connected vessels was observed in the Nicaragua by Lancaster 1988).

Jewish Men as Western Others

Arab masculinity delineates collective boundaries and positions the Western "foreigner" in relation to it. This cultural mapping is done by translating questions of collective identity into terms of the body and sexuality and by linking sexual discourse with political-national discourse. This process is intensified by the semicolonial, intercultural "contact zone" (Bowman 1996; Gluzman 1998; Pratt 1999) in Jaffa.

These hierarchies are expressed in many cases in terms of masculinity. The Israeli context that brings together dominated Palestinians and dominating Jews reveals a counterexample. In the Palestinian discourse, whether in the Occupied Territories (the West Bank and Gaza) or in Israel, Arab superiority over the Western is emphasized precisely by defining the cultural "coming toward Jews" as becoming female and a betrayal of one's heritage (Kressel 1996, 64).

In the sphere of gender discourse, the stereotype of the Western person, and the Jew as a special case of this, represents an inversion of the ideal gender roles in the family. This person does not control his wife and tolerates exaggerated manifestations of permissiveness. He is therefore often derisively labeled as a tartur. According to this stereotype, the Jewish man reveals cowardice in the public sphere, as well as lack of assertiveness, resolution, and other characteristics valued as vital masculine traits (see Peteet 1994).

The combination of overpermissiveness and lack of male domination is a leitmotif in Jaffa men's remarks about their Jewish neighbors. The common accusation: "The Arabs started dressing worse than the Jews [*Al-'arab saru yilbasu azrat min al-yahud*]," shows how the Jews are perceived as markers of alterity and feminization. This perception emphasizes the potency of the Palestinian who is de facto in a structural situation of financial, political, and cultural impotence. The heroic narrative of Arab masculinity is an expression of resistance (Scott 1990) that symbolically humiliates Jewish masculinity and challenges the state institutions that represent it (particularly the police and the prison service). It does so by constituting Arab masculinity as hypermasculinity.

As in other patterns of stereotyping in Jaffa, sexual labeling is not free of contradictions. The contempt for the masculinity of the Jew stops when it comes to IDF: "To the Arabs," a young student told me, "all the Jews are like women until they go into the army. They become more like men, they build themselves in the army. We miss out on that. There, you are committed to something serious, not just weapons, but also responsibility and strength." Paradoxically it appears that the aggressive masculinity of the Palestinian citizens of Israel relates precisely to the images of Israeli military masculinity. It stems from the structural similarity between Arab masculinity and military combat masculinity (compare Si'on 1997). The two types of masculinity share many characteristics: aggressiveness, a rigid hierarchy, objectification of the woman, fear of her infidelity, phobia about homosexuality, homoerotic physicality, and so on.

CONCLUSION: SITUATIONAL MASCULINITY AS A RELATIONAL FORCE FIELD

Stories from the cultural world of working-class men in Jaffa help us understand the cultural mechanism that orders this world. These stories sketch out a cognitive-social map that classifies objects of existence according to the constitutive categories of the gender culture. The set of stories places the category of dominant masculinity in the center, between four loci of power: the woman, the failed man, the homosexual, and the Western man. The vectors that mediate between the categories are two-directional: masculinity constitutes every antithesis but is also constituted by it and by the actual act of constituting. The product of these vectors is the category of masculinity. Masculinity is cultural idiom that is not "present" in any concrete place but is constructed dialectically out of its expressions in discourse and in praxis. The map of masculinity presents an interaction between seemingly static categorical borders that are actually in flux.

Despite its oppressive character, masculinity [*rujula*] in Jaffa is not an ideology in the Marxist sense of the word. It is not merely a system of false ideas and mystification of economic-political exploitation. It is above all a cultural power that organizes relations between the sexes. *Rujula* is a political economy of the body in which the male body is measured and evaluated through social actions in relation to other men and women.

The Jaffa cultural scene presents two opposing trends with regard to hegemonic masculinity. On the one hand, a centripetal force forms an ordered ideology and an "authentic" and essentialist masculine identity. On the other hand, a centrifugal force cracks the appearance of homogenous masculinity. Men's occupation with the concept of masculinity is an infra-political response (Scott 1990) to macro-political marginality. In this sense, masculinity permits men to tell an "authentic" and "Arab" metanarrative about themselves as a way of coping with the reality of political and social inferiority. Constructing a rigid ideology of masculinity is a way in which men in Jaffa can find identity and meaning as a compensation for their humiliating political predicament. At the same time, there exists a reverse trend of breaking that notion of masculinity. Such contradictions constitute masculinity as a paradoxical, situational, and conflictual set of practices and meanings. Masculinity in this context is defined primarily at and through the borders of Jewish and Palestinian Arab identities. In the Jewish-Arab mixed town of Jaffa, itself a laboratory for the constitution of social boundaries, masculinity serves as a boundary-setting mechanism that separates, mediates, and relates between self and other, individual and collective; namely, between different types of men and women and between Arabs and Jews.

NOTES

1. This hypothesis was confirmed by two longtime social workers whom I interviewed.

2. When I asked why women are expected to restrain themselves while the men's weakness is greeted with tolerance, my informant told me, "man is man, that's his nature. The woman has to restrain herself because she is meant to be a mother and take care of the children—that's what nature prepared her for. She has to be more careful and if she slips she will pay for it."

3. The saying goes: "A real man is one who never takes advice from a woman [*al-rajul ibn al-rajul illi 'omro ma yishawer mara*]."

4. Like many of the quotes above, this saying draws on a *hadith*, but it is commonly heard in folk culture. It is often followed by the complementary saying that preceding the mother is your wife "who lies under you" [*illi btunghuj tahtak*]."

5. The sanctified image of the mother is in total contrast to the demonic image of woman in contexts in which she does not function as a mother. This perception finds many expressions in Palestinian folklore in Jaffa; for instance, in the proverb: "If not for their evil tongues, their feet would reach paradise [*lola lisanathon sabaqat qdamathon*]."

6. It is important to note that despite the importance of the birth of sons in patrilineal families, the situation in Jaffa is very different from that of Arab villages in Israel as described, e.g., in Hassan (1991). The changing structure of the nuclear family in the city is beyond the scope of this paper.

7. As in the proverb: "The man said, you are looking for trouble, woman. She answered him, it will fall on your head, man [*jatak dahya ya mara. Qalat: 'ala rasak ya rajul*]." In other words, the woman's troubles fall on her husband in the end. This fate was dramatically rendered in the recent Palestinian film *'Atash* (2005), which tells the story of a patriarchal tragic figure who exiled himself, along with his family, out of his native village due to a certain indecent incident involving his teenage daughter.

8. On women who breach the borders of the feminine role, see the study by Ghanem (1995), who analyzes the cultural position of female Palestinian political prisoners who are perceived as masculine [*mustarjalat*]. After their release, they are the object of admiration, but also of alienation and distance, clearly demonstrated by the difficulty in finding suitable matches for marriage.

REFERENCES

Bourdieu, P. 1990. "La Domination Masculine," *Actes de la Recherche en Sciences Sociales* 84: 4–31.

———. 1997. "Masculine Domination Revisited." *Berkeley Journal of Sociology* 189–203.

Bowman, G. 1996. "Passion, Power, and Politics in a Palestinian Tourist Market." In *The Tourist Image: Myths and Myth-Making*, ed. T. Selwin. London: John Wiley and Sons.

Brandes, S. 1981. "Like Wounded Stags: Male Sexual Ideology in an Andalusian Town." In *Sexual Meanings*, ed. S. Ortner and H. Whitehead. New York: Cambridge University Press.

Connell, R. 1996. "New Dimensions in Gender Theory, Masculinity Research, and Gender Politics." *Ethnos* 61 (3–4): 157–76

Cutileiro, J. 1971. *A Portugese Rural Society.* Oxford: Clarendon.

Douglas, M. 1969. *Purity and Danger: An Analysis of the Concepts of Pollution and Taboo.* London: Routledge and Kegan Paul.

El-Haj, M. 1989. "Changes in the Texture." *Politics* 21: 14–20.

Ghanem, H. 1995. "Female Political Prisoners Between Two Worlds." Master's thesis, The Hebrew University.

Gilmore, D. 1990. *Manhood in the Making: Cultural Concepts of Masculinity.* New Haven, CT: Yale University Press.

Gluzman, M. 1998. "The Body as Text, Masculinity as Language: The Language of the Body in 'The Book of Internal Grammar.'" In *Literature and Society at the 20th Century*, ed. Y. Schwartz and Y. Bar-El.

Hassan, M. 1991. "Growing Up Female and Palestinian in Israel." In *Calling the Equality A Bluff: Women in Israel*, ed. B. Swirski and M. Safir. New York: Pergamon Press.

Hilu, N. 1992. "The Effect of the Environment, the Family and Friends on Youth Delinquency in Jaffa." Master's thesis, Tel Aviv University.

Kandiyoti, D. 1991. "Islam and Patriarchy: a Comparative Perspective." In *Women in Middle Eastern History*, ed. N. R. Keddie and B. Baron. New Haven, CT: Yale University Press.

Kressel, G. 1996. "Mentality, Intelligence, and Morality." *Theory and Criticism* 8: 47–72.

Connell, B. 1995. *Masculinities.* Cambridge: Polity Press.

Lancaster, R. 1988. "Subject of Honor, Object of Shame: The Construction of Male Homosexuality and Stigma in Nicaragua." *Ethnology* 27 (2): 111–25.

Mahfouz, N. 1990. *Palace Walk* [Bayn al-Qasrayn]. New York: Anchor Books.

Mer'i, M. 1989. "The New Class." *Politics* 21: 22–34.

Mernissi, F. 1975. *Beyond the Veil: Male-Female Dynamics in a Modern Muslim Society.* Cambridge, MA: Schenkman.

Monterescu, D. 2006. "Stranger Masculinities: Gender and Politics in a Palestinian-Israeli 'Third Place.'" In *Islamic Masculinities*, ed. L. Ouzgane. London: Zed Books.

Monterescu, D. and D. Rabinovitz. 2007. *Mixed Towns, Trapped Communities: Historical Narratives, Spatial Dynamics, Gender Relations and Cultural Encounters in Palestinian-Israeli Towns.* London: Ashgate Publishing.

Mosher, D. L. 1991. "Macho Men, Machismo, and Sexuality." *Annual Review of Sex Research* 2: 199–247.

Peteet, J. 1994. "Male Gender and Rituals of Resistance in the Palestinian Intifada: A Cultural Politics of Violence." *American Ethnologist* 21 (3): 31–49.

Pratt, M. L. 1999. "Arts of the Contact Zone." In *Ways of Reading*, ed. D. Bartholomae and A. Petroksky. New York: Bedford/St. Martin's.

Sa'ar, A. and T. Yahia-Younis. 2006. *Masculinity in Crisis: The Case of the Israeli-Palestinians.* Paper presented at the Seventh Mediterranean Social and Political Research Meeting, Montecatini Terme and Florence.

Schneider, D. 1968. *American Kinship.* Chicago, IL: University of Chicago Press.

Schutz, A. 1964. "The Stranger: An Essay in Social Psychology." In *Collected Papers: Vol. II.* The Hague: Martinus Nijhoff.

Scott, J. 1990. *Domination and the Arts of Resistance.* New Haven, CT: Yale University Press.

Sharabi, H. 1988. *Neopatriarchy: A Theory of Distorted Change in Arab Society.* New York: Oxford University Press.

Shokeid, M. 1997. "Ethnic Identity and the Status of Arab Women in an Israeli Town." In *The Intercultural Experience*, ed. M. Shokeid and S. Deshen. Tel Aviv: Shoken Press.

Simmel, G. 1971. *On Individuality and Social Forms*, ed. D. Levine. Chicago: The University of Chicago Press.

Si'on, L. 1997. *Images of Masculinity Among Combat Soldiers: Infantry Service as a Rite of Passage from Adolescence to Adulthood*. The Shein Center for Studies in the Social Sciences. Jerusalem: The Hebrew University.

Somekh, S. 1982. "Introduction." In *Bayit be-Qahir* [Bayn al-Qasrayn] by N. Mahfouz. Tel Aviv: Hapo'alim Press.

Tapinc, H. 1995. "Masculinity, Femininity and Turkish Male Homosexuality." In *Modern Homosexualities*, ed. E. Plummer. London: Routledge.

8

From Water Abundance to Water Scarcity (1936–1959)

A "Fluid" History of Jewish Subjectivity in Historic Palestine and Israel

Samer Alatout

INTRODUCTION: WATER ABUNDANCE, SCARCITY, AND JEWISH SUBJECTIVITY

Since the early 1950s, water resources in Israel have been continually described as scarce, less than 1,850 million cubic meters per year (mcmy). Indeed this number is frighteningly low, to the point that different Israeli leaderships since the early years of the state have been willing to go to war over water. Witness, for example, the military skirmishes between Israel and Syria during the 1950s and up to the mid 1960s. Some even argue that these two countries fought the war of 1967 largely, if not exclusively, over the water resources of the Jordan River.[1]

Is this narrative accurate? Has water been so scarce in Israel since the state's inception? Was it scarce before then, as the story goes? "[Historic] Palestine always had a water scarcity," Mordechi Virschubski, the legal advisor of the Water Commission of Israel from 1954, told me in an interview in 1997. Virschubski is the man credited with passing the water law through parliamentary hurdles by 1959.[2] Is it true that "everyone knew that water in Palestine was scarce," as another influential figure, Aaron Wiener, the director general of Tahal Water Company of Israel between 1953 and 1977, also told me in a different interview (Aaron Wiener, interview, August 25, 1997)?

Upon further investigation, however, the assumption that an absolute consensus over water scarcity has existed since time immemorial does not hold true. In fact, it was only towards the mid 1950s, when a variety of factors collided, that water scarcity became the dominant view we witness today. These factors included the establishment of Tahal in 1952; the resignation of Simcha Blass, its first director general and the leading Zionist water

199

expert before the state, in 1953; and the passage of the water law between 1955 and 1959. I was surprised to discover that before 1953, especially before the establishment of the state in 1948, there was an equally dominant view among Zionist water experts that water in historic Palestine was, in fact, abundant. Experts estimated water sources to be at a level more than 3,000 and approaching 4,000 mcmy (Lowdermilk 1944; Nachum Gross, interview, September 8, 1997; Wiener, interview, August 26, 1998). Zionist water and political experts struggled long and hard against British estimates of the water potential of Palestine, which reached about 1,500 mcmy. They claimed that these estimates were "meager" and "politically motivated" (Great Britain 1946; Wiener, interview, August 25, 1997).

Thus the historical question can be raised: what created this shift from a perception of water abundance to one of scarcity? How did that shift occur and solidify in a water law within a decade, 1948–1959, and what were the reasons behind that shift?

Surprisingly, the great majority of water experts in Israel, even those who worked in the water apparatus since the late 1950s, had no recollection of the struggles between advocates of abundance and advocates of scarcity.[3] The rhetoric of scarcity, in other words, became so powerful a perception that it erased the notion of abundance from memory. Even those few experts who remembered the dominant belief in abundance were, for the most part, dismissive of it (scientifically unsound, politically motivated, etc.) (Meir Ben Meir, interview, August 14, 1997; Hillel Shuval, interview, July 30 1997). Only two experts, Aaron Wiener and Menachem Kantor (the water commissioner of Israel between 1959 and 1977), were aware of the serious struggles in early statehood over the issue of water potential of Israel (Wiener, interview, August 25, 1997; Menachem Kantor, interview, August 9, 1997).

The explanation for the shift from water abundance to scarcity often relies on what historians of science call an "internalist" explanation of scientific knowledge and practice. In this view, scientific knowledge has no relation to the political and social worlds outside of it. Changes in scientific knowledge result from the scientific logic itself, following solely from scientific methods, rules of evidence, and progress in techniques.

This vision of science (and engineering for that matter) came under immense scrutiny from the 1970s onward, but especially during the 1990s.[4] Such scrutiny came under the influence of what eventually became known in the early 1990s as science and technology studies. Science and technology studies is an interdisciplinary approach to scientific practice and to the production of knowledge. The field benefited from a number of disciplinary studies of science that included sociology, politics, anthropology, history, and philosophy of science and technology. The dominant view of this field, despite differences of methods and conclusions, is that science and scientific practice are not isolated phenomena, that they are connected in particular to the ways we live and organize our political and social lives (Alatout 2006; Jasanoff 1996 and 2004; Latour 1993).

The implications for the debate about water scarcity are great. From this perspective, what we take as a scientific "fact" cannot be seen as an unfiltered representation of nature. Fact can be, and often is, as much a statement about politics as it is about nature. From a science and technology studies perspective, issues of scarcity, abundance, and other environmental categories are more complex than what meets the eye. Their genealogy, their historical origin, and their construction have to do with social, political, and cultural factors as much as with scientific disciplines, their rules of methods, and their conceptions of evidence.

This chapter is greatly informed by the approach of science and technology studies. It starts with the assumption that the world and the way we organize ourselves in it are coconstitutive (Jasanoff 1996; Latour 1993). I argue that the shift from a notion of abundance to one of scarcity in the Israeli context was a sign of another shift that was being promoted by water research and practice: a shift in the conception of Jewish identity in historic Israel-Palestine from the Jew as settler to the Jew as a citizen of the modern state. This crossover of identity borders proved crucial in its impact upon scientific research on water.

The story of water knowledge and institutions in Israel provides a clear example of the struggles in the beginning years of the state over the boundaries of the state, its limits vis-à-vis civil society, and its role in the making of Jewish identity. This chapter specifically explores the links between shifts in knowledge about water resources, their management apparatus, and shifts about the concept of Jewish subjectivity.

Serving as a background to all these shifts—indeed, in some ways constituting their basic reference—was the negation of the Palestinians as a national community with political, economic, social, and cultural rights to Palestine's water resources. The discursive erasure of Palestinians in Zionist and Israeli water policy is similar to the discursive erasure of Palestinians that was a prominent feature of architectural, town planning, and other developmentalist discourses explored by Abowd and LeVine in other chapters of this volume.

IMPORTANT NOTES ON
HISTORIOGRAPHY, DATA, AND ERASURE

When doing research on water politics since the beginning of the British Mandate period of Palestine (1918–1947), two problems become apparent that need to be addressed from the start: the absence of Palestinians from direct involvement in water politics and the lack of Palestinian sources that explore these issues. Regarding the first problem, Palestinians are predominantly absent from the direct involvement in water politics between 1918 and 1948. They are briefly active actors in resistance to the expropriation of land for Israeli water projects during the 1950s. Their general absence in no way deflects from their significance for what was occurring before and after the establishment of the Israeli state. To be sure, erasure does not mean the absolute absence of those defined as "other" but rather their constant presence on the margins and the sidelines. In other words, we must see erasure as an active process rather than a state of being; it points to the exercise of power at the level of the body and of the population (Foucault 1979). It also points to power's ability to shape perceptions of populations at large (Lowdermilk 1944; cf. LeVine 1995, 2005).[5]

Since 1967, when Israel gained the West Bank and the Gaza Strip as a result of war, it has been much harder to erase Palestinians from water discourses. They have been engaged directly with the Israeli production of knowledge about water resources and very attentive to documenting that knowledge as their legal and human rights are entangled in those resources.[6] Such a task, however, has been hampered by the lack of Palestinian archival records. The efforts on the part of Bier Zeit University and other institutions in Palestine to collect and maintain as many of those records as possible have been countered by continuing Israeli attacks. Sometimes these attacks include the ransacking of Palestinian institutional archives in the West Bank, Gaza, and Lebanon.[7]

Water's importance as a written historical record linked to questions of identity did not acquire importance for the Palestinians until after the war of 1948. Before then, water seems to have been a local concern for the Palestinian community. Issues of water only acquired nationalist dimensions amongst the Palestinians after the mid 1930s, when they did for the Zionist movement.

THE POLITICS OF ABUNDANCE
AND DECENTRALIZATION (1918–1948)

Technicizing (Depoliticizing) Jewish Immigration

After the British occupation of Palestine solidified itself in 1918 and Palestine's borders were opened to Jewish immigration, a few small Palestinian revolts took place in 1920 with basic demands of political representation, the halting of Jewish immigration, and the building of Palestinian institutions of governance. The 1922 Churchill White Paper linked the annual level of Jewish immigration to the technical category of the "economic capacity" of Palestine. This category came to be known as the "absorptive capacity of Palestine." In such fashion, Churchill made a double move: on the one hand, he insisted that the Jews were in Palestine "out of right not of sufferance," yet he kept immigration decisions under British control, subject to British rather than Zionist politics. The absorptive capacity of Palestine became a yearly technical measure that estimated the number of Jewish immigrants that would be allowed into Palestine the subsequent year.

This technicization of Jewish immigration attempted to depoliticize the struggle over immigration—immigration from then on was displaced from the political field to the technical apparatus of Mandate power (cf. LeVine 1995). This shift succeeded to a certain degree, although not fully. On the Palestinian Arab side, utilizing the British category of absorptive capacity was a clear rejection of their participation as a political community and of their historic-moral basis for rejecting Jewish immigration en masse. This rejection had its roots in the 1917 Balfour Declaration's description of Palestine's non-Jewish inhabitants as having full "civil and religious," but not political, rights. This definition stood in sharp contrast to the recognition of the world Jewish community's political rights to the country.

In a way, the coinage of the technical category of the absorptive capacity of Palestine constituted a further attempt at erasing the Palestinians from effective politics by creating a shared, technical language over Jewish immigration that could be maneuvered between the British and the Zionists. This dynamic resulted in the disruption of Palestinian political aspirations. Participating in debates over the absorptive capacity of Palestine would then undermine Palestinians' essential demand: to be considered a political community that should develop and control institutions of government and that should decide on significant questions like immigration.

Between 1922 and the mid 1930s, the Zionist leadership's relationship with water was somewhat ambiguous. On the one hand, there was great benefit to be gained from modernizing and intensifying agriculture. Zionists often argued that the absorptive capacity of Palestine was a flexible category that could be extended endlessly by modernization (cf. LeVine 1995; Sufian 2007). This claim had the potential to open up Palestine to unlimited Jewish immigration.

On the other hand, in their struggles with Jewish plantation owners, modernization threatened the ideology of Zionist Labor leaders; modern, intensive agriculture would diminish the need for Jewish labor and would strengthen plantation owners' positions vis-à-vis wages, labor politics, and against Zionist labor more generally (Gross 1984).[8] These ambiguous relations between Labor Zionism and water resources played out until the mid 1930s. This focus left water without any particular national political meaning. In this sense, water was treated as a local or a regional concern in research and in practice—for a settlement, a group of settlements, or a mining

Table 8.1. Jewish Immigration During the First Half of the 1930s

Year	1931	1932	1933	1934	1935	1936
Number of immigrants	4,075	9,553	30,327	42,359	61,854	29,727

company (Muenzner 1947 and 1945; Picard 1931). There was no real sense in which water was a national concern.[9]

This emphasis changed after the large waves of Jewish immigration from Europe between 1933 and 1935 (see table 8.1) and with the beginning of the Great Palestinian Revolution of 1936. The Revolution of 1936 lasted intensely for six months and moderately until 1939. It was so intense that it required the largest deployment of British forces outside of India in the history of British colonialism. The British appointed the Peel Commission to investigate the reasons behind the Palestinian Revolution of 1936. A year later, the government published the Peel Commission Report. The Peel commissioners, with only one dissenting voice, blamed the revolt on what they deemed irreconcilable objectives of the British Mandate. These included the dual obligation of establishing a Jewish National Home in the country while simultaneously protecting the civil and religious rights of the Palestinian indigenous population. Moreover, the commissioners pointed to the inappropriate negation of the Palestinians as a political community in British Mandate politics (see Great Britain 1937a). The only fair conclusion, the Peel Commission argued, was to partition Palestine into two states, one Palestinian and another Jewish.

The relevance of the Peel Commission Report to the issue of water scarcity lies in the process of evidence collection. Through interviews, Zionist water and settlement experts revealed the importance of the report for understanding the shifting place of water for the Zionist project at the time. They claimed that water capacity was raised as a technical instrument for determining the absorptive capacity of Palestine and thus served as an important political instrument for deciding the level of Jewish immigration. The often contentious debates between the commissioners and Zionist political and water experts focused on whether the water potential of historic Palestine was one of abundance or scarcity.

For its part, British scientific culture was committed to a geological interpretation of the world. Empirical evidence was crucial. Geologists during this time were committed to field investigation and to testing rock formations in the field itself, especially since geophysics was a new discipline still struggling for recognition from geology (Bowler 1992; Picard 1936, 1940). From a British viewpoint, the empirical evidence was clear: water resources were very meager in Palestine (Great Britain 1946; Great Britain 1937b).

For the Zionists the story was different. Zionist geologists (most famously Leo Picard, who was a world-renowned professor of geology at the Hebrew University of Jerusalem) and geophysicists, despite their disagreement on methods, agreed on the existence of water abundance. Picard argued that as long as there were more spaces to explore for water, the water potential could be higher than experienced. He did not challenge British ways of knowing. Rather, he gave an example that was very relevant to those committed to empirical and geologic observations. While he insisted that his well sinking in the western Emek did not produce water, he thought there might be water in the eastern Emek as well as in some parts of the western Emek. When asked if he was being speculative, he answered, "Not so much in this country, because you see the country is exposed and you have sufficient exposure to find the lines of these faults" (Great Britain 1937b). He based his argument on the intriguing and unique geological structure of historic Palestine.

When evidence from geophysicists was ushered in by a number of Zionist experts, the reaction of the commissioners was extremely hostile. The antagonistic exchange between the Zionist experts and the Peel commissioners addressed the question of what constitutes a fact. Was a fact based on empirical and observable outcomes or theoretical outcomes? For instance, one of the commissioners, Sir Laurie Hammond, became incensed by answers to his inquiries about the possibility of intensive farming that would require elaborate irrigation systems. At one point in the investigation, Hammond flatly rejected Hexter's and Ruppin's approaches as speculative and deductive. In a response to Hexter's demand that the Mandate administration encourage immigration, Sir Hammond argued that the question of immigration heavily, and rightfully, depended on the availability of water for intensive farming. In a spirited exchange with Hexter, he repeatedly dismissed his interlocutor's arguments as nothing but unsubstantiated hopes.

> *Sir Laurie Hammond*: You want them, the government, to look at it with the eyes of *hope and faith* rather than to take the actual view as it is and say, "We know that at the present moment there is so much land that can be irrigated; from experiments made we believe there is a certain amount that can be irrigated, but beyond that we are not prepared to go?"
>
> *Hexter*: No, that is not what I say. Let me have the *hope and faith*, but let the Government help me to intensify the cultivation of this country, to the extent that there is irrigation and water. . . .
>
> *Sir Hammond*: And then you are prepared to accept, as a condition of your getting those extra lands, the actual presence of irrigation, that is, that it has actually been proved, not hoped for?
>
> *Hexter*: No (Great Britain, 1937b).

Extending irrigation for Hexter did not rely on proven empirical presence of water. It relied on its theoretical potential. If water were theoretically available, then Zionists would find a way of extracting it (cf. Penslar 1991).

Defining and restating the most legitimate opinion within Zionist colonization institutions, the manager of the Palestine Jewish Colonization Association, H. L. Wolfson offered the reasons for (some) Zionist suspicion of geological insistence on empirical knowledge:

> Take, for instance, the district of Upper and Lower Galilee. There are areas there where in the opinion of geologists the prospects of finding water would have been quite improbable and negative. In spite of that, owing to the general concept of colonization and our willingness to make expenditure *a fonds perdu*, we have gone on and made these drillings, and, curiously enough, found water. . . . We have found you cannot make any definite statement about the possibilities of not finding water. . . . We must therefore start out on our settlement plans with the assumption that, given sufficient capital which we are willing to invest, in most areas water can be found; there is no certainty of course. . . . We have found in our experience the geologists do not err very much in saying there is water and then find that there is not, but they have erred in the reverse direction. (Great Britain, 1937b)

In another exchange, Hexter attacked the empirical biases of the British geologists' search for water as limited. In his testimony he gave an example in which the boring at Pardes Hanna for a depth of more than six hundred meters failed to yield any water. He added quickly that this well is in the same vicinity as the "famous well of Karkur." He continued that "even in the coastal plain within relatively small distances one can dig and have a successful well and one can go down six hundred meters and have a failure" (Great Britain, 1937b). In other words, empirical observations and, by association, geological conclusions could never be conclusive, at least with respect to the unavailability of water.

Despite disagreement among Zionist experts on what counted as legitimate evidence, these professionals all thought of the water resources of historic Palestine as abundant. Most of these experts, among them Simcha Blass and the American Christian Zionist Walter Lowdermilk, put that estimate at 3,000 mcmy at the lower end. They sometimes argued that the estimate reached as far as 4,000 mcmy (Lowdermilk 1944). Perhaps part of the reason for this belief in abundance was that Judeo-Christian Biblical narratives about Palestine were often taken to be the true representation of Palestine's history, climate, and geology. A more politically strategic conclusion, and perhaps a bit more cynical one, is that Zionist experts deliberately articulated their methodological viewpoints about abundance in order to open up Palestine for unlimited Jewish immigration (Alatout forthcoming).

By 1948, almost all Zionist water and settlement experts believed that water was an abundant resource. They thought that the practical problem of reaching those resources was one of governmental will. They claimed that the British Mandatory government did not desire to have more water and therefore did not invest in finding more resources because they wished to keep Jewish immigration extremely limited. All that was needed to access more resources was to have a government willing to invest in surveying the water resources of Palestine and waterworks (American Friends of the Middle East 1964).

Decentralized Water Institutions before 1948

Like much of Jewish life in Palestine before 1948, and especially before the Peel Commission's suggestion to partition Palestine, water institutions were highly decentralized. All water supply and extraction companies were local and regional. The legal system inherited from the Ottoman period, the *Mejelle*, which allowed private ownership of water resources, shaped this local/regional framework. By 1937 there were two water companies, neither of which had a national mandate. They were each owned by different communal settlements. The Jordan River Valley Society was jointly owned by five settlements in the Jordan Valley and the Harod Valley Water Society was owned by seven settlements in the Harod Valley. There were also sixteen water cooperative societies in smallholder villages (Muenzner 1947).

Only after the 1937 Peel Commission's partition plan and after the emergence of water as a strategic political instrument did the Zionists start to think about water in national terms. In 1937, three national institutions—the Jewish Agency, the Jewish National Fund (land-buying agency), and the Histadrut (labor organization)—founded Mekorot. These national institutions founded Mekorot for the purposes of "planning, executing, and running waterworks for irrigation and consumption" throughout Palestine (Muenzner 1947, 63–65). Within a few years, Mekorot grew from supplying 1 mcmy in 1939 to supplying 14 mcmy in 1945.

The centralization of water institutions was slow but not limited to water by any means. To appreciate the fact that this was a major transformation in Zionist thinking, one should note that the only three companies managed jointly by different national institutions (the Jewish Agency, the Jewish National Fund, and the Histadrut) were established in the years 1936–1937 (Muenzner 1945). Besides Mekorot, those included the air transportation company, Aviron Ltd., established in 1936, and the national employment fund, Bizur, also established in 1936.

This progressive nationalization of Jewish life in Palestine was hardly complete at the time of the establishment of the state in 1948. Jewish life was still highly decentralized in the areas of education, security apparatuses, settlement, and even water itself. Centralization was the focus of the new Israeli leadership under Israel's first Prime Minister, David Ben-Gurion.

THE POLITICS OF SCARCITY AND CENTRALIZATION

Constructing Water as a Scarce Resource

By 1948, almost all Zionist experts agreed that the water potential of Israel was high. There was one exception to this consensus and that was the water engineer Martin Goldschmidt. He immigrated to Palestine as a young civil engineer in the early 1930s. He was unsuccessful in securing a job in the water sector with the Jewish Agency or other Zionist institutions in Palestine. This was the time when the Zionist movement had an ambiguous relationship with water and waterworks. Instead, Goldschmidt worked in the Water Department of the Mandatory government until 1948. He was a self-proclaimed Zionist, but also believed water was a scarce resource (1,200–1,500 mcmy) in Palestine. In fact, he was behind British water potential estimates for more than a decade. According to Wiener, Zionist water and political experts of the time were "unkind" to him (Wiener, interview, August 25, 1997). They accused him of all sorts of things: of being a "self-hating Jew" and an "anti-Zionist" (Virschubski, interview, September 11, 1997). After the establishment of the State of Israel, Goldschmidt worked in the Department of Water in the Ministry of Agriculture. Simcha Blass, the one expert who believed water was abundant in Israel until his death in the 1980s, headed this department.

In 1950, the Israeli government charged the Ministry of Agriculture and its water department with turning the Lowdermilk-Hays plan into a workable one. This meant conveying the waters from the Jordan River in the north of the country to the Negev desert in the south.[10] The purpose seemed simple enough; since Israel was to keep its borders open to Jewish immigration and new immigrants were to be dispersed throughout Israel (especially in empty spaces thought of as lacking security and under foreign military threat such as the Negev and border towns), new waterworks were urgently needed to make immigrants' settlement possible.

There were two important water institutions in the country, the Water Department under the Ministry of Agriculture run by Simcha Blass and Mekorot Water Company, whose chief engineer was Aaron Wiener.[11] The two institutions had a number of problems about jurisdiction. Questions remained about which institution would plan the National Water Carrier and which agency would be responsible for quotas, prices, and the construction and maintenance of waterworks (Kantor, interview, August 9,

1997; Wiener, interview, September 25, 1997). By 1951, the Water Department issued three Interim Reports for the Water Master Plan. In the second (1950) report, the water potential was estimated at more than 2,800 mcmy. In the third (1951) report, the same potential was estimated at more than 2,600 mcmy. The latter report, however, added a note that it was most probable to find more groundwater resources that were not yet tapped. Blass (1952) talked about a water potential of more than 3,000 mcmy.

In 1952, turf problems intensified between the Water Department and Mekorot to such a level that the cabinet intervened. They created an inter-ministerial committee to find a solution to the institutional problem. The committee decided to establish a third water institution charged exclusively with water planning. This institution was named the Tahal Water Company for Israel. This arrangement was both less than Blass wanted (he wanted a cabinet position for water affairs) and more than Wiener wanted. Wiener desired to limit the Water Department in the Ministry of Agriculture to deciding quotas and prices. He wanted to leave planning and execution of the National Water Project in the hands of Mekorot, which he thought would be more careful and efficient.

Ironically, Simcha Blass became director of Tahal and Aaron Wiener served as its deputy. This was a negotiated position between the two old institutions. The new company's first task was to issue the Fourth Interim Plan in 1952. It failed to do so precisely because of the disagreement over the water potential of Israel. Tahal sank more than two hundred exploratory wells in order to survey groundwater resources in the country. It found those resources much less than the Third Interim Report claimed.[12]

The positions taken by different water experts are worthy of note. Blass (1952) believed that more resources should be put into better surveying of groundwater resources. For him, the water potential could be calculated in theoretical terms and deduced from the rainfall, the rate of percolation, the rate of evaporation, etc. This approach led him to estimate the water potential in Israel at 3,000 to 4,000 mcmy.[13] On the other hand, Wiener and other water experts within Tahal concentrated on empirical evidence. They believed that water potential was only the water that you could actually deliver. Deliverable water was estimated at less than 1,800 mcmy.

Such disagreements on what constitutes scientific evidence (theoretical versus empirical) proved incommensurable. They led to a final showdown in which Blass stepped down from his position in Tahal and Wiener took over.[14] This shift in leadership paved the way for the Fourth Interim Report, which came out in 1953 after Blass's resignation. From then on, the estimate of the state's water potential was gradually reduced until it was estimated in the Master Plan of 1955 and the Updated Master Plan of 1957 at no more than 1,850 mcmy.

Moving toward Centralization

As stated previously, prior to the establishment of the Israeli state, water was regulated through a set of legal codes that were inherited from the Ottoman era (the Mejelle) and the British Mandate Ordinances. Rights to water mostly followed property rights to land. A person owned the water on his/her land—and only that much—whether it was a river passing through or a groundwater resource. Landowners could not claim ownership over groundwater aquifers or rivers, but only over the *use* of those aquifers within or rivers passing through their land. The British High Commissioner's Ordinance of 1940 was another important element of prestate water regulation. This ordinance declared that rivers were common property that could not be privately owned. This ordinance failed miserably, however, because of Zionist objections. Zionists feared that this ordinance would limit their access to surface water resources (Laster 1976).

After the establishment of the Israeli state, the Constituent Assembly—the governing body of the new state—declared all the regulations preceding the state valid until repealed by law. In 1950, the Israeli government adopted the High Commissioner's Ordinance of 1940 in order to make possible the construction of the National Water Carrier. This ordinance declared surface water resources, including rivers, public property. It authorized the state to use those resources for public waterworks. The ordinance also authorized the state to appropriate private property if needed in the process of constructing those public works.

After the resignation of Blass and the consolidation of power under Wiener, the centralization of water resource management under one institution ensued. Even though the position of water commissioner was established by 1953 (first as the director of the Water Department in 1949), its powers were gradually increased from 1954 onward. The justification given for this increase in power was water scarcity.

Soon after his hire in 1954, the new law graduate Mordechi Virschubski was charged with studying international as well as different national water laws for the purpose of regulating water in the Israeli State (Virschubski, interview, September 11, 1997). Beginning in 1955, the Knesset passed a few provisional water laws. By 1959, the Knesset passed a comprehensive Water Law, which included the Water Drilling and Water Metering Laws of 1955, the Drainage and Flood Control Law of 1957, and the Water Law of 1959.

Each of these laws concentrated more power within the state, namely in the person of the water commissioner. But each of these laws also regulated people's access to the state's water resources. Such resources could no longer be privately owned and access to them required a permit application from the water commissioner. The Commissioner held the power to grant, reject, and modify the conditions of the permits. Moreover, the water commissioner defined the exact uses, quantities, and qualities permitted to people.

He was also empowered to monitor people's compliance with the conditions under which permits were issued. Monitoring included a number of technical and legal instruments, including the installation of water meters, the right to inspection, and the right to revoke any license. The Water Law, as well as the institutions it built and legitimized and the technologies it deployed, became an instrument for constructing citizens that would follow the law but were also subject to state surveillance and taxation. The citizen took on a new identity, expected to help the state in some sense but also subject to the state's power. This shift in notions of citizenship was not limited to or only inherent in water policy making. It extended to other areas such that it became part of a general debate within Israel on the nature of the state and the nature of Jewish identity.

A word on scarcity, the state, and its Palestinian citizens is warranted here. Even though Israeli Palestinians never constituted a serious military threat to the state, the Israeli political and military establishment constructed them as such. They were placed under extreme security measures, curfews and movement constraints and were subject to outright violence at times for more than a decade and a half (Kimmerling 1983; Troen and Lucas 1995).

The Israeli state offered scarcity, along with population dispersal and immigration, as the main justification for the transfer of the water resources of the Jordan River out of its basin—going against the customary laws of rivers at the time—to irrigate other lands at a distance. In 1954, the state decided to draw water from the Beit Natufa reservoir. This reservoir was adjacent to a number of Palestinian villages and withdrawal of water from it required the confiscation of 12,000 dunums of land from the village of Kafr Mandeh and the displacement of most of the inhabitants of the village. Not surprisingly, the attempt to do so met strong resistance, so a large police presence was required to carry out the water extraction (*Jerusalem Post*, 16 December 1954, 7 June 1955). The Israeli government argued that in Israel, like in all democratic states, "the national or greater interest has always had to prevail, and no one has seriously criticized the necessary use of compulsion in the final instance when all argument, reason, and explanation had failed." This reference to compulsion in democratic states was disingenuous since Palestinians in 1954 were still considered an enemy presence in Israel, subject to emergency regulations. In addition, the technical necessity of broadening Beit Natufa was not established nor agreed upon at the time (Alatout 2003).

THE BOUNDARIES OF THE STATE: JEWISH SUBJECTIVITY FROM A ZIONIST SETTLER TO A CITIZEN OF THE MODERN STATE

What took place in water policy making and politics—the increasing centralization of water policy in the institutions of the state and the redefining of the relationship between the state and its citizens—was not a unique event. It was part of a general trend in Israeli society. Paying attention to the broader shifts in Israel helps contextualize water policy as a politics of identity.

With the signing of the Declaration of Independence in May 1948, the construction and definition of a new Jewish identity became of paramount concern. This concern took into consideration the changing institutional context of its expression; that is, living under the authority of British Mandate rule to living in an independent state that is defined as Jewish. In this era, the most relevant factor was defining the relationship between Zionist and statist institutional structures. Defining the respective roles each would play in constructing and defining the new Israeli-Jewish identity was vital.[15]

Two major approaches were articulated with regard to identity politics and the extent to which the state could intervene in their formation. Ben-Gurion exemplified the statist position in his elaboration of the concept of *mamlakhtiyut*.[16] For him and many of his colleagues in Mapai,[17] the boundaries of the state were, or were supposed to be, coextensive with the boundaries of civil society. In that sense, the state was to become both the main source of the new political identity and its most central institutional expression. With this conception, the new Israeli identity emerged as one of a Jewish citizen in a Jewish liberal-democratic state.

Mamlakhtiyut was not the only vision of what Israeli political life should look like. Challenges emerged in varying degrees not only from within political parties in opposition to the dominant Mapai party, but also from within older Zionist institutions. The latter included those closely identified with Mapai such as the Histadrut[18] and the *kibbutzim*[19] movements. Even within Mapai itself, many voices disagreed with the totality of the state as presented in Ben-Gurion's political thought. These disagreements constituted the bulk of Ben-Gurion's own troubles with his party, both during his temporary retirement (1953–1955) and after his permanent retirement in 1964.[20] Ben-Gurion's position in favor of strong state institutions was matched by Ultra Orthodox Jewry's anti-state positions (Friedman 1995; Strum 1995).

This divergence in positions does not mean that Jewish identity was stagnant or remained the same. The shift toward Ben-Gurion's demand for a strong identification with the state manifested itself in a number of ways, not the least of which included the nationalization of a number of decentralized elements of Jewish life like the unification of the different paramilitary groups into one force, the Israeli Defense Forces; the centralization of education (even though some provisions were made for religious education); and the centralization of the water apparatus of the state.

One important point to note here is that Palestinians living in Israel were wholly outside the discussions over the relationship between the state, civil society, and Israeli citizenship. They were not considered part of any of these notions; in contrast, they were constituted as the other, the threat, and the problem.[21] The Israeli public was mostly concerned with containing their level of threat. The Emergency Regulations gave the military immense powers to deal with the presumed threat.

CONCLUSION: ABUNDANCE, SCARCITY, JEWISH SUBJECTIVITY, AND THE ERASURE OF THE PALESTINIANS

The way we understand our world and the way we organize our lives in it are mutually constitutive. In this sense, scientific facts are not the mere unfiltered representations of nature. They are indicative of a sociopolitical process of construction. They are, in other words, the conclusion of a political process of interpretation and contestation. In this sense, unpacking the black boxes of scientific facts through historical and genealogical work may tell us a great deal about social and political life.

Once an assertion becomes scientifically certified as fact, it becomes an immensely powerful instrument in shaping the world we live in. As we have seen in this chapter, water abundance during the Mandate period of Palestine implied and determined a certain politics of Jewish immigration and political decentralization. The same can be said about water scarcity in the state period. A belief in water scarcity became the "true" perception of the water potential of Israel in the 1950s. It became an instrument for the centralization of water institutions and for the concentration of power in state apparatuses. The legal system facilitated this shift in part through the legitimization of a number of elements in law: resource appropriation, surveillance, discipline, and control.

Although many Middle East scholars tend to assume a static notion of identity in which, for example, Jewish subjectivity remains fixed throughout historical changes, the evidence presented here demonstrates that political identity is always transient and subject to relations of power and knowledge. Its borders are contingent upon the changing relations between power and knowledge. In the Israeli case, the assumption that Jewish subjectivity continued unaffected with statehood and that Zionist parameters continued to shape that subjectivity in the same ways is fundamentally unsound. Jewish identification depends to a large degree on the knowledge produced during a specific time (i.e., whether historic Palestine is a land of abundance or scarcity matters in how Jewish subjects relate to one another and to the land). It also depends upon the form of institutionalization that accompanies that knowledge (i.e., decentralization provides a different conception of self and other than the strong centralized state). So, for example, the shift in our understanding of water (from abundance to scarcity) was coconstitutive with a shift in forms of institutionalization (from decentralization to centralization) and a shift in forms of identification (from the Jew as immigrant settler to the Jew as a citizen of the modern nation-state).

What is interesting about borders is precisely the work that constructs and shapes them—the way they are established, contested, stabilized, and reconstituted in a number of fields and ways. The issue of water scarcity in Israel centers around the following moving boundaries: scientific (geological versus geophysical), political (Zionists versus Israelis, among others), and organizational (decentralization/non-statist versus centralization/statist). None of these boundaries were fixed and all of them were subject to transformation in one form or another. Nor did these borders exist in isolation from one another. Indeed, the scientific, the political, and the organizational were all and continue to be constituted in extended networks of relations.

What about the Palestinians and water politics? What role or roles did they play in the making of these borders? Even though historical detail is somewhat wanting, the Palestinians constituted the demographic and political space, literally and figuratively, within which all these struggles over borders took place. It was against their rejection of Jewish immigration that the notion of abundance emerged and it was against their demand for more water that the notion of scarcity came about. Yet while all of these processes were was taking place, they were deemed invisible, at least as a political community. They were considered undeserving, as a farming community; and wished away, as an other. It is also against this background, the conflict between the Israelis/Zionists and the Palestinians, that the Jew as settler and the Jew as the citizen of the modern nation-state developed.

NOTES

1. A number of scholars have mentioned this as a possibility, some more certain than others (Gleick 1988; Star 1991). Some, however, like Wolf (1995), take a more sophisticated view, that even though water scarcity could be a reason for war, it could also be a reason for cooperation. This position, however, is equally problematic since it still regards water scarcity, the biophysical condition, as the main force for either war or cooperation, isolating it from the social and cultural contexts that constitute the interpretative schemes for concerns about water resources.

2. Mordechi Virschubski, interview, September 11, 1997. Virschubski went on to become a member of the Knesset for more than a decade in the early 1980s and 1990s and, at the time of the interview, he was a council member for cultural affairs in the city of Tel Aviv.

3. For example, in an interview, Jacobo Sack, a senior engineer at Mekorot water company, insisted he had no memory of a struggle over water potential of Israel

even though he had worked at Mekorot since the early 1960s. "Really?" he asked, "I have no idea because I'm not familiar with those figures. This is the first time I hear about this" (Jacobo Sack, interview, July 22, 1997).

4. For studies that were published in the 1970s or conducted in the 1970s and came out in the early 1980s, see Barnes and Edge (1982); Bloor (1976); Collins (1982 and 1985); Knorr-Cetina (1982); Latour (1983 and 1987); Latour and Woolgar (1979); Pinch (1986). For more recent studies, published in the 1990s, see Ezrahi (1990); Jasanoff (1990 and 1995); Jasanoff et al (1995); Kleinman (1995); Latour (1993 and 1997); Yearley (1994); Pickering (1992).

5. Witness also the more dramatic pronouncement of Golda Meir, often cited, that "there are no Palestinians."

6. See, for example, the emergence since the late 1960s and early 1970s of a large number of nongovernmental organizations focusing on agriculture, water research, and environmental and social justice issues. To mention just a couple of important examples, the Palestine Hydrology Group and the Applied Research Institute of Jerusalem have been active in these fields of research for more than two decades and both maintain large research archives that are extremely beneficial to all sorts of researchers.

7. There is a small, but expanding, archive on water resources in historic Palestine at Bier Zeit University that I visited a number of times between 1997 and 1999. A number of institutions lost their records through the years in direct Israeli action that is meant precisely to destroy any Palestinian basis for memory. For example, the offices of the Institute for Palestine Studies were attacked in the Lebanon War of 1982 (along with a number of PLO institutions). Even more recently, the attack on the Department of Statistics and the Ministry of Education in Ramallah in 2004 point to the same deliberate and violent politics of erasure.

8. In an interview, Nachum Gross restated his position (1984) that Labor Zionists were especially sensitive to irrigation technologies that would reduce demand for labor. Interview, September 8, 1997.

9. Many might object that water was as a matter of fact very political from the very beginning of Zionist immigration into Palestine (Garfinkle 1994). This objection is true to some degree, but not completely. The fact that the Zionist Organization was aware of the importance of water for Palestine while drawing the boundaries of the country—Zionists tried their best to include the whole of the Jordan River and the Litani River within the borders of Palestine—does not mean that water remained political or that water's politics stayed the same. More specifically here, I argue that water's importance to the politics of Jewish immigration was acquired only toward the mid to late 1930s.

10. James Hays was a TVA engineer who worked on turning Lowdermilk's (1944) plan of transferring the Jordan River waters from the north to the Negev desert in the south. He published the plan (Hays 1948) just before the establishment of the state.

11. Even though Mekorot was not the largest water company in Israel at the time (it was ranked the third as a matter of fact), it was considered the national water company because of its ties with the Jewish National Fund, the Jewish Agency, and the Histadrut. In addition, those who established the company became very important in Israeli politics during the first decade including Levi Eshkol, who held a

number of cabinet positions during the 1950s and became the Prime Minister of Israel after Ben-Gurion's final resignation in 1963; and Pinhas Sapir, who also occupied a number of cabinet positions in the 1950s including finance minister.

12. Wiener described this as the ultimate proof of the limited water resources of Israel. Interview, August 25, 1997.

13. In the 1970s, when large fossil aquifers were discovered under the Negev, he famously told Menachem Kantor, then the water commissioner, "See, here is the water I was always talking about." Kantor, interview, August 9, 1997.

14. This was not as simple as might be inferred from this narrative. As a matter of fact, Blass's resignation had everything to do with another political battle that was fought on a different front. At the same time in 1953, Ben-Gurion went into his temporary retirement in the Negev and the "more practical" cabinet members like Levi Eshkol were instrumental in tipping the tide in favor of Wiener and against Blass. Wiener, interview, September 25, 1997. However, the full implications of this story are beyond the purview of this chapter. For more on Ben-Gurion's temporary retirement see Troen and Lucas (1995).

15. The relationship between the Palestinian minority and state institutions was vaguely defined in the Declaration of Independence. On the one hand, the state was proclaimed Jewish and on the other, it was proclaimed democratic. The deployment of water policy in the definition of the Palestinian minority as "other" is very important. Even though it is somewhat out of the purview of this chapter, one example should be sufficient to point to this process. The Mekorot water company, as I said before, was owned by three "national institutions," but at the same time was officially appointed by the state as its water company. The fact that Mekorot was owned by these institutions meant that their bylaws dictated its business practices. Those bylaws demanded that Mekorot was to exclusively serve the development of the Jewish inhabitants of the state, not all of its citizens. This became a basis for discrimination not only by Mekorot, but by a number of companies that were in similar positions.

16. Normally translated as "statism." However, it is often argued, and rightly so, that *mamlakhtiyut* is a broader concept than statism. On the notion of *mamlakhtiyut*, Gorny (1995); Don-Yehiya (1995); Horowitz and Lissak (1989).

17. The Hebrew abbreviation stands for *Mifleget Poalei Eretz-Yisrael* [Party of the Workers of the Land of Israel]. This party was established in 1930 by the merging of *Ahdut Ha'avoda* [Unity of Labor party] and *HaPoel Hatzair* [the Young Worker party]. It embodied the more moderate factions of socialist Labor Zionism. The main competitor of Mapai in socialist labor politics was Mapam [the United Workers' Party], which was established in 1948 by the merging of *Hashomer Hatzair* [the Young Pioneer] and the left-leaning members of *Ahdut Ha'avoda*.

18. The English translation of the Hebrew acronym *Histadrut*, is *The Jewish Federation of Labor*.

19. The *kibbutzim* (plural form of *kibbutz*) are agricultural Jewish settlements in Palestine and have been in existence since 1908, when the second *aliyah*, heavily Eastern European, deployed radical socialist politics. Kibbutzim are linked to the Zionist project of the "regeneration" of the Jewish people by working the land; they became the symbol of its success. On the kibbutzim movement and its struggles with the state, see Henry Near (1995); Ben-Rafael (1995); Lucas (1975). Other valuable resources are a number of biographies of Ben-Gurion.

20. The position for or against the presence of a strong state extended to include positions in foreign policy including those of the Arab-Israeli conflicts. Ben-Gurion and his supporters, such as Moshe Dayan and Shimon Peres, were known as hawks; while others, Moshe Sharett, Golda Meir, and Yitzhac Rabin, became known as doves. See Lucas (1975).

21. See Elia Zureik (1979) for an excellent account on Palestinian conditions within the Israeli state. See Connolly (1996) on the transformation of "difference" into "othering" and the political consequences of that process on political identity.

REFERENCES

Samer Alatout (2000), "Water Balances in Palestine, Regional Cooperation, and the Politics of Numbers," in David B. Brooks and Ozay Mehmet (eds.), *Water Balances in the Eastern Mediterranean*. Ottawa: International Development Research Centre, pp. 59–84.

Samer Alatout (2003), "Imagining Hydrological Boundaries, Constructing the Nation-State: A 'Fluid' History of Palestine." Ph.D. diss., Department of Science and Technology Studies, Cornell University, Ithaca, NY.

Samer Alatout (2006), "Towards a Bio-territorial Conception of Power: Territory, Population, and Environmental Narratives in Palestine and Israel," *Political Geography* 25 (6): 601–21.

Samer Alatout (forthcoming), "Beyond a Sociology of Translation—Networks, Articulation, and Power: Constructing a Zionist Network of Abundance and Settlement in Palestine, 1918–1948," *Social Studies of Science.*

Barry Barnes and David Edge (eds.) (1982), *Science in Context: Reading in the Sociology of Science*. Cambridge, MA: The MIT Press.

David Ben-Gurion (1954), *Rebirth and Destiny of Israel*. New York: Philosophical Library.

Eliezer Ben-Rafael (1995), "The Kibbutz in the 1950s: A Transformation of Identity," in S. Ilan Troen and Noah Lucas (eds.), *Israel: The First Decade of Independence*. Albany: State University of New York Press, pp. 265–78.

Simha Blass (1952), *Ha-Mayim BiMdinet Yisrael: Skira* [Water in the state of Israel: a survey], [in Hebrew] Central Zionist Archives 5594/4707/*Gimel.*

David Bloor (1976), *Knowledge and Social Imagery*. Chicago: University of Chicago Press.

Harry Collins (1982), "The Replication of Experiments in Physics," in Barry Barnes and David Edge (eds.), *Science in Context: Reading in the Sociology of Science*. Cambridge, MA: The MIT Press.

Harry Collins (1985), *Changing Order: Replication and Induction in Scientific Practice*. London: Sage.

Eliezer Don-Yehiya (1995), "Political Religion in a New State: Ben-Gurion's *Mamlachtiyut*," in S. Ilan Troen and Noah Lucas (eds.), *Israel: The First Decade of Independence*. Albany: State University of New York Press, pp. 171–94.

Yaron Ezrahi (1990), *The Descent of Icarus: Science and the Transformation of Contemporary Democracy*. Cambridge, MA: Harvard University Press.

Menachem Friedman (1995), "The Structural Foundation for Religio-Political Accommodation in Israel: Fallacy and Reality," in S. Ilan Troen and Noah Lucas (eds.), *Israel: The First Decade of Independence*. Albany: State University of New York Press, pp. 51–82.

Adam Garfinkle (1994), *War, Water, and Negotiation in the Middle East: The Case of the Palestinian-Syrian Border, 1916–1923*. Tel Aviv: Tel Aviv University.

Peter Gleick (1988), "The World's Water," *Issues in Science and Technology* 14 (4): 80–88.

Great Britain (1937a), *Palestine Royal Commission Report*, July 1937. London: HMSO.

Great Britain (1937b), *Palestine Royal Commission: Minutes of Evidence Heard at Public Sessions*. London: HMSO.

Great Britain (1946), *A Survey of Palestine: Prepared in December 1945 and January 1946 for the Information of the Anglo-American Committee of Inquiry*. Palestine: Government Printer.

Nachum Gross (1984), *Deep Water and the Absorption of Academic Immigrants in the Twenties* [*Mai Tehom VeKlitet 'Olim Academa 'im BeShenot Ha'Isrim*] [in Hebrew] Jerusalem: Institute of Economic Research in Israel.

James Hays (1948), *The TVA on the Jordan: Proposals for Irrigation and Hydroelectric Development in Palestine*. Washington, DC: Commission on Palestine Surveys.

D. Horowitz and M. Lissak (1989), *Trouble in Utopia: The Overburdened Polity of Israel*. Albany: State University of New York Press.

Sheila Jasanoff (1990), *The Fifth Branch: Science Advisors as Policymakers*. Cambridge, MA: Harvard University Press.

Sheila Jasanoff (1995), *Science at the Bar: Law, Science, and Technology in America*. Cambridge, MA: Harvard University Press.

Sheila Jasanoff et al. (1994), *Handbook of Science and Technology Studies*. Thousand Oaks, CA: Sage.

Sheila Jasanoff (ed.) (2004), *States of Knowledge: The Co-Production of Science and Social Order*. New York: Routledge.

Baruch Kimmerling (1983), *Zionism and Territory: The Socio-Territorial Dimensions of Zionist Politics*. Berkeley, CA: Institute of International Studies.

Karin Knorr-Cetina (1982), *The Manufacture of Knowledge: An Essay on the Constructivist and Contextual Nature of Science*. Oxford: Oxford University Press.

Richard Laster (1976), *The Legal Framework for the Prevention and Control of Water Pollution in Israel*. Jerusalem: Ministry of the Interior.

Bruno Latour (1983), "Give Me a Laboratory and I will Raise the World," in Karin Knorr-Cetina and Michael Mulkay (eds.), *Science Observed: Perspectives on the Social Studies of Science*. London: Sage.

Bruno Latour (1987), *Science in Action*. Cambridge, MA: Harvard University Press.

Bruno Latour (1993), *We Have Never Been Modern*. Cambridge, MA: Harvard University Press.

Bruno Latour (1999), *Pandora's Hope: Essays on the Reality of Science Studies*. Cambridge, MA: Harvard University Press.

Bruno Latour and Steve Woolgar (1979), *Laboratory Life: The Construction of Scientific Facts*. Princeton, NJ: Princeton University Press.

Mark LeVine (1995), "The Discourse of Development in Mandate Palestine," *Arab Studies Quarterly* (Winter): 95–124.

Mark LeVine (2005), *Overthrowing Geography: Jaffa, Tel Aviv, and the Struggle for Palestine, 1888–1948*. Berkeley: University of California Press.

Walter Lowdermilk (1944), *Palestine: Land of Promise*. New York: Harpers and Brothers.

Noah Lucas (1975), *The Modern History of Israel*. New York: Praeger.

Gerhard Muenzner (1945), *Jewish Labor Economy in Palestine*. London: Victor Gollancz.

Gerhard Muenzner (1947), *Labor Enterprise in Palestine: A Handbook of Histadrut Economic Institutions*. New York: Sharon Books.

Henry Near (1995), "The Crisis in the Kibbutz Movement, 1949–1961," in S. Ilan Troen and Noah Lucas (eds.), *Israel: The First Decade of Independence*. Albany: State University of New York Press, pp. 243–64.

Derek Penslar (1991), *Zionism and Technocracy: The Engineering of Jewish Settlement of Palestine, 1870–1918*. Bloomington: Indiana University Press.

Leo Picard (1931), *Geological Researches in the Judean Desert*. Jerusalem: Goldberg's Press.

Leo Picard (1936), "Conditions of Underground-Water in the Western Emmek (Plain of Esdraelon)," Jerusalem: Hebrew University, *Bulletin of the Geology Department* 1, no. 1.

Leo Picard (1940), "Groundwater in Palestine," *Bulletin of the Geology Department* 3, no. 1. The Hebrew University of Jerusalem.

Andrew Pickering (ed.) (1992), *From Science as Knowledge to Science as Practice*. Chicago: Chicago University Press.

Trevor Pinch (1986), *Confronting Nature: The Sociology of Solar Neutrino Detection*. Dordrecht, The Netherlands: Reidel.

Philippa Strum (1995), "The Road Not Taken: Constitutional Non-Decision Making in 1948–1950 and Its Impact on Civil Liberties in the Israeli Political Culture," in S. Ilan Troen and Noah Lucas (eds.), *Israel: The First Decade of Independence*. Albany: State University of New York Press, pp. 83–104.

Sandy Sufian (2007), *Healing the Land and the Nation: Malaria and the Zionist Project in Mandatory Palestine*. Chicago: University of Chicago Press.

S. Ilan Troen and Noah Lucas (eds.) (1995), *Israel: the First Decade of Independence*. Albany: State University of New York Press.

Aaron Wolf (1995), *Hydropolitics along the Jordan River: The Impact of Scarce Water Resources on the Arab Israeli Conflict*. Tokyo: United Nations University Press.

Steve Yearley (1995), "The Environmental Challenge to Science Studies," in Sheila Jasanoff et al. (eds.), *Handbook of Science and Technology Studies*. Thousand Oaks, CA: Sage.

Elia Zureik (1979), *The Palestinians in Israel: A Study in Internal Colonialism*. London: Routledge and Kegan Paul.

Part III

SHAPING CITIZENS AND SPACE IN ISRAEL-PALESTINE

9

Seizing Locality in Jerusalem

Alona Nitzan-Shiftan

Like most of Israeli society, Israel's planning administration was unprepared for the country's victory in the 1967 war; specifically, the conquest of the biblical homeland of Eretz Israel comprised by East Jerusalem and the West Bank. The experience of 1948, however, taught imperative lessons regarding the importance of creating "facts on the ground," and nowhere was it more important than in Israel's "eternal capital" after East and West Jerusalems were unilaterally reunified. LeVine's chapter on Tel Aviv and Jaffa in this volume demonstrates the wide range of administrative, legal, and aesthetic tools that were developed during the pre-1948 period to enable the creation of facts on the ground in Palestine, particularly through the use of built space. This chapter demonstrates how the professional architectural discourse complemented those tools after 1967 to help cement the reunified Jerusalem's place as the symbol of Jews' return to their mythical biblical origins.

Jerusalem's centrality to the ur-myths of Judaism (and through it, Zionism) made it difficult for Israel's modernist planners and politicians to express architecturally powerful symbols related to these myths and ideologies. Rather than using the opportunity to push for the development of an autochthonous Israeli style that would still be rooted in the local environment, the minister of housing simply advised his planners to give the unified city[1] an "Oriental character."[2] The prefabricated concrete arches that were soon after superimposed on the completed design of East Jerusalem's first neighborhood illustrate the confusion that permeated the architectural establishment in this period.[3]

This situation changed dramatically, however, when a younger generation of architects entered the planning scene. During the 1970s, these

Figure 9.1.   Ram Karmi, Gilo, Cluster 6, 1970s, General View. Courtesy of Ram Karmi, Architect.

architects created a coherent architectural image that depended heavily on the readily accessible Palestinian vernacular. What was ironic in this endeavor, as explained by Elinoar Barzaki, the former head of the Jerusalem Region in the Ministry of Housing, was that the "post-'67 architecture of power absorbed the symbols of the conquered rather than those of the conqueror" (see figure 9.1).[4] This chapter will explore why architects chose to Israelize a contested city with architectural forms of the conquered nation, and how they were able to separate the Palestinian vernacular architecture from the culture that produced it in order to make it constitutive of "an Israeli architecture."

This process is particularly interesting since, in the period before 1967, beginning in the 1930s and continuing for the next thirty years what would become the "Israeli architectural tradition" was specifically modernist, both aesthetically and ideologically.[5] Yet with the conquests of 1967, Israel was forced to confront, and in many ways, adapt to a local architectural vernacular. This vernacular intersected with the cultural and professional formation of the Israeli architects that were entrusted with the national mandate of Israelizing Jerusalem. Concomitantly, modernist architecture experienced several unrelated crises across the globe (including Israel), crises that questioned the foundational discourse of "progress and development," that was shared by the heretofore hegemonic Labor Zionist elite.

As the first "natives" of the Israeli state, Israeli-born *sabra* architects naturally sought to critique both architectural and Zionist modernisms. What is so fascinating here, is how and why this process led them to the Palestinian vernacular, and in particular to "the Arab village," which had fascinated them for almost a decade by the time post-1967 construction was underway.

SEARCHING FOR AN ARCHITECTURE OF PLACE

In the late 1950s, sabra architects launched a campaign to localize Israeli architecture. They saw in the territory of the decade-old Israeli state a homeland that was fundamentally different from what had been envisioned by the preceding generation, the founders of Labor Zionism. Since the early 1930s, Zionist architects in Mandate Palestine had embraced a modern architecture, which promised a new beginning, a departure from both bourgeois and "Oriental" life, which they believed had contaminated Jewish life in the diaspora.[6] Sabra architects claimed that the resultant "international architecture"—by then identified with the Israeli state—disregarded the Zionist promise of "a national home."

Architects voicing this criticism, known also as the "Generation of the State,"[7] were committed primarily to professional, rather than political, action.[8] Their cultural formation was strikingly uniform—they were native-born, urban, and socialist.[9] Most members of this group were born or grew up in Tel Aviv and attended one of three high schools there during the 1940s.[10] These schools were ideological hubs, cultivating "men of European culture in the East" while investing them with the value system of the so-called "working settlement"—the elite of Labor Zionism.[11]

By the 1960s, the new generation of architects had formed an identity and agenda of its own. "Bound with issues of the nation,"[12] this generation focused particularly on housing in the state's periphery.[13] Their social and professional capital in the Israeli habitus gave the new cohort enough power to lead the building of a so-called "united Jerusalem" after 1967.

Enthusiasm for vernacular architecture, as opposed to the more uniform modernist style of the 1930s–1950s, typified the new generational strategy that sabra architects shared with their colleagues overseas. Instead of the modernist will to re-form society, they sought "the spatial expression of human conduct."[14] The crucial belief here was that an unmediated form of this expression could be found, they believed, in indigenous architecture, where life, rather than architects, dictated the form of building.[15] As a result, architects shifted their focus to man, with structuralist anthropology providing the theoretical ground for their belief that "man is always and everywhere essentially the same."[16]

Such a sentiment leads to a belief that man's environment must be expressed by similar architectural principles. Postwar architectural discourse presented a wealth of mostly "primitive" examples of this correlation between man and the built places that clothed his life. This architecture was felt to be uncontaminated by Western historical conventions or by spurious Western progress. Moreover, unlike regional architecture of (the European) home, it risked no nationalistic interpretation. Rather, the prototypical generic inhabitants of these environments saw their history, culture, and politics ignored in favor of a universal truth in which vernacular architecture was "nearly immutable, indeed, unimprovable, since it serves its purpose to perfection."[17]

Heideggerian phenomenologists similarly found in vernacular architecture ontological definitions of place, of being "at home" in the world. They complemented the social ethics of the European Team 10 and the concurrent New Brutalism trend,[18] which bears so effectively on the architectural discourse of sabra architects. The sabra architects founded new venues for using architecture to socialize new immigrants into a national community and at the same time to connect this imagined community to its place, i.e., the Land of Israel.

Makom (Hebrew for place) refers to "the encounter between man and the place where he is."[19] The notion of makom is fundamental to sabra art and architectural discourse because, as Gurevitz and Aran have argued, Israeli Jews did not succeed in resolving the ambiguities of their place: the tension between the text and the territory. The Land of Israel, according to this argument, has always been an abstract homeland, an idea, an aspiration the Zionist movement inherited from the Jewish religion. At the same time, however, it was also an actual place laden with history, authenticity, and sacredness. If the founding generation was devoted to the idea, the sabra generation embraced the territory itself. The schism between the two constantly disturbed the process of inhabiting the land. Because the idea, according to Gurevitz and Aran, preceded the place, the efforts of sabra architects to substantiate the idea in the land were not as spontaneous as they imagined. On the contrary, they were conscious, determined, and ideologically charged— fundamentally different from the effortless nativeness that is gained by birthright and direct ancestry.[20]

This nativeness was readily found for sabra architects in Arab culture, the vernacular architecture of which, inseparable from the place in which it was created, evinced the rootedness they sought. When Yoram Segal published in the inaugural issue of the journal *Tvai* a cover story on "The Traditional House in the Arab Villages of the Galilee,"[21] he stressed this unmediated connectedness. He saw in the ties of the *fellah* to his house, which he builds and maintains with his own hands, "a relationship of belonging, of identification, and of strong emotional attachment."[22] It was precisely this sort of relationship that the sabra architects were seeking. In his recent book, Ram Karmi suggests that "emulating the local gave birth to an empathy toward the lifestyle of the Arabs and the Bedouins, and led to a renewed examination of different identity options."[23] Like Arab words in Hebrew slang, Arab attire for Israeli youth, or Arab food in Israeli cuisine, the evocation of "the Arab village" in Israeli architectural culture was a protest through which sabras aimed to identify themselves as natives by appropriating "the Arab village," which functioned as a set of formal and functional characteristics conducive to a harmonious built environment and a cohesive community. Naturally, the Palestinian inhabitants of these villages play little part in the picture. Their presence is at best generic and their communal life is typically Mediterranean.

In fact, the goal was not to mimic Palestinian Arab architecture, but rather to "translate" regional values and molds. In so doing, Israeli architects sought to create a sense of "homeness" which challenged the founders of the state's insistence that a home for the new Jew be free of past memories—a modernist new beginning on a clean slate.

Put simply, Zionist revolutionary socialism, which attempted to redeem the country through its modernization, did not accord with the sabra generation. It had emerged in Europe, and its sweeping Judaization of Mandate Palestine intentionally ignored indigenous architecture. It also operated from the top down, locating at the top the Zionist pioneers who "salvaged" a land conceived as a tabula rasa. However, the sabra approach (turning to the local vernacular in order to build from bottom up) was no less confusing. A genuine national architecture required an unmediated expression of the place, but the search for authentic expression yielded perplexing results: native architecture was mostly Palestinian Arab.

The Israeli search for an alternative to Zionist modernism in the local Palestinian vernacular was contradictory: at exactly the time when Arab culture was most denigrated by the Israelis, its secret code for local connectedness was deeply admired. In the wake of this contradiction, notions of colonizer/colonized or Western/Oriental gave way to the ambivalence of colonial subjectivity. Scholarly analysis of this condition emerged in critical response to binary oppositions, such as in Edward Said's seminal *Orientalism*.[24] It habitually focused on the incapacity of the colonized to retrieve an "authentic" identity that was not always already entangled in colonial subjugation.[25] My interest here is in a similar yet inverted ambivalence, for the study of which I look at the dominant professional discourse rather then at the "natives" as the object of ethnography.[26] Accordingly, I focus on the colonizer's dependency on the identity of the colonized in order to define an "authentic" national identity of visceral ties to the place. The Israeli desire to achieve the "Arab's" nativeness, which was seen as the ultimate expression of locality, sheds new light on a subject seldom frequented by postcolonial scholarship.

The national and professional sentiments of the sabra, I argue, underlay the Israeli architectural praxis that shaped the urban landscape of post-1967 Israeli Jerusalem. These sentiments were developed as an internal Israeli debate lodged between post–World War II architectural culture, the modernist crisis of which echoed in the sabra generational revolt against Zionist modernism; and a national identity built on a formative lack, which provoked a desire for and fantasy about the intimate relationship of the Arab native with the place, its landscape, stone, and light. After the 1967 war, when the object of this fantasy, the Arab habitat, became tangibly present and heavily populated with the Palestinian residents of the Occupied Territories, this seemingly internal professional debate was caught in the urgent politics of the Palestinian-Israeli conflict. Three strategies for Israelizing the Arab vernacular would ultimately be deployed: it could be read as biblical architecture, as an uncontaminated primitive origin of architecture, or simply as typically Mediterranean.

"BIBLICALIZING" THE LANDSCAPE

After the 1967 conquest of Jerusalem's Old City, Israeli Jews rejoiced in a metaphorical return home, especially to the Western Wall and the Jewish Quarter, the symbolic centers of the Jewish people. The consequent increased focus on the vernacular architecture of the Jewish Quarter prompted a national strategy that weakened the authority of Arab architectural forms over Israeli architecture. When Segal wrote on the Arab village in the Galilee in 1966, or when sabra architects simultaneously launched a preservationist approach to the reconstruction of Old Jaffa, they expressed admiration for the human values and identity embedded in what they saw as generic examples of the region's vernacular architecture. But when architects of this generation started reconstructing the Jewish Quarter immediately after the 1967 war, this vernacular was no longer generic; it was seen by Israelis as an embodiment of Jewish history. The tangible presence of the Quarter and the Wall substantiated for Israelis their national confidence and anchored their claim over a disputed land. "The Wall," said architect Karmi, "symbolizes the place in which I feel direct roots to King David. I can greet him *shalom.*"[27] Cutting-edge archeological research authenticated this biblical connectedness. While architects were seeking locality on the ground, archeologists sought Jewish history underneath its surface. The two were combined in the reconstructed Jewish Quarter, where archeological finds were embedded, as Nadia Abu El-Haj recently demonstrated, in the physical fabric and spatial experience of the Quarter.[28]

If the architecture of the Quarter testified to the continuity of Jewish habitation since biblical times, the new sense of locale could be applied to the surrounding Palestinian villages, whose architecture was perceived as biblical, with the inhabitants as its custodians. Indeed, the "special zone"— the planning unit of Jerusalem's most symbolic part—reached beyond the Old City. It included the Palestinian rural hinterland of East Jerusalem, the

Figure 9.2. Model of Jerusalem during the Second Temple Period, Scale: 1:50 from Safdie in Jerusalem, RIBA Lecture, Courtesy of Professor Avi-Yona.

planning of which often fell under the rubric of landscape design. The central feature of the national landscape scheme was a green belt around the Old City, previously a British colonial dream, which would visually arrest the Old City of Jerusalem. The Arab village of Silwan was included in this park because "its character gives us a good picture of how the landscapes and villages of Biblical times looked."[29] Publications of the army's educational system compared this village to the archaeologically informed open-air model of Herod's Jerusalem.[30] This 1:50 scale monumental reconstruction of the so-called Second Temple Period—itself a major tourist attraction—confirmed the sameness of Sillwan and Herod's Jerusalem, again emphasizing the continuity of ancient building traditions (see figure 9.2).[31] At the same time, however, there was an explicit effort to deploy a scientific methodology to the task at hand rather than the romanticism of nineteenth-century Orientalism.[32]

THE NOBLE SAVAGE AND THE ORIGIN OF ARCHITECTURE

Moshe Safdie, an Israeli-born architect, emigrated during his youth to Canada. There he became internationally known for his groundbreaking Montreal Habitat (Expo 1967). Endorsed by the Israeli administration upon his return home in December 1967, he designed the (unrealized) prefabricated Jerusalem Habitat. Safdie called the Arab village site of his project by its Hebrew/biblical name, *Manchat*. (See figures 9.3 and 9.4 for a comparison between Safdie's Jerusalem Habitat and the Arab village of Manchat.) "Here," he stated, "was the prototype, the ancient village, with which any modern development would have to co-exist."[33]

Figure 9.3 The Ancient Village of Manchat. Dilapidated and Housing Immigrants Since 1948, the Village Would Be Restored and Reconstructed. From Moshe Safdie, *Jerusalem: The Future of the Past* (Boston: Houghton Mifflin Company, 1989), Unpaginated.

Realizing the absolute dichotomy between the Arab village and the Israeli superblock, he clearly intended to emulate the former, to contrast an architecture derived from abstract intellectual premises with one stemming from the primal instincts of habitation. Furthering the roots of these instincts in primary habitation, such as the structures built by "the tree people," Safdie

Figure 9.4. Habitat Jerusalem, Close-Up. Note the Prefabricated Boxes, the Convertible Domed Gardens, and the Pedestrian Bridgeways Clustered on the Steep Topography. Courtesy of Arnott Rogers Batten Ltd.

advanced a Darwinian logic that directly revoked his inspiration, the semi-nal *Architecture Without Architects* of his acquaintance, Bernard Rudofsky.

The Arab village, untouched by Western sophistication, exemplified for Safdie the true origin of architecture. To his eyes, even villages of 1948 Palestinian refugees, built with "fairly limited resources" and devoid of his-torical depth, were "awesome environments."[34] They proved for him that habitation was a product of "the compassionate search for the way people live their private and public life."[35] Inspired by this perception, Safdie sought to build something that was "wholly contemporary, an expression of life today, but that would be as if it had always been there."[36] In so do-ing, he sought to fulfill the Zionist dream of fusing the ancient with the modern. In Jerusalem "the origin" was biblical, the modern progressive, and the combination of both a validation of a people enduring from a re-mote past to an unforeseen future.

MEDITERRANEANISM

Inspiration from indigenous architecture similarly underlined the ordinary housing that defined Jerusalem's post-1967 vernacular. 1977 saw the pub-lication of Ram Karmi's essay "Human Values in Urban Architecture." Es-sentially a manifesto, the essay prescribed a list of Mediterranean architec-tural forms as guidelines for future planning. They were intended to help architects resolve the most pressing question: that of belonging. How could architects establish an architectural language that encouraged personal ex-pression but also defined a vernacular for the national community? Karmi's reference for such active re-rooting was the revival of the ancient Hebrew language, which addressed biblical origin, kinship, and blood. Israeli ar-chitecture, Karmi contended, should connect those attributes to the land.

In different contexts, scholars have termed the strategy Karmi chose for this task *Mediterraneanism*.[37] He invoked the timeless patterns of Mediter-ranean architecture as guidelines for a hierarchical ordering of the built en-vironment, from the house to the cluster, quarter, square, street, bazaar, and, finally, to the entire system. Then he compiled a manual of Mediter-ranean structural elements that should constitute the alphabet of the He-brew built landscape: the wall, the gate, the balcony and porch, the stairs and threshold, the streets and alleyways. Finally, under the banner of "val-ues," he discussed the application of the lessons learned from Mediter-ranean architecture to the present day, advocating such post–World War II trends as the separation of pedestrians from vehicles and the creation of public spaces between buildings.

The architectural precedents that Karmi looked to were no longer tied to the Arab village, his prime reference of the 1960s, but to the Old City and

Greek villages, on the one hand, and to architects such as Le Corbusier and
Safdie on the other. Karmi's precedents go back to his architectural training
in Britain. The architectural historian and critic Reyner Banham, who was
closely associated with Alison and Peter Smithson, has chronicled the emergence of New Brutalism. He writes that at the Architectural Association of
the early 1950s, where the Smithsons taught and Karmi was a student, a
new generation "saw in Mediterranean peasant buildings an anonymous architecture of simple, rugged, geometrical forms, smooth-walled and small
windowed, unaffectedly and immemorially at home in its landscape setting."[38] Hence, Karmi's search for homeness in Mediterranean, or earlier in
Arab, built culture, had strong European roots that associated him with the
interests such as of Aldo van Eyck, James Stirling, and the regionalism of his
friend Kenneth Frampton.[39]

Politically, the idea of Israeli participation in a larger Mediterranean culture divested Palestinian architecture of its authority over a style that was
previously its own. Instead, it was subsumed within the historical and spatial narrative of Israeli architecture.[40] It could thus relieve the Israeli architect of the disturbing conflict between admiring native architecture and dis-
regarding the larger Arab culture that produced it. The association with
Europe's cradle of civilization was pacifying and flexible, and could accommodate the early modernism of which Karmi's father was a major proponent.

THE ETHICS OF ISRAELI PLACE MAKING

When Karmi moved from the private sector to the heart of bureaucracy, he
was making an ideological claim on behalf of the architectural profession
for the right to shape the physical image of the state. It was, as Karmi suggests, an attempt to manage the identity of the "national home" bureaucratically.[41] Karmi first distinguished between *building* and *architecture*, and
then between *space* (or *roof*) and *place*. His claim was that the extant government buildings fell short of being architecture at all, that they were
merely a system of roofs that failed to create any sense of place. Only such
a sense would enable the creation of a true national home in Eretz Israel.[42]

That is, Karmi identified the *makom* [place] his Israeli-born generation
was seeking with the national home Zionism promised. Makom, Karmi
argued, is a prerequisite for a national home because only an identifiable
Israeli place can provide the moral basis for the ownership over the land.
Seeking "the physical and spiritual right to . . . that land," was for Karmi
at the heart of Israeli place making. "Creating a 'place,'" he reminded us,
"is a qualitative, symbolic and emotional process," a task that architects—rather than planners or bureaucrats—should undertake. Architec-

ture, as distinguished from building, "can reflect and represent the cultural aspiration of a community;" that is, it can create a symbolic place rather than a mere conglomeration of dwelling units. Making the built landscape into a makom was a way to nationalize the territory. It was a way to Israelize Jerusalem.

TRAPPED IN THE CROSSFIRE
OF ARCHITECTURE AND POLITICS

During the 1970s and well into the 1980s, this generation of architects created a recognizable style that spread from the reconstructed Jewish Quarter to the new housing settlements on the outskirts of the city. Inspired by the aforementioned Brutalist and regionalist architectural trends, the stone-clad buildings were broken into small terraced masses that tried to echo Jerusalem's mountainous landscape and emulate its vernacular. Densely laid out, these buildings typically form groups of row houses facing into courtyards. The buildings are thus said to mark "a shift from architecture of facades to architecture of [communal] interior spaces" in Jerusalem.[43] The State of Israel and its architects promoted this architecture of "united Jerusalem" in official exhibitions and numerous publications that celebrated locality through housing clusters and various preservation projects.[44] Intriguingly, the devaluation of this architecture in Israeli professional consciousness coincided with the First Intifada of 1987–1993, which staged the Palestinian-Israeli contest over locality.

Located in the midst of political tension, the residential neighborhoods in Jerusalem were microcosms of the Israeli reality. They consolidated its Jewish population and instead of becoming the slums contemporary critics were dreading, they encouraged a social mobility that significantly upgraded the Jewish inhabitants of Jerusalem's low-income housing.[45] At the same time, building on confiscated land undermined the possibility of sharing locality with Palestinians. The combination of local architectural motives and the presence of massive bulldozers turned this local "place-sensitive" architecture into the hallmark of the Israeli occupation for Palestinians. In spite of the successful social program of these housing estates, the Palestinian-Israeli conflict started to erode the architectural reputation of post-1967 neighborhoods, whose style, even in Israeli culture, was derogatively coined neo-Oriental, crusade, or—worst of all—postmodern.

The architecture of post-1967 Jerusalem, particularly that of its residential neighborhoods, is a manifesto of the dominant generation of Israeli architecture. The larger-than-life architectural commissions of post-1967 Jerusalem offered architects of this generation a vast testing ground for implementation of their architectural program. The unprecedented power that sabra architects exercised during the decade following the 1967 war has established them as leaders of the architectural profession in Israel to this day.

The team working on the satellite neighborhood of Giloh, for example, was based in Tel Aviv and had little regard for the national romantic depiction of Jerusalem. Their initial schemes of high-rise buildings or radical row house mega-structures in Giloh were intended to evade what they dismissed as "Jerusalemism."[46] The Ministry of Housing favored instead the so-called neo-Oriental style, with its four-story stone buildings, arguing that they would suit Jerusalem and also sell better than the proposed housing mega-structures. The head of the team, Avraham Yaski, decided, "if you're raped, relax and enjoy it."[47] Responding to the Ministry of Housing's demand, he tried to strike a compromise between the Brutalist architecture they had previously built and the stone to which they had now to surrender. The rough tubsa stone and the concrete arches are evidence of this drama.

The story Yaski told me was deliciously laden with the contradictions that characterize his generation. After the 1967 war, state officials invested Jerusalem's architecture with Jewish symbolism and adhered to the British colonial rule of stone cladding, evoking as a result a romantic style that embarrassed Yaski's secular and socialist team. But the criticized romantic Jerusalemism that the Ministry of Housing imposed on his team was the product of the architects' own sabra architectural program: the cluster, the courtyard, and the lessons learned from the Arab village and the Palestinian vernacular. Throughout the 1970s, Yaski admitted, they continued to explore the city's traditional neighborhoods in order to find inspirational models for Jerusalem architecture. But nobody noticed the Arab village that was caught between the bulldozers preparing the ground for Giloh and the City of Jerusalem because "nobody talked about these things in those days."[48] "These things" referred to the Palestinian dispossession, and "those days" were the days of the post-1967 euphoria. Yaski honestly admitted that architects, unlike the writers and the artists with whom they associated, were confined to an institutional framework, which eroded their critical perspective.

Does institutional dependency explain the contradictions that the sabra architectural program inherited? Or do we need to look more closely at the Israeli identity, which was suspended between Zionist modernism and Palestinian rootedness? This cultural location had a significant effect even on architects and artists who were ardent critics of the Israeli occupation. In a contested territory, the powerful desire of one culture to "belong" to the place, to adopt as its own the physical surroundings and the cultural trappings of that place, can be, in itself, part of a process of alienating the other.

This holds true even for those who recognize the legitimacy of the other's claim to the territory.

Take, for example, Itzhak Danziger, whose sculptural forms and materials communicated to sabra architects local identity and the essence of the Israeli landscape, and who led the basic design studies at the Technion from 1955 until his death in 1976. Danziger leveled harsh criticism at the Zionist project not as an idea, but as an expression of a typical modernization process. For Danziger, the East embodied potential resistance to the injury caused by Labor Zionism. The makom for which Danziger searched for years was found in Palestinian religious sites, many of which were linked to a Jewish past. This place was an environment, a landscape, a ritual, and an opportunity for connected Israeliness.[49] Connected to what? To Palestinian authenticity that had not yet been "spoiled" by the Zionist project. Danziger's admiration for Arab culture, as Sarah Hinsky insightfully demonstrates, was often incompatible with his commitment to the Zionist cause. His land-healing memorials for fallen soldiers were undergirded, she argues, by the same culture of dispossession that uprooted the Palestinians whose connectedness he admired.[50]

Micha Ullman, an acclaimed Israeli artist, followed Danziger's teaching at the Technion architectural school. For the 1988 exhibition "To the East: the Orient in Israeli Art"[51] Ullman prepared a striking buried house of perfectly ordered residential elements made of iron and earth. The work was situated at the dead end of a gallery dedicated to "the villages hidden from sight," a dedication which criticized Israeli blindness to the Palestinian forced exile. Ullman's inclusion in the category of hidden villages is intriguing because his own identity was concealed despite his obviously critical voice. An earlier exhibition catalog prepared by Yigal Zalmona, the curator of "To the East," characterized Ullman as "a digging man: farmer-soldier-archeologist."[52] If one had to define the Zionist equation of displacement, its components would include conquering the land through agricultural, military, and historical means, which the farmer, the soldier, and the archeologist employed during the process. My interest lies exactly in this ambivalence resulting from dual identity—the artist criticizing the products of the same Israeliness that defines him and his work.

The work of the internationally renowned artist Dani Karavan further illuminates this complexity. In the same exhibition, Karavan displays an uprooted olive tree hanging upside-down in the air by its roots. He invokes the olive tree as a Palestinian emblem of rootedness and dispossession, as the same tree had been repeatedly uprooted and replanted. Replanted finally in the museum's sculpture garden, it became a living document, tormented and charged with the memory of uprooting, exhibition galleries, indoors and outdoors, politics and art.

Karavan's questioning is appropriate and corresponds to the layers of meaning in his works. The displayed early sketches of abandoned villages pay no heed to the ugliness, distress, and pain of the desertion. They arouse instead a certain romantic feeling, a unity of structure and landscape, perhaps even a sense of archaeology (see figure 9.5). These are the villages that sabra architects, who warmly embraced Karavan long before he was recognized by the art world, referred to repeatedly in the context of the localism that they attempted to create.

At the heart of this inability to see the distress that the abandonment of these villages must have occasioned is a yearning to be "of the place." The very localities that Israeli-born artists and architects identify as points of connectedness to a place—the familiar landscape of the abandoned village—are sources of pain and alienation for the former inhabitants. What is more Israeli than an abandoned Palestinian area? What conveys local Israeli ambience more than Ein Hod, old Jaffa, or Ein Kerem—all populated by artists who incorporated the abandoned villages into their existence and their lifestyles and made them as beautiful as can be?[53] The beautification of abandoned areas dulls the pain of the battle. These villages of exile, the heart of Palestinian pain, were transformed by their hands into artists'

Figure 9.5. Dani Karavan, Catalogue Page Showing Drawings of Beit Jiz, 1953. Reprinted from Gila Blas and Ilana Tatenbaum, *Social Realism in the 1950, Political Art in the 1990s* (Haifa: The New Haifa Museum, 1998), p. 97.

colonies or, more significantly, into inspirational models for "local" Israeli building.

This predicament indicates a need to examine the founding generation of Israeli sabra culture, the generation that today bemoans the byproducts of its yearning for a local, connected Hebrew nativeness that was in many cases constructed on the ruins of the localness of the other. In some intriguing way the housing of Giloh, which is regularly targeted by the gunmen of Beit Jala during the current Palestinian intifada, may be the most accurate chronicle of Israeli architecture. It brings together the process and the result. It combines Brutalist aesthetics and the image of traditional stone building, therefore reversing the traditional use of concrete and stone. The arches in Giloh are made from exposed concrete while the prefabricated panels are covered with tubsa stone. This reversal can be read as a metaphor for Giloh's political position: it was industriously produced by a centralizing state on confiscated land, yet succeeded in fostering a sense of community and securing the Jewish middle class of Jerusalem. The architecture of Giloh is indeed both hospitable and brutal, simultaneously building the nation and divulging its colonial practices.

The roots of this architecture are a great concern for the integrity of human life in the age of progress, and technology sheds light on its problematic focus on man. In post–World War II architectural culture, the notion of man, by and large, implied a generic identity. This man was real, invulnerable, and entertained essential sameness across cultures and times. In Israel, however, when this generic man was a new immigrant, when his community had roots in foreign countries, and when his place was a contested territory that he had to conquer and protect through military power, his identity had to take on a host of different and more complex meanings. Local architects, trying to construct for this man a coherent and identifiable Israeli home, drew on the ethics of New Brutalism and the nascent regionalism of Team 10.

Ultimately, the home they constructed was intended to house the personification of the Zionist dream of a New Jew in the image of the native sabra. The model of the native Jew that the sabra embodied, however, was itself the result of an insecure possession of place. Sabra architects defined themselves vis-à-vis a modernization project that they thoroughly criticized and a place for which they longed but the "genetic code" of which was defined as Arab once it was juxtaposed with the Zionist project's strictly modernist path. Eventually the efforts of Israeli architects to crack the Palestinian code for local habitation on unequal political grounds diverted their focus on the structuralist man of post–World War II architectural culture away from its humanistic path. It deprived other men of the symbolic ownership of their built heritage.

POSTSCRIPT

Recent architectural critics enumerate the political pitfalls of this localist architectural tradition, which they want to divest of its leading role in Israeli architectural practice. According to this view, "concern with localness after 1967 reflects the release of dark tendencies that are fundamentalist in essence."[54] The clear separation between the social role of this architecture and its aesthetics characterizes the production of criticism during the politically charged time of the Palestinian intifadas. But does this criticism mark the end of "the tradition of the place," of the search for locality? Not necessarily. The "true" locality is now being attributed to Israel's modernism—the Bauhaus style of the 1930s and 1940s as well as the state's "gray" modernism of the 1950s. Recent exhibitions and monographs clearly indicate that the tradition of the modern, uncontaminated by the conflict or the Orient, is taking command. This recovery has a global appeal. A proponent of gray modernism explains that for a younger generation, that "knows that the 1950s are now in style" and whose "memory works in megabytes," it offers escape: "plain and simple—they are sick of fabricating 'local' architecture and getting bogged in the provincial swamp." The global in this happy reversal prompts the local to redefine a modernist tradition for Israeliness in a state of crisis.

NOTES

1. Israel performed the act of unification unilaterally by expanding the city's municipal boundaries and changing Israeli municipal law in order to enact Israeli jurisdiction in the newly defined Israeli capital. The Palestinian population of Jerusalem refused to participate in the state practices of the new regime, an act that was intended to validate their resolute demand to recognize in East Jerusalem the occupied capital of Palestine.

2. The Minister of Housing Mordechai Bentov explained on the Knesset [Israeli parliament] podium: "the planning principles are: building in stone, relatively low rise building, within the limits of three stories, in accordance with the neighborhood that border the area under development. Also incorporated are elements of Oriental building such as arches, domes etc; building types are especially adjusted to the topographic condition and the slopes of the sites (terraced building). . . . The architects and planners are exerting extra efforts to bestow on these neighborhoods an image that accords with the landscape and character of Jerusalem." See "Planning and Building Methods in East Jerusalem," *Haaretz*, February 2, 1968. Also Yehuda Drexler, interview with the author, September 2, 1998; and David Kroyanker, *Jerusalem Architecure—Periods and Styles: Modern Architecture Outside the Old City: 1948–1990* (Jerusalem: Keter, 1991), 41–42.

3. The Ministry of Housing was eager to build quickly on land confiscated immediately after the war in order to create a continuous built area between North

Jerusalem and Mount Scopus. They therefore recruited completed housing plans, which Itzhak Perlstein had designed for another site, and added to them prefabricated arches in order to provide Eshkol Heights with the appropriate Oriental look.

4. Elinoar Barzaki, interview with the author, August 20, 1998. Barzaki studied in Europe during the 1968 events and was recruited by Ram Karmi upon her return to join his team at the Ministry of Housing. Later she became the city engineer of Jerusalem and, at the time of the interview, the head of the architectural school at Tel Aviv University.

5. Aviah Hashimshoni, "Architecture," in *Art of Israel*, ed. Benjamin Tamuz (Israel: Massada, 1963), 199–229. The English edition is "Architecture," in *Art of Israel*, ed. Benjamin Tamuz, Max Wykes-Joyce, and Yona Fischer (Philadelphia: Chilton Book Co., 1967).

6. For the triple negation of the Jewish diaspora, the bourgeoisie, and the Orient, which preconditioned the adoption of modern architecture as a Zionist expression, see: Alona Nitzan-Shiftan, "Contested Zionism—Alternative Modernism: Erich Mendelsohn and the Tel Aviv Chug in Mandate Palestine," *Architectural History* 39 (September 1996), 147–80.

7. See: Joseph Mali, ed., *Wars, Revolutions and Generational Identity* (Tel Aviv: Am Oved: Merkaz Yitzhak Rabin le-heker Yisra'el, 2001), particularly Menachem Brinker, "The Generation of the State: a Cultural or Political Concept?" 143–57.

8. Dan Etan, interview with the author, July 29, 1998. Etan pointed out that the founders of Labor Zionism did not entrust his sabra generation with political duties but instead assigned them professional tasks. Indeed, one of the main questions facing scholars of this sabra generation is its members' political inefficacy in comparison to the founders of Labor Zionism. See: Yonatan Shapira, *An Elite without Successors* (Tel-Aviv: Sifriyat Po'alim, 1984). Anita Shapira argues that this generation conformed to the activist message of Labor Zionism and saw in politics a field of verbal articulations rather than accomplishments. Following her comment that they turned instead to professional careers, this study questions the political efficacy of their action through "the professions," see: Anita Shapira, "'Dor Baaretz,'" in *Old Jews, New Jews*, ed. Anita Shapira (Tel Aviv: Am Oved, 1997), 122–54.

9. Not all the protagonists I study were actually born in Mandate Palestine. However, interviews have revealed that the great majority of the group under focus was indeed native-born. Others assimilated to the culture of the sabra at an early age, being young enough to study in the appropriate high schools and to participate in the activities of Zionist youth movements, which led to the required cultural path I describe below.

10. The high schools were Tichon Hadash, Gimnasya Herzlia, and Bet Hinuch Tichon. Each of them was a hub for different youth movements.

11. Interviews with Dan Etan (July 29, 1998, May 15, 2001, and June 6, 2001) and with Avraham Vachman (August 8, 1998, and ongoing personal communication).

12. Moti Sahar, phone interview with author, July 2001.

13. Particularly important was the Model Housing Estate in Beer Sheva (1959–1964), where a team experimented with different housing types ranging from a kilometer-long housing block (Yaski and Alexandroni) to *casba*-inspired carpet housing (Havkin and Zolotov). The unrealized plans for the new town of Bsor

(1961–1964) generated new ideas that were strongly influenced by the British plans for Hook. Avraham Yaski headed both teams. Other examples of influential experiments are Etan and Yashar's Victory Housing in Dimona of the mid 1960s (the name of which was inspired by the Six Day War that immediately preceded the population of the housing complex); Yaakov and Ora Ya'ar's housing and commercial center in Givat Hamoreh (1958–1961); and David Best's plans for housing quarters in Arad (Yeelim, 1961, Avishur, 1965).

14. Jacob Bakema, in *Team 10 Primer*, ed. Alison Margaret Smithson and Team 10 (Cambridge, MA: MIT Press, 1968), 24.

15. Stanford Anderson, "Memory without Monuments: Vernacular Architecture," *Traditional Dwellings and Settlements Review* 11, no. 1 (1999): 13–22.

16. Aldo van Eyck in *New Frontiers in Architecture; CIAM '59 in Otterlo*, ed. Oscar Newman (New York: Universe Books, 1961).

17. Bernard Rudofsky, *Architecture Without Architects: An Introduction to Nonpedigreed Architecture* (New York: Museum of Modern Art, 1964), caption for illustration 1.

18. Early New Brutalism stressed reverence to materials, affinity between building and man, and inspiration from peasant architecture (particularly from the Mediterranean vernacular). Aesthetically, the trend is known for its brute materials, especially its characteristic exposed concrete. The building that most inspired this trend is Unite d'Habitation in Marseilles, a monumental housing complex by Le Corbusier late in his career. The first history of this trend by a contemporary critic is Reyner Banham, *The New Brutalism: Ethic or Aesthetic* (New York: Reinhold, 1966).

19. Dani Karavan in *Social Realism*, ed. Blas and Tatenbaum.

20. See Zali Gurevitz and Gideon Aran, "Al Ha'makom," [Israeli Anthropology] *Alpayim* 4 (1991).

21. Yoram Segal, "The Traditional House in the Arab Villages in the Galilee," *Tvai* 1 (1966): 19–22.

22. Ibid., 20.

23. Ram Karmi, *Lyric Architecture* (Israel: Ministry of Defense, 2001), 12.

24. In the wake of Said's *Orientalism* of 1978, many studies have demonstrated the Western/Oriental dichotomy in different contexts and locales. For the Israeli context, see Ella Shohat, *Israeli Cinema: East/West and the Politics of Representation* (Austin: University of Texas Press, 1989); Gil Eyal, "On the Arab Village," *Teoria ve Bikoret* 3 (1993); and Yigal Zalmona and Tamar Manor-Fridman, *Kadima: The East in Israeli Art* (Jerusalem: Israel Museum, 1998). Particularly important in this context is Dan Rabinowitz, *Anthropology and the Palestinians* (Raanana: ha-Merkaz le-heker ha-hevrah ha-'Arvit, 1998).

25. See, for example, Russell Ferguson, *Out There: Marginalization and Contemporary Cultures* (New York and Cambridge, MA: New Museum of Contemporary Art and MIT Press, 1990); Homi K. Bhabha, *The Location of Culture* (London and New York: Routledge, 1994).

26. For critical discussions of the object of ethnography, see James Clifford and George E. Marcus, *Writing Culture: The Poetics and Politics of Ethnography* (Berkeley: University of California Press, 1986); Talal Asad, *Anthropology and the Colonial Encounter* (London: Ithaca Press, 1973); George W. Stocking, *Observers Observed: Essays on Ethnographic Fieldwork* (Madison: University of Wisconsin Press, 1983).

27. David Cassuto, *The Western Wall: A Collection of Essays Concerning the Design of the Western Wall Plaza and Its Surroundings* (Jerusalem: The Jerusalem Post Press, 1975), 95.

28. Nadia Abu El-Haj, *Facts on the Ground: Archaeological Practice and Territorial Self-Fashioning in Israeli Society* (Chicago,: The University of Chicago Press, 2001).

29. Arieh Dvir [architect], "Overall Plan for the Jerusalem National Park," in The Jerusalem Committee, *Proceedings of the First Meeting, June 30–July 4, 1969* (Jerusalem), 24.

30. The publication of the Israel Defense Force, *Bamahane*, preached the love of the country. It published stories and detachable centerpieces of images from "the Land of Israel." These posters became major visual stimuli in the military physical environment, service in which is obligatory. Many of these features were compiled in Irit Zaharoni, *Israel, Roots and Routes: A Nation Living in Its Landscape* (Tel Aviv: MOD Publishing House, 1990). This edition is based on the Hebrew book *Derech Eretz: nofe artzenu*.

31. The open-air model was reconstructed and largely imagined in the absence of accurate archeological data by the archeologist Professor Avi Yona. A recent appraisal of it in a publication dedicated to "knowing the country" is: Gavriel Barkai and Eli Shiler, "A Tour in Second Temple Jerusalem in the Holyland Hotel Model," *A Periodical for the Study of the Land of Israel* 2001, 21–50.

32. Yoram Tzafrir, preface to *The Eretz-Israeli Residential House*, by Yizhar Hirschfeld (Jerusalem: Yad Ben Tzvi, 1987).

33. Moshe Safdie, *Jerusalem: The Future of the Past* (Boston: Houghton Mifflin, 1989), 27.

34. Moshe Safdie, *Safdie in Jerusalem*, Slidcas no. 3, extracted from a talk given to the Royal Institute of Architects in May 1979 (London, Pidgeon Audio Visual).

35. Moshe Safdie, *Jerusalem: The Future of the Past*, 29.

36. Safdie, *Beyond Habitat*, 216. For Safdie's design for the Western Wall Plaza see Alona Nitzan-Shiftan, *Israelizing Jerusalem: The Encounter between Architectural and National Ideologies 1967–1977*, Ph.D. diss., MIT, 2002.

37. This concept was particularly important in the context of Italian colonialism in North Africa, where architects integrated European and North African built traditions under the banner of the Mediterranean tradition in which Romans had rights of authenticity. For a succinct and illuminating account of the term in architectural culture, see Mia Fuller, "Mediterraneanism," *Environmental Design* 8, no. 9/10 (1990); and Mia Fuller, *Colonial Constructions: Architecture, Cities, and Italian Imperialism in the Mediterranean and East Africa* (New York: Routledge, forthcoming). For an in-depth study of this phenomenon and its remarkable influence on Italian modernism, see Brian Lloyd McLaren, "Mediterraneita and Modernita: Architecture and Culture during the Period of Italian Colonization of North Africe (Lybia)," Ph.D. diss., MIT, 2001.

38. Banham, *The New Brutalism*, 47.

39. Kenneth Frampton, who studied together with Karmi at the AA and worked in Israel for a while, invested these British regionalist attitudes with critical theory. The resultant *Critical Regionalism* turned into one of the most influential texts in late twentieth-century architectural culture worldwide.

40. For Mediterraneanism in the Israeli context, see Yaakov Shavit, "The Mediterranean World and 'Mediterraneanism': The Origins, Meaning, and Application of a Geo-Cultural Notion in Israel," *Mediterranean Historical Review* 3:2 (1998), 96–117, and Yaakov Shavit, "Culture Rising From the Sea," [Tarbut Ola Min Hayam] *zmanim* 34–35 (1990), 38–47.

41. For the bureaucratic management of national identity see Michael Herzfeld, *The Social Production of Indifference: Exploring the Symbolic Roots of Western Bureaucracy* (Chicago: University of Chicago Press, 1993).

42. Karmi, "Human Values in Urban Architecture," in *Israel Builds*, ed. A. Harlap (Tel Aviv: Ministry of Housing, 1977), 44.

43. Interview with Amir and Ofer Kolker, July 27, 1998. The Kolkers were deputies to Ram Karmi, the head architect of the Ministry of Housing from 1974–1979. They were part of a large team that Karmi assembled in order to devise strict design guidelines for the entire country. Ofer was responsible for the central region while Amir was responsible for the Jerusalem region.

44. For example, Gil'ad Duvshani and Hari Frank, *Build Ye Cities: An Exhibition of Israeli Architecture*, Institute of Architects and Town Planners in Israel AEAI, 1985; Yoseph Kiriaty, special issue, "Contemporary Israeli Architecture," *Process: Architecture* 44 (1984).

45. During the fierce debate over the building of Nebi Samuel, later known as Ramot, Yehuda Drexler convinced Prime Minister Golda Meir to violate the 1968 Jerusalem Master Plan, which recommended building a suburb of 2,000 units on the site of Nebi Samuel, where Drexler intended to build a neighborhood of 20,000 units. His argument was as follows: Why not upgrade lower income families that previously lived in frontier neighborhoods instead of settling Jerusalem's wealthy population in a luxurious suburb? Golda Meir accepted this logic and approved the project. See protocol of the State Council for Planning and Building, the Subcommittee for Principal Planning Issues, The Ministry of Interior Affairs, February 1, 1971 (courtesy of Yehuda Drexler).

46. Avraham Yaski, interview with the author, August 23, 1998.

47. Ibid.

48. Ibid.

49. For texts by Danziger, see Mordechai Omer (curator), *Yitzhak Danziger* (Tel Aviv: Gan ha-taasiyah Tefen, Tel Aviv Museum of Art, The Open Museum, 1996).

50. Sarah Hinski, "The Silence of the Fish: Local and Universal in Israeli Art Discourse," *Teoria Ve'bikoret* 4 (1993): 105–22.

51. Tzalmona and Manor-Friedman, *Kadima*.

52. Yigal Zalmona, (curator), *Mikhah Ulman: 1980–1988* (Jerusalem: Israel Museum, 1988).

53. For the case of Ein Hod, see the excellent anthropological study Susan Slyomovics, *The Object of Memory: Arab and Jew Narrate the Palestinian Village* (Philadelphia: University of Pennsylvania Press, 1998).

54. Esther Zandberg, "The Lost Dignity of the Shutters," *Haaretz Weekend Supplement* October 27, 2000, 42.

10

Present and Absent

Historical Invention and the Politics of Place in Colonial Jerusalem

Thomas Abowd

Jerusalem is a place where geography, memory, and historical invention have interacted in myriad ways through successive waves of foreign domination. As the primary site of confrontation between Palestinians and Israelis since 1948, Jerusalem is an urban center where an intense conflict of two opposing national visions has continually—and often violently— raged. The city is a place where religious groups clash most intensely and where communal grips on myths, ideologies, and places are least- readily loosened.[1]

Though a demonstrated parity of desire for Jerusalem exists, I suggest that in the ability to comprise and reconfigure the space and history of the city, there has been no parity of power between Palestinians and Israelis. Nothing underscores this disparity more potently than the fact that this struggle for land is not simply a national conflict but also a colonial one. Palestinian Muslims and Christians have lived since 1948 (and well before) as an occupied and colonized people, vulnerable to policies of ethnic cleansing, exclusion, and wholesale dispossession. Israeli Jews, though diverse in their views about their government's illegal possession of Palestinian territory, often find themselves as direct occupiers of another people's land. Even many Israeli peace activists live in the homes of or on land stolen from the indigenous Arab population.

Colonial power has remade Jerusalem over the last several decades not simply through the instruments of superior arms, force, and coercion, but also through more subtle forms of historical invention and myth making. By looking at the politics of place in Jerusalem under Israeli occupation, I show how specific locales in this divided metropolitan area have simultaneously served as sites of remembrance and of forgetting. The chapter details how the

Israeli state has forcefully appropriated homes from Palestinian families and transformed them into distinctly Israeli places, ones dedicated to the memory of Israeli national achievement, sacrifice, or belonging.

As the Israeli state commandeered thousands of Arab homes throughout Jerusalem in the spring and summer of 1948, the city was reconfigured both discursively and physically.[2] Not only were tens of thousands of Palestinian Jerusalemites driven out of their familial places by Zionist forces, but these familial places were taken over and settled with new Israeli residents. The budding Jewish state also utilized such properties (and the neighborhoods they comprised) to construct new histories and assertions about belonging to the city.

One particular Jerusalem home, belonging to the Palestinian Baramki family, has possessed an emblematic and distinctive history.[3] Taken as a case study for investigating the borders of remembering and forgetting, this once-familial site has served multiple functions convenient to colonial rule. These various functions point to the ways in which the dominant national community has reconfigured Jerusalem and the larger country in which it is so centrally embedded. The fate of the Baramki home (and that of the Arab family who still claim it) tells us about the politics of history, place, and the construction of nationalist myths. The Baramkis' property is significant because it has since 1967 been used by the Israeli state to help legitimate its rule over the city. It stands at the site between the border of active forgetting and of steadfast remembering.

THE PRODUCTION AND DESTRUCTION OF THE PAST: HOMES AS SITES OF REMEMBERING AND FORGETTING

All nationalisms and national movements have been assembled upon a foundation of elaborate and refined myths—stories about peoples and places. Israeli nationalism is no different. The builders of Zion have often mobilized supposed "eternal" connections between the Jewish people and Jerusalem to assert an exclusive Israeli right to the city.

The nationalist notion of Jerusalem as the exclusive province of the Israeli state has been advanced in particular through the articulation of potent narratives of Israeli independence [*komimeyot*], defense [*gonen*], and redemption [*geula*]. These ideas have special resonance for millions of Jews and Christians globally, for the city retains an immense symbolism for these groups, often grounded in biblical myths and involving figures such as King David. One illustration of the discursive construction of an Israeli Jerusalem is the fact that independence [*komimeyot*], defense [*gonen*], and redemption [*geula*] are the names authorities have given to three former Arab neighborhoods in today's West Jerusalem, once home to several thousand Palestinian exiles. These places, though still containing hundreds of former Palestinians homes, are formally off-limits to Palestinians today.

A number of prominent scholars of colonialism, citing "re-naming" strategies of the sort described above, have written about the cultural dimensions of colonial rule. Many have examined the usefulness of ideas and ideologies for facilitating the project of controlling and dominating other peoples and their lands. Describing the role of knowledge construction in the formation of colonial rule, Nicholas Dirks (1996) notes, "[I]t has not been sufficiently recognized that colonialism was itself a cultural project of control. Colonial knowledge both enabled conquest and was produced by it; in certain important ways knowledge was what colonialism was all about."[4]

Indeed, Jerusalem's potent symbolism and enduring myths have played a central role in assembling Israeli national histories and identities. For several decades now, the Israeli state has used a strategy to assert that Jerusalem belongs solely to the Israelis because it is the eternal and unified capital of the Jewish people. This strategy, one meant to assert transhistorical ownership over a contested territory, has been advanced on the land of and even within the very homes of uprooted Palestinian families.

The Israeli state has appropriated some Arab homes and turned them into kindergartens, centers for psychoanalysis, clubs for new Jewish arrivals to the country [*olim*], Holocaust memorials, restaurants, and even shelters for animals. In a few cases, the actual structures of the houses have served a strict ideological function. For example, the Israeli state seized a partially destroyed Arab home on the road from Tel Aviv to Jaffa and later remade into what is today known as the Etzel Museum. The remnants of this damaged Palestinian structure have been utilized to memorialize the role Menecham Begin's paramilitary organization, Etzel, played in the ethnic cleansing of Palestine's Arabs.

Palestinian refugees' memories of flight and exile have been narratives all too often relegated to an intellectual no man's land. Scholars of the Arab-Israeli conflict have frequently ignored oral sources, regarding them as subjective renderings that necessarily deviate from the one "true story." In attempting to relate some of Jerusalem's hidden histories over the last several decades, it is precisely oral sources from which scholars need to draw more substantially.[5]

Memory is mediated through a host of present-day issues, political concerns, and prejudices, and is thus often highly contested and fluid. The sometimes clouded and selective ways in which people often remember their pasts are indeed real issues for which a historian must account. But past events are also not completely up for grabs or "undecidable." Though the memories of both national communities must be examined critically, limitations of memory do not necessarily discount what those affected by traumatic events have to say about their experiences.

THE BARAMKI HOUSE

The Baramki home, not far from Jerusalem's Old City, has served various functions for the Israeli state since it was taken from its owners in the spring of 1948.

The home was built in 1934 in the neighborhood of Sa'ad Said. During the first Arab-Israeli War in 1948, a no man's land of barbed wire, mines, and fences split this neighborhood and the places that comprised it between the Jordanian-held east and Israeli-held west sides of the city. This divide physically fractured the city for the next nineteen years. The Baramkis were one of thousands of Arab families in Jerusalem who fled their places of residence during the violent spring of 1948 for what they believed at the time were temporary havens. Like thousands of other Palestinians families, they gathered only a few items as they fled, believing that they would return after a few weeks.

Andoni Baramki, a Palestinian architect of renown trained in Athens during the latter years of Ottoman rule, designed this large home. Like the many other structures in Jerusalem that were also his creation, this one featured a distinctive hybrid use of Corinthian columns and Arab-style arches and verandas. Baramki experimented with the use of red and white stones, which he often utilized in the same arch or facade. These would become his architectural trademarks. Homes with his signature still dot Jerusalem's landscape of loss, particularly in the neighborhoods of West Jerusalem, which were once home to tens of thousands of Palestinians.

Sixty to seventy years after many of these homes had been constructed and fifty-three years after his family's flight, the son of the architect told me about the Jerusalem his father and mother lived in under the British colonial government. He related how, in his words, his father's work had been "mutilated" by many of the current Israeli occupants of these homes. Original living spaces have been subdivided and former verandas that graced the fronts of properties have, on occasion, been enclosed with glass or sheet metal to create an additional room. Some of the former homes have been crowned with unattractive add-on floors, erected carelessly on the former flat rooftops of these structures and often with little if any regard for the original aesthetic.

The story of this family's flight was typical in many ways. They were unable to remain in Sa'ad Said as the spring of 1948 arrived. "We left with very little in April [1948]," relates one family member. "All our pictures, our carpets, everything was left behind. Sa'ad Said became a very dangerous place so we moved to Qatamon and then that became dangerous. So, we finally went to Bir Zeit [a Palestinian village north of Jerusalem] to wait for the fighting to end. It ended but then the city was cut in two and we lost everything and could not go back."

The Baramki home, as it happened, came to rest precisely on the edge of the emerging frontier between the Israeli- and Jordanian-ruled segments of the city. It straddled the territorial border. These two sides came to be known after 1948 as East and West Jerusalem, spatial designations born of an artificial division. These designations had never meant anything before the city was violently partitioned. This arbitrarily defined boundary, drawn in a perfunctory manner across a formally undivided landscape by Israeli and Jordanian generals, actually ran along the outer edge of the Baramki home's front garden. Not a few of the structures in the vicinity (usually Palestinian) were actually divided by the width of the pen used to draw the border, a potent metaphor for the disruptions that partition has repeatedly engendered in colonial contexts.

The unsightly frontier slithered through the center of this neighborhood like an ugly serpent of barbed wire and concrete walls. This enforced order of separation between Jews and Arabs in the city eventually resulted in a situation in which the boundaries of rule simultaneously created and hid the traumas of displacement and exile. The partition of Jerusalem put an end to many areas of Arab-Jewish "mixed" life in the city, including the area where the Baramki family once resided.

Only weeks after its Arab owners had fled, the sentinels of the budding Jewish state commandeered the mammoth, well-fortified, imposing, three-story, and strategically positioned stone structure of the Baramki home. The Israeli military transformed the house into an army post in the weeks after the 1948 War began. They placed weapons behind the home's thick limestone walls and aimed them across the mixture of mines and barbed wire. They reinforced the doors and sealed the home's front entrance. They filled the structure's exquisite arched windows with concrete and made them into turrets so that only a thin aperture, narrow enough to accommodate a gun and the gaze of a marksman, remained.

Israeli forces stationed at this house turned military post were positioned, in part, to help stem what the new Jewish state referred to as "Arab infiltration" across the newly crafted frontier. However, as Israeli historian Tom Segev describes, these efforts to traverse the new frontier were usually attempts by Palestinian exiles to return to their homes in areas conquered by Israel during the 1948 War.[6] The use of the term infiltration itself was a rhetorical move that served to criminalize Palestinian attempts to return to their homes while at the same time solidifying Israel's presence in and control over the western segment of Jerusalem. Palestinian efforts to secretly cross this dividing line could be regarded as acts of hostility, illegality, or even terrorism only once this segment of the city was secured as Israeli national space.

With very few exceptions, neither Jews nor Arabs were permitted to cross over to the other side of the city over the next nineteen years. Though the division of Jerusalem prevented Israeli Jews from visiting the Old City and the Wailing Wall, sealing the border also ensured that the Arab homes on Jerusalem's west side from which tens of thousands of refugees had fled could not be contested because the families were deemed "absentees" by Israeli law.[7]

Emptied of its Arab occupants, the structure began to assume new uses and take on new meanings. Those on the Israeli side of the border began, for example, to refer to the property as the Tourjaman Army Post.[8] This vital border post's significance was bound up with the Mandelbaum Gate complex, which existed just north of the property and served as the one crossing point between the east and west sides of the city.

Elements of the Baramki home's exterior and interior that signified a familial presence began to disappear as Israel transformed the site from home to military outpost. Most of those who knew the house as belonging to the Baramkis were dispersed from this region in 1948 as the neighborhood became a hostile frontier zone. In the months and years that followed, Jewish immigrants who knew little or nothing of the pre-1948 city were housed in the vicinity of the Baramki home and in other emptied Arab neighborhoods that ran along the East-West frontier. They had no memory of the house's previous ownership. Musrara (a few dozen meters south of the Baramki home), parts of Abu Tur (just south of the Old City), and the Mamilla neighborhood below the Jaffa Gate [*bab el-Khalil*]—all were major sites for settling new (and usually poor) Jewish immigrants to Israel. This despite the fact that these quarters were contiguous to the border and could be dangerous places to walk, let alone live in.

MEMORIES OF WAITING

Exile has been a condition shared by many Palestinian Jerusalemites with whom I spoke during fieldwork. During the course of interviews with them in East Jerusalem, many would point in the direction of a lost familial house, sometimes just a few kilometers to the west. These were places that many still referred to as home and they had not given up the struggle to return. However, few were confident that they would ever reclaim the homes of their parents and grandparents. Those I interviewed would bring out old photos of their homes and occasionally would show me old titles and keys to these lost properties.

Though I came to see commonalities between these different Palestinian experiences of exile, there always seemed something quite distinct about the Baramki case. Unlike nearly all other Palestinian families pushed out of their homes by Jewish forces in 1948, the Baramkis had the dubious privilege of being able to see their property on the Israeli-held side of the no man's land during the years of the divided city (1948–1967). For better or worse, they were able to witness its transformation. The son of the home's owner remembers ascending seven flights of steps to the top of the East Jerusalem YMCA, the tallest building on the east side at the time and situated only one hundred meters from the city's dividing line. From this vantage point, he and his father would gaze down across the frontier and assess the condition of their crumbling property. Family members such as this man, now in his seventies, relate that having the opportunity to reconnect visually with their house did not assuage the uncertainty generated by being separated from it.

He and other Palestinians relate that in the years that followed the division of the city, they were confident that they would return. But that optimism began to evaporate with the passing of time. "I could see this place where I grew up, full of Israeli soldiers, being destroyed little by little. That was hard. And it was worse to see my father who was so sad when he would look at it because he built this place."

Much mystery existed among Palestinian exiles concerning Jerusalem's division and their return to their homes. Questions of *when* they would return over the years gradually became questions of *if*. For many Palestinian exiles and refugees, the barbed wire and concrete walls that divided Jerusalem into two parts served as a continual reminder of their condition of displacement. But what could not, for the most part, be seen from East Jerusalem vantage points were the multiple ways in which former Arab neighborhoods on the Israeli-controlled west side (e.g., Talbieh, Qatamon, Baqa, and Musrara) were being altered and reconfigured, renamed and redefined.

Many refugees I spoke with recall how rumors began to seep across the border concerning the fate of their properties. Such news suggested that their homes, lands, and neighborhoods were not waiting still and untouched for their eventual return.

"Were you confident then that you would eventually get the house back?" I asked the son of the architect in his office outside of Jerusalem one summer morning.

"No, no, not at all," he recalls gloomily, "Not as the years went by. Actually, I told my father to forget about the house. By the mid 1960s it was clear to me that if we were ever going to reclaim that property, it would not be in my father's time." Though from the heights of the YMCA he and his family could stand within one hundred meters of their property, they and their property resided on either side of a political abyss. The family could more easily travel to Baghdad, Beirut, or Boston than return to the place they once called home, just a stone's throw away across the frontier.

JUNE 1967: MAKING THE LAND "WHOLE"

The years of the "divided city" were to end suddenly and dramatically. During six days in June 1967, Israeli forces conquered East Jerusalem in lightning fashion. Within a few weeks of invading this side (and after some internal Israeli debate), the victors brought down the division of walls and barbed wire that had for nineteen years split Jerusalem into two. The city, Israeli officialdom euphorically declared, had now been "reunified" and "liberated."

Once the physical partition was removed, thousands from either side of the former divide quickly streamed across to the other side in curiosity. Palestinian refugees who had waited nineteen years to return made their way back to their former neighborhoods and homes. Hundreds of thousands of Israeli Jews streamed to the Western Wall and the Jewish Quarter of the Old City. The Israeli conquest of the east side of Jerusalem had brought down the barrier, which many initially believed opened up possibilities for Palestinian exiles to reclaim their stolen properties.

Several dozen refugees I interviewed related that a pervasive belief existed among the displaced that they would finally be able to repossess their homes after nearly two decades of exile. After all, they had not repudiated their claims to these properties. United Nations Resolution 194 acknowledged their right to return; a broad international consensus supported this notion. But the prospect of reclaiming homes and lands was more complex. Palestinian Jerusalemites would, ironically, remain exiles within the newly reconfigured Israeli municipality; what the Israeli state—in its juridical remaking of the city—would term "present absentees." Upon returning to their old neighborhoods, many described feeling the same ambivalence that the Israeli juridical category embodies; that condition of being present and absent at the same time. The boundary between presence and absence was, in a sense, dissolving.

These returnees had never left the city they referred to as home but were precluded from reclaiming their homes. They discovered that their residences were usually still there, discernable from the street, but that they had been altered in various ways. Remarking on their initial return, many refugees told me that the social and physical landscapes of their former neighborhoods, like the properties themselves, were at once familiar and foreign. Hala Sakakini (1990), who visited her family home in Qatamon in the days immediately after the border was taken down, relates her experience of return: "It was a sad encounter, like meeting a dear person whom you had last seen young, healthy and well groomed and finding that he had become old, sick, and shabby. Even worse, it was like coming across a friend whose personality had undergone a drastic change and was no more the same person."[9]

The ambivalence of these sentiments underscored the manner in which the city had become simultaneously unified and fractured. The Israeli government gave new Hebrew names to streets, squares, and locales. They also numbered these sites in different ways. Arabic was absent from this segment of Jerusalem and refugees describe the pervasive strangeness and inscrutability of a Hebrew that had taken over and become emblazoned on everything they once knew.

Old, formerly empty lots and locales had been filled in with an architecture of concrete and faux stone, built for utility and the needs of new Jewish immigrants. Trees stood ten feet taller, were chopped down, or were no longer within the province of properties, whose gated perimeters had occasionally been reapportioned. Many Arab exiles, returning to their former familial places, relate discovering an Israeli family residing there—often more than one. Different children now played on the same front lawns they once played on as children.

Though the physical wall had finally come down in June 1967, other emerging legal divides were erected in their place. Jerusalem came under sole Israeli control after 1967, and in this way the city was physically "unified." However, the conquest and subsequent occupation of East Jerusalem had left the Christian and Muslim populations over whom Israel ruled on the other side of a *juridical* boundary. These legal strictures and the social boundaries the occupiers drew would prove to be, in many respects, as impenetrable as the former physical frontier.

One Palestinian exile, a Christian woman named Mounira, returned to see her family's home in Qatamon only in the mid 1990s, some forty-five years after she and her family fled and twenty-eight years after the wall had come down. She explained to me that she did not want to go back to see the place where she spent her first eleven years. Mounira described still feeling "emotionally fractured" in a city that Israeli authorities claimed was "unified," but where social and political divisions remained constant. She related harboring cynical feelings, then and now, concerning the return of the property:

> During the years when the city was divided, we heard that more and more [Jewish] refugees were coming and more refugees were coming and that they

were being put in our homes. The Jordanians kept giving us a kind of "mor-phine," telling us that we would go back and that they would make sure of this. They kept saying this but I did not have much confidence. I was always very skeptical. My mother went back *right* after 1967 and found four Jewish fami-lies living in our house. The house was sub-divided and I remember my mother telling me that the house was well looked after and that the families there were very nice and let her in to see the house.

"Why didn't you go back and see the house earlier?" I inquired, some-what astonished that she had waited so long to travel the few kilometers across the former frontier to visit the place she had spent her childhood years.

"I didn't want to go back," she replied without hesitating, "you see, be-cause my house was no longer my house. I couldn't take seeing it as a stranger. Better not to see."

Many other exiles returned and knocked on the doors of their homes. Several met with the Israeli Jews who were living there. In another legal move typical of colonial power, an entirely different land law had been put in place. Israeli law declared such homes as "state land" and, as such, ear-marked for Israeli Jewish use only. Old keys were of no value in opening present-day doors and gates. British Mandate–era deeds were useless in pushing forward claims on stolen properties. Both items to this day remain useful only in evoking memories of a former life and livelihood. They are props in a cruel stage play of loss.

The Baramkis, too, crossed over the old frontier with their keys and deeds. They made the short walk through the former no man's land that they once peered across. As the owner and his son approached the battle-scarred structure and entered the remains of what had been their front gar-den, one family member describes feeling a genuine sense of confidence that they would soon be able to reclaim their property. Most, however, were far less confident. They were forbidden to enter their properties by military authorities still stationed there. The Baramkis, with the help of an Israeli lawyer, made attempts to reclaim their property. However, the Israeli state refused to hand over the badly damaged property to the family, claiming alternately that it was still required for purposes of Israeli "secu-rity," that it was in need of repair and thus a physical hazard, and finally, that ownership of the property had shifted since the Israeli grid of legality had been imposed on Jerusalem beginning in the early 1950s. If Palestini-ans like the Baramkis stood any chance of retrieving their properties under Israeli occupation, the onus was placed on them to prove (to Israeli offi-cials, in Israeli courts) that they were wrongly classified as absentees.[10] Few were able to do so.

RECONFIGURING JERUSALEM: THE DISCURSIVE CONSTRUCTION OF A REGIME OF POWER

Following the 1967 war, the city began to undergo significant alterations, discursive as well as physical. Only weeks after seizing East Jerusalem, Israeli law was extended to this segment of the city and this territory was now referred to as Israeli land. The sixty thousand Palestinian Jerusalemites who came under Israeli rule in the wake of the conquest of East Jerusalem were transformed almost overnight from citizens of the Jordanian monarchy into "permanent residents" within the enlarged Israeli municipality.

The physical division that had fractured Jerusalem was now gone. But the elimination of that form of forced separation between Arab and Jew gave way to emerging practices of drawing other kinds of frontiers within a physically unified urban space. These acts included extending Israeli segregationist legislation over the whole of Jerusalem, East and West. An emerging order was being imposed. These alterations across the city's legal landscape, I argue, underscore the distinctly colonial dimensions of Israeli rule.[11]

Israeli intentions of forging institutional forms of separation between Arabs and Jews were underscored and made evident by the ways these authorities redrew the municipal boundaries in June 1967. Unilateral alterations of the city's borders inflated the area newly redefined as Jerusalem by a factor of five.[12] A number of Israeli historians and Jerusalem city planners have asserted that the Israeli intention and guiding principle in enlarging the city's municipal boundaries after the June war was the desire to ensure the maximum of Palestinian land under Israeli control with the minimum of Palestinian populations. In other words, it aimed at taking in as much occupied Palestinian land as possible within the Israeli municipality borders while including within those newly constituted boundaries the fewest number of Arabs who lived in and around the Jerusalem area.[13]

The state sought to exclude certain populations and implicitly include others as it expanded. In some cases, hundreds of acres of a particular Arab village became incorporated within these newly defined borders of the city while the Arab owners or users of that land were driven off or left on the other side of the arbitrarily drawn municipal divide.[14] The creation of a radically gerrymandered city border, weaving around dense Arab population concentrations, mirrors historical desires among Zionist leaders for a state as free of Palestinians as possible. This strategy can be seen as part of a broader design to guarantee Jewish demographic dominance in the city. Two former Israeli planners who helped comprise these post-1967 policies have written that they meant to ensure that the Arab population in the area Israeli state defined as Jerusalem would never surpass 28 percent of the total population.[15]

Whereas in 1948 tens of thousands of Palestinians were removed by force from Jerusalem, in the wake of the 1967 war thousands more were excluded and denied residency in the city through a careful redelineation of borders and redefinition of what constituted Israel. Israeli policy in the post-1967 period in Jerusalem, therefore, has been about defining boundaries of the city that keep Palestinians outside while simultaneously extending legal exclusions that police the various internal frontiers within the city's municipal limits.

In addition to the vast reordering of spaces in Jerusalem, a parallel ideological effort—a policy of knowledge construction—was equally at work in the "reunified" urban center. As the borderlands were swept away and military emplacements were dismantled, one such border post was kept intact along the line of the previous divide: the Baramki house, the site that had come to be known by Israelis as the Tourjeman Army Post.

Former Israeli deputy mayor of Jerusalem Meron Benvenisti recounts that this locale, resting as it did on the edge of the former frontier, was retained "for posterity."[16] However, nowhere in his extensive writings on the city does Benvenisti mention that the structure was originally a home. That, it seems, is to be forgotten. The property had become, in the dominant order of naming things, the former Tourjeman Army Post or the Tourjeman Building. It was to be left as a monument, but one that pointed to only one national history, one collective memory, and one geographical imagination. The other was forgotten.

What precisely such a memorial was meant to convey symbolically for succeeding generations of Israelis—"for posterity"—was not clearly articulated at the time. But what was certainly evident was that two mutually exclusive visions of this structure and its past converged on the same locale. One was brought to the foreground and the other silenced. The Baramki property was no longer seen simply as a home or even as a home at all. Weathered by war, stripped of elements and traces that would indicate that this was once a familial space (including the removal of the family who owned it), the structure's role as a military garrison—and then former military garrison—had begun to assume a "taken for granted" quality for Israelis as well as many Palestinians.

DOMINATION ON DISPLAY: THE BARAMKI HOUSE AND "THE TOURJEMAN POST MUSEUM"

The encounter between the Baramkis and the Israeli state is emblematic of the ways in which Palestinians are simultaneously present and absent in Jerusalem. The Israeli law defining Palestinian exiles as absentees underscores the legal marginality Arabs inhabit in the Jerusalem of Israel's imagination. But this marginality also points to the ways in which certain understandings of the city are remembered and recognized, while others are simply "absented" or forgotten.

The initiation of Israeli plans to reconfigure the city physically after 1967 also brought the material construction of the depiction of Jerusalem as a space uniquely vital to the Jewish people. Jerusalem is constructed as a sacred place, an eternal place, the "heart of the Jewish people," the city of King David. These notions of heritage anchor Israeli national identity more firmly in the "history" of—and desire for—Jerusalem.[17] Such concepts have also entailed the construction of monuments and museums intended to remember Jerusalem in ways that naturalize the Israeli presence in a city that others consider a decidedly occupied territory.

These dynamics affected the Baramki house. Members of the Baramki family were permitted to cross the former divide to West Jerusalem in 1967. But they were not allowed access to their home until the early 1980s. The circumstances of their return were as odd as they were painful for the owners. As was the case with hundreds of other Palestinian homes, the Israeli office of what is referred to as the custodian for absentee property had turned the house over to the Israeli government for "public purposes." In the early 1980s, the home underwent another transformation. Without notice or the permission of the owners, the Israeli municipality stealthily reconstituted the dilapidated former "Tourjeman Post" into what became known as the Tourjeman Post *Museum.*

This site, the Israelis declared, would now serve as a monument meant to memorialize the "reunification of Jerusalem." The structure's interior and exterior were designed in ways that recall what life was like in the city during the nineteen years it was fractured between east and west sides. The museum's layout accomplishes this solely from the perspective of those on the Israeli side of the frontier. Museum brochures and the plaque placed on the front door referred to the structure as: "Dedicated to the Theme: Jerusalem—A Divided City Reunited."

The home's crumbling exterior was left for the most part in its damaged state—"for posterity" (i.e., to remember)—while a donation from an American family enabled the Israeli municipality to reconfigure the interior. By maintaining the structure in the condition it had been in between 1948 and 1967, those who appropriated the home sought to call attention to its history as one of military garrison, not as familial space. The museum qua military garrison no longer had a history prior to 1948. In the literature that the city produces for external consumption, it is never mentioned that the structure was in fact the home of a Palestinian family. That history is utterly silenced within this representational space.

Leaving the structure in a state of disrepair reminds those who come across it of the sacrifices the embattled defenders of the budding Jewish state claim

Baramki House, Jerusalem, 1990, in its Early Years as the Israeli "Tourjeman Post" Museum. Courtesy of the Author.

to have endured as hostile forces sought to destroy them. Leaving the home not as it had been during the years of the divided city calls attention to traces of a former existence as "defense post" and this strategy has, to a significant extent, helped divert the onlookers' gaze from the site's other pasts.

I often had occasion to pass by the Baramki home during my various research stays in Jerusalem. The appearance of the building from the outside reminded me of Salvador Dali's *Slave Market with the Disappearing Bust of Voltaire*, a painting that depicts the revolutionary Voltaire's head as comprised of two slave merchants standing in a market. Here, in this one image, the two seem almost parasitically bound up together. One can observe two different ideas of history (one opposed to slavery and one in favor) converging on—in fact, comprising—the same site. The two images and the two meanings in a sense battle it out for visual superiority and historical prominence. Two unequal forms of knowledge drive the perception of this place.

Gazing at the Baramki house/Tourjeman Post offered the same sort of visual confusion and ideological tension. As I gazed at the Baramki house, fully knowing its Palestinian genesis, it was almost impossible *not* to observe a structure that resembles a (former) military compound, a museum, and a (former) home. Traces and details of all exist but they somehow cannot be viewed simultaneously, even if one possesses the knowledge of what the structure once was. A convergence and discordance exist at the same time. The Israeli municipality has been intent on projecting the place as one that has served as an essential role in the defense of the nascent and beleaguered Israeli state.

This is, in the official narrative, a place of military glory, a launching pad from which Jerusalem was "liberated," a site of noble defense and purity of arms—but nothing else. By memorializing this locale in the way that it has been commemorated, the memory of the building as an Arab home is silenced. Here, as in so many other appropriated Palestinian homes across this colonial urban space, there exists a layering of meaning that paves over as much as it, perhaps unintentionally, highlights.

The damaged facade of the Baramki home was retained to aid in the elaboration of a very specific narrative of power. The retention of these military elements aid in the silencing of the home's Palestinian family and their past as well as the larger historical narrative of Palestinian loss. This fusing of signifier (a dilapidated stone structure) and signified (Israeli military outpost and site of defense), as Barthes explains in his brilliant semiotic exploration of myth, forms an association. This association or sign is meant to take on a natural quality and does so as the events or histories that complicate the mythic representation are effaced. In Barthes's words, history continually "evaporates" as myths ossify and become the taken-for-granted reality.

This sign ("the Tourjeman Army Post") in turn is meant to serve what Barthes (1957) regards as a "second order" signifier, one that represents a former time of division and denial, siege, and yearning for "wholeness." Therein lies a myth central to Israeli power, one that has since 1967 included the idea that the city was "liberated" by Israeli forces, and is the eternal capital of the Jewish People. This signification of domination—this unhealthy sign—Barthes regards as vital to the production of mythologies.[18]

Crucial to the construction of this particular monument to Israeli defense [*gonen*], independence [*komimyot*], and redemption [*guela*] is the memory of the former frontier that this army post once policed. Drawing attention to this former reality primes one for reading the landscape in a particular (and historically quite partial and nationalistic) way. Those who come into contact with the structure are meant to remember the Israeli longing for return

One of the Windows of the Baramki House, Transformed into an Israeli Army Turret in 1948. Courtesy of the Author.

across the frontier and for the right to "reclaim" what is said to have always belonged to the Jewish people.

The city's present ("united" under sole Israeli authority) is depicted, therefore, as legitimate and natural—legitimate precisely because it is natural. Making Jerusalem "whole," and keeping it intact as the sole province of the Israeli state, necessitates evoking at key times and places the former frontier, lest that division is reinstituted (i.e., lest the Palestinians are able to establish their own national claims to the city). In this way the future and the present are dependent upon, and in a constant dialectical relationship with, a peculiar reading of the past.

Descendents of the home's original owner recall feeling totally violated when word reached them that their property had been transformed into an Israeli museum. They recall how such designs on the home not only undermined their efforts to retrieve it but contributed to erasing their history in Jerusalem, too.

"How did you hear that the Israelis were going to establish this museum?" I asked the son of the original owner several years after it had been established. "There was an article about the house in the Israeli press right after it became a museum and it was written that I, the former owner, refused to come to the opening celebrations. Well, I had not even been *told* that the house would become a museum—not that I would have even considered attending the opening. But they [the Israeli municipality] did not even have the decency to inform us that they were turning our home into this museum."

It was only after the transformation of the property into a "public space," however, that the family was able to obtain access to their property for the first time since their expulsion. The tale of his return speaks to the forms of representational and legal power that have remade his city since 1948. Upon setting foot in the structure after more than thirty years of exile, the Israeli curator of the museum—a middle-aged, rotund American—approached him and informed him that, should he wish to enter, he would have to pay the admission fee. Baramki responded angrily, replying that he was the owner of the property and that he returned neither as guest nor as tourist. He relates how he steadfastly refused to buy entry into his home. But the curator, apparently unfazed by the irony of the circumstances (or perhaps incredulous that the building had ever been a home), insisted that Baramki—"like all other visitors"—pay for admission. A short standoff ensued after which the entry fee was finally "waived" and the owner was permitted to pass into the museum. Baramki would not yield to the new identity of visitor as opposed to owner.

In this moment, this interaction, one could see parallels with the ways space in the city as a whole is organized and controlled. Today, in an age of layers upon layers of Israeli checkpoints across a colonized Jerusalem, Palestinians may refer to the city as *home* all they wish. They may not, however, enter unless "permitted" to do so by the occupying authorities. Ultimately, Israeli authorities alone determine who may gain access and, indeed, what the price of entry will be.

NAMING THE FACT

Like the Jewish-American who regulates entry into the Baramki's own home, the Tourjeman Post Museum itself also serves as a gatekeeper of sorts, a sentinel guarding over historical truth. The museum/memorial is a component of Israel's use of historical invention. Trouillot (1995) describes dynamics by which the politics of naming can aid in the silencing of certain historical narratives while ensuring that other discourses are privileged, foregrounded, and advanced as history. "The naming of the 'fact' is itself a narrative of power disguised as innocence. . . . Naming the fact thus already imposes a reading and many historical controversies boil down to who has the power to name what."[19]

Walking through the home for the first time in nearly four decades, the owner remembers feeling a simultaneity of curiosity, powerlessness, and rage. Mostly, however, he relates experiencing tremendous sadness as he sought to reconnect with that which he and his family once knew as a place most intimate. His dismay at the state of the property, he tells me, was intensified with each discovery of how those who had built the museum had stripped it of its pre-1948 history. Tiled floors were damaged or altered; the outlines of the arched windows he once peered out of are now filled in with concrete.

Baramki cheerlessly recalls that visit fifteen years later, as we sit in his office on the outskirts of Jerusalem.

"What was it like to go back?"

"Well, it was awful, actually," he relates almost inaudibly, as he reclines into silence for several moments in his enormous leather armchair. "This place that was a part of my childhood was just a shell of something we all remember, just a shell." He describes entering and searching for traces of his family's former presence using the coordinates of memory. But the act of walking this reconfigured place was often disorienting. His memory was "jammed" by alterations in the building's design and by changes in its construction. Even he walked the line between remembering and being made to forget. Observing the structure's remade interior for the first time since he was in his early twenties, Baramki notes how those responsible for this museum had completely altered the interior.

"The home on the inside," he tells me, "they destroyed like the outside." The foyer was where the Israelis had placed a ticket booth and sold postcards and literature about their history of this locale. The former dining room was converted into a library of sorts. Illuminated by long uncovered fluorescent lights hanging from the high ceilings, this room held a number of books, sources, and maps about the history of the city.

The space that had served as bedrooms on the top floor was transformed into one dimly lit gallery, housing an exhibit of images, artifacts, and items of Israeli military material culture. Guns, mortars, and other weapons used during the 1948 and 1967 wars are exhibited, a sort of display of "purity of arms."

The story the museum wishes to tell is teleological, as the plague on the museum door denotes: "Dedicated to the Theme: Jerusalem—A Divided City Reunited." The various moments that comprise this telos are integral to the narrative of Israeli liberation and redemption [*geulim*] in the city. That narrative is related in images displayed along a linear, representational path on the top floor of the museum. From a time of division and separation and longing, the story culminates in the liberation of the city in June 1967. The representations are oddly quite "clean," not sullied by images of "collateral damage" or death (save for the pictorial memorials of the Israeli soldiers who died during the war). But no images of Palestine's dead were displayed, no pictures of their destroyed buildings were featured, no mention made of captured political prisoners or the tens of thousands more made refugees. Most importantly, there was nothing about what the fractured city meant for the Palestinian exiles forced to leave their homes and unable to return. They do not exist.

The pictorial history exhibited in the area formerly divided by bedrooms and now turned into a spacious gallery was drawn both from the years Jerusalem was physically divided as well as from the moments of fighting that engulfed the city in June 1967. Visitors are told of the transformation of the city from a "backwater" to a modern, enlivened, "unified" capital of the Jewish state. Pervasive representations include those of triumphant Israeli soldiers parading through the newly pacified streets of East Jerusalem, storming and "liberating" the Old City, and bringing down the physical divide that formally fractured the city.

Texts and images venerate Israeli military power. But one central message of the exhibit also seemed to be about the historical connection "the Jewish people" have had to the city and the centuries-long wait they have had to endure to "reclaim" that which has always been theirs. This is the "eternal" capital of the Jewish people stretching back to the time of King David, the literature asserts. As one Israeli professor at Hebrew University once explained to me, "The Jewish people are not *returning* to this land. That is what the Arabs do not understand. We are not returning here, we never left! We never left!"

A transhistorical notion of Jewish identity and entitlement to the city is deployed powerfully at this locale. The claim to ownership of the city has, by this account, a biblical basis stretching back 3,000 years. No other people's notion of connection to Jerusalem, maintain Israeli officials and much of its citizenry, has nearly the same legitimacy. In a document produced by the Israeli government press office and distributed at the museum, it is asserted, "In weighing ostensibly competing claims to the city, it must be recalled that the Jewish people bases its claims to Jerusalem on a link which dates *back millennia* and to King David, and that there is no legal basis for the 'historical' Palestinian claim that Jerusalem was their capital. Moreover, though the Palestinians may have a strong *emotional* attachment to Jerusalem, it does not necessarily follow that Jerusalem should become the capital of any Palestinian political entity."[20]

The son of the home's architect told me that he did not—could not— spend even a moment looking at these images and photographs displayed in a gallery comprised of his family's gutted bedrooms. What he did not stay to scrutinize (but what visitors to this museum have been shown) is a cleverly constructed representational place.

The museum allows the visitor to use the actual physical structure of this home turned outpost turned museum to better understand the Israeli narrative of longing and redemption. At the end of the exhibit, all are invited to gaze out from the narrow slits in the filled-in windows of the top floor, apertures that once served as turrets and where, during the dark days of the divided city, Israeli soldiers peered out bravely at an enemy as apparently faceless today as they were then. From this vantage point, looking out in the direction of the fortressed hilltop campus of Hebrew University, one can view the spread out Jerusalem landscape, and within this representational context, one can imagine the former terrain as Israel's brave defenders and Jerusalem's "liberators" once did.

By reenacting the practice of gazing across a once-divided landscape, visitors are meant to understand the significance of this site for the security of the budding state. Today, though, those who gaze out from behind these former turrets (themselves former windows), see a seamless whole, a unity achieved through Israeli victory. One sees just what the beleaguered Israeli nation is said to have once seen and which it now memorializes. From this vantage point, Israeli collective memory and the myths that inform it ossify into "historical truth."

The practice of peering out from the former turrets of this once familial space, however, is not as benign and straightforward an exercise as visitors to the museum might imagine. As with other texts or representations, one never simply "sees" them outside of an ideological context, and the ideological context all too often determines how texts and representations are viewed, read, and received. In an analysis of the multilayered character of ideological work, Zizek (1994) notes, "One of the fundamental strategies of ideology is the reference to some self-evidence—'Look, you can see for yourself how things are!' 'Let the facts speak for themselves' is perhaps the arch statement of ideology—the point being, precisely, that facts *never* 'speak for themselves' but are *made to speak* by a network of discursive devices."[21]

What the Israeli municipality does not wish visitors to see or to come to terms with is the reality that when we look at the former house, its crumbling exterior, the representations of the museum, and the view of the landscape from the turrets, we "see" all of these things against the background of a "discursively pre-constructed space."[22] When we peer out from these minimally opened windows, we view a minimally articulated historical account. This is Jerusalem's history related through turrets, not the windows of an exiled Arab family.

As I walked the representational space of the Tourjeman Post Museum, I was reminded of the innocent quality that myths so consistently possess. Assessing the home as a site of loss and denial, I was reminded as well of a powerful component of ideological domination: that ideology all too often functions most powerfully in its silences and absences; a work or text or building is tied to ideology not so much by what it says as by what it does not say. In the case of the Baramki home, the gaps and absences within the structure are as significant and vitally important to Israeli nationalism as that which is proudly proclaimed to be present. The house, like the displaced family members it once belonged to, is both present and absent at the same time.

CONCLUSION

The story of the Baramki house and the transformation of Jerusalem shows the complex ways in which memory is made "usable" for contemporary political concerns in a colonial city. "Policing" the past and determining what is permitted to be seen as the past has allowed dominant Israeli communities to control the present and the future of Jerusalem and beyond.

The home of the Baramki family is emblematic of other places in Jerusalem where Palestinian populations have been disappeared and their attachments to particular places silenced. Like myriad other sites, it is a locale where opposing national imaginations converge. Israeli efforts toward constituting and fostering particular visions of Jerusalem at and in the Baramkis' home are a vital component of the kind of colonial rule that pervades across the contested and violent landscape of Israel-Palestine. Such practices of historical production can themselves be violent and they have eventuated in a highly politicized landscape that denies as much as it affirms, that paradoxically affirms in its denials and that speaks through its silences.

The Baramki house and the Tourjeman Post Museum exist simultaneously. The utilization of the home historically embodies two different but interconnected modes of domination. Serving first as an instrument of military conquest, it policed the borders imposed on the city by the dominant national community. Today, the once familial space is deployed in the service of epistemic violence, used to produce and police certain ideological and historical boundaries. The monument to Israeli military victory does more than simply deny the home's familial past. It elaborates a series of myths that evaporate the history of the Palestinian people more generally while at the same time providing legitimacy for Israel's presence in the Jerusalem of its imagination.

A Palestinian family home of former architectural splendor, designed by a now deceased master of Palestinian architecture, now serves as a component of a different architecture of knowledge production, a scaffolding of truth-making, a foundation for epistemic violence. It continues to rest on the frontier of competing historical imaginations and memories, anchored in place but simultaneously on the moving edge of Israeli colonial power.

NOTES

1. Twenty-four months of fieldwork and research in Jerusalem were generously funded by the Fulbright-Hays Dissertation Fellowship, The Social Science Research Council, and a summer grant from Columbia University's Middle East Institute. I would like to thank Sandy Sufian, Mark LeVine, Glenn Bowman, and Salim Tamari for their invaluable help and comments on many drafts of this chapter.

2. For excellent Palestinian and Israeli sources on this period, see Salim Tamari, "The Phantom City," in Tamari 1999 and Segev 1998.

3. As will become evident, like thousands of other homes, this home is not recognized as Arab-owned by the Israeli state, which has denied these former inhabitants

the right to reclaim or reenter their properties. However, unlike Slymovics 1998, who worked on the appropriated Arab village of Ein Hod near Haifa, I shall refer to the rightful owners as "the owners" throughout this chapter in a modest attempt to unsettle the Israeli state's "settled fictions" about ownership and entitlement.

4. Dirks 1996, ix.

5. Much of the reliable information concerning the Palestinian exodus in 1948 has been reconstituted by a judicious examination of declassified Israeli archives. These scholarly works from both Israeli and Palestinian historians have unearthed the fact that Israeli authorities sought to expel as many Palestinians from their land as possible and prevent their return. Because of this vital research, an entire artifice of Israeli myth has been disproven. Despite the hugely important interventions that have been made in understanding these historical events, scholarship based on archival sources can not alone flesh out the daily lived experiences of dispossession and dispersal most Palestinians have known and tens of thousands of Israelis have witnessed or taken part in. For that one must turn to the imperfect but vital realm of oral sources, particularly life histories. See Segev 1998, Flapan 1987, Pappé 2006.

6. See Segev 1988.

7. During the course of the 1948 hostilities, over 40,000 Palestinians from the West Jerusalem area had been pushed out of their homes and neighborhoods. Roughly 1,500 Jews fled their homes in what became East Jerusalem. The 1949 Rhodes Agreement between Israel and the Arab states called for bringing down the partition between Jerusalem's two sides. Israel refused to implement this and also refused to adhere to the UN Resolutions calling for the return of the nearly 800,000 Palestinians removed from their land during the 1948 hostilities.

8. Tourjeman was an Arab man who lived and owned property in the area of the home before 1948.

9. Hala Sakakini, *Jerusalem and I* (Amman: The Economic Press Company, 1990), xi. Though there was a desire to reclaim the property, these exiles were unable to do so and they knew it. They knew that these homes were now in a different political reality.

10. Meeting this Israeli standard for ownership was accomplished by Palestinian exiles in only a handful of known cases. To be successful, the Arab owner had to demonstrate sufficiently to the Israeli state in Israeli courts that when he or she fled West Jerusalem in 1948, they had not gone to a country "at war with Israel." Such read the provisions of Israel's Absentee Property Law (originally the Enemies Property Law). I came upon only one family, the Daouds, who owned a property in Talbieh and were able to reclaim it after a several year battle after they proved that they had fled in 1948 to El Salvador, not a state "at war" with Israel at the time of her birth.

11. See Asad 1993, Scott 1999, and Mitchell 1988.

12. See Chazen and Khalidi 1991, Dumper 1997, and Sarah Kaminkar 1997.

13. This is fully acknowledged by Israeli city planners involved in planning Jerusalem after 1967. See Chesin and Malamud 1999 and Benvenisti 1996.

14. *Lands* of the villages of Beit Iksa and Beit Hanina became the site of the sprawling Jewish hilltop settlement of Ramot while the *populations* of these villages were almost completely left outside of Israel's newly defined "eternal capital."

15. See Chesin and Malamud 1999.

16. Benvenisti 1976.
17. See Hobsbawm and Ranger 1983. See also Asad 1991 for a discussion of the ways tradition and modernity are often parasitically bound up with one another.
18. Barthes 1957, 114–115.
19. Trouillot 1995, 114.
20. See Israeli Government Press Office Report 1996, 12 [emphasis mine].
21. Zizek 1994, 11.
22. Ibid.,11.

REFERENCES

Asad, Talal. *Genealogies of Religion* (Baltimore: Johns Hopkins University Press, 1993).

——. Afterword in *Colonial Situations,* ed. George W. Stocking Jr. (Madison: University of Wisconsin Press, 1991), 314–24.

Barthes, Roland. *Mythologies* (New York: Noonday Press, 1957).

Benvenisti, Meron. *Jerusalem: The Torn City* (Jerusalem: Isratypeset, 1976).

Chazen, Naomi and Rashid Khalidi. *Negotiating the Non-Negotiable: Jerusalem in the Framework of an Israeli-Palestinian Settlement* (International Security Studies Program: American Academy of Arts and Sciences, 1991).

Cheshin, Amir S., Bill Hutman, and Avi Melamed. *Separate and Unequal: The Inside Story of Israeli Rule in East Jerusalem* (Cambridge, MA: Harvard University Press, 1999).

Dirks, Nicholas. Foreword to *Colonialism and its Forms of Knowledge: The British in India.* By Bernard S. Cohn (Princeton, NJ: Princeton University Press, 1996), ix–xvii.

Dumper, Michael. *The Politics of Jerusalem since 1967* (New York: Columbia University Press, 1997).

Hobsbawm, Eric and Terrance Ranger. *The Invention of Tradition* (New York: Cambridge University Press, 1983).

Kaminkar, Sarah. "For Arabs Only." *Journal of Palestine Studies* 26, no. 4 (Summer 1997): 5–16.

Mitchell, Tim. *Colonizing Egypt* (Berkeley, University of California Press, 1988).

Sakakini, Hala. *Jerusalem and I* (Amman: The Economic Press, 1990).

Scott, David. *Refashioning Futures* (Princeton, NJ: Princeton University Press, 1999).

Segev, Tom. *1949: The First Israelis* (New York: Owl Books, 1998).

Tamari, Salim, ed. *Jerusalem, 1948: The Arab Neighborhoods and their Fate in the War* (Washington, DC: Institute of Palestine Studies, 1999).

Trouillot, Michel-Rolph. *Silencing the Past: Power and the Production of History* (Boston: Beacon Press, 1995).

Zizek, Slavoj. Introduction to *Mapping Ideology* (London: Verso, 1994).

11

Framing the Borders of Justice

Sharia Courts in Israel and the Conflict between Secular Ideology and Islamic Law

Moussa Abou Ramadan

INTRODUCTION

The relationship between the *sharia* [Islamic] courts in Israel and the Israeli state is not as discrete as it may seem at first glance. Although the sharia courts portray themselves to the public and to the state as autonomous institutions that implement the sharia [Islamic law] in a complete and perfect way, they actually employ a discourse that obscures their position as an integral part of the country's legal establishment. The court's position is based on the notion that there exists a pure sharia, devoid of any traces of secular Israeli territorial law, or any other non-Muslim religious law. Such a stance, however, is incompatible with the legal reality inside Israel: it ignores the processes of secularization that have, for over a century, diminished the assumed "purity" of the sharia applied in the territory that has become the State of Israel.

The secularization process began, as it did in many Arab countries, with the Ottoman codification of the sharia in the early twentieth century. The codification process gave the state a set of laws that it could order the religious authorities to enforce, thereby diminishing the power of the religious establishment ['*ulama*] to articulate religious norms. A special form of secularization, which this author refers to as Israelization, began after 1948 when the state of Israel replaced some religious personal status law with territorial civil law. It did this not only for the Muslim community but for Israel's other religious communities as well.

The Israeli Sharia Court of Appeals has not only ignored this secularized reality but has resorted to a process of Islamization in order to mask it and bolster its own religious discourse and standing. Islamization here occurs as a strategy that repackages secular Israeli legal norms as norms that already exist in Islamic law. These legal norms are then applied in the sharia courts as pure, authentic Islamic law. The processes of Israelization and Islamization are therefore actually dialectical, occurring simultaneously. As the Israelization of the sharia courts increases, so does the process of Islamization. These two processes, seemingly distinct with defined borders of conceptualization and implementation, actually merge and overlap.

The Islamization of Israeli civil law was intended to strengthen the Muslim community inside Israel by presenting it as governed, at least in matters of personal status, by autonomous courts applying authentic Islamic law. The actual consequences of Islamization, however, have generally resulted in increased Israeli state control over the sharia courts. First, the courts accept and apply codified Ottoman family law, denying their own power to establish the personal status norms that govern their community. The Israeli territorial law repackaged as Islamic is also often at odds with classical Islamic law. In the case of the waqf, or endowed property, Islamization has legitimated the dispossession of Islamic holy places. Whether these consequences are positive or negative depends on one's position on classical Islamic law governing Israel's Muslim minority. As a significant consequence of the discursive process of Islamization, the practical governance over the holy places has been lost.

I do not argue that secularization has rendered the law applied in the sharia Courts "un-Islamic," or that it is impossible for an Islamic legal system to exist inside a secular, non-Muslim state. Yet it is equally clear that there is no such thing as a purely Islamic legal system, as laws throughout history have been consolidations of several systems. In this context, sharia courts in Israel must acknowledge the compromises that a religious court must make in order to operate within a secular state. They must also acknowledge the consequences of these compromises on the religious community. The boundaries between secular and religious law in Israel (and as a byproduct, between secular and religious identities) will continue to be crossed without due consideration of their implications until such an acknowledgement is made.

THE DISCOURSE OF THE SHARIA COURT OF APPEALS

The most important and visible processes that are taking place in Islamic law today are secularization and Islamization. Taking place simultaneously, these dialectical processes of "secularity" and "holiness" influence each other and create a new hybrid product. The principles that the sharia courts apply come from two sources, one religious and one secular. In the process of secularization, religious norms interact with secular norms. Together they create a new norm that is different from both secular and religious law. This hybridization process is also present in the process of Islamization, in which an Israeli secular norm is introduced as an Islamic one. Although its source is secular, its external attire is seen as Islamic.[1]

The sharia courts in Israel try to maximize an autonomous Islamic space of operation/jurisprudence within the secular state of Israel. In Muslim societies, there is a similar tension between secular and religious legal systems. In Israel, this relationship is intersected by another axis, majority-minority relations. Within these relations, the population accessing the sharia court is a structurally discriminated group that has to simultaneously legitimize itself before its own population and the state.

The Sharia Court attempts to accomplish this differentiation and legitimation by employing a discourse/language that represents the courts as relying directly on the Qur'an (the Holy Book in Islam) and sunna (the path of the Prophet Mohammed; religious actions instituted by the Prophet) alone. This discourse does not consider the history of Islamic law applied in Israel. Islamic law applied in Israel has in fact confronted considerable historical developments, including the interpretations of the Hanafi religious scholars [*fuqaha'*], the Ottoman experiments in sharia codification, and the establishment of the State of Israel as a Jewish state. Due to the latter, the Court's claim of direct influence from Islamic texts and early Islamic practice insulates the Islamic religious establishment in Israel from external criticism, because it says it is relying directly and exclusively on Islam's primary sources. But the boundaries in law and practice are not so clear. The sharia courts present themselves as applying law that is pure, immaculate, and void of any secular stain. They theoretically prohibit dependence on Israeli civil legislation because the sharia is considered complete and comprehensive. The courts claim, through application of the sharia, to have already addressed any legal situation that could possibly arise. The following examples, drawn from decisions of the Sharia Court of Appeals (the Court), illustrate this position. In 1994, the Court pointed out in another decision that a lower court's decision "depends on Clause 25 of legal capacity and guardianship, which is a positive one, and the court can judge according to the rules of the Islamic law only. It is unnecessary to point out that the rules of the original sharia are complete and comprehensive and give answer to any wondering or question."[2]

Finally, in 1997: "Here we repeat and confirm that the Sharia Court of Appeals applies the Orthodox *sharia*, and it sees the *sharia* as a full and comprehensive judicial system. We have explained this several times before."

The Sharia Court of Appeals has even banned in its jurisdiction the application of the basic law of Israel: human dignity and freedom, a piece of legislation that is part of Israel's constitution.[3]

In addition to emphasizing their Islamic purity, the sharia courts in Israel present themselves as historically continuous entities, despite having operated under several different political regimes—Ottoman, British, and Israeli. The courts argue that the sharia applied during these times has not been harmed or modified. They make this claim as they present the history of Islamic law in Israel as progressing linearly and uniformly.[4]

This discourse of Islamic and historical purity is the product of a new era at the Sharia Court of Appeals that began with the appointment of three judges, or *qadis*, to permanent positions at the Sharia Court of Appeals in 1994. One qadi of the Sharia Court of Appeals was interviewed by the magazine *Sawtt al-Haq wa al-Hurriyah*.[5] The qadi belongs to the northern branch of the Islamic Movement.[6] In one interview he stated, "I believe that the Sharia Court has applied only the *Sharia* rules, and this is its role; I wonder how the Sharia Court can adopt the positive law [law enacted by the state and subject to amendment or change], and anyone of the citizens who would like to be judged according to the positive law can go to a civil court, and we, on our side, will act to remove this mixture at the Sharia Court of Appeals."[7] Such statements are misleading because the Sharia Court is not autonomous. It does not apply a "pure" sharia, and the qadi's claims do not reflect the legal reality in which the sharia courts function. Instead, such words ignore the ways in which secularization and Islamization have shaped Israeli sharia.

SECULARIZATION AND CODIFICATION
OF ISLAMIC LAW IN ISRAEL

Secularization of Islamic law in Israel is taking place on two levels: partial codification and Israelization. The departure from the classical conception of Islamic law began in the 1917 Ottoman Family Law. Codification is performed by the state rather than religious scholars, or *fuqaha'*. The consequences of this process are especially strong in Israel, a non-Muslim country that, since the flight of almost every member of the Supreme Muslim Council in 1948, lacks a representative Muslim body to supplement or modify the codified law. Moreover, the High Court of Justice, having the power to review the decisions of the sharia courts, can turn to Ottoman Family Law in order to determine the correctness of a decision. It can do this without reference to the rich history of the sharia outside of the Ottoman Family Law or even to the sources of sharia itself, like the Qur'an, sunna, or classical treatises on Islamic law. These experiments are not considered part of the secularization process, but remain within the religious realm, similar to the supposedly nonsecular codifications of Christian law by the Catholic Church in the Holy Land.[8]

Most of the Islamic law that applies to Muslims in Israel has been codified not only on the substantive level but also on the procedural level. In addition to the substantive codification of the Ottoman Family Law, the sharia courts apply the laws of evidence taken from the Mecelle, the civil code enacted in 1879 by the Ottoman Empire government.[9] They also apply the Sharia Procedural Law, codified in 1917.

Leaders and religious scholars often debated the issue of codification in the history of Islamic law, particular during the Ottoman period. They argued whether codification was part of the process of renewal, and ultimately staving off the erosion of—or even increase—the state's power.[10] Codification, however, is more than a process for organizing legislation or modernizing a legal system. The code turns into a symbol, an instrument in the hands of the government, and a sign that expresses control. Before the Ottoman Mecelle, this form of state control was unknown in the Islamic world. Some state control of legislation was legitimate in Islamic society. Examples of legitimate state control of legislation include the influence of state-appointed *fuqha'* in designing the legislation or the enactment of *qanun* and non-sharia laws related to issues not covered by Islamic law. The codification of the sharia, however, is a relatively new phenomenon. Modern scholars of Islamic law have continued the codification debate. Scholars across the spectrum have argued that codification is a "radical departure" from traditional practice that can only supplement, and perhaps even bring an end to, Islamic law.[11]

There is no doubt that any law that undergoes a process of codification does not remain the same. The mere procedure of codification changes the law. This does not mean that codified law ceases to be Islamic. The Islamic aspect of the law is an issue connected to time and circumstances within a historical context. According to a dynamic conception, codification is likely to lead to a law that is different from the classical law but is still Islamic law. The difference lies in the transfer of authority from the *'ulama* [religious leaders/scholars] to the state. In another conception, there is an implicit assumption that codification is a sign of modernism.[12] Here Islam is considered antimodern and therefore it is not possible to mix these two contradictory elements.

In a similar manner, the application of the Ottoman Family Law, itself, codified in the last years of Ottoman rule and then implemented by the British rulers, demonstrates the degree to which codification transfers legislative power from the qadis to the state. Codification transforms the nature of the Islamic law being applied in the courts by removing Islamic law from the context of the classical sources, by subjecting decisions of the sharia courts in Israel to the review of the Israeli High Court of Justice, and by rendering codified Islamic law applied in Israel static. The latter is static because there is no representative body that can amend or supplement it.

This process of codification has, however, been going on since the late Ottoman period, and continued in Palestine under the British Mandate period (1918–1947).

We can see the interpenetration and validation of the two streams of law, Israeli and Muslim, in the application of Clause 130 of the Ottoman Family Law. The Israeli High Court of Justice has interpreted the Family Law without consulting the Qur'an or the classical Islamic legal sources. It interpreted the law in such a way as to support and legitimize the judgments of the Sharia Court of Appeals.[13]

The example of Clause 130 demonstrates how codification of Maliki law (one of the four dominant law schools of Sunni Islam) departed from classical Maliki practice and facilitated the secularization of Islamic law. The judgment of the Sharia Court of Appeals developed and changed Islamic law without reference to the classical sources.[14] The High Court of Justice further endorsed the changes by separating the interpretation of Clause 130 from Maliki law.

The High Court of Justice believes that ordinary interpretation should lead to the conclusion that the arbitrator reached. At the same time, it is important for him to point out that this is also an interpretation of Sharia Court of Appeals. The High Court does not feel at ease in its role as a "high interpreter" for a sharia decision. Therefore, it supports its position with the reference to the Sharia Court of Appeals. It is possible to see various judgments as a kind of dialogue between the Sharia Court of Appeals and the High Court of Justice. This dialogue has also taken place in the areas of divorce and marriage law. In all these cases, the state laws derive legitimacy for its judicial review of sharia court decisions from the Sharia Court itself. The Sharia Court has ruled that there is no *ijtihad* when there is a *nass* [text]; that is, when it can derive a decision from the Qur'an or other basic religious texts.[15]

SECULARIZATION AND ISRAELIZATION (EMPTYING)

The term emptying, like the term secularization, is a problematic one, because this term can refer to a change in the essence of Islamic law. Any deviation from this essence can constitute an emptying of classical Islamic law through the process of secularization. I am not referring to the end of Islamic law but rather to a change in its essence. Emptying refers to those parts of classical Islamic law that have undergone a process of secularization through codification in the Ottoman Family Law as well as other parts of law that did not undergo a process of codification. Issues of maintenance and alimony of children are examples of the latter.

Emptying takes place in different stages. In the first stage, Islamic law is limited in its application to issues of personal status and endowment. The second stage empties these issues of their content by issuing unified, territorial legislation that binds all members of the various religious communities, including Muslims. In many fields, the application of unified territorial laws has replaced the application of religious personal status law.

Several examples can help us understand this dynamic. The issues of marriage, divorce, and management of *waqfs* [religious endowments] are three areas that are all allegedly under the exclusive jurisdiction of the sharia courts. In all three cases, we find myriad examples of classical religious law being emptied of its content by the Ottoman Family Law. This latter law changed existing laws to fit more modern sensibilities. One could argue that the Ottoman Family Law went so far as to nullify many of the patriarchal features of classical Muslim family laws.

Polygamy is an especially useful example because of its powerful ideological implications. The Ottoman Family Law obviously acknowledges polygamy. However, it allows the wife to contract for limitations on polygamy by demanding that if the husband tries to marry another wife, the existing marriage will be considered nullified. This stipulation exists in Clause 38 of the Ottoman Family Law. The clause partially depends on the Hanbali school (another dominant law school in Sunni Islam).[16]

The law in Israel employs a dualistic approach to polygamy. Although there is aversion to polygamy, expressed in normative prohibition on the criminal level, polygamous marriages are acknowledged on the civil level. This dichotomy exists in the Woman's Equal Rights Law. Clause 8(a) of this law nullifies the defense which existed in Clause 181 of the Penalty Law. Clause 5 holds that "this law is not intended to harm prohibition laws and permission to marriage and divorce."[17] Despite condemnations, the courts do not give severe penalties; fines are often imposed in lieu of jail time. This difference between rhetoric and practice reflects a dualistic approach to bigamy. On the one hand, bigamy is classified as criminal trespass, but on the other, it is not punished accordingly.

Civil judgments show that judges do not always recognize the legal results of polygamous marriages. In the case of family unification, it is impossible to demand the unification of a polygamous family because the cultural purpose of the law is to eradicate polygamous marriages. The High Court of Justice confirmed the Ministry of the Interior's policy not to approve applications for family unification when these applications are submitted by polygamous families. Approval would encourage people to commit such a trespass.[18]

A division between the criminal level and the public level gives rise to an ambivalent discourse that acknowledges some, but not all, of the special ramifications of polygamous marriages. An ambivalent discourse allows the state to ignore the unification of families, especially Muslim families. It also allows the state to disallow entitlement to allowances of income. This entitlement ensures payment of high sums by the Institute of the National Insurance to these families.

Divorce is within the exclusive jurisdiction of the sharia courts. Like polygamy, however, we find that the integration between the criminal order and the interpretations of the High Court of Justice regarding the tortuous aspects of divorce have emptied the institution of divorce of its content.

Marriage is made by consent between an adult man and a sane woman. According to Hanafi Law, a husband can dissolve the marriage without his wife's agreement.[19] Hanafi religious scholars spent a great amount of effort on deciding the type of phrases that can lead to divorce. Even divorce by joking, divorce by coercion, and divorce of a drunkard can be valid divorces.[20]

Clause 181 of the Penalty Law of 1977 holds that he who dismisses his wife without her agreement and without the interference of an authorized court is subject to five years of imprisonment. Though the wording of the clause is general and theoretically applies to all the different religious communities in Israel, in practice it is intended for Muslims, since classical Muslim law acknowledges unilateral divorce. The High Court of Justice interpreted the term "in spite of the woman" to mean that the divorce is made against her will.

The District Court differentiates between religious law and criminal law. Criminal law is interpreted independently for criminal offenses. Even if it is possible according to the religious law to issue a judgment retroactively, divorce of the wife by coercion and without a court judgment is considered a criminal offense.[21]

Israeli Law acknowledges that divorce of a woman against her will and without a court decision gives her right to compensation. The legislatures in some Arab countries have introduced similar articles in their personal status law to compensate women for unilateral divorce. This measure is called in Arabic talaq ta'asufi.[22] The article is based on the idea of abuse of rights. The premise to this article of law is that the right to divorce unilaterally is accorded to a man but he should not abuse this right.[23] The Sharia Court of Appeals in Israel refused to follow this line of thinking for two reasons.[24] The first was that this rule of talaq ta'asufi has no accepted sharia basis. The second is that a Muslim woman can sue her husband in civil court and the man could be persecuted by the state for crime.

Integration between criminal and civil sanctions leads to emptying the essence of Clauses 102 and 118 of the Ottoman Family Law when they deal with divorce [talaq] as unilateral divorce. Today, Muslim divorce in Israel is decided according to Clause 130 of the Ottoman Family Law.[25] This law has also undergone a process of secularization. It is possible to say that codification decreased the use of books of Islamic law on the issue of divorce. Integration between tort orders and criminal orders increased the clauses in the Ottoman Family Law that deal with the issue of talaq. It routed the laws of Muslim divorces to Clause 130, which itself has undergone a process of secularization.[26]

THE WAQF

A final example of Israeli territorial law interfering with the exclusive jurisdiction of the sharia courts is the case of the waqf. Such interference ultimately empties the sharia courts' jurisdiction of its religious significance. Although the Israeli state eventually gave jurisdiction over waqf management to the sharia courts, this jurisdiction is of little significance since most endowment property underwent a process of dispossession. After dispossession, the rules of endowments no longer apply to such property. The sharia courts are given exclusive jurisdiction over the endowments, but they are unable to apply the classical rules of endowment management.

The waqf [Islamic religious endowment] plays a central role in Muslim societies in areas such as help to the poor and support of education.[27] The waqf is a judicial institution, recognized by Islamic law, through which an individual can endow some property to a specific purpose. The endowed property cannot be passed as legacy or be sold or given as a gift. The endowed property is no longer owned by the endower and becomes God's property.[28] The mutawalli or ma'mur is in charge of the endowments and manages them. The endower himself can act as a mutawalli, but if he does not work for the benefit of the endowment, he will be dismissed. The endowments have played an important social role in various Muslim societies and have acquired a collective richness over hundreds of years.

The role of the sharia courts regarding endowments has changed. While in the 1960s and 1970s the sharia courts legitimized the dispossession of parts of the endowments, in the nineties they erased the memory of the dispossession by manipulating the Muslim public imagination. Qadis now speak about keeping the endowment property through a legal regulation signed in 1994 by the qadi staff. The Muslim endowments were first included within the frame of applying the Law of Absentee Property. In 1965, the process of dispossession was completed.

The issue of endowments is different from the issue of personal status. Personal status issues center on identity, but endowment issues focus on the control of lands and identity. It turns out that the institution of Muslim endowment collided head-to-head with the Zionist project to purchase Palestinian Arab-owned land.[29]

Subjection of Waqf Property to the Law of Absentee Property

Under British Mandatory rule, waqf property was managed by a government-created endowment committee. The ma'mur was appointed to be in charge of the endowment of public property. The other mutawallis who were in charge of private endowment property left the country in 1948. After 1948, endowment property, like all property left behind by individuals who fled during the war, was classified as absentee property and transferred to the care of the Custodian of Absentee Property.[30]

Classifying waqf property as absentee property was not the only option available. Another alternative solution was one in which the Israeli state would appoint other individuals to the Supreme Muslim Council to replace those who had fled. It was possible to appoint other people to the Council. In *Hassouna*, however, the High Court of Justice rejected this option declaring, "We do not think that the Muslim Religious Court was able to change an absentee property into non-absentee property by nomination of the demander to be a custodian."[31]

Still another option was to treat waqf property like property belonging to the Christian communities. For example, Bishop Hakim, the head of the Greek Catholic community in Israel, moved to Syria, but the property registered in his name was not classified as absentee property.[32] Similarly, the head of the Greek Orthodox community resided in East Jerusalem, which before 1967 was not considered part of Israel. Nonetheless, the property of the Greek Orthodox Church was not considered absentee property. The Israeli state treated Christian and Muslim religious property differently.

The High Court of Justice eventually reversed its position on the waqf property, holding that new mutawallis may be designated to replace those who fled. Waqf property would no longer be considered absentee, the court explained in *Bulus v. the Minister of Development and others*. "Not the waqf property, nor the rights of the beneficiaries were changed to become vested to the custodian on [the mutawalli's] absence, but only the authorities of the absentee Mutawalli were moved to the custodian."[33] The sharia courts were given the power to appoint the new mutawallis.

In 1964, the Israeli state published a proposed amendment to the Law of Absentee Property that accomplished several things.[34] First, it dispersed any doubt about control and possession of waqf property. Second, it removed control of waqf property from the religious community by releasing private (family) endowments to the intended beneficiaries. It also set up boards of trustees to manage public endowments. Finally, it characterized the endowments as property that hindered modernization, thereby making it necessary to remove the Islamic legal limitations that kept this property out of the commercial sphere.

People in other Arab countries raised similar debates about the incompatibility of the waqf and modernity.[35] Some authors claimed that this reform was similar to what was happening in the neighboring countries such as Egypt and Syria.[36] In Egypt and Syria, however, the goal of modernizing the waqf was to redistribute the land to the community.[37] In contrast, the practical effect of waqf policy in Israel has been to dispossess the Muslim community of its land for the benefit of the state. The trustee committees in Israel[38] often consisted of people who did not always follow the rules of accountability. They mostly sold the endowment property that was in their trust.[39]

The sharia courts participated in this process. Boards of trustees frequently asked the sharia courts to issue *fatwas* [religious opinions] abolishing the holiness [*izalat al-qudsiyya*] of some waqf property and permitting its commercial sale. The courts repeatedly obliged. The sales contracts authorizing the commercial sale of waqf property usually stipulated that the return on the sales was to benefit the Muslim community by funding different projects. In many cases, however, the returns were divided among the trustee board members and the projects were never fulfilled.

There are two examples in which the High Court of Justice dealt with such issues. The first example concerns a Muslim cemetery in Jaffa registered to the name of the man in charge of the waqf.[40] On May 15, 1966, the cemetery was registered in the name of the custodian of absentee property. The custodian transferred the cemetery to the Board of Trustees in Jaffa, which signed a contract selling the property to a company in 1973. The Sharia Court of Jaffa facilitated the sale with a 1973 fatwa, effectively abolishing the holiness of the cemetery and freeing it for commercial sale. The company committed to pay a specific amount of money to the Board of Trustees and to exhume and relocate the bones. Several months later, one of the board members submitted a claim against the company to the district court, claiming that the sale should be have been done by public offer. He was not invited to the meeting for approving the sale.[41] In the end, a compromise was reached by which the private company raised the price of the transaction. During this period, the members of the Board of Trustees were changed.

The Sharia Court of Appeals ultimately canceled the fatwa in 1974. The court held that qadis lack the authority to issue fatwas; they have the power to issue legal decisions only. The Jaffa Board of Trustees subsequently petitioned the district court for the cancellation of the sale. The Board of Trustees claimed in court that the contract of sale was signed because it included a condition holding that the land was no longer a holy place.[42] The Board argued that the contract did not fit the public order and interests of the Muslim community in Jaffa since it harmed the members of this community. The land was the last Muslim cemetery where people could bury their dead. Additionally, this contract injured the holiness of the dead. They argued that a contract for sale contradicted the law of the absentee property because it involved building houses, a goal that is not clearly present in the law of absentee property.

The district court rejected these arguments. An appeal was submitted to the High Court of Justice, which confirmed the district court's ruling. The High Court of Justice decided that the board of trustees, which earns returns on the sale of absentee property forwarded to them, can use the returns for things beyond the stated goals in the law. Building houses for Muslims can be a goal included in this list, though it was not mentioned explicitly. The Israeli Supreme Court held that the contract was not against public order and interest because the aim of the contract, building houses, was a legal interest.[43]

In other cases, the High Court supported the Sharia Court decisions without explicitly acknowledging that it did so. In several high-profile cases involving development of cemetery land, this allowed the Sharia Court to abolish the holiness of a place. This procedure has been applied in a few cases involving cemeteries, but not to all endowments. From a legal point of view, the State of Israel was not obliged to use this procedure. In the Law of Absentee Property of 1965, there was an emphasis on the point that the custodian of absentee property is the owner of the property.[44] Therefore, as soon as the custodian of absentee property takes over endowment property, it is no longer subject to the restrictions and conditions of the endowment.

The emphasis is therefore again on the fact that property that is transferred to the trustee board is free from any conditions or restrictions; the property can thus be freely transferred. The law does not differentiate between a cemetery and another kind of land. It is true that the law prohibits the board of trustees from selling mosques,[45] but it does not prohibit the sale of cemeteries. It is therefore not clear why the procedure of *izalat al-qudsiyya* [abolishment of holiness] was used in these instances, as many cemeteries had been transferred without resorting to this procedure.

These examples show that the jurisdiction of sharia courts over endowments has been emptied of its content. Endowments were treated like absentee property and transferred to the custodian of absentee property. Rules of waqf do not apply to these types of property. They are treated as ordinary property. Therefore, the exclusivity of jurisdiction is actually an exclusive jurisdiction upon the endowments but without substantial endowments belonging to the Muslim community.

ISLAMIZATION AND LEGITIMACY

In addition to restricting the space of classical Islamic law, the sharia courts in Israel have also engaged in a dialectical process whereby they attempt to expand the Islamic legal space through the Islamization of secular Israeli law. When we talk about Islamization, we generally mean the attempt of certain states, such as Egypt, to insert Islamic norms into the secular judicial system and to change norms that are conceived of as secular. This change involves using norms that are conceived of as Islamic. The amendment of Clause 2 of the Egyptian constitution, which declares that the sharia is the main source of law,[46] represents the climax of Islamization.

Islamization in Israel has occurred in the opposite direction. Norms derived from Israeli secular law are introduced as norms that exist in Islamic law. This process of Islamization is actually a reinterpretation of classical Islamic law. It does not represent a new process in Islamic law. Islamic law has long been influenced by foreign law systems, the influences of which have been introduced in a blurred way that obscured their foreign source and emphasized their Islamic aspects.[47]

Parallel to the process of secularizing Islamic law, there is a process of Islamization of secular law that challenges the borders officially delineating their separation. This process can be observed in the context of child guardianship. Israeli law acknowledges the principle of the best interest of the child. It obliges the religious courts, including the Sharia Court, to apply this principle.[48] The Sharia Court is bound to these principles, but rather than admit that it was applying Israeli law, the Court decided that consideration of the child's welfare is actually a norm drawn from an Islamic source. In a long series of decisions, the Sharia Court of Appeals decided that the rules that scholars use to decide child custody cases constitute refutable presumptions. If it is proven that the principle of child custody requires deviation from these presumptions, the Sharia Court will also deviate.[49]

Traditional Hanafi law is different.[50] It rules that, in general, children will stay with their mother up to age seven for boys and age nine for girls. The mother must fulfill certain conditions, and if she does not, custody of the child will be transferred to one of a long list of relatives dictated by Hanafi law. After the period of nursing [*hadana*] finishes, the custody of the child is transferred to the child's father.

Some Hanafi legal texts mention consideration of the child's welfare, but it is not treated as an overriding principle as it is defined in Israeli law. In Islamic law, the issue of child custody is settled by dividing the roles of the father and the mother according the needs of the child. The male child has to be in his father's home at the age of seven so that he will not learn women's habits and ways of talking.[51] The daughter must move to her father's home so that he will protect her.[52] The rules of nursing [hadana] soften the patriarchal approach, but they do not abolish it.[53]

Laws exist in some Arab countries that consider the child's welfare, but only with respect to specific events. The principle of child welfare is not an overarching principle that is applied to all child custody cases.[54] Recently, the Moroccan legislature changed the principle of consideration of the child's welfare into a guiding principle,[55] but the defining division remained as it is. The decisions of the Israeli court actually constitute Islamization of the secular law in Israel.

Islamization of Israeli law takes place in the sharia courts because these courts have ostensibly prohibited reliance on Israeli secular law. Instead, the sharia courts argue that the court should rely on the words of God alone. The Islamic method is introduced as a complete and perfect one in which reliance on secular law is not necessary.[56] After establishing the nonreliance on Israeli secular law, the Sharia Court of Appeals decided that in matters of custody the best interest of the child is the guiding principle.[57] The Sharia Court read the *fuqaha'* texts on hadana as having the purpose of protecting the best of interests of the child. In instances where one demonstrates that the case is not in the best interest of the child, the rule can be changed.

The sharia courts are attempting here to build an Islamic legal identity that is different from Israeli secular law while covertly applying territorial norms. The Sharia Court of Appeals put a special emphasis on the idea that sharia procedure is different from Israeli civil procedure. Islamic civil procedure in Israel, however, is actually based on the Ottoman Civil Procedure, which is commonly known to be a copy of the French Procedure with a change in numbering only.[58] The High Court of Justice decided according to Clause 62 of the Ottoman Civil Procedure that the application of Ottoman law must be carried out "on the background of principles of the foundation of our modern law."[59] As such, the claim that the sharia courts are applying the Qu'ran without any change is completely refuted. This contention is an ideological presentation that has no connection with reality in any way. Even in classical Islamic law, the Qu'ran did not cover all the issues. In such instances, there is no connection between it and certain specific rules.[60]

One of the functions of Islamization is to obscure Israeli legal reality and to create the false impression that there *is* sharia in its stead. The hidden function of Islamization is to legitimize the secularization of Islamic law by legitimating governmental activities through another context.

It is possible also to expose the connection between Islamization and legitimacy in the field of endowments. The fatwas that legitimized the sale of waqf property created a negative impression of qadis in Israel. To challenge this impression, all the working qadis signed onto Judicial Decree [*marsum qada'i*] Number 1 in 1994.[61] The *marsum* attempts to establish the autonomy of the sharia courts. The decree does not even mention the State of Israel. Instead, it addresses the Muslim community inside Israel as an *umma*, or nation. Its title reads: "In the name of God the most merciful." Below the title it reads: "The Sharia High Court for Appeals" (it should be noted that according to the law, the accurate name is "The Sharia Court of Appeals").

The decree [*marsum*] opens by acknowledging that it deals with painful events regarding religious endowments. It includes orders that are obligatory for the rest of the qadis. The marsum draws its authority from the principle of *maslaha* [interest], which is considered to be one source of Islamic law.[62] The marsum mentions both the Law of Absentee Property and amendment number 3 as steps toward the dispossession of Muslim endowments. The marsum gives examples of certification of long-term rents. The marsum also differentiates between holy waqfs, such as a mosque or cemetery, and nonholy waqfs. It should be noted that this differentiation is not accepted in Hanafi law. Hanafi law does not distinguish between holy and nonholy endowments.

The marsum then gives four orders. The first prevents the qadi from issuing a fatwa whose purpose is to use a holy or nonholy endowment in a manner contrary to the purpose for which it was originally set up. Any opinions found in classical Islamic law that contradict such a prohibition are considered as contradictory to *maslahat al-umma*. The second order prohibits any use for any purpose. Similarly, there is a prohibition of agreements that will affect the ownership of an endowment, such as leases, equitable liens, exchange deals, or a license that deals with the use of an endowment. The third order mandates an evaluation and criticism of waqf management every six months. The fourth order deals with cemeteries and mosques, holding that the holiness of cemeteries is "part of the consciousness of the nation and its faith." It even emphasizes the holiness of unused mosques. The marsum's purpose is to give legitimacy to qadis and to move beyond past acts in which permission and license to sell endowments were given. The marsum refuses to acknowledge the fact that Muslims in Israel long ago turned into a religious minority.

To accomplish this, the marsum turns to classical Islamic law for legitimacy, but utilizes these classical concepts in a new way. It specifically does this with the status of maslaha as a source of legislation. Here, the qadis take the role of *fuqaha'* [jurists] in order to be able to make a legal interpretation [*ijtihad*] and change regulations. Maslaha is actually a secondary source of legislation, which modern writers have used to modernize or reform the application of Islamic law.[63] This marsum was issued and publicized in the magazine *Sawtt al-Haq wa al-Hurriyyah* [The Voice of Right and Freedom].[64]

The ideological role of the marsum is clear when we understand that most endowments have been confiscated from the Muslim community in Israel. Besides, the fatwa that the qadis are required to give in order to legitimize a deal is not obligatory on the legal level. The sharia courts do not have jurisdiction over special activities such as *ijaratayn* because jurisdiction is given to the district court only. In most of the orders of the marsum regarding registration, transparency was not required. No reports seem to have been sent to the Sharia Court of Appeals as the marsum stipulates.

CONCLUSION

The sharia courts created a discourse that argues that there is a clear theological, legal, and epistemological separation between Islamic and secular law in Israel. The evidence presented here reveals that this claim is misleading. At the very least, the boundaries between "religious" and "secular" law in Israel are socially and politically fluid. These delineations between religious and secular are therefore often misleading. Despite their claims, the sharia courts do not apply the sharia in a "pure" way.

To be sure, there has never been a pure Islamic law. Instead, like other laws, Islamic law has influenced and has been influenced by various cultures. Islamic law has gone through a process of secularization, not only in Israel. Within the State of Israel, there are religious courts that are expected to apply a pure form of religious law. Yet such expectations of religious courts are met most often in the breach. To understand the nature of law, identity, and citizenship in Israel, the borders between the secular and the sacred need to be readjusted to match the complex and often contradictory realities on the ground.

NOTES

Dedicated to the memory of my father.

1. The hybridization in the Israeli context is a combination of Israeli secular law and religious law. On hybridization in another context, see Ihsan Yilmaz, "Marriage Solemnization among Turks in Britain: The Emergence of a Hybrid Anglo-Muslim Turkish Law," *Journal of Muslim Affairs* 24 (2004): 57. On the concept of hybridity and its critics, see Floya Anthias, "New Hybridities, Old Concepts: The Limits of 'Culture.'" *Ethnic and Racial Studies* 24 (2001): 619.

2. [NB: "A" plus a reference number refers to the number of the appeal in the Sharia Court of Appeals and 13/10/1994 is the date of the decision] See A 63/94 of 13/10/1994. See also A 106/94 of 19/4/1995, 100, 106 regarding the amendment law of family laws (alimony), 1959 and A 59/95 of 19/7/1995, *Al-Kashshaf* 1995,

193. See A 37/95 of 30/7/1995, *Al-Kashshaf* 1995, 232, 234; A 84/94 of 31/3/1995, *Al-Kashshaf* , 1995, 73, 74; and *Al-Kashshaf* 1995, 352, 357. [*Al-Kashshaf* is the official publication of sharia courts decisions from 1992 to 1992, compiled by the interdisciplinary center in Herzlia in 1999]

3. A 194/99 of 22/11/1999 and A 247/98.

4. A 106/94 of 19 April. P. 1021995

5. *Sawtt al-Haq wa al-Hurriyah*, 1/7/1994, 4.

6. On this movement, see Thomas Meir, *The Muslim Awakening in Israel* [in Hebrew] (Givat Haviva: The Arab Studies Institute, 1988); Reuben Paz, *The Islamic Movement in Israel Following the Municipal Elections*, research report [in Hebrew] (Tel Aviv: Dayan Centre, Tel Aviv University, 1989); Alisa Rubin Peled, *Debating Islam in the Jewish State: The Development of Policy Toward Islamic Institutions in Israel* (New York: State University of New York Press, 2001), 121–46; Nohad 'Ali, "Political Islam in an Ethnic Jewish State: Historical Evolution, Contemporary Challenges, and Future Prospects," *Holy Land Studies* 3 (2004): 69.

7. *Sawtt al-Haq wa al-Hurriyah*, 1/7/1994, 4.

8. See Alain Seriaux, *Droit Canonique* (Paris: Presses Universitaires de France, 1996); John D. Faris, *The Eastern Catholic Churches: Constitution and Governance according to the Code of the Eastern Churches* (New York: Saint Maron Publications, 1992), 67–106; René Metz, *Le Nouveau Droit des Eglises Orientales Catholiques* (Paris: Éditions du Cerf, 1997).

9. For the text and commentary, see Salim Rustum Baz Al-Libnani, *Al-Majalla* (n.p., 1986).

10. Dominique Sourdel, "Droit Musulman et Codification,"*Droits* 26 (1997): 33–50; M. Morand, *Avant-projet du code du droit musulman en Algerie* (n.p., 1916). Also see Norman Anderson, *Law Reform in the Muslim World* (London: Athone Press, 1976), 14–19. On the codification in the Ottoman Empire, see Jacques Lafon, "L'empire ottoman et les codes occidentaux," *Droits* 26 (1997): 69.

11. Joseph Schacht, "Problems of Modern Islamic Legislation," *Studia Islamica* 99 (1960): 12; Khaled Abou El Fadl, "Islam and the Challenge of Democratic Commitment," *Fordham International Law Journal* 27 (2003): 4, 63, 70–71.

12. Bruno Oppetit, *Essai sur la codification* (Paris: Presses Universitaires de France, 1998), 8.

13. Ibid., 600.

14. See for possibilities of interference in the arbitrators' ruling the Shariasharia Court can interfere if the report of the arbitrators contradicts justice (A 197/97 from 28/12/1997) or if the arbitrators ignore facts and evidence (A 161/97 from 24/12/1997).

15. A 6/96 of 27/2/1996, *Al-Kashshaf*, 19.

16. Ibn Qudama, *'Umdat al-fiqh ala-madhab al-hambali* (Beirut: Al-Assriyyah lil Tiba"a w al-Nashr, 2001), 95. See also Ibn Qudama, *Al-Mughni* (Cairo: dar al-hadith, 2004), 9:246, 346.

17. S.H., 1951, 248.

18. H.C.J 1226/02 *Nimr bin Abdallah Abu Issa and Others v. The Minister of Interior* (of 23/10/2002). See application of this decision at Ministerial Courts, A.M. (Jerusalem) 951/02 *Abdallah Maraqa and Others v. Minister of Interior* (of 17/2/2003); A.M. (Jerusalem) 510/03 *Tabahi and Others v. Minister of Interior* (of 22/7/2002).

19. Al-Muwsilli, *Al-Ikhtiyar li-ta'lil al-mukhtar*, (Beirut: Dar al-Khayr, 1998), 2:193.

20. Al-Muwsilli, 3:166–7.

21. T.P (Tel-Aviv) 775/79 *State of Israel v. Diab Issawi*, P.M, 1980 (2): 381.

22. Article 134 of the Jordanian Law of Personal Status of 1976, Article 117 of the Syrian Law of Personal Status of 1953 as amended in 1975. See Jamal J.Nassir, *The Islamic Law of Personal Status* (The Hague: Kluwer Law International, 2002), 135–36; Mustafa al-Siba'i, *Sharh qanun al-ahwal al-shakhsiya* (Beirut: Dar al waraq, 2001), 9 ED: 243–244.

23. When one exercises his rights, he cannot be responsible for harm caused to another (*"nemimen laedit qui suo jure utitur"*). But the theory of abuse of rights relativizes one's exercise of one's rights and limits these rights, particularly when the rights are used to harm a third party. This concept was developed by the French civil doctrine; see Francois Terre, Philippe Simler, and Yves Lequette, *Droit Civil. Les Obligations* 661–66 (Paris: Dalloz, 1993). Some scholars tried to anchor this theory in Islamic law; see Mahmoud Fathy, *La notion de l'abus des droits dans la jurisprudence musulmane* (Sainte-Etienne: Société de l'Imprimérie A.Mulcey, 1912).

24. A 259/2003 from 27/1/2004.

25. Regarding religious law sources of this clause and the interpretation of the Sharia Court of Appeals, see Moussa Abou Ramadan, "Divorce Reform in the Sharia Court of Appeals in Israel (1992–2003)," *Islamic Law and Society* (forthcoming).

26. Ibid.

27. Mariam Hoexter, *Endowments, Rulers, and Community: Waqfs al-Haramayn in Ottoman Algiers* (Leiden: Brill, 1998). On a survey of the issues of waqfs, see Miriam Hoexter, "Waqf Studies in the Twentieth Century: The State of the Art," *Journal of the Economic and Social History of the Orient*, 41 (1998): 474–495.

28. Al-Marghinani, *Al-Hidaya* (Beirut: Dar al-arqam, n.d.), 3:15; Zayla'i, *Tabyin al-haqa'iq* (Beirut: Dar al-kutub al-'ilmiya, 2000), 4:266; Ibn 'Abdin, *Hasshiyat rad al-Muhtar* (Beirut: Dar al-fikr, 2000), 4:533.

29. As Michael Dumper argues, the waqf was a "bete noir (sic) of the Zionist movement." Michael Dumper, "The Waqf Revisited," *Journal of Palestine Studies* 27 (1998), 106–7. On the process of dispossession of Israeli Arabs see: Alexandre (Sandy) Kedar, "The Legal Transformation of Ethnic Geography: Israeli Law and the Palestinian Landholder 1948–1967," *NYU Journal of International Law and Politics* 33 (2001): 923, 993.

30. H.C.J 332/52. *Hassouna v. Custodian of Absentee Property and Others*, PD 1198.

31. Ibid., 1198

32. David Neuhauss, "Between Quiescence and Arousal: The Political Functions of Religion. A Case Study of the Arab Minority in Israel: 1948–1990" (PhD diss., Hebrew Univerity, 1990), 48.

33. H.C.J 69/55. *Bulus v. Minister of Development and Others*. PD 147,151.

34. Proposal of Absentee Property Law, Amendment 3: Liberation of endowment property and its use. 1964, H.H 629, 1964, 48.

35. A. Sekaly, *Le problème des wakfs en Egypte* (Paris: Librairie orientaliste Paul Geuthner, 1929). In Israel itself this was used to dispossesses the Arabs in the South of Israel. See Ronen Shamir, "Suspended in Space: Bedouins Under the Law of Israel," *Law and Society Review* 1996: 231.

36. Aharon Layish, "The Muslim Waqf in Israel," *Asian and African Studies* 2 (1966): 41–76, 53–66.

37. G. Baer, *Studies in the Social History of Modern Egypt* (Chicago: University of Chicago Press, 1969), 70. R. Deguilhem, "Le Waqf en Syrie indépendante" in *Le Waqf dans le monde musulman contemporain (XIX–XX siècles)* ed. F. Dilici (Istanbul: Institut français d'études anatoliennes, 1994), 123–44.

38. Article 3 of the Law of Absentee Property (Amendment 3) states: "A board of trustees shall be a body corporate competent to acquire and transfer any right, enter into any obligation and be a party to any legal proceeding and to any contract."

39. See Yitzhak Reiter, "A Reform Assessment in the Muslim Waqf Institution in Israel: The waqf in Acco," [in Hebrew] *Hamizrah Hakhadash* 21 (1989): 44; Michael Dumper, *Islam and Israel: Muslim Religious Endowments and the Jewish State* (Washington: Institute for Palestine Studies, 1994), 50–62. Many reports have been written by the Israeli State Comptroller on the irregularities of financial administration in the Boards of Trustees. See Report No. 24, 190; Report No. 27, 170; Report No. 34, 73; Report No. 35, 496; Report No. 38, 83.

40. I.E. 3997/91 *The Trustee Committee of the Muslim Waqf v. Yosi Investment Company.* PD 49 (5), 766.

41. I.E. 205/74 *Board of Trustees of Jaffa v. Zuhdi Siksik,* PD 28 (2), 545.

42. Ibid.

43. I.E. 3997/91 *The Trustee Committee of the Muslim Waqf v. Yosi Investment Company.* PD 49 (5), 766.

44. Text of the Law in English in Aharon Layish, "The Muslim Waqf in Israel," *Asian and African Studies* 2 (1966): 41, 73.

45. Clause 29C states that "a board of trustees shall not in any manner transfer immovable property which includes a mosque." Although there is such prohibition an attempt to sale Hassan Bik Mosque in Jaffa to a private company. In 11/9/1974 the Trustee of absentee properties of Hassan Bik waqf to the Trust committee of Jaffa and the title was registered on the name of this committee. In the same day, the waqf was given in long-term rent for forty-nine years to an Israeli company. According to the agreement between the company and the Trust Committee of Jaffa, the company has the right to destroy parts of the mosque but to leave one room and the minaret. After the opposition of the local Muslim community in Jaffa, the agreement was not executed. See Samih Hamouda, "Masjid hassan bik:khuyut al-muamara," *Markaz ihya al-turath al arabi* (1985): 37–39.

46. See C.B. "Islamic Law as a Source of Constitutional Law in Egypt: The Constitutionalization of the Sharia in a Modern Arab State," *Columbia Journal of Transnational Law* 37 (1998): 81.

47. Gideon Libson, *Jewish and Islamic Law. A Comparative Study of Custom During the Geonic Period* (Cambridge, MA: Harvard University Press, 2003).

48. H.C.J 8906/04 *Bellah Levi and Others v. The Rabbinical High Court in Jerusalem and Others,* on 8/9/2003. PD 55; See also: H.C.J 8906/04 *Ploni v. Ploni and Others,* on 20/7/2005, judgments 9 and 12.

49. A 37/97 on 28/2/1998; A 28/98 on 26/5/1998; A 248/98 on 29/11/1998; A17/00 on 14/5/2000.

50. See Abi Layth al-Samarqandi, *Fatawi al-nawazil* (Beirut: Dar al-kutub al 'ilmiyya, 2004), 221–22; Al-Quduri, *Mukhtassar al-Quduri* (Beirut: Dar al-kutub

al-'ilmiyya, 1997), 173–74; Al-Sarakhsi ,*Al-Mabsut,* vol. 5 (Beirut: Dar al fikr, 2000), 182–87; Al-Kasani, *Bada'i' al- sana'i* (Beirut: Dar al-fikr,1996), 4:59–66; Ibn Nujaym, *Al-Bahr al-ra'iq* (Beirut: Dar ihya' alturath al 'arabi, 2002), 4:256–65; Ibn 'Abdin, *Hashiyat rad al-muhtar* (Beirut: Dar al-fikr, 2000), 3:610–28; Qadri Pacha articles and commentaries: Muhammad Zayd al-Abyani, *Sharh al-ahkam al-Shar'iyya fi al-ahwal al-shakhsiyya,* vol. 2 (Cairo, 1992), 65–80.

51. Al-Sarakhsi, *Al-Mabsut,* vol. 5 (Beirut: Dar Al-Fikr, 2000), 183.

52. Ibid.

53. See also the conclusion that Tucker reached in another period. Judith E. Tucker, *In the House of the Law: Gender and Islamic Law in Ottoman Syria and Palestine* (Berkeley: University of California Press, 1998).

54. Dina Charif Feller, *La garde (Hadanah) en droit musulman et dans les droits égyptien, syrien et tunisien* (Genève: Librairie Droz, 1996).

55. Clause 186 of the New Law of the Moroccan Family.

56. For example, 91/99 on 31/5/1999, A172/00 on 3/9/2000. See also A282/2004 on 29/11/2004: "This is so in addition to the fact that this court had expressed its opinion regarding the law (it means the Law of Legal Validity and guardianship of 1962. M.A.R.) in A. 93/99."

57. A 48/94 from 1/12/1994; A 53/2003 from 23/3/2003; A 278/2004 from 14/12/2004; A 138/2005 from 20/6/2005; A 58/92 from 9/2/1993; A 268/2003 from 18/8/2003.

58. Young, *Corps du droit ottoman.*

59. H.C.J 1089/90 *Assi v. The Sharia Court, Middle Region,* PD 45(5), 152.

60. Y. Linant de Bellefonds, *Traité de droit musulman comparé* (Paris: Mouton,1965), 1:31–32; Chafik Chehata, *Etudes de droit musulman* (Paris: Presses universitaires de France, 1971), 35.

61. www.justice.gov.il/MOJHeb/BatiDinHashreim/MaagreiMeida/Minsharim/.

62. See later on this concept.

63. Felicitas Opwis, "Maslaha in Contemporary Islamic Legal Theory," *Islamic Law and Society* 12 (2005): 182.

64. *Sawt al-Haq wa al-Hurriyah* on 8/7/1998, 7.

12

Modernity and Its Mirror

Three Views of Jewish-Palestinian Interaction in Jaffa and Tel Aviv

Mark LeVine

This chapter returns us once again to the space of Jaffa–Tel Aviv that Willen and Monterescu also discuss, to explore how the spatial, ideological, and economic development of these neighboring towns reflect the tension of erecting and then penetrating multiple boundaries between Palestinian Arabs and Jews in the country. More specifically, I explore how the technocratic fields of architecture and urban planning came to be reflected in and have a mutual influence upon the literary and artistic productions of the two communities and the material relations between those people on the ground.

The cultural and material relations that existed in Jaffa–Tel Aviv also touch upon the deeper functioning of modernity in these two towns. Through this example of Jaffa–Tel Aviv we find out about how modernity operated in Israel-Palestine's conflicted history.

One founder of Tel Aviv recalled almost twenty-five years after the city's establishment that it was "from the overthrow of geography that Tel Aviv was born."[1] Such a creation ex nihilo in fact reflected the Zionist obsession with ensuring the success of its nationalist movement, and later the Israeli state, as a success that was as modern as possible. This impulse put Zionism in direct competition with Palestinian Arab nationalism which itself was involved in a decades-long interaction with the modern world's economy, politics, and cultural products and values.

A CITY AND A NATION BORN OUT OF THE SANDS?

Since 1949 (after the Israeli state was born), Tel Aviv and Jaffa have officially been administratively considered one city: Tel Aviv–Yafo (the Hebrew term for Jaffa). Yet when Tel Aviv was founded in 1909, the motivation of the city fathers was in fact to create a separate modern suburb that would provide its residents with a European style of living. This vision of Tel Aviv was presented as a contrast to Jaffa, which they felt to be dirty, noisy, overcrowded, and essentially Arab.[2] For their part, Jaffa's residents and municipal leaders considered the region surrounding the city, including the Jewish suburb (at least until the late 1920s) and the surrounding Arab farms and Bedouin communities, to be administratively and (specifically for the Arab areas) culturally part of Jaffa.

Ironically, today the situation is reversed. While officially municipal leaders consider Jaffa to be an integral part of a united city, the majority of Arab residents consider Jaffa to be historically and culturally distinct from Tel Aviv, even as they struggle to gain greater political representation. As demonstrated by the intercommunal violence of late 2000 and 2001 centered in Jaffa and other mixed cities of Israel, Jews also see the Palestinian residents of Jaffa, if not the space of Jaffa itself, as being outside their communal boundaries. Despite the early twinning of Tel Aviv–Yafo in 1949, Tel Aviv–Yafo is now as divided as it was in the 1920s and 1930s, after the British Mandatory government granted the Jewish city municipal independence.

From the start, the Tel Aviv municipality had a problem with marginal populations who did not, or could not, respect the official boundaries of the town; people who refused to be pushed to the territorial margins of the city. After its founding, the local Bedouins, who had long used the land for pasture and farming, continually "plagued" the new town. Soon thereafter it was Palestinian Arabs from the surrounding villages who resented the extension of Tel Aviv's boundaries as increasing encroachment on their lands. While municipal leaders considered most non-Jewish Arabs as problematic, they also considered certain Jews populations as a challenge—Yemenites who refused to conform to the Ashkenazi-European version of Zionism and Eastern Europeans who violated Zionist moral norms (usually because of their involvement in prostitution or similarly disreputable activities). Neighborhood residents and town leaders considered these populations outside the boundaries of Tel Aviv's society.

Despite the modern, exclusively Jewish vision upon which Tel Aviv was founded and built, the various "subaltern" populations remained or eventually became woven into the social, economic, and cultural fabric of the region. From the 1880s through the 1940s, Jews and Palestinians of all varieties worked and did business together in vineyards, family factories and restaurants, and brothels; in work that involved carting sand for cement, in the port, and in selling land. In response, the leaders of Tel Aviv extensively deployed the most modern strategies of spatial manipulation, particularly through the mechanisms of architecture, town planning, and associated legislation and regulations. Leaders employed these fields to enforce the declared or desired boundaries. Because of these dynamics and the attempts to manage them, I argue that an examination of residential frontier regions of these borderland populations reveals Jaffa's relationship with Tel Aviv and proves an especially profitable site for understanding the complex and problematic nature of modernity.[3]

The role and dynamics of modernity within the larger Zionist and Palestinian nationalist discourses were not unique to the territory of Palestine. The modernization of Paris was premised upon "cleansing the large cities" and even more powerfully in the "backward" colonies, "cleansing the entire country" was a crucial component of modernizing it.[4] The process of modernization consequently enabled the creation of a conceptual tabula rasa from which a new and modern nation could grow.[5]

In Palestine specifically, the modernist discourses deployed by the Zionists and the British were part of a larger developmentalist impetus brought by both groups to Palestine. This impetus clashed with an indigenous move toward development that was equally modern but not colonial in nature. European colonial modernity, however, was a doubly asymmetrical process that sustained its own borders. This ideology designated a break with an older, traditional age and, just as important, "a combat in which there are victors and vanquished . . . [where] Other cultures 'bec[o]me pre-modern by contrast.'" Through the process of being cleansed, these assumed pre-modern cultures are then deemed ready to be "civilized" and are "given form."[6]

Such a modernist ideology allowed for a discursive erasure of the Palestinian Arab presence in the Jaffa–Tel Aviv region in the Mandate period. The rhetoric used, whether in literature, poetry, or art, to describe the region upon which Tel Aviv would be built most powerfully achieved this erasure. The narratives that governed the town's architectural and town planning development focused on the land being "nothing but sand," before the arrival of Zionist Jews, as empty and remote as the Sahara desert. The Palestinian Arabs who lived there were deemed "primitive" and "without any law," even when their living conditions or other aspects of life closely mirrored those of the Jewish and nascent Zionist community. All these depictions made possible an idea of Tel Aviv as standing apart from Jaffa as a pure Jewish city. Such a conceptual separation, in turn, facilitated the perception of Tel Aviv as a modernist project and space sine qua non.[7]

Such perceptions of actors who were involved in the struggle over land and identity in the Jaffa–Tel Aviv region demonstrate how and why the production of modernity "occurs *only* by performing the distinction between the modern and non-modern, west and non-west." This practice of demarcation between modern and nonmodern always carries the danger of "contamination and disruption by the latter on the former."[8] The need to prevent such contamination and the threat to the larger nationalist project it symbolizes led to the creation of all sorts of borders between the two communities during the last century. These borders spanned the ideological and the physical.

COMPETING IMAGINATIONS OF JAFFA AND TEL AVIV IN THE LITERATURES OF THE TWO MOVEMENTS

Nationalist leaders, poets, writers, and artists on both sides of the constructed divide articulated fantastical descriptions of Jaffa and Tel Aviv. Such descriptions of the two cities reflected the larger imaginations of the two movements. In the fall of 1936, while Palestine was still reeling from the violent strikes that had begun in April of that year, the official *Tel Aviv Gazette* featured an article promoting tourism to the city. Ignoring the ongoing hostilities, the article explained that "Tel Aviv is not a city, but rather a house of cures, a house of health. If I was a doctor, I would send all the sick Jews . . . for three years [to] in Tel Aviv, because this is a one hundred percent Jewish city, it is the best [place to] rest for all sicknesses. Tel Aviv isn't just Eretz Israel, Tel Aviv is life."[9]

As the chapters by Sufian, Davidovitch, and Willen have demonstrated, issues and symbols related to health were crucial to Zionist, and later Israeli, discourses and policies. Clearly one of the main justifications for the Zionist enterprise in Palestine was the belief that Jewish life in the diaspora had become inherently unhealthy, even sick, and that the establishment of a "national home" on the ancestral soil of Palestine was the cure for this illness. If Zionist adherents believed settlement in Palestine to be the cure for what ailed European Jews of the late nineteenth and early twentieth centuries, Tel Aviv, as we see here, was one of the sites where that cure could be administered in its purest and most potent form.

The problem with this pathway to cure was, of course, that another people inhabited the Promised Land. If the land was well populated and sustaining a growing and productive population, how could Zionist leaders justify Jewish resettlement of the country after so many centuries of absence? Thus out of necessity, as much as in imitation of other European colonial discourses, the Zionist movement began to portray Palestine as largely vacant, its land as barren or sterile, and its Arab inhabitants backward and unproductive, in this way creating the discursive and physical space for Jewish colonization and settlement.[10] A verse from the book of Amos, prominently displayed above the entrance to the home (now a museum) of Tel Aviv's first and longest-serving mayor, Meir Dizengoff, explained that God "will restore the fortunes of my people Israel, and they shall rebuild the ruined cities and inhabit them."[11] This restoration, however, necessitated a double conceptual negation, negating both the Jewish diaspora and the Palestinian Arab presence in the country. Against such forces Tel Aviv would have to be[come] a "perpetuum mobile, dynamic, [full of] tempo and movement."[12]

To capture this dynamic, numerous songs and poems refer to "the sands of Tel Aviv." These texts are often juxtaposed with well-known, almost iconic photographs or drawings of the sands on which Tel Aviv was born.[13] In fact, as the city developed and expanded into the 1920s, "Tel Aviv on the sands" remained an important theme in poetry and songs,[14] symbolizing a quiet, romantic space of diversion and amusement for the busy town.[15] As one poem from 1922 exclaimed:

> If you want, habib
> to waste an hour
> Run quickly to Tel Aviv.
> Go to the hills; there in the evening
> on the Sand, there you will see,
> You will find everything.[16]

Moreover, as opposed to what the novelist Shai Agnon would describe as the "desert of Jaffa," in his seminal *Tmol Shilshom*,[17] once the landscape was consecrated as the Zionist project, "the sands" that supposedly comprised the area that would become Tel Aviv became "the gardens of love of Tel Aviv, like the threshing floor in the moshav, and the vineyards of Ein Gedi;"[18] that is, the sands were pregnant with life and waiting for their "cultivators," as Ben-Gurion similarly described Jewish immigrants to Palestine.[19] In fact, in a manner that reminds us of the temporal borders discussed by Sufian in her chapter on the construction and future of a distinct Hebrew medical language, the seemingly ancient sands were linked to the future of Tel Aviv: "Tel Aviv, Tel Aviv, City of the Future, filling [everything] with its brightness. On the sands of the sea, noisy from all the people."[20]

When poets described regions where Arabs lived or worked in the Jaffa–Tel Aviv region, their presence is either ignored or appropriated;[21] that is, symbolically and discursively the Jewish immigrants became the original Arabs. One poem about the Nordiah neighborhood (located in what is now the Dizengoff Center area) describes how "the Bedouins that came from Poland" spread out over Balfour Street and lived in tents.[22] As for the real Bedouins, as a 1937 children's story about a boat trip on the Yarkon river explains, they live just "as it had been hundreds of years ago"—that is, "primitively."[23]

The depictions in literature of Tel Aviv as modern and dynamic versus backward and stagnant Palestinian Jaffa continued into the post-1948 period. Writers like Ya'akov Shabtai (in his well-known novel *Past Continuous*) strove to depict the perpetual creative destruction fueling Tel Aviv's development, in good measure through the continual "separati[on] of the Arabs from their Arabness";[24] that is, by removing any Arab presence from the narrative. Similarly, films such as the 1987 *Late Summer Blues*, a coming of age movie set in Tel Aviv about the summer before Israeli teenagers entered army service, featured much of the same imagery as the earlier literary texts just noted and, ironically, was filmed at least in part on the beach in Jaffa.[25]

"WE ARE IN A STATE OF WAR":
TEL AVIV AS PERCEIVED BY ITS OTHER

Similarly to Tel Aviv, the city of Jaffa was, during the half century until 1948, both the economic and cultural center for Palestine's Arab community, its "gate of entrance and liberation."[26] Several of the most important literary clubs, part of dozens of Palestinian Arab cultural and educational organizations, were located in Jaffa. Writers such as Muhammed Izzat Darwazah and Muhammad Rafiq al-Tamimi, although not born in Jaffa, lived and did much of their writing there.

For Palestinian Arab writers, there was a clear conceptual and epistemological distinction between life in Jaffa before and after Tel Aviv was established. Writers particularly highlight this narrative break after World War I, when the Jewish town began to develop rapidly, threatening Jaffa's economy at the same time that it contributed to its growth.[27] On the one hand, the Arab press described Tel Aviv as "the modern Jewish city," or as one Arab journal described it, "the most advanced city in Palestine."[28] Yet the rapid economic expansion of Tel Aviv and the "entrance of Jews into the commerce of Jaffa" led Jaffans to fear losing an increasing number of jobs to Jews.[29] Jaffa's leadership further accused the Tel Aviv Municipality of being involved in national Jewish politics—that is, of basing municipal policies on the need to pursue Zionist goals that were detrimental to the interests of Jaffa and Arab Palestine as a whole.[30]

Arab leaders also felt that the British Mandatory government showed much favoritism to the development of Tel Aviv. Thus one article in *Falastin*, titled "Tel Aviv Municipality: God's Contentment Upon It," explained how Jaffa faced continuing hardship while the government lowered Tel Aviv's debt. The author used this economic issue as an example of the government's unequal treatment of the two cities.[31] Moreover, the Jaffa press portrayed the Tel Aviv municipality as playing a major role in the taking of "Arab national land."[32]

In light of this belief, and perhaps in response to the positive Jewish portrayal of Tel Aviv as well, the Palestinian Arab press described Tel Aviv as "the most corrupt city in Palestine," or "the one pure Jewish city in Palestine but at the same time the city in which we see the most corruption."[33]

Given the rampant corruption believed to be endemic to the Jewish city, the Arab media further described the Tel Aviv municipality as "encouraging [the] transgression of public security in ways that are not found in other cities, linked to Jewish immigration."[34]

What's more, the historical connection between communist activity and violence in Jaffa and Tel Aviv (e.g., the violence of May Day 1921 that began on the border between the two towns after a demonstration by Jewish communists) meant that Tel Aviv was seen as a hotbed of "communism." The Arab press blamed Jews for "bringing Communism to this Holy Land.[35] Indeed, Tel Aviv's corruption was represented as contagious. Furthermore, the Arab press negatively viewed the entrance of Arabs, or Arab symbols, to this Jewish space unless such penetration was an act of defiance against the city and what it symbolized. For instance, in an article entitled "The Fez in Tel Aviv," in *al-Jam'iah al-Islamiyyah,* the author explained that "we are in a state of war . . . , and [can not] deny ourselves of any weapon or means to defend ourselves. And there is no [better] weapon than . . . holding on to our Eastness. And I will confirm for you that the presence of the fez in Tel Aviv will be a great influence . . . and I am the first to hold on to the fez."[36]

As Sandy Sufian has argued elsewhere, political cartoons helped shape Palestinian Arab and Jewish popular/public opinion, especially during the times of heightened tension such as the 1936–1939 Revolt.[37] Cartoons in the Palestinian Arab press helped to shape and reinforce visual markers of separation in the larger popular culture. As a 1936 cartoon showing Tel Aviv Mayor Dizengoff presenting the High Commissioner, Lord Wauchaupe, reveals, Tel Aviv symbolized the evils of the Balfour Declaration and the continued cooperation between the municipality and the British government. In another cartoon, also featuring Dizengoff, the Mayor of Nablus replies to the mayor's "Shalom" (Hebrew word for hello/goodbye/peace) by exclaiming "No Shalom, No Salam (Arabic word for peace), and no negotiation till Jewish immigration ends."

Other cartoons depicted virtuous and traditionally dressed Palestinian women confronting Zionist harlots in a court of law or utilized a standard technique of European physiognomy, theriomorphism, to represent Jaffa and Tel Aviv as, respectively, a mouse and a cat about to pounce on it.[38] In all these cartoons, the goal was to both publicize and popularize the struggle and sacrifices of individual citizens with the larger community.[39] Cartoons, like journalistic articles and literary works, played a central role in building and maintaining communal borders.

The views and values depicted in the cartoons extend to those reflected in Palestinian literature before 1948 (and, of course, after 1948 as well). Thus the writer Najati Sidqi wrote a collection of stories titled *al-Akhwat al-Hazinat* [*The Sad Sisters*], all of which discuss the social and political problems faced by the Arabs of Palestine and others through the prism of the Jaffa experience.

In the title story, Sidqi describes the transformation of Jaffa from a quiet, romantic Arab place into a busy city inhabited by aliens—Jews—who have introduced strange habits and ways of life.[40]

Even more important is Muhammed Izzat Darwazah's story, *al-Malak was al-Simsar* [*The Angel and the Land Broker*]. Darwazah describes the methods used by Zionists to entice Arab landowners to sell their lands. The story begins with a description of a typical Palestinian Arab family from sometime in the late Ottoman period through the mid 1920s.[41] The head of the family, who is about forty years of age, has spent all his life as an illiterate farmer and has never been exposed to the attractions of life in the cities. Under the influence of a Jewish land broker, he makes his first visit to Tel Aviv. There he is introduced to a Jewish girl—no doubt resembling the one in the cartoon described earlier—who encourages him to spend himself into debt. The yield of the land he owns is not enough to meet his obligations and the land broker arranges for a mortgage. When the payment falls due, the protagonist cannot meet it. He has to sell the land to the broker for a price far below its value. Within a short time, he spends the money and deserts his wife and children, turning into a beggar. Ultimately, the illiterate farmer ends his life in a lunatic asylum, having gone crazy as a result of his tragic experience. Darwazah's frankly political aim becomes clear toward the end of the story, when he describes in great detail the way in which other villages decide to create a fund to save land threatened by Zionist buyers.[42]

Memorial books and other memoirs of diaspora Palestinians also reflected such views of both Jaffa and Tel Aviv. These literary genres should be considered as "village histories," belonging to a hybrid category of texts that in the past might have been conventionally assigned to the disciplines of anthropology or folklore yet are today being seen as important sources for the history of the country.[43] These texts also remind us, as one memorial book about the large village of Salameh on the outskirts of Jaffa does, how Palestine before the war was a generally vibrant and living Palestinian space intimately connected to the surrounding landscape.[44]

The memorialization of Jaffa and through it, Palestine, not only serves the purpose of preserving a history of loss. Indeed, the memoirs of former (mostly bourgeois) citizens of the city reveal these people's imagination of the city as the "wide-open gate to Palestine." These authors depict Jaffa as the country's "gleaming city," the "center of Palestine's politics and national spirit," and even, with "its advanced ways of life and fertility of its lands" (i.e., the "sands" upon which Tel Aviv was built), "the greatest city in terms of culture and civilization."[45]

Depicting their city as a space of "rebirth," Palestinian writers mirror the Jewish depictions of a Palestinian-free Tel Aviv by completely ignoring the long-standing Jewish presence in Jaffa and its surrounding region.[46] But the contemporary Palestinian Jaffan community has more pressing concerns: not just to memorialize the once "thriving, flourishing, and blossoming city that always loved the stranger" and not just to teach children "how beautiful are the memories."[47] Equally important is the community's need to explain the much more troubled present situation of the city and to help motivate residents to take action to improve their situation. To do so requires a two-part process. The first is to express sorrow for the loss of Jaffa by depicting the city as symbolizing what the martyrs of 1948 fought and died for, and by depicting the city itself as a symbol of the *Nakba*, the disaster of 1948.[48]

> Jaffa, my poor city . . . Jaffa, my wounded city . . .
> Jaffa, my slaughtered country.
> Jaffa, to forget [you] my city, is to cut my throat.[49]

There is a telling difference between the poetry and larger descriptions of Jaffa written by exiles from Jaffa and the descriptions of neighborhood's contemporary residents. For the former, the most important refrain is perhaps that of the famous song of Fairuz, "Mina Yafa" [Jaffa Port], in which she sings "And we will return, we return, Oh Jaffa; we will return, we return, Oh Jaffa."[50] The latter, however, cannot wait for the second coming of the Jaffa's original inhabitants. As a 1997 brochure from the Jaffan Palestinian community organization *al-Rabita* explains in a poem that concludes the booklet:

> Shall we begin in the destruction of Jaffa and its culture and Arab civilization or in its judaization?
> From where shall we begin, when Jaffa has been judaized for so many years.
> Tel Aviv, this city that makes you really feel like you want to vomit when you write "Tel Aviv-Yafo Municipality."
> Where is Tel Aviv from Jaffa, here it embraces your history in longing, for entering and enfolding your originality.
> Will it think that this "Tel Aviv" was created in the culture of the city of Jaffa, and swallowed her blood and sweet nectar in this, what symbolizes for us "Tel Aviv"?
> Is it possible that this unplanned/random city to swallow the ancient Cana'anite city, cleaving to its history and culture?

It is ironic that Tel Aviv, the "first modern Hebrew city in the world," whose identity is intertwined with town planning and architectural discourse, is derided here as random or unplanned. This irony is most likely not lost on the local Palestinian Arab community, which is in the midst of a fifty-year struggle with the Tel Aviv municipality over control of the planning and development in what today is Tel Aviv's Arab quarter.

FROM REFLECTION TO REALITY: LABOR AND THE
PRODUCTION OF SPACE IN THE JAFFA–TEL AVIV REGION

The works of Palestinian Arab and Jewish poets, storytellers, novelists, artists, and journalists reveal the various ways the two communities saw themselves and the other during the century-long conflict between them. They do not, however, necessarily represent an accurate portrayal of the lived reality on the ground in the Jaffa–Tel Aviv region. These literary works keep portrayals at the level of representation. In contrast, by exploring two material practices and relations—the production of space and the repro-duction of labor in the two cities—we see how much of the two nationalist ideologies were made concrete in the relations between the two communi-ties on the ground.

If the people of Tel Aviv imagined their city to be born out of the over-turning of the local geography, then the best way to analyze the impact of this process is by looking at the urban planning and architecture of the city. In the Zionist imagination, at least, Tel Aviv was the modern antithesis to backward, dirty, and stagnant Jaffa. The latter represented not only the Palestinian Arab "other" but the Jews of the pre-Zionist diasporic condition as well. So when the Zionist founders of the city imagined their new neigh-borhood as a modern space, this vision was in contrast to the windy, cramped, and seemingly chaotic streets of both the Palestinian and old Jew-ish neighborhoods of Jaffa (or of Jerusalem for that matter). Instead, Tel Aviv's development would be strictly planned and regulated to follow the most modern and scientific understandings of urban living, to ensure a proper amount of space between houses, and to offer aesthetic confirma-tion to the growing power of Zionism in the country. As Herzl wrote in *The Jewish State* years earlier, "We shall not dwell in mud huts; we shall build new, more beautiful and more modern houses." Similarly, one of the founders of Tel Aviv explained that while they didn't have money, "a plan we do have."[51]

In contrast to the "complete anarchy" and aesthetic ugliness of Jaffa, the founders of Tel Aviv sought to build a "clean and healthy" Jewish city, built for Jews and Jews only. The city was meant for Jews who "possessed energy and vigor" and who would therefore appreciate the fact that it would be "beautiful, arranged according to laws, all of it Hebrew."[52] Paying attention to all the modern facilities of Europe, Tel Aviv was to be segregated spatially, economically, aesthetically, and politically from the existing Arab city. Even more interestingly ironic or paradoxical, the *galut* [diaspora] Jewish envi-ronment, accomplished by adopting Ebenezer Howard's garden city/suburb paradigm, was considered the most modern planning system in Europe.[53]

Adoption of the garden suburb style was reflected in the straight streets, the arrangement of houses, and the style of building. What is important here, however, is that while the Jewish leaders described this process as unique to Tel Aviv, the same process of town planning and architectural development was happening in Jaffa. Indeed, the developments in Jaffa were largely along the same lines as those in Tel Aviv, whether it was the trees being planted for Jamal Pasha Boulevard—to which Tel Aviv leaders actually contributed money and trees and which mirrored Tel Aviv's own Rothschild Boulevard—or the evolution of architectural styles from the Mediterranean style common to both towns (and similar to houses across the Mediterranean in this period) to the eclectic style of the 1920s. Such parallel development was sufficiently apparent that when the Tel Aviv municipality invited the eminent Scottish planner Patrick Geddes to create a town plan for Tel Aviv in 1925, Geddes's introduction explained that however impressive Tel Aviv's growth and energy was, the "natural" development for the town would be to continue growing for the "good of greater Jaffa."[54]

The Zionist movement and Tel Aviv leaders in particular made a more concerted effort to separate themselves from Jaffa and the larger Palestinian Arab community with the onset of the 1930s, largely in response to the countrywide eruption of violence in 1929 (although even before this episode, by several accounts around 1927, Zionist architects had begun to turn back to Europe for inspiration). In response to this renewed threat to the emerging Jewish hegemony in Palestine[55] and the concomitant needs for both increasing separation and justification of Zionism as uniquely civilized, modern international style (IS) architecture quickly became the dominant style of the 1930s. This eclectic style came under criticism for bad architectural form and lack of culture or planning.[56] The closing of the Bauhaus school—where seven Jewish/Zionist architects studied—with the onset of Nazism in Germany in 1933 also contributed to this trend.

It is thus no surprise that in the environment of the 1930s Zionist architectural discourse became ever more militantly modernist. Similarly, the larger Zionist argument that the Palestinians were incapable of developing the country, and thus undeserving of ruling or even remaining in it, became ever more vigorous. The IS/Bauhaus vernacular accorded so well with the Zionist spirit of renewal that by the early 1930s modernism became the visual mold for the Zionist project.[57]

At the same time, town planning would become perhaps the most important discourse to ensure the expansion of the town in this period. Tel Aviv's rapidly growing population required ever more land, which in turn demanded that Tel Aviv's boundaries would extend to gain control of the territory of the six villages that surrounded it. What made this possible was that Zionist planning resonated with the British authorities, who enacted numerous town planning ordinances that facilitated Tel Aviv's expansion even when other policies aimed to curtail Jewish acquisition of and control over Arab land.

Here again, while Tel Aviv's builders engaged in an extremely self-conscious modernization in the urban sphere—so much so that UNESCO recently declared it a World Heritage Site in recognition of its astounding collection of IS/Bauhaus style buildings—Jaffa in no way escaped this development. In fact, while the UNESCO listing completely ignored Jaffa's architectural heritage, the town was also home to a great many buildings in this style, including perhaps the most modern house in the whole Jaffa–Tel Aviv region. Many of the structures in Jaffa seem to have been designed by Italian rather than German architects.

But Jaffa's similarities to Tel Aviv did not end at the level of architecture. In the 1940s, the city commissioned the chief architect of Cairo to design a town plan that would have made Jaffa into one of the premier seaside cities of the Eastern Mediterranean. The design, which I have discussed in detail elsewhere,[58] was never realized, as the Israeli authorities had little incentive to develop Jaffa after 1948. The plan reveals, however, the intentions of the municipal authorities to do everything possible to keep up with its neighbor to the north.

As important as the development that occurred in Jaffa was, it is clear how well the Palestinian Arab residents of the Jaffa–Tel Aviv region understood the implications of the Zionist-cum-British discourses of development generally and their implementation through town planning schemes. To take just one example from the Jaffa–Tel Aviv region, when the Tel Aviv Municipality attempted to build a road on Arab land, the Jaffa-based religious daily *al-Jam'iah al-Islamiyyah* complained:

> [I]n reality the plan in the Town-Planning Commission now including Sheikh Muwannis is not really a 'plan,' but rather a plan to take the land out of the hands of the owners. . . . We have farmed land north of the Auja for a long time and then Jews came and wanted to buy it because it is close to Tel Aviv, and we said no, and they tried to get it through various means, including using the Government to push a plan to open a road through our farmland . . . after it proved incapable of gaining ownership through [other] means. [We declare] that this project has no benefit returning to the village, either from a planning or moral perspective.' Moreover, the project 'has no benefit returning to the village, either for planning or from moral perspective.'[59]

The above quote points to the sometimes intense conflict between the two communities; it suggests that while the development of the two cities mirrored each other, there was little positive interaction or cooperation between the cities and the people who lived there.

However, the reality is quite different. In fact, it was almost impossible to keep the two communities apart, economically as well as culturally, a fact which led the mayor of Tel Aviv to exclaim in frustration in 1940 that he would "blow up with bombs" a new market scheduled to be built on a mutual border between Tel Aviv and Yafo because it would allow cheaper Palestinian Arab–made goods and foodstuffs to flood into Tel Aviv and therefore threaten the Jewish economy.[60]

Moreover, despite Tel Aviv's self-proclaimed status as a "Jewish" city, not only did a small number of Palestinian Arabs live in Tel Aviv (in contravention of the original bylaws of the town) but many Palestinian Arabs worked in Tel Aviv throughout the late Ottoman and Mandate periods. When the authorities cracked down on the employment of Palestinian Arab labor, Jewish businessmen began to "smuggle factories into the Palestinian Arab village (Summel), thus freeing themselves from the obligation to employ Jewish labor."[61] This is likely one reason why the Tel Aviv Municipality became so interested in annexing the land of Summel and other villages adjoining Tel Aviv in the ensuing years. This case demonstrates the increasing importance of administrative borders for policing the more porous national boundaries that were supposed to separate the Arab and Jewish communities and economies in the Jaffa–Tel Aviv region.

Not surprisingly, one of the best indicators of the everyday relations between Arabs and Jews in Jaffa comes from their workplace interactions. Scholars such as Baruch Kimmerling, Gershon Shafir, Barbara Smith, Zachary Lockman, me, and other authors in this volume have clearly demonstrated the deep connection between economic and territorial dimensions of the conflict. All of this research has demonstrated how the conquests of labor and land became among the most important tools of the Zionist enterprise in Palestine. The conquest of land and labor occurred in the rural sectors, as epitomized by the kibbutz, and in the urban sector, as epitomized by Tel Aviv (established in 1909, the same year as the first kibbutz, Degania).[62]

But such conflict needs to be contextualized within the rapid growth of the Palestinian economy in the years after the British conquest in 1917, growth in which the working class of the two communities played a crucial role. Although Tel Aviv was established by sixty bourgeois families from Jaffa, working-class Jews and Palestinian Arabs also held an important presence in the neighborhood turned city from the beginning of the city's foundation. It could not be otherwise, given the centrality of the Jaffa–Tel Aviv region as a destination for the majority of Jewish immigrants and capital.

Beyond mere propaganda, the local and national leadership devoted significant energy throughout the Mandate period to developing ties with Arab workers. The records of their successes and failures provide the best, and often the only, documentation about labor conditions in Arab Jaffa. In 1921, for example, Jewish woodworkers sought, with varying degrees of success, to develop ties with Palestinian Arab carpenters, bakers, government (railway, postal, and telegraph) workers, and camel drivers. In the latter case the woodworkers hoped to work together to get rid of the Bedouin camel drivers, who were nicknamed the "fifth aliyah."[63] For their part, Palestinian Arab port workers sought help from the Histadrut to improve working conditions at the port and combat the influx of cheap "foreign" workers from Egypt and Syria.[64]

As the 1920s ended, it appears that Arab workers began to heed warnings that the Histadrut was helping them only to further Jewish interests.[65] Yet with the economic upturn of the early 1930s, the Histadrut once again focused concerted energy on organizing Jaffa's Palestinian Arab workers.[66] These workers used the Histadrut's interest to press the leadership of its "Arab union," the Palestine Labor League (formed in 1932, hereafter PLL) and to promise that the Histadrut would not seek to bring Jewish workers into Jaffa port.[67] The Histadrut's success in organizing Arab workers in Jaffa prompted the Arabic newspaper *Falastin* to issue a public call for the creation of an Arab union in 1934. This call led to the establishment of the Arab Workers Society (AWS) in Jaffa in October 1934.[68]

Despite intense efforts by the local press and Arab bourgeoisie to stop the cooperation between the working classes of both communities and, in particular, between the Palestinian Arab working class and the Zionist unions, Palestinian Arab workers continued to approach the Histadrut into the early part of 1936.[69] This continued gesture led trade unionists to convene a national conference in Jaffa in February of that same year. Although the outbreak of the strike and revolt in 1936 severed connections between the Histadrut and Arab workers, these workers recontacted the Histadrut regarding worsened conditions at the port after it reopened in October of that year.[70] By the end of 1937, relations were much improved and a "strong tendency" to organize Arab workers resumed in Jaffa, and throughout the country as a whole.[71]

The dynamic of relations between Palestinian Arab workers and the Histadrut (Zionist labor organization) would not have been possible without some level of cooperation with the leaders of the Palestinian Arab community. Of note, the Histadrut rented a house from the son of Jaffa's mayor at one point and the Jaffa Municipality signed labor agreements with the Histadrut representing Palestinian workers. These cooperative relations reflected a reality where, even as the nationalist conflict intensified, the Histadrut, in the interest of labor relations, sometimes acted more constructively toward Palestinian Arab workers than did the latter's nationalist "leaders." Because of this, the deputy mayor of Jaffa complained to a representative of the Palestine Labor League (the Arab union established by the Histadrut): "Why do you bother us and meddle every day in the interests of the workers?" The PLL (Histradrut) representative replied: "Times change, there is democracy, there is freedom to organize, justly and honestly." The deputy mayor did not appreciate this line of reasoning, answering "What democracy, we don't have democracy, we scorn democracy. . . .

We only understand one thing: the worker that puts forth demands to us is a worker that wants to be lord over us and this we will not suffer."[72] At this point another official entered the room and the conversation, declaring that the PLL only wanted to "upset our order" by getting involved with workers, which would hurt the unity of the Arabs and make it harder to have a united front against the Zionist movement as a whole.[73]

This exchange clearly reveals the contradictory position of the PLL/Histadrut within the larger arena of Palestinian Arab labor politics in Jaffa. Whatever its role in securing the overall "conquest of Hebrew labor" in Jaffa, the Histadrut's aims and activities were in many cases closer to the interests of Jaffa's Palestinian Arab workers than those of the Arab national leadership. The literature of the two communities, however, rarely reflects such a complex reality.

CONCLUSION

The history of the Jaffa–Tel Aviv region, on both a cultural and material level, clearly demonstrates that the attempt to rigidly establish and police the spatial, communal, economic, and cultural boundaries between the two nations-in-the-making demanded continual vigilance. Palestinian Arabs and Jews continuously challenged these boundaries through constant communication, coexistence, and occasional practical "solidarity." This muddier reality is not meant to suggest an "if only" narrative that offers a glimpse of what could have become of Palestine had the militant nationalisms of the two communities not achieved political hegemony by the 1920s. It does remind us, however, as Michelle Campos's chapter also points out in this volume, that while nationalist mythologies often masquerade as history, a genealogical approach to the modern history of Palestine and the Palestinian-Israeli conflict demonstrates how hard the leaders of the two communities had to work to achieve their aims. These leaders were the most invested in establishing and policing a firm border between the two communities. By reapproaching the innumerable borders separating Palestine and Israel today through the history that has brought us to this point, it is not impossible to imagine that glimpses of a way forward, towards peaceful coexistence in the future, could be recovered.

NOTES

1. "Tel Aviv," *Yediot Tel Aviv*, 1933 (3): 61.
2. As Argyrou points out, a society is modern and civilized only insofar as it is a European society, which accounts for the consistent portrayal of Tel Aviv as a

European space. Vassos Argyrou, *Anthropology and the Will to Meaning: A Postcolonial Critique* (London: Pluto Press, 2002).

3. Walter Mignolo utilizes a similar strategy with his "border thinking" as a way of upsetting the dominant epistemology of "colonial difference" in analyzing colonial modernity in the Americas. Walter Mignolo, *Local Histories/Global Designs: Coloniality, Subaltern Knowledges, and Border Thinking* (Princeton, NJ: Princeton University Press, 2000).

4. Quoted in Gwendolyn Wright, *The Politics of Design in French Colonial Urbanism* (Chicago: University of Chicago Press, 1991), 16, cf. 319, note 8.

5. James Holston, *The Modernist City: An Anthropological Critique of Brasilia* (Chicago: University of Chicago Press, 1989), 83. The planners possessed a teleological view of history in which capitalist modernity signified an advance in human civilization that began in Europe and would spread to the "backward" regions.

6. Bruno Latour, *We Have Never Been Modern*, trans. Catherine Porter (Cambridge, MA: Harvard University Press, 1993), 39; Holston, *The Modernist City*, 68.

7. See Mark LeVine, *Overthrowing Geography: Jaffa, Tel Aviv, and the Struggle for Palestine, 1880 to the Present* (Berkeley: University of California Press, 2005).

8. Tim Mitchell, "The Stages of Modernity," in *Questions of Modernity* (Minneapolis: University of Minnesota Press, 1999), 26, his italics. That is, there are two registers of difference, one providing the modern with its characteristic indeterminacy and ambivalence and the other with its enormous power of replication.

9. Shalom Esh, "Tel Aviv," *Yediot Tel Aviv*, 1936 (3–4): 116.

10. See Shafir for how this process in the labor market led to the emergence of a "militant nationalism" within Zionism already by 1909. Gershon Shafir, *Land Labor and the Origins of the Israeli-Palestinian Conflict* (Berkeley: University of California Press, 1989).

11. Amos, 9: 14. Isaiah 58:12 reads "And your ancient ruins shall be rebuilt; you shall raise up the foundations of many generations; you shall be called the repairer of the breach, the restorer of streets to dwell in." See also Ezek 36:10.

12. *Hapo'el Hatza'ir*, 3/xi/33, 3.

13. Cf. Eliyahu Hacohen, *Bkhol Zot Yesh Bah Mashehu: Shirei Hzemer Shel Tel Aviv* [The Songs of Tel Aviv, 1909–1984] (Tel Aviv, 1985), 22–23.

14. Rafael Klatzkin, "Tel Aviv on the Sands," *Hacohen*, 1985, 31.

15. Ibid.

16. "Tel Aviv," *Haaretz*, Purim 1922 (Tel Aviv Municipal Archive [TAMA], 20/18, newspaper clippings file).

17. A. B. Yafeh, "Writers and Literature in Little Tel Aviv," in *The First Twenty Years: Literature and Art in the Little Tel Aviv, 1909–1929* (Tel Aviv: Tel Aviv Fund for Literature and Art, 1980), 22–23; Shai Agnon, *Tmol Shilshom* (Tel Aviv: Schocken, 1957), 42–43.

18. Hacohen, *Bkhol Zot Yesh Mashehu*, 22.

19. Quoted in Joseph Gorny, *Zionism and the Arabs, 1882–1948* (New York, Oxford University Press, 1987), 140.

20. Amnoel Harusi, "Himnon Tel Aviv," in *Bkhol Zot Yesh Mashehu*, ed. Eliyahu Hacohen (Tel Aviv: Hevrat Dabir, 1985), 60.

21. Cf. Shlomo Tanai, "On Dizengoff Street," and Asher Dayakh, "Agav Tiyul Le-yad Hayarkon," in *Shirei Tel Aviv Aviv* [Poems and Songs of Tel Aviv], ed. Dalyah Haretz and Ozer Rabin (Tel Aviv: Hakibbutz Hameuhad, 1982), 45, 63.

22. Avot Yisharon, "Eresh Poem for Shchunat Nordiah," quoted in Tamar Berger, *Dionysus Basenter* [Dionysus at Dizengoff Center] (Tel Aviv: Kibbutz Hameuchad Publishing, 1998), 143. Emphasis added.

23. Libbie Braveman, *Children of the Emek* (New York: Furrow Press, 1937), 68–69.

24. Tamar Berger, *Dionysus Basenter* [Dionysus at Dizengoff Center] (Tel Aviv: Kibbutz Hameuhad Publishing, 1998), 86.

25. Renen Schorr, *Late Summer Blues* (Israel: Blues Productions, 1987).

26. Cf. A.S. al-Domaniki, "Nathra fi Ta'rikh yafa" [A View of the History of Jaffa], *al-Mashriq* 10 (1928): 729. He further (on page 833) describes Jaffa as "beautiful" in myriad ways, "important" strategically, and very "fertile."

27. Cf. *al-Jam'iah al-Islamiyyah*, 25/12/32, 8.

28. *Falastin*, 13/3/29, 1; TAMA, 3/145 (al-'Umran, n.d.), 605.

29. "The presence of ten thousand Jews in Jaffa is cutting the Jaffa Municipality off from us and from our workers" (*Falastin*, 26/10/32, 9). Cf. *Falastin*, 7/vii/31, 7. Also, cf. 31/5/34. 3.

30. *Falastin*, 5/ix/29, 4.

31. *Falastin*, 20/7/30, 1.

32. *Falastin*, 24/9/32, 6.

33. Ibid.

34. *Falastin*, 8/xii/33, 7.

35. "Mr. Dizengoff Goes On Doting," *Falastin*, 12/viii/36, 3.

36. *al-Jami'a al-Islamiyyah*, 6/ix/32, 2.

37. See Sandy Sufian, "Anatomy of the 1936–1939 Revolt: Images of the Body in Political Cartoons of Mandatory Palestine." *Journal of Palestine Studies*, forthcoming.

38. Sufian, ibid.

39. See, for example, *Falastin*, 24/4/36 for a special photographic issue devoted to the rebellion (cf. Ali al-Najjar, "The Arabic Press and Nationalism in Palestine, 1920–1948" (Ph.D. diss., Syracuse University, 1975), 138.

40. Najati Sidqi, *al-Akhwat al-Hazinat* [The Sad Sisters] (Cairo: Dar al Maarifa Bi-Misr, n.d.).

41. The story appears to be set in the 1920s, but the grandson of the author has informed me that it was written in the late Ottoman period, around 1913 (Dr. Izzat Darwazeh, e-mail communication, 3/2000, citing information provided by his father, the author's son). I was not able to locate any surviving copies; my discussion is based on the detailed description in Abu-Ghazaleh, 1973.

42. Recounted in Adnan Abu-Ghazaleh, *Arab Cultural Nationalism in Palestine During the British Mandate* (Beirut: Institute of Palestine Studies, 1973), 63.

43. Susan Slyomovics, *The Object of Memory: Arab and Jew Narrate the Palestinian Village* (Philadelphia: University of Pennsylvania Press, 1998), 1.

44. Thus photocopies of the diary of one of the village leaders from 1947 tell of his being prevented from commencing a trip because of an important call from the mufti of Jerusalem Sahrah Dirbas, *Salameh: Ihda al-Qura al-Kabira Qada Yafa* [Salameh: One

of the Biggest Villages in the Jaffa District] (n.p.1998), photostat of diaries of Sheikh Muwannis.

45. Yusef Heykal, *Ayyam al-Sabba* [Days of Juvenility] (Amman: Dar al-Galil Press, 1988), 82–85; Imtiyaz Diyab, *Yafa: Utr Medinah* [Jaffa: Perfume of a City] (Beirut: Dar al Fati al-Arabi Publishing, 1991), 14; Hana Malak, *Al-Juzzur al-Yafiyyah* [Roots of Jaffa] (Jerusalem: privately printed, 1993), 43; Culture Committee of the Fund for a Free Jaffa, *Yafa, Haqaiq wa-Maalumat* [Jaffa: Facts and Information], (Kuwait, 1990), 15; Ahmed Zaki al-Dajani, *Medinah Yafa wa-Thawrah 1936* [Jaffa and the Revolt of 1936] (n.p., n.d.), 84–85.

46. Cf. Culture Committee of the Fund for a Free Jaffa, *Yafa*, 14. Abbas Nimr, "Jaffa . . . The Eternal Longing," *al-Quds*, 17/5/97, no page number on offprint.

47. Muhammad Badarna, *Yafa: Urus al-Bahr* [Jaffa: Bride of the Sea] (Jaffa: Rabita Publications, 1997), 13, 56.

48. From a poem by Mahmud Salim al-Hawt, title not given, in al-Dajani, *Medinah Yafa*, 212–13. Cf. Walid al-Hilias, "Yafa of the Martyrs," in al-Dajani, *Medinah Yafa*, 214.

49. M. S. Ishkantana, *Israr Sukut Yafa* [Secrets of the Collapse of Jaffa], (n.p.: 1964), pp. 3–4.

50. From the album "Nejma al-'Arab al-Awali." Lyrics in Badarna, *Yafa: Urus al-Bahr*, 11–12.

51. See LeVine, *Overthrowing Geography*, ch. 6.

52. 15/9/25 meeting of the Tel Aviv Town Council, *Yediot Tel Aviv*, 1925 (no. 2), 3; *Yediot Tel Aviv*, 1934 (nos. 11–12), 43; Dizengoff, undated, 2; Droyanov, 1935, 188.

53. Central Zionist Archives (CZA), L51/71, bylaws of the Nahalat Binyamin society; quoted in Kark, 1990, 121; TAMA, *Protocols of Achuzat Bayit*, 1908, 21.

54. Patrick Geddes, *Town Plan for Tel Aviv* (Tel Aviv, 1925). Copies at the TAMA and Tel Aviv University Department of Geography Map Room.

55. By this I mean that 1929 violence and many official investigations it prompted (such as the Shaw Commission and Passfield white paper of 1930 and the Hope-Simpson and French reports of 1931) constituted the first real threat to British support for Zionist policies in the country (cf. Mark LeVine, "The Discourse of Development in Mandate Palestine," *Arab Studies Quarterly* Winter 1995, 95–124.).

56. Mishar ve-Te'asia, ibid., p. 100.

57. Alona Nitzan-Shiftan, "Contested Zionism-Alternative Modernism: Erich Mendelsohn and the Tel Aviv Chug in Mandate Palestine," in *Architectural History* 39 (1996): 147–80, 151.

58. LeVine, *Overthrowing Geography*, ch. 7.

59. al-Jam'iah al-Islamiyyah, 21/12/37, 3. The consolidated town planning regulations of 1930 gave a local town planning commission the right to build roads as a first step toward executing a town plan.

60. CZA S25/5936, meeting of representatives of Jaffa's Jewish neighborhoods with leaders of Tel Aviv and Zionist representatives, dated 16/5/40.

61. CZA, S25/4618, clipping from Davar, 26/3/35.

62. The "conquest of labor" [*kibush ha-'avoda*] sought the successful insertion of Jews into various occupation that had previously been largely Arab either by lowering the standard of living of the Jewish immigrants or raising it for Palestinians so

that in either case Jews would be in a better position to demand jobs from the Jewish bourgeoisie that controlled the burgeoning Zionist economy of the late nineteenth and early twentieth centuries. When this strategy failed to produce the intended results by the end of the first decade of the twentieth century, the Labor movement developed the "conquest of land" [*kibush ha-karka'a*] as an alternative strategy that was based on acquisition of land upon which Jewish settlements (epitomized by the famous kibbutz system) could be established. These exclusively Jewish spaces would foster a Jewish economy where Palestinian Arabs would, by virtue of their physical absence, be unable to compete for jobs.

63. Zachary Lockman, *Comrades and Enemies: Arab and Jewish Workers in Palestine, 1906–1948* (Berkeley: University of California Press, 1996), 74, 129, 155. These attempts were spurred on by the low wages paid to Arab workers, whose low wages made them natural competitors for their Jewish counterparts.

64. The willingness of these workers to work for very low wages naturally pushed down the already low wages of local Palestinian Arab workers (Labor Archives [LA], IV/208/1/4487b, 14/6/34 letter; LA, IV/208/1/4495, several letters in Arabic in this file; cf. Lockman, *Comrades and Enemies*, 217; cf. LA, IV/208/1/4487b, 19/10/34 letter from Zaslani to Crosby).

65. Cf. Lockman, *Comrades and Enemies*, 1996, 95, citing *Falastin*, 19/8/27. Hapo'el Hatza'ir felt negotiations held during this period were entered into hastily and recklessly, to protect the status quo and prevent the Arab camel drivers from establishing a foothold in Jaffa (Hapo'el Hatza'ir, 13/xi/25, 15).

66. The PLL shifted its focus to Jaffa from Haifa because of the importance of the citrus industry and the port, where workers were increasingly discontented and ripe for organization because of the long hours and low pay given to them by Arab contractors, as well as by the aforementioned foreign competition (Lockman, *Comrades and Enemies*, 217).

67. The Palestinian Arab dock workers and lightermen were the main force behind this drive (Lockman, *Comrades and Enemies*, 226). Needless to say, this was a promise they certainly could not make since the raison d'être of the Histadrut activities in Jaffa, and the PLL in particular, was specifically to facilitate the conquest of Hebrew labor there and elsewhere in Jaffa.

68. The AWS was established in July 1934 in Jerusalem by a member of the Nashashibi family, and was thus supported by *Falastin*, which also had ties to the Nashashibi camp. The call by *Falastin* led to a large public meeting with more than four hundred workers from different industries (*Falastin*, 19/9/34, 2; 21/9/34, 3; 23/9/34, 7).

69. For example, help was sought in securing promised (but undelivered) wage increases from a member of one of the most prominent nationalist families in the city, Azmi Bey Nashashibi (LA, IV/208/1/4495, Arabic list of workers with Hebrew notes).

70. LA, oral Memoir of Eliyahu Agassi, 22/2/72.

71. CZA, S25/2961, PLL, report of activities, June–Dec, 1937.

72. LA, IV/219/239, 23/5/44, protocol of Arab Secretariat.

73. Ibid. Cf. Hagana Archive, *Yediot me Yafo*, 28/11/43.

Conclusion

Reapproaching the Border

Whether exploring history, law, health, or architecture, the contributions to this volume point to the instability and permeability of the myriad boundaries that have separated or (more infrequently) brought together the Palestinian Arab and Jewish communities of Israel-Palestine. As mentioned in the introduction to this volume, such fluidity of borders has been a feature of the relations between the two communities since the emergence of the two national movements over a century ago. Unfortunately, the continuing intensity of the Palestinian-Israeli conflict (which now includes intra-Palestinian fighting verging on civil war) as this volume goes to press highlights how much more successful both sides (leaders and ordinary members of the two people alike) have been at building rather than removing the innumerable walls between them.

At the same time, however, the evidence presented here reminds us of how much work and effort has had to go into building and reinforcing the borders between Israelis and Palestinians. The scholarship presented in this volume illustrates how these borders often served the seemingly opposite functions of including or excluding various groups depending on the circumstances of the moment. We are reminded that other kinds of relations among the many communities that call Israel and Palestine home were and are possible. Indeed, such relations occasionally existed amidst the larger framework of intercommunal conflict between Jews and Palestinian Arabs. They also exist today within the relational framework of Russians, Ethiopians, Africans, Central Europeans, Filipinos, Bedouins, and migrant Arab workers in Israel as well.

Significantly, the lessons of this volume extend beyond Palestinian-Israeli political relations to explore other kinds of borders. These still underappreciated borders have impacted, often through their intersection, the historical trajectory of Israel-Palestine. For instance, the state, technocratic experts, and the public have all played a part in establishing borders about citizenship—who belongs, who does not, and what the contours of state citizenship should be. The theme of citizenship has emerged as central to several of our contributions: from Abowd's exploration of defining architectural space as belonging to a particular family or the state "public" to Alatout's investigation into the beneficiaries of water resources and the shifts in the territory's water capacity. In the processes of defining, encouraging, and policing the boundaries of citizenship, these authors (as well as Campos and LeVine) remind us that the negative act of erasure is just as important to consider as the positive act of establishing the qualities of state identity. Willen's research on a marginalized population, the "illegal" migrant workers, touches upon the issue of people not given Israeli citizenship who still need health and human services. Her insights are especially important in this regard because they teach us that even in the cases of acute intercommunal conflicts (the Palestinian-Israeli conflict), other groups outside the body of the conflictual parties can have an important influence on (and be influenced by) the internal dynamics of the two dominant societies entangled in political conflict. These migrants' identity as an "illegal" presence in Israel puts them in a precarious position with regard to work, residency, and health. Willen's investigation also points to the paradoxes that illegality poses, especially with regard to health policies and practice. The borders of citizenship, therefore, are not predetermined or without challenges but are part of a process of constantly defining and redefining the state and dealing with its new demographic changes.

Besides the theme of citizenship, space is an important tool for maneuvering theoretical and concrete boundaries. Some of the most important scholarship of the last generation on Israel-Palestine has been grounded in spatial, urban, or related theoretical concerns. As Abowd and Forman have shown us, naming a space gives meaning to it and either allows certain functions of a given locale to proceed or disallows others. Naming a space also conveys ownership and control over that space, demarcating who can gain the benefits from that place and who cannot. Naming, however, is only one of a series of steps necessary toward grasping a territory. As Alona Nitzan-Shiftan and each of our authors who deal with space shows, architecture—the field which defines spatial relations—reiterates borders for particular interests and constitutes the most material intersection of spatial ideologies, discourses, and politics of identity. Sites of daily interaction—homes, infant care centers, and immigration absorption centers—not only serve their primary function but are also places of identity formation. They are often places where various borders collide; where the penetration and negotiation of borders occurs.

Spaces are also intricately related to memory. As we have learned from Abowd and Campos, some of the most important spaces are sites of forgetting and remembering. The employment of particular memories—collective or otherwise—enables the creation of certain kinds of power over territory. Having power over what is worthy of remembering carries with it the ability to disable other memories; it forces a forgetting of certain parts of one's own past, including the ramifications one's actions may have had on other groups or places. In the cases that we have seen in this volume, enabled memories have privileged certain narratives of citizenship and solidified particular nationalist stories. At the same time, they have implicitly and explicitly delegated other memories to oblivion. These memories are not inert or irrelevant for contemporary living and practice. LeVine's chapter on Jaffa and Tel Aviv, for instance, clearly demonstrates the continuing political and ideological saliency of a century-old imagination about the space of the region in which the two cities developed.

Indeed, how borders are drawn often reflects ideology, whether nationalistic, religious, or scientific. The chapters that deal with health and the body (section 2) show us that ideologies rarely remain at an abstract level but are most often inscribed in practice (whether spatially, linguistically, aesthetically, or even corporally) onto people's bodies. For instance, Davidovitch et al's examination of who was deemed a fit immigrant in 1950s Israel details which persons were considered desirable Israelis; here interests concerning the body and (potential) citizenship collide. These authors also demonstrate the ways in which this ideology is put into practice through the use of vaccination. Transforming people's bodies into an ideal (or the opposite process of taking what exists and creating associative models) involves a journey of back-and-forth shifts, of border crossings between the extant and the imaginative. Sufian's contribution touches upon those kinds of shifts when she discusses how medical professionals in Palestine wanted to be accepted into the international medical arena while also trying to establish a particularistic language to promote their nationalist agendas. Sufian's piece helps us understand how professionals (here medical practitioners, like the Israeli state and contemporary Palestinian medical counterparts) similarly drew upon ideologies of scientific positivism and modernization to set up and enforce boundaries of identity. In this case, geographical borders of East/West and temporal concerns of the past, present, and future of the Jewish nation inform practical decisions about which words the medical professional should use in their daily practice. Language becomes the conduit through which ideology is put into practice; language conditions the doctor/patient relationship as well as the relations between the Zionist medical professionals and their international colleagues.

Indeed, as many of the contributions here demonstrate, nationalist movements constantly play with notions of time—the borders between past, present, and future are constantly appropriated. In all of the cases set forth in this volume, the past is forever alive in that it is used to make sense of the present and find possibilities for the future.

Language plays an important role not only in medical practice but in notions of sexuality, gender relations, and the relations between religion and the state. As Monterescu notes, the words used to describe men's and women's behavior in contemporary Jaffan Arab society denote the underlying disintegration of Palestinian patriarchy. Language and typologies of character are responsive actions taken by Palestinian men to reestablish their dominance in a changing, globalizing world. Abou Ramadan extends the discussion of language and the borders it reflects by showing that, despite claims of purity and Islamic rootedness, Shari'a courts do not and cannot separate their judgments from the overarching legal system of Israel. Despite language that promotes division, legal practice is hybrid and fluid; it shapes the identities of majority and minority populations alike in ways that contradict official discourses of law.

Certain policies, like those dealing with health, immigration, or law, provide particularly useful areas for interrogating the concept of borders. They offer insights into state policies and their often paradoxical relationship with human practice. Israel's two-tiered health system, like that of many other countries, impacts the delivery of care (and health status itself) between and among citizens and noncitizens. Willen's contribution, however, illustrates that local conditions, including the political leanings of local government, occasionally override state policy. Local conditions are central to understanding particular borders between citizen and noncitizen or between healthy and nonhealthy. Locality is crucial to understanding how distinctions are put into practice.

Still, locality is framed by the larger phenomenon of modernity. Many contributions to this volume explored the specific and conflicted trajectory of modernity in Israel and Palestine, and through them, the Middle East more broadly. Nitzan-Shiftan's discussion of the Israeli use of the "Palestinian vernacular" in East Jerusalem architecture and housing after 1967 shows us how locality and modernity came together during this time in interesting ways. Here again, notions of past, present, and future—notions of rootedness—are employed and reshaped for building in a newly conquered land.

Other contributions show us that the changing dynamics of modernity are particularly important for understanding the transition from Ottoman imperial to British imperial rule. Discussions by Baram, Campos, and LeVine highlight the importance of giving equal weight to the triangular relationship between the local Arab population, the Zionist settlers, and the Ottoman state as is given to the far more widely studied dynamic between Palestinians, Zionists, and the British. At the same time, Forman's discussion of state mechanisms of power and their role in establishing territorialized space reveals the depth of the power of modernist and modernizing discourses.

In conclusion, it is worth recalling Samer Alatout's observation that "what is interesting about borders is precisely the work that constructs and shapes them—the way they are established, contested, stabilized, and reconstituted in a number of fields and ways." As we articulated in the book's introduction, this volume has reapproached various methodologies of certain academic disciplines. It has also looked at the history and present of Palestinian-Israeli relations in new ways. By reapproaching these borders, we have hopefully opened up new avenues for further, fruitful inquiry.

Index

About the Editors and Contributors

Moussa Abou Ramadan received his Ph.D. from Aix-Marseille III (2001). He is lecturer of the Faculty of Law of Haifa University. His research interests include Islamic law, religious minorities rights, Shari'a courts, and international human rights.

Thomas Abowd received his Ph.D. from Columbia University (2003). He is assistant professor of anthropology at Wayne State University, Detroit Michigan. He has conducted research in Palestine and Israel for over a decade and has written extensively on urban politics in Jerusalem and Detroit. He is the author of "National Boundaries, Colonized Spaces: The Gendered Politics of Residential Life in Contemporary Jerusalem," forthcoming in *Anthropological Quarterly* and is completing a book on colonialism, the politics of space, and contemporary Jerusalem, titled *Landscapes of Loss: The Spatial Construction of Identity and Difference in Jerusalem*.

Samer Alatout is assistant professor of rural sociology and environmental studies at the University of Wisconsin, Madison. He completed his Ph.D. in Science and Technology Studies at Cornell University in 2003. He also was a postdoctoral fellow in the Geography Department at Dartmouth College. He is interested in scientific knowledge and practice as forms of power, discursive constructions of identity, the mutual production of political and ecological orders, state formations, governmentality, and, most recently, b/order studies. He worked extensively on water politics in the Middle East, especially on water as a site for constructing and imagining Zionist identity in historic Palestine, as well as Israeli identity and state building after 1948. His most recent publication, "Towards a bio-territorial conception of power: Environmental narratives in Palestine and Israel," appeared in *Political Geography*. A number of articles are forthcoming and will appear in *Israel Studies Forum, Social Studies of Science,* and other academic venues. His most recent research is a multi-cited project on b/order zones, focusing attention on the mutual shaping of political and ecological orders on the border. His comparative attention is focused on Israeli-Palestinian borders, U.S.-Mexico border zones, and Native People's shifting borders in Wisconsin.

Uzi Baram is an anthropologist whose studies revolve around material culture, power, and social identity, particularly as those elements relate to the emergence of the modern era and representations of peoplehood. As a historical archaeologist, his principle area of research has been the Middle East, focused on the period the Ottoman Empire ruled Palestine. He is editor and contributor to *A Historical Archaeology of the Ottoman Empire: Breaking New Ground* (2000), *Marketing Heritage: Archaeology and the Consumption of the Past* (2005), and *Between Art and Artifact: Approaches to Visual Representation in Historical Archaeology* (2007). Baram is an associate professor of anthropology at New College of Florida.

Michelle Campos is assistant professor of modern Middle East history at the University of Florida. She is currently completing a book manuscript on political culture in late Ottoman Palestine and has published several articles on this topic. Campos earned her Ph.D. from Stanford University in 2003.

Nadav Davidovitch, M.D., Ph.D., MPH is a public health physician and historian of medicine and public health. He is a senior lecturer in the Department of Health Systems Management, Division of Public Health, Ben Gurion University and an adjunct lecturer at the Center for the History and Ethics of Public Health at Columbia University's Mailman School of Public Health. He is currently studying the varied consequences of immigration within the health domain. He is also working on various notions of contested science in environmental health and vaccination policy. Among his recent publications on health and immigration are: "Medical Borders: Historical, Political and Cultural Analyses" (*Science in Context,* with Rakefet Zalashik), and "Health Care as a National Right? The Development of Health Care Services for Migrant Workers in Israel" (*Social Theory and Health,* with Dani Filc). He has coedited, with Michal Alberstein and Austin Sarat, *Trauma and Memory: Reading, Healing and Making Law* (forthcoming).

Dr. **Geremy Forman** teaches and researches the historical, legal, and geographical dimensions of the Israeli land regime at Tel Aviv University and the University of Haifa. His articles have appeared in international journals such as *Environment and Planning D: Society and Space*, *The Journal of Historical Geography*, *Theoretical Inquiries in Law*, *Israel Studies*, and *The Journal of Israeli History*.

Mark LeVine is professor of modern Middle Eastern history, culture, and Islamic studies at the University of California–Irvine. He is the author or editor of half a dozen books, including *Overthrowing Geography: Jaffa, Tel Aviv and the Struggle for Palestine*, *Why They Don't Hate Us: Lifting the Veil on the Axis of Evil*, *Religion, Social Practice and Contested Hegemonies: Reconstructing the Public Sphere in Muslim Majority Societies* (with Armando Salvatore), *An Impossible Peace: Oslo and the Burdens of History* (forthcoming) and *Heavy Metal Islam* (forthcoming)

Daniel Monterescu is assistant professor of urban anthropology at the Central European University in Budapest and a postdoctoral fellow at the European University Institute. He received his Ph.D. in cultural anthropology from the University of Chicago (2005). Monterescu studies ethnic relations and urban space in Jewish-Arab mixed towns as part of a larger project on identity, sociality, and gender relations in Mediterranean cities. His previous projects interrogated the construction of Arab masculinity and the narration of life stories in Jaffa. His publications feature articles in the *Journal of Mediterranean Studies*, *Theory and Criticism*, *Israeli Sociology*, *IJMES*, and contributions to numerous edited volumes in English and Hebrew including *Islamic Masculinities* and *Tel-Aviv-Jaffa Studies*. He is author (with Haim Hazan) of *Twilight Nationalism*, a bilingual study of autobiographical narratives of Palestinian and Jewish elderly in Jaffa, and editor (with Dan Rabinowitz) of *Mixed Towns, Trapped Communities: Historical Narratives, Spatial Dynamics and Gender Relations in Jewish-Arab Mixed Towns in Israel/Palestine*.

Alona Nitzan-Shiftan holds a Ph.D. and an S.M.Arch.S from MIT and teaches at the Technion's Faculty of Architecture and Town Planning in Israel. Her work on the politics of architecture, particularly in Israel and the United States, won many interdisciplinary awards. She is currently working on a manuscript tentatively titled *Designing Politics: Architecture and the Making of "United Jerusalem."*

Rhona Seidelman is a Ph.D. candidate in the Faculty of Health Sciences at Ben Gurion University of the Negev. She is writing her dissertation on health and immigration at the *Shaar Haaliya* processing camp, 1949–1952. Her fields of interest include cultural and social history of the State of Israel, and the history of quarantine. Among her recent publications is "Herzls *Altneuland*: Zionist utopia, medical science and public health," (*Korot:*

The Israel Journal of the History of Medicine and Science, with Nadav Davidovitch).

Shifra Shvarts, Ph.D. is associate professor of the history of medicine at the Moshe Prywes Center of Medical Education, Faculty of Health Sciences, Ben Gurion University and a guest professor in the Sackler School of Medicine, Tel Aviv University and in the Gertner Institute for Epidemiology and Health Policy Research, Sheba Medical Center. Her research is focused on the social history of medicine and public health of Israel during the nineteenth and twentieth centuries. She is currently studying the activity of international health organizations and movements in Israel during the early years of the state. She published five books on the subject of the development of Israel's health care system. Her sixth book *Health and Zionism—The Shaping of the Israeli Health System in the Early Years of the State, 1948–1960*, is forthcoming.

Sandy Sufian is an assistant professor of medical humanities and history in the Department of Medical Education, University of Illinois at Chicago School of Medicine. She has a Ph.D. in Middle East history from New York University and a master's of public health from Oregon Health Sciences University. Sufian works on topics in the history of medicine during the British Mandate of Palestine. She is the author of *Healing the Land and the Nation: Malaria and the Zionist project in Palestine, 1920–1947* and founder of the Global Network of Researchers on HIV/AIDS in the Middle East and North Africa (GNR-MENA).

Sarah S. Willen, Ph.D., MPH is a Postdoctoral Research Fellow in the National Institutes for Mental Health (NIMH) Training Program within the Department of Social Medicine at Harvard Medical School. She is editor of *Transnational Migration to Israel in Global Comparative Context* (Lexington Books, 2007) and guest editor of a special issue of *International Migration* titled, "Exploring 'Illegal' and 'Irregular' Migrants' Lived Experiences of Law and State Power" (July 2007). Among her publications are recent articles in *International Migration*, the *Revue Européene des Migrations Internationales*, and the *Journal of Middle East Women's Studies*.